D0162793

THE ECONOMIC
ANALYSIS OF
UNIONS

THE ECONOMIC
ANALYSIS OF

UNIONS

New Approaches and Evidence

BARRY T. HIRSCH
University of North Carolina at Greensboro

JOHN T. ADDISON
University of South Carolina

Boston
ALLEN & UNWIN
London   Sydney

© Barry T. Hirsch & John T. Addison, 1986
This book is copyright under the Berne Convention.
No reproduction without permission. All rights reserved.

Allen & Unwin Inc.,
8 Winchester Place, Winchester, Mass. 01890, USA

Allen & Unwin (Publishers) Ltd,
40 Museum Street, London WC1A 1LU, UK

Allen & Unwin (Publishers) Ltd,
Park Lane, Hemel Hempstead, Herts HP2 4TE, UK

Allen & Unwin (Australia) Ltd,
8 Napier Street, North Sydney, NSW 2060, Australia

First published in 1986

Library of Congress Cataloging-in-Publication Data

Hirsch, Barry T., 1949–
   Economic analysis of unions
Bibliography: p.
Includes index.
1. Trade-unions – United States.   2. Wages – United
States.   3. Cost and standard of living – United States.
4. Industrial relations – United States.   I. Addison,
John T.   II. Title.
HD6508.H48   1985   331.88'0973   85–18690
ISBN 0–04–331097–4 (alk. paper)
ISBN 0–04–331098–2 (pbk.: alk. paper)

British Library Cataloguing in Publication Data

Hirsch, Barry T.
   The economic analysis of unions : new approaches
and evidence.
1. Economic history – 1971–   2. Trade-unions
I. Title   II. Addison, John T.
330.9'048   HC59
ISBN 0–04–331097–4
ISBN 0–04–331098–2 Pbk

Set in 10 on 12 point Sabon by Columns of Reading
and printed in Great Britain by Butler & Tanner Ltd,
Frome and London

Contents

86-2437

Preface

Research on labor unions has made rapid advances during the last decade. Most notable has been an emerging synthesis of choice-theoretic microeconomic analysis and traditional institutional approaches to unions, combined with the application of modern econometric techniques. In this book, we attempt to survey, synthesize, and evaluate these new approaches to the economic analysis of unionism. Our book is intended not only for specialists in the area, but also for interested students and scholars with training in economics. The book can also serve as a primary or supplemental text in graduate and advanced undergraduate courses dealing with the economics of unions.

As in any collaborative effort, the relative contribution of the authors varies across chapters. BTH provided initial drafts of Chapters 2, 3, 5, and 6; JTA of Chapters 1, 7, 8, and 9; and both of Chapter 4. Chapters 4 and 7 involved the most extensive collaboration. Broad coordination of the manuscript was the responsibility of BTH. We extend our thanks to William J. Moore, who reviewed and made numerous suggestions on an earlier draft of the manuscript, and to Clifford Donn and Bruce Kaufman, who provided comments on Chapter 4. We are of course responsible for any errors that remain. We also thank our copyeditor, Liz Paton, who provided invaluable assistance with the final typescript. Finally, we especially appreciate the cheerful and expert assistance of Sharon Nowell, Rebecca Askew, Vicki Sparrow, and Marilyn White, who typed numerous drafts of the manuscript.

Barry T. Hirsch
John T. Addison
March 1985

CHAPTER 1

An Overview

In his progress report on the economic analysis of unionism, George Johnson (1975) noted the Cinderella-like status of the subject within the corpus of labor economics. He reported that the proportion of articles dealing with unionism in the three major US journals (the *American Economic Review*, *Journal of Political Economy*, and *Quarterly Journal of Economics*) had fallen steadily from around 9 percent in the 1940s to just under 0.5 percent in the first four years of the 1970s. Pencavel (1977) pointed to a similar dearth of union articles in the top two British journals: of the 350 major articles published in the *Economic Journal* and *Economica* between 1970 and 1975, only three could be classified as analyzing the causes and consequences of union behavior. By contrast, labor economics net of unionism had enjoyed a modest renaissance on both sides of the Atlantic during this same period.

Since then there has been a dramatic surge of interest in the economic analysis of unionism, so much so that even comparatively recent survey treatments (e.g. Parsley's, 1980, widely cited review of union relative wage effects) have a curiously dated air. Some indication of the pace of development is indicated by the fact that of the approximately 600 references in this book, well over half appeared either during or after 1980. It is ironic that interest in unionism has heightened precisely at the time when unions are in decline. Moreover, in a sharp conceptual break with the traditional monopoly view of unionism, much of the new literature has explored the potentially beneficial role of unions.

As we shall see, a large part of the modern literature has also focused on improved measurement of familiar union effects. The development and application of well-articulated behavioral models of the union have lagged behind these technical improvements in the empirical literature. But this too is changing. While Johnson (1975, pp. 23–4) concluded that, after almost three decades of research, "the problem of modeling trade union behavior has proved to be virtually intractable", the current view is aptly summarized by Dertouzos and Pencavel (1981, p. 1163) as follows: "There is nothing about the trade union as an institution that makes its central features impossible to characterize in a framework

1

analogous to purposive models in economics."

This is not to argue that there is necessarily any greater unanimity today about the objective function of the union but, rather, to indicate that theoretical progress has been reported along a number of fronts. Thus, some of the early maximizing models have been tested within an orthodox utility-maximizing framework whereby outcomes are constrained to lie on the labor demand curve, while other studies have explored the possibility of 'efficient' bargaining outcomes off the demand curve. Yet others have exploited the notion that there is a divergence of interests between the union leadership and the rank and file, drawing on the property rights literature and public choice theory (i.e. the economics of politics). However, the simple median voter model, in which the union as agent accurately represents the preferences of the 'average' union member (or principal), remains the prevailing analytical approach. In short, the current literature provides an altogether richer theoretical mix than existed at the time of Johnson's survey.

This book provides a detailed review and analysis of what we believe to have been the major developments in the economic analysis of labor unions over the past decade. We focus on the economic modeling and goals of unions, the determinants of union membership and growth, union bargaining and strikes, the impact of unions on relative wage and nonwage outcomes, unions and the distribution of income, the effects of unions on productivity and profits, the union role in inflation, and union activity in the political marketplace.

As is inevitable in any such undertaking, some topics are either excluded or receive more limited attention than they perhaps deserve. The thrust of our book is micro-theoretic, concentrating on theoretical and empirical work by economists in both traditional and new areas of labor economics and industrial relations. The emerging synthesis of an institutional and descriptive-based industrial relations literature with neoclassical microeconomic theory and modern econometric techniques is evidenced throughout the book. This synthesis is still at an early and exciting stage, however, and at numerous points in the book it is clear that much work remains. Our primary focus is on unionism in the US, although British and Canadian evidence also is covered. Robert Gordon (1982, p. 13) once remarked pithily that the theoretical ingenuity of American economists is matched only by their institutional chauvinism. While there is some truth in this observation, there can be little doubt about the technical and theoretical sophistication of many of the US studies reviewed here. Moreover, the new synthesis of choice-theoretic and institutional frameworks has progressed much further in the US than elsewhere.

In what follows, we provide a brief overview of the book's contents. Chapter 2, which sets the scene for much of our subsequent analysis, presents unionism as resulting from individual and collective choice. We begin with a review of attempts to model the union maximand in situations where the wage and employment outcome lies on the demand curve. Union attempts to improve the compensation–employment constraint are discussed in this framework. Simultaneous bargaining over the wage *and* employment may make possible an outcome off the demand curve that is preferred by both the employer and the union. We analyze this case, and also the possibility that unions facilitate industry cartelization. The routes through which unions pursue their members' interests are next identified, distinguishing between the conventional monopoly model and modern notions of competitive unionism in which the union is portrayed as an instrument of collective voice and as such not necessarily incompatible with economic efficiency.

It is implicit in our discussion up to this point that unions perfectly represent members with median preferences. This assumption is next formalized, with the arguments for and against the median voter model documented. The chapter concludes with some observations on public sector unionism and a detailed discussion of the demand for and supply of unionism.

Chapter 3 draws directly on this latter discussion in analyzing the determinants of union membership and growth. After first summarizing sources of union data, we turn to time-series models of union growth and cross-section models of union status determination. While the empirical regularities in the two literatures can be interpreted within the demand–supply framework presented in the preceding chapter, the fact remains that neither literature has estimated the underlying structural demand and supply equations. Since the arguments employed in the cross-section material are more closely allied to the theoretical determinants of unionism, we devote more space to this literature. Specifically, we examine the role of personal, industry, and labor market characteristics in explaining membership and, importantly, the contribution of right-to-work laws and the legal structure. Moreover, since many of the studies estimating union membership equations have been motivated by a concern to model the effect of unions on wages, we devote some time to the simultaneity arising from the joint determination of union status and the union–nonunion wage differential. Drawing on our analysis, we then speculate on the future course of union membership.

In Chapter 4, we tackle the intriguing question of unions and strike activity. After outlining some stylized facts on strike frequency and discussing the costs to both parties occasioned by work stoppages, we turn to an examination of the theoretical determinants of strikes. A basic dilemma here is how to explain strikes since they are inefficient *ex post* (i.e. both parties could be better off settling without a strike at the post-strike outcome). We focus on several recent Pareto optimal 'accident' models emphasizing *joint* strike costs, imperfect information, and negotiation costs as determinants of strikes. We are careful to distinguish between factors affecting relative bargaining power – which primarily affects the final wage settlement – and factors affecting the probability of a strike. Other models have viewed strikes as providing a necessary learning process, during which mutually inconsistent claims are moderated, or as a means of reconciling the expectations of rank-and-file members with those of union leaders and management.

While our analysis of strikes is primarily concerned with economists' models, we also consider other explanations and, in particular, the suggestion that strikes may vary systematically with the political complexion of governments and the structure of the union movement. Having confronted the various theoretical approaches with the empirical evidence, we provide a critical appraisal of the alternative strike models. Finally, we consider third-party settlements as an alternative to strikes, paying special attention to public sector impasse resolution, conventional and final-offer arbitration, and settlement outcomes under compulsory arbitration.

Despite allegations encountered in the early strikes literature that strikes are a symptom of bargaining power, the main effect of this power – at least within the private sector – is to raise wages. In Chapter 5, therefore, we consider the definition, sources, scope, and measurement of the union–nonunion wage differential. Estimation of the wage advantage of unionized workers constituted the best-researched topic in the area of union impact at the time of Johnson's survey. Much of the subsequent analysis of unionism has continued to focus on this familiar terrain. The hallmark of the new literature is its use of microdata sets, allowing the analyst to control for a myriad of factors that affect wages, and the application of new econometric techniques. Problems of specification and estimation again attach to much of this new literature, however, and much of the chapter is given over to a discussion of technical issues. Unfortunately, careful attempts to model the endogeneity of union status and to control for sample selection bias arising from unmeasured differences between union and nonunion workers have produced estimates that lack robustness and are often implausible.

The trail leads to yet newer studies exploiting longitudinal data sets. Such studies purge unmeasured quality differences between union and nonunion workers (if they are fixed over time), but are themselves plagued with several serious problems. Nevertheless, the use of longitudinal data represents an important step forward in the quest for improved estimates of union relative wage effects. Accordingly, this body of literature is given close attention.

Having spent some time on questions of measurement, we next

4

discuss the variation in the relative wage advantage of unionized workers by market, industry, occupation, and demographic group. The role of industry and job characteristics is also discussed, as is the emerging literature on fringes. Other topics covered include the effect of union membership versus coverage, union wage effects in the public sector, and changes in the differential through time. We finally examine recent micro studies estimating union wage differentials in the UK and Canada. Interestingly, many of the quantitative and qualitative findings of these studies correspond closely to the US evidence.

A logical extension of the preceding discussion of union relative wage effects involves an examination of union impact on wage dispersion and the income distribution (Chapter 6). Having discussed the incentives for wage standardization in the union sector, we examine the empirical evidence. First, we compare the wage distributions of union and nonunion (male) production workers and assess the component contributions of worker characteristics, earnings function parameters, and wage standardization to the observed differences. Separate findings on wage dispersion by establishment and industry are also reported, as are findings on unions and the size distribution of family incomes. Second, we consider the possibility of simultaneous determination of unionism and earnings dispersion. We then assess union impact on the shape of the age–earnings profile, explaining union–nonunion differences alternatively in terms of the median voter model, a human capital training model, and an 'incentive' model rooted in contract theory. Finally, we discuss briefly the largely neglected issue of union impact on labor's share and the functional distribution of income.

The remaining three chapters of the book encompass some of the most controversial and tendentious issues in the economic analysis of unions, namely their impact on economic performance, inflation, and politics. In none of these areas is the role of unionism well defined.

Chapter 7 investigates the union impact on productivity, productivity growth, and profitability. Much of the controversy here centers on a series of studies emanating from Harvard, the message of which is that unions frequently raise productivity over and above those micro-theoretic 'improvements' recorded when firms react to a higher union wage by substituting capital for labor and hiring labor of higher quality. It is no exaggeration to say that the orthodox view of unions as monopolies pure and simple has been shaken by this new and largely empirical literature. The new view, while accepting that unions have a monopoly 'face', emphasizes their positive role in work settings involving continuity, shared working conditions, and worker complementarities in production. Indeed, it is argued that the potential gains in productivity often offset the acknowledged allocative costs of unionism generated by the union wage premium.

Our own evaluation of this important literature is based on evidence not only on productivity, but also on productivity growth and profitability. Discussion begins with a restatement of the orthodox view of unions as monopolies and a review of the very limited empirical evidence with a bearing on the allocative costs and technical inefficiencies traditionally ascribed to unionism. We then examine the theoretical underpinnings of the new view of unionism. The balance of the chapter is given over to a detailed discussion of the empirical evidence. In order to assess the generality and robustness of the Harvard findings, we begin with a review of all the production function studies examining union impact on total factor productivity, distinguishing between manufacturing or economy-wide studies and industry-specific studies. There follows a discussion of time-series studies of total factor productivity growth and the attempt to reconcile important differences between this literature and the largely cross-sectional findings of the Harvard analysts. Finally, so as to shed more light on the productivity growth findings, we examine the emerging literature on unions and profitability.

Our concluding remarks are motivated by the need to explain the disparate findings of the productivity studies. First, we tackle those empirical patterns that are discernible in that literature. Second, we interpret the rationale of such positive union productivity effects as exist. Third, we distinguish between static and dynamic union effects. Finally, we address the necessary agenda for further research seeking to isolate unions' nonwage effects.

The role of unionism in the inflationary process has occasioned no small controversy, more so in Britain than the US. In any assessment of union impact in this area, we have to look to two basic issues. The first is to establish the sense in which unions may be identified as a 'cause' of inflation. The second is to investigate how the mechanics of the inflationary process interact with or are complicated by unionism. This structure underpins the analysis of Chapter 8.

Investigation of the first question requires that we distinguish between the proximate and fundamental causes of inflation. It is quite possible to exonerate unions as a proximate or direct cause yet indict them as a fundamental or indirect cause. It has long been argued, particularly in Britain, that unions are indeed a direct cause of inflation. We consider three principal variants of this argument and compare their performance with that of the standard monetarist model in which inflation is 'always and everywhere' a monetary phenomenon. While it is concluded that unions are not a direct cause of inflation, it is equally clear that the standard monetarist treatment fails adequately to address union influence on the mechanics of the inflationary process.

Much recent theoretical inquiry has attempted to explain wage and price contracts, and hence a sluggish adjustment process, without any recourse to unionism, while much empirical literature has meanwhile focused on micro contract (and hence union) data, making only obligatory homage to the contracts literature. The rather opaque position of unionism in contract theory thus receives considerable attention in Chapter 8. It is shown that union contracts add to inertia in the economic system, thus complicating the task of economic management. Unfortunately, little attention has been paid to contract endogeneity, but what evidence there is suggests that policymakers cannot exploit inertia by over-expansionary policies in the recovery phase. In short, contracts will change if the assumptions upon which they are predicated change. Within this context, we examine cost-of-living adjustment clauses (COLAs) and contract length.

In the final section of the chapter, we return to the issue of fundamental causation and examine the fragmentary evidence on the exogeneity of wage change. We conclude that there is little or no indication of autonomous union wage push and that the dominant direction of causation is from money growth to wage change rather than the converse. Are we to conclude, therefore, that unions are neither a direct nor an indirect cause of inflation? The answer is in the affirmative if union rent seeking is restricted to pecuniary markets. However, unions are also active participants in nonpecuniary markets and it is entirely possible that the expenditure demands that they make on government lead to over-expansionary macroeconomic policies.

The political activities of unions are the subject of our final chapter. Only recently has this 'third face' of unionism attracted theoretical and empirical scrutiny, largely at the instigation of public choice theorists. Such theorists have been concerned with both the internal operation of unions and their wider political context, although little progress has been made in fusing the two. Among the questions we consider in Chapter 9 are the following. Do unions have influence in the political process? How is this influence measured? What form does this influence take? Do unions act in the wider interest of workers in general? What is the impact of union-favored legislation?

We begin by discussing the most obvious case, namely the operation of public sector unions. Here, we expand somewhat on discussion in previous chapters. Next, we examine the rationale for the involvement of private sector unions in the political marketplace, and discuss the relative mix of rent-seeking activities in the two markets. Union influence, proxied by membership penetration and/or financial contributions, is then analyzed in terms of specific pieces of legislation voted on or enacted by legislators at state and congressional levels. We finally range even more widely, albeit at the price of considerable imprecision, to consider the effect of unions on economic growth, public expenditure, and inflation. The key to this general discussion is that unions are but one of a number of sectional interest groups engaged in rent seeking in the political marketplace. Frankly, the union contribution is opaque, but it is argued that we can ascribe to unions, *inter alia*, a partial role in retarding growth and in increasing government expenditure.

We believe very considerable progress has been made in the economic analysis of unionism in the decade following Johnson's survey. That said, much imprecision still attaches to the union effects charted in the book. We have attempted at all times to provide a balanced appraisal not only of what we now know unions do, but also of the many aspects of unionism where our understanding is weak. The new synthesis of microeconomic theory, institutional industrial relations, and econometric analysis is still in an early stage of development. That this new synthesis has contributed enormously to our understanding of the role of unions is, we trust, evident in what follows.

CHAPTER 2

Unionism:

Individual and Collective Choice

2.1 Introduction

The trade union typically is viewed as an association of employees whose primary goal is to improve the well-being of its members. A union pursues its members' interests by acting as their exclusive agent in collective bargaining and via the political process. Union effects on wage and nonwage outcomes include both monopolistic and competitive aspects, or, more precisely, aspects that are both consistent and inconsistent with economic efficiency.[1] The union, in its role as members' bargaining agent, provides a collective voice for worker preferences. As a result, a union can cause wage and nonwage outcomes to diverge from competitive levels, primarily although not exclusively through the use of the strike threat and other restrictions on factor supplies. Alternatively, some outcomes associated with unionism – for example, seniority systems, structured work rules and schedules, and relatively larger fringe benefits – have aspects that may be consistent with an efficient labor market.

Union status results in part from individual choice in that workers choose utility-maximizing jobs, and in part from collective choice since union representation for any job is determined collectively by past and present workers. Union members and jobs covered by collective bargaining agreements are likely to differ from nonunion members and uncovered jobs; hence, empirical analysis of union effects on economic outcomes must account appropriately for these inherent differences. Accordingly, economists have given increased attention recently to the determination of union status and the interrelationships between union determination and observed outcomes in unionized labor markets.

In this chapter we examine the union status and collective bargaining outcomes among workers, as determined by individual and collective choice. We briefly summarize alternative models of the trade union, contrasting models assuming outcomes on the labor demand curve with bargaining models pointing to outcomes off the demand curve. The role

9

of the union as workers' agent is then discussed with attention focused on the monopoly and competitive aspects of unionism.

The median voter model is developed in order to analyze union status determination and the structure and mix of union services provided to workers. We examine critically the applicability of the median voter and agent–principal models to labor unions. We then develop within a demand–supply framework the determination of union status, analyzing those factors that systematically affect the benefits and costs of unionism. Finally, unionization in the public sector is contrasted with private sector unionism.

2.2 Union Goals and Outcomes: Modeling the Trade Union

On the demand curve: the wage–employment tradeoff

Despite numerous attempts at modeling, there is still no universally accepted model of union goals or behavior.[2] It is generally agreed that the utility of a union and its members is a positive function of real wage and nonwage compensation and union employment. And, because labor demand is downward sloping, there is a tradeoff between compensation and employment. However, in the absence of a clearly specified union objective function – for instance, wage bill maximization or union wealth maximization – the existence of a wage–employment tradeoff provides few unambiguous predictions. Moreover, since workers and union officials (workers' agents) usually have limited property or ownership rights in their unions, specification of a simple maximand in the union objective function is less acceptable. Rather, unions are likely to exhibit diverse objectives and the weights attached to these objectives will differ across unions (Martin, 1980, examines the implications of ownership rights on union behavior).

Central to trade union models specifying outcomes on the demand curve is the assumption that the union unilaterally determines the wage and the firm is then free to adjust employment to the profit-maximizing level on the demand curve. Empirical evidence on the curvature of the union indifference curve is then brought to bear in order to infer trade union objectives. Recent contributions developing this approach include Farber (1978b, c), Dertouzos and Pencavel (1981), Pencavel (1984), and Oswald (1982). Whereas in this approach, the *method* of wage–employment determination is assumed (i.e. unions set the wage and firms subsequently determine employment), we later examine 'off-the-demand-curve' models that take trade union objectives as given (e.g. rent maximization) and then explore the nature of the bargaining process through which settlements are achieved.

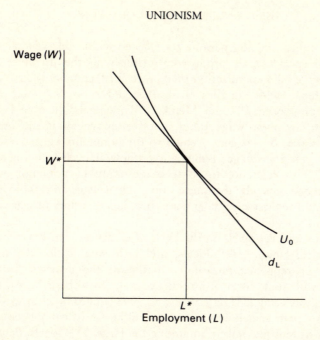

Figure 2.1 Wage and employment outcomes: on-the-demand-curve case

An attractive feature of on-the-demand-curve models is that they lend themselves to conventional constrained maximization techniques. Figure 2.1 shows the wage–employment outcome of such a model as the tangency of the union's indifference curve, U_0, and the firm's labor demand curve, d_L. The union is assumed to set the wage at W^* and the firm adjusts employment to L^*. Any outward shift of d_L will unambiguously increase union utility by allowing increases in W^* and L^*. A decrease in the elasticity of d_L will lower the employment cost of acquiring wage increases. As Lazear (1983a, b) notes, however, for a given displacement of workers from the union to nonunion sectors, a more inelastic labor demand in the *nonunion* sector implies a larger wage reduction. And the larger the union–nonunion wage differential, the greater will be employer resistance to unions.

Empirical evidence about union goals remains meager, although several recent papers provide some suggestive results. Dertouzos and Pencavel (1981) specify a particular union objective function, a Stone–Geary utility function of the form:

$$U(W,L) = (W - \gamma)^\theta (L - \delta)^{1-\theta}, \qquad (2.1)$$

where W is the wage, L is employment, $\partial U/\partial W$ and $\partial U/\partial L > 0$, and γ, δ,

11

and θ are utility function parameters. Nested within this general form are several special cases proposed previously in the literature. For example, wage bill maximization (maximize WL), commonly associated with Dunlop (1944), implies $\theta = 0.5$ and $\gamma = S = 0.$[3] Rent maximization (Rosen, 1970; de Menil, 1971), whereby the excess of the union over nonunion wage times union employment is maximized, implies $\theta = 0.5$, $\delta = 0$, and γ equal to the nonunion wage. Letting γ equal some reference wage permits a hypothesis whereby a union sets a wage goal with reference to some other union or nonunion wage. Finally, a model whereby the union's objective is wage and employment *growth* would suggest specifying γ and δ as lagged values of wages and employment.

Dertouzos and Pencavel, on the basis of evidence from International Typographical Union (ITU) locals, find little support for the simple wage bill or rent maximization hypotheses; the evidence is most consistent with some form of a reference wage hypothesis. In a closely related analysis using ITU data, Pencavel (1984) finds no clear evidence supporting a particular union maximand, although he cannot reject the hypothesis of rent maximization among the larger ITU locals. Pencavel estimates the curvature of the union indifference curve, or, more precisely, the union's marginal rate of substitution between wages and employment (i.e. $(\partial U/\partial W)/(\partial U/\partial L)$), which in equilibrium equals the slope of the firm's labor demand function. His most consistent empirical finding is that the elasticity of substitution between wages and employment is between 0 and 1, implying that these union locals exhibit relatively little substitutability between wages and employment (i.e. indifference curves are rather flat over the relevant range). Thus, differences in labor demand elasticities can account for little of the intercity variation in real wages; rather, intercity differences in the level of demand must explain the large differences in the wage across locals. Pencavel finds significant differences in objective function parameter estimates between a group of large and small ITU locals, suggesting that using the results from any single study or sample to make generalizations about typical union behavior must be done with caution.

In two earlier papers, Farber (1978b, c), who explicitly assumes that union policies maximize the utility of the median member, also rejects the hypothesis of wage bill maximization, on the basis of data from the United Mine Workers (UMW). He finds that UMW members exhibit a high degree of risk aversion, value fringe benefits significantly more than wages, display relatively low discount rates, and place a relatively high weight on employment. This latter finding of course runs counter to the conventional wisdom that the UMW historically has pursued wage gains at the expense of employment (Farber, 1978b, p. 935n). Oswald and Carruth (1984) estimate a constrained maximization model using data for the post-war British coal industry and also report significant risk aversion by miners (although not so much as in Farber), plus general support for the neoclassical on-the-demand-curve model.

While empirical analysis of union goals remains limited, we believe much union behavior can be explained by focusing attention on union effects on demand and supply that improve the compensation–employment constraint facing it. That is, most union policies aim to increase or maintain demand for union labor, to make labor demand in the union sector more inelastic, or to restrict factor supplies. In order to understand the logic of these union policies, it is worth remembering that demand for union labor is derived from product demand for which labor is an input and that the tradeoff between compensation gains and employment losses will be more favorable for unions the more inelastic is union labor demand. Following the Marshall–Hicks laws of derived demand, demand for union labor will be more *inelastic*: (1) the more inelastic is demand for the product, (2) the more difficult is substitution in production between union labor and capital or nonunion labor (i.e. the lower the elasticity of substitution), (3) the smaller the share of union labor cost to total cost (this condition is reversed if the elasticity of substitution is greater than the product demand elasticity), and (4) the less elastic the supply of other factors of production.[4]

It is typically argued that the likelihood of unionization and the potential gains from union representation are greater the less elastic is labor demand. For example, Oswald (1982) shows that in general the expected gain from unionism *decreases* with the price elasticity of product demand, the elasticity of substitution between capital and labor, and the relative cost of labor in the final product, as well as with workers' degree of risk aversion. He also shows that the union's optimal or preferred wage increases with an increase in alternative opportunities (e.g. unemployment benefits), but is ambiguously affected by changes in other product and input prices, income taxes, and even by increases in product demand (although this will always increase union utility).

Lazear (1983a, b), by contrast, contends that an inelastic labor demand has ambiguous effects on expected union utility. While it lessens the displacement associated with any union wage gain, any given displacement will cause a larger decrease in the nonunion wage. In Lazear's model, a larger union–nonunion wage differential increases optimal firm resistance and lowers the probability of union representation. Thus, the extent of union coverage is predicted to be inversely related to the union–nonunion wage differential. What is important, according to Lazear, is the *convexity* or curvature of the labor demand schedule around the relevant wage, because a more convex d_L implies both a smaller displacement effect and smaller decrease in the nonunion wage. Lazear then shows, quite interestingly, that a more inelastic *product* demand implies a more convex labor demand schedule and thus greater union utility. By extension, one could argue that any action that reduces the elasticity of demand for union labor, but not for nonunion labor, unambiguously improves union welfare.

A number of union policies intended to improve the welfare of union workers can be understood by considering their effects on product and labor demand. Union-negotiated contract provisions such as work rules specifying minimum labor inputs for given jobs or capital inputs (crew sizes, number of musicians, etc.), limitations on tasks performed by union workers, restrictions on substitution of nonunion for union labor, and effort level or output limits for workers act either to increase demand for union labor or to decrease its elasticity by making substitution in production more difficult. Such provisions generally are inefficient in that potential output obtained from given amounts of capital and labor is reduced (however, see discussion in the subsequent section).

Political lobbying by unions also can be understood by reference to this economic framework. Typically, organized labor has supported restrictions on many foreign imports (both final goods and inputs) while opposing limitations on exports, opposed the building of plants in foreign countries (which substitute foreign for domestic labor), supported strict restrictions on immigration, opposed relaxation of child labor and work-in-home laws, and strongly supported higher minimum wages while opposing a lower youth differential. Each of these policies, while detrimental to society's total output, benefits identifiable groups of union members via their effects on the demand for union labor. While organized labor does not represent, at least by intent, the interests of labor in general, it clearly seeks to act in the interest of its members. Apparent exceptions to this statement – for example, union support for income maintenance programs – often can be explained as part of a logrolling strategy to form majority coalitions for policies in members' interest. These issues, touched on only briefly here, are analyzed in some detail in Chapter 9.

Off the demand curve: bargaining models of the union

The previous discussion has assumed that wage and employment outcomes under collective bargaining lie on the labor demand curve. However, if unions and management bargain simultaneously over wages and employment (either explicit or implicit bargaining) so that firms are not free to adjust freely to a point on the demand curve, it can be shown that outcomes on the curve are unlikely to be Pareto optimal. That is, for any given wage–employment combination on the demand curve there generally exists some combination off the curve, with lower wages and greater employment, preferred by both the union and the firm. This point, traced back at least to Leontief (1946), has been resurrected recently in articles by Hall and Lilien (1979) and McDonald and Solow (1981) and is now receiving much attention from labor economists.

Following McDonald and Solow (1981), we show in Figure 2.2 how any point on the labor demand curve is suboptimal for the two bargaining parties. Panel (a) of the figure shows the firm's family of isoprofit curves. For any given wage, say W_1, profit is maximized on the

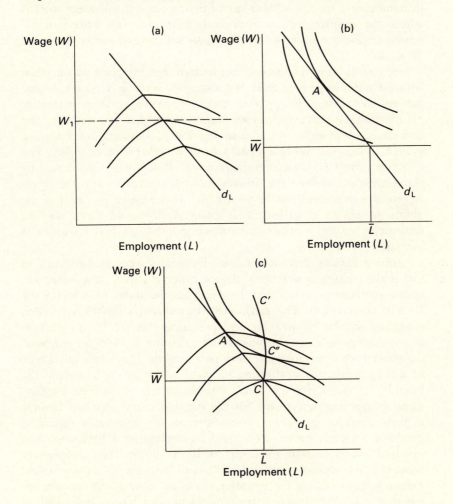

Figure 2.2 Wage and employment outcomes: off-the-demand-curve case

labor demand schedule d_L. However, identical profits can be made at a lower wage rate with either greater or less employment. The firm attempts to maximize profits (i.e. get on as low an isoprofit schedule as possible), subject to constraints. If the firm is free to adjust employment for any given wage, profits will be maximized at a point on the demand schedule. Panel (b) of the figure shows a particular indifference curve mapping for the union, following the customary assumption that its utility is an increasing function of wages and employment (and that the objective function is twice continuously differentiable and strictly concave). If the union is constrained to points along or inside the demand curve, but can achieve any of these points, it will select point A where the indifference curve is tangent to d_L. The wage rate $\bar{W}$ represents the nonunion wage; the union will not, of course, settle for $W < \bar{W}$.

From panel (c) of the figure it can be seen that any point on the labor demand curve is suboptimal. For example, starting at point A and moving southeast, it is apparent that both parties prefer a settlement off the demand curve with lower wages and higher employment. The firm can achieve higher profit than at point A, although lower than at point C. Likewise, the union can achieve a higher level of utility. The contract curve CC' represents the locus of efficient bargains formed by the tangencies between the union's indifference curves and the firm's isoprofit curves, bounded below by $\bar{W}$.[5] If the union in fact has the ability to obtain a settlement at point A, it would agree only to settlements on the contract curve above point C'', where its utility is increased further.

Nothing ensures that institutional bargaining arrangements will in fact make possible a settlement on the contract curve. At a minimum, such a settlement requires that the union has the ability to influence the level of employment. This can occur either through explicit agreement regarding number of workers and provisions for layoffs or, alternatively, through work rule arrangements regarding workers per machine, adoption of new technologies, work pace, and the like. These latter type of arrangements, while affecting the *ratio* of capital to labor and the intensity of effort, are less likely unambiguously to increase employment. Bargaining agreements off the demand curve need not involve explicit contract provisions. Implicit contract agreements regarding employment levels conceivably could be binding on a firm since it is involved in repeated negotiations with the union. Yet, cooperative solutions are typically unenforceable and unstable; thus we would expect settlements on the contract curve to survive only in settings where a 'mature' collective bargaining relationship has evolved. And, as shown by Oswald (1984) in a survey of US and British union contracts, explicit agreements on employment are rare.

Does 'efficient' contracting necessarily imply settlements off the demand curve? As shown by Oswald (1984), this need not be the case. Assume that the union represents the median worker, that employment and layoffs are determined strictly by seniority, and that the median worker's utility, *given employment*, is a function only of his wage rate. Union indifference curves therefore will be *horizontal* at employment levels beyond the one that ensures the employment of the median worker. In this case, union indifference curves will be tangent to the firm's isoprofit curves at points *on* the demand curve. In other words, the contract curve coincides with the labor demand curve at all wages below which the median worker's employment is secure. While both casual and more rigorous (e.g. Farber, 1978b, c) empirical evidence show that unions do care about the wage–employment tradeoff, Oswald's analysis does remind us that on-the-demand-curve and efficient settlements may not diverge greatly where the union places a low weight on employment.

Recent papers by Eberts and Stone (1983). Ashenfelter and Brown (forthcoming), Card (1984a), and MaCurdy and Pencavel (forthcoming) attempt to distinguish between the alternative views of settlements on the demand curve and on the contract curve. Using data for public school teachers in New York for 1972 and 1976, Eberts and Stone contend that the adoption of employment-related contract provisions (such as limits on class size and reduction-in-force procedures) should *reduce* wage compensation if settlements are constrained to lie on the demand curve, while being positively associated with wage gains if they are measures of bargaining strength and there exist settlements on the contract curve. They obtain positive coefficients on variables measuring the presence of such provisions in a salary equation, providing support for the view that settlements occur off the demand curve. By contrast, they do find significant compensating salary differentials (i.e. negative coefficients) for non-employment-related job attributes (e.g. changes in leave provisions, health benefits, and other fringes). While we find the Eberts and Stone evidence persuasive in rejecting the hypothesis of a settlement on the demand curve, we are reluctant to generalize their results. More specifically, because the output and employment levels of public schools are not highly variable, particularly *within* a contract period, and because public schools are not-for-profit, settlements off the demand curve seem much more likely than in the private sector.

Ashenfelter and Brown (forthcoming) utilize ITU data (provided by Pencavel) to test the alternative models. They show that a vertical contract curve, beginning at point C in Figure 2.2(c), would imply a negative relationship between employment and workers' alternative wage (since the contract curve would shift outward as the alternative wage falls), but *no* relationship between employment and the actual

17

wage, holding constant the alternative wage. They consistently find a negative relationship between employment and the actual (i.e. contract) wage, however, thus rejecting the hypothesis of settlements on a vertical contract curve. Card (1984a) employs a similar methodology with data for airline mechanics during the period 1969–76. He also finds that employment is related to the contract wage and rejects both the labor demand and vertical contract curve models.

MaCurdy and Pencavel (forthcoming) attempt to distinguish between the two models using a new data set consisting of ITU locals in 13 smaller towns for the period 1945–73. Employing a more general and powerful test than do Ashenfelter and Brown, MaCurdy and Pencavel reject the hypothesis of settlements on the labor demand curve and of settlements on a vertical contract curve. And, as found in Pencavel (1984), MaCurdy and Pencavel find that employment is given a low weight relative to wages (i.e. a very flat union indifference curve) and that the hypothesis of union rent maximization can be rejected.

The very limited empirical evidence to date thus suggests that settlements off the demand curve are likely to exist in some bargaining situations. However, there is no evidence that a vertical contract curve exists or that settlements off the demand curve in fact lie on the (presumably nonvertical) contract curve. That is, evidence of settlements occurring off the demand curve does not imply that these settlements are efficient. The most important conclusion to be reached from these studies may well be that further work is necessary. And, as pointed out by MaCurdy and Pencavel (forthcoming), 'neither of these models is the relevant one in *all* labor markets at *all* times'.

A final situation worth mentioning, similar in many respects to the off-the-demand-curve analysis discussed previously, is the 'union-controlled' firm (Kotowitz and Mathewson, 1982). Assume that the union can unilaterally choose the wage and employment combination for *all firms* in an industry: in other words, offer settlements on an 'all-or-nothing' basis. In this case, settlements will occur at points off firms' labor demand (marginal revenue product) curves and on 'all-or-nothing' demand curves which lie to the right. The union in effect provides a mechanism whereby workers capture all of producers' surplus. As seen in Figure 2.3, settlements in this situation may occur at higher wage and employment levels (W_2, L_2) than in the case where the union chooses a wage and the firm is free to adjust employment (W_1, L_1). By contrast, the bargaining model of McDonald and Solow predicts greater employment but a *lower* wage in situations where wages and employment are simultaneously determined by collective bargaining, as compared to a situation where firms are free to adjust employment to the union wage.

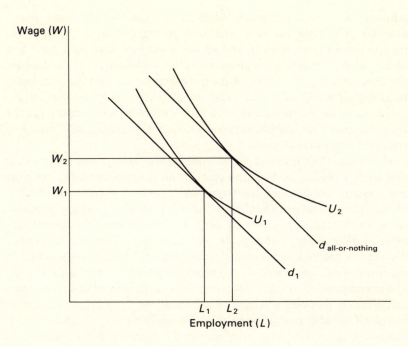

Figure 2.3 The all-or-nothing demand curve

Unions as a cartelizing mechanism

While labor–management relations are typically viewed as adversarial, it is important to realize that the profitability of firms is in the common interest of both parties. Thus, some writers have emphasized the role of unionism as a means of achieving cartel profits in an industry. This argument goes back at least to Henry Simons (1944); more recent analyses along these lines include Warren-Boulton (1977), Maloney, McCormick, and Tollison (1979), and Thompson (1980).

Central to the cartelization argument is the union's right to strike. The strike makes possible a reduction in industry output so that monopoly price and profits can be obtained. Maloney *et al.* (1979) propose a cooperative labor–management arrangement in which joint profits are maximized (this amounts to the existence of vertical integration between the output and labor input markets). Collective bargaining determines the division of joint profits, although the union will not accept less than it could have gained by taking a noncooperative stance.

As with most cooperative situations, the cartel solution does not

19

represent a stable equilibrium. Such an outcome will be more likely, however, where the union is organized throughout an industry, where the number of firms is small and all are willing to 'take their turn' at a strike, where output has high or prohibitive storage costs, and where the short-run supply curves of competing firms are relatively inelastic. In addition, work rules and other contractual provisions that significantly increase the marginal costs of production for outputs greater than the monopoly output may substitute for the strike as a means of restricting output and entry.

Thompson (1980) assumes that cooperation exists among firms such that each is willing to bear the costs of an occasional strike, but does not assume cooperation between labor and management. Rather, management acts periodically to induce a strike by offering below-competitive wages. In order to keep workers organized, the industry must subsequently compensate workers for their strike losses. Thompson predicts lump-sum payments from industry to workers in the form of pension, medical, and other fringe benefit payments, but *not* above-competitive wages. This contrasts with the alternative union cartelization theories whereby industry output is reduced because of increased variable costs (due to above-competitive wages), and in which lump-sum payments from workers to the industry are predicted. As Thompson points out, we typically do not observe the latter payment pattern.

Unionism as a cartelizing device has the advantage of not being illegal and may be particularly attractive for industries that are otherwise unable to restrict output − for example, through regulatory entry restrictions. While empirical tests of this theory are difficult, Thompson suggests several industries (airlines, automotive, rubber, and electrical equipment) where strikes occur on a revolving firm-by-firm basis and unionism appears to act as a cartelizing device. (Linneman and Spiller, 1983, attempt such a test using strike data from the airline industry.)

For a number of reasons, we are skeptical as to whether industrial unionism and strikes generally serve as an effective method for industrial cartelization. Our primary reservation stems from the substantial instability involved in all cooperative behavior, whether among firms or between management and labor. Moreover, empirical evidence supporting such a theory (and inconsistent with other explanations) is not readily available. Strikes constitute a very small proportion of total workdays in all but a few industries. Moreover, if unions were effective as a cartelizing device, profitability should be greater in highly unionized industries, *ceteris paribus*. As will be seen in Chapter 7, exactly the opposite is true. If industrial unions do act as a cartelizing device to restrict output (other than that restriction induced by wage increases), labor apparently captures all of the returns.

Despite our skepticism, the cartel literature does focus attention on the important point that industry profitability is in the interests of both labor and owners of capital. As with the bargaining models introduced previously, it is likely that in some instances production decisions on output and inputs are made *ex ante* in such a way as to maximize joint profits, while bargaining outcomes regarding compensation and employment are in effect *ex post* arrangements for distributing those profits.

2.3 Monopoly Unionism, Competitive Unionism, and Collective Voice

In its role as workers' agent, the union pursues its members' interests in a variety of ways. The routes by which unions affect the workplace typically are catalogued as being either monopolistic or competitive aspects of unionism. These terms can be misleading. Commonly used in this literature, they refer to aspects of unionism that, respectively, decrease or increase economic efficiency. This is the manner in which we use these terms in the discussion that immediately follows. (An alternative approach is to analyze the competitively determined equilibrium level of monopoly unionism – see Section 2.5 below.) While the distinction between the monopolistic and competitive aspects of unions is useful, it should be emphasized that these categories are not mutually exclusive. To the contrary, we should expect unions to pursue members' interests in all possible forms; thus, union effects will have significant components that are both competitive and noncompetitive. And, as noted previously, unions can also be expected to pursue members' interests through the political marketplace.

We briefly introduce the monopoly and competitive views of unionism here; a fuller treatment of these issues is reserved for Chapter 7. Union actions in the political marketplace are examined in Chapter 9.

Monopoly unionism

The monopolistic view of unionism, firmly held by most economists, begins with the presumption that unions raise wage rates above competitive levels in the union sector. Unions' ability to raise wages depends on the existence of monopoly or Ricardian rents in the product market and results from a restriction on factor supplies, primarily although not exclusively through the threat of strikes. Union-induced wage increases prompt predictable price-theoretic responses by firms; in particular, increases in the capital-to-labor ratio and an upgrading of

21

worker quality. Society suffers net welfare losses from unionism owing to the resulting inefficient factor mix and the misallocation of resources between the union and nonunion sectors. Further losses result from strikes, inefficient work rules, decreases in managerial discretion, and a standardized compensation structure that does not provide optimal work incentives.

The monopoly view of unions assumes that settlements occur on the demand curve. That is, once union wages are determined, firms are free to adjust to a new profit-maximizing level of employment and factor mix. However, if settlements occur off the demand curve, as in the bargaining and cartel models outlined previously, there is little we can say *a priori* regarding economic efficiency. For example, a union and firm that bargain simultaneously over wages and employment may maximize their joint surplus and employ the factor mix that would obtain in the absence of unionism. One other instance where unionism may not be associated with allocative inefficiency is the case of monopsonistic firms. While monopsony is not believed to be pervasive, other than in the short run, a union wage increase in such a setting can lead to increased rather than decreased employment (Viscusi, 1980, provides a formal analysis).

Note also that the possibility of obtaining an above-competitive wage, either on or off the demand curve, presumes the existence of excess profits or quasi-rents, differential (pre-union) costs among firms in an industry, or union organization of the entire industry. If there is free entry into the industry, *marginal* union and nonunion firms should be making equal (i.e. zero) economic profits. If none of the conditions listed above are met, unionized firms could not survive in the long run, unless unionism has positive productivity effects that fully offset the increased wage costs.

Competitive unionism and collective voice

While economists have traditionally focused on the anticompetitive monopoly effects of unionism, increased attention has been given recently to the alternative view, closely associated with Richard Freeman and James Medoff (1979b, 1984), that union collective voice, combined with firms' responses to unionism, helps to improve productivity and the functioning of internal labor markets. They argue that the positive aspects of unions, in addition to their anticompetitive monopoly effects, must be weighed carefully in any appraisal of US unionism. We might add that Freeman and Medoff have been reluctant to apply their analysis to countries other than the US.

According to the collective voice view, unions allow workers to communicate collectively to management or exercise 'voice' in the shaping of internal industrial relations policies. This contrasts with the market mechanism whereby exit and entry provide the primary signals to management and which requires the firm to be responsive to the marginal or most mobile workers. Unionism thus causes a firm to be more responsive to the preferences of average and less mobile workers. (There is of course no difference between average and marginal workers in the pure neoclassical model.)

Collective bargaining may be more effective than individual bargaining for two reasons. First, individuals who protest or try to alter any aspect of the work relationship may bear significant costs and possess incomplete legal protection from employer retaliation, yet receive only a small share of the benefits from a changed work environment. Workers acting collectively, on the other hand, are granted extensive protection under the labor laws of all western countries. Secondly, many important aspects of the workplace environment may be public or collective goods, implying that all employees are affected similarly and exclusion is difficult. This may render individual bargaining inadequate and make collective organization relatively more attractive.

In Chapter 7, we analyze the collective voice view of unionism in greater depth within the context of union effects on productivity and profits. Below, we examine a public choice view of the union as agent for its principals (members), as derived from the individual and collective choices of workers.

2.4   Unions and Public Choice Theory

The median voter model, collective goods, and union status determination

Unionism can be treated as the outcome of both private and collective choices. Union status results in part from private choice since individuals sort into jobs that maximize their utility. Union-provided services and collective bargaining outcomes can be thought of as a part of the bundle of job characteristics that individuals take into account when choosing their optimal job path. Even though individual workers have little effect on union coverage, services, and outcomes within any given workplace, the extent and goals of unionism across the labor market are affected by the job choices of mobile workers. This process is similar in many respects to the well-known Tiebout (1956) mechanism, whereby locational mobility may allow efficiency in the size and mix of local public goods, even though individual voters cannot affect collective choice outcomes within any given locality.[6]

Within given jobs, union representation has been determined

collectively by past and present workers. We initially treat union coverage and union services as representative of the collective preferences of the workforce. While current workers are not likely to have participated in past voting for union representation, they have exercised choice in their acceptance of jobs, and, once on a given job, possess at least limited ability to decertify the union as their bargaining agent. More importantly, union leaders have an incentive to respond to the expressed preferences of their members. Union leaders who fail to reflect the preferences of a majority of workers increase the risk of defeat in union elections or of a takeover by a rival union.

Union membership or collective bargaining coverage can be treated as a public or collective good: once provided it is nonrival in consumption so that use by one person does not prevent its use by another. If low-cost exclusion of non-payers is not possible, free-rider problems and non-optimal preference revelation will cause less than an optimal amount of a public good to be produced by the market (national defense is of course the classic example).

Many of the services that union membership or collective bargaining coverage provide are nonrival and exclusion is difficult, given the framework of existing labor law wherein all workers within a bargaining unit are typically covered by a single contract. Thus, similar workers will receive equivalent compensation packages and individual workers cannot generally be excluded from contract provisions covering layoffs, work-sharing, promotion, and the like. Moreover, such job characteristics as safety, hours, speed of work, lighting, temperature, and noise are shared or collective goods to the extent that workers face similar working conditions. Of course some union services – for example, assistance in carrying out grievance procedures – may be rival among covered workers or may be denied to covered workers who do not join the union (Reynolds, 1980b). Moreover, maintenance of wage gains or other rents typically may require that employment or the number of union members be restricted, thus calling into question the assumption of nonrivalry (M. Olson, 1980). Despite these qualifications, we believe it is useful to treat collective bargaining coverage as a type of (local) public or collective good whereby similar workers receive an equivalent bundle of services.

While all workers within a bargaining unit are subject to a single contract, their preferences as to the mix of contract provisions are not likely to be identical. Unlike a private good, where individuals can adjust their consumption until marginal valuation equals price, the output of a public good is determined collectively and any individual worker is unlikely to realize exactly his preferred contract or working conditions among those contract and job bundles that are achievable through collective bargaining.

24

The equilibrium output of a collective good, when determined democratically (either by referendum or via representatives), can be treated as if determined by the preferences of the median voter. Although the median voter model is simplistic and will subsequently receive qualification, it is useful in explaining union membership determination, union goals, and collective bargaining outcomes. Indeed, the collective voice view of unionism summarized above accepts the median voter model without qualification. The model predicts that maximizing union leaders will propose to workers a bundle of services that tends toward the preferred bundle of the median voter. Any alternative package could be defeated by a proposal closer to the preferences of the median voter, and, once the median package is achieved, no alternative could gain a majority vote. That is, an equilibrium outcome exists and it is stable.

The essential elements of the median voter model are illustrated in Figure 2.4. The horizontal axis measures the quantity of union services. We assume that the quantity can be ordered from 'less' to 'more' even though unions provide a composite good comprised of a bundle of attributes, including potential wage and nonwage gains achievable through collective bargaining, working conditions, grievance procedures, structured seniority systems, institutionalized work rules, etc.

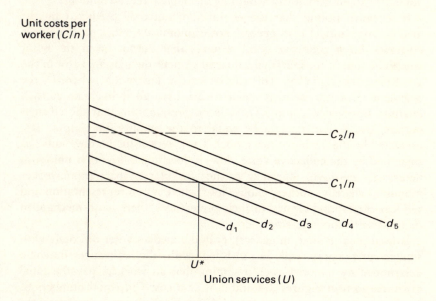

Figure 2.4 Median worker equilibrium for the collective union good

This is the same simplifying assumption made in demand analysis for most goods. The vertical axis measures the per unit price or cost of union services per worker (C/n), and includes such things as union dues and expected loss from strikes. It is assumed that individual workers pay an equal amount for union representation. The demand curves d_1 through d_5 represent five individual worker demands (willingness to pay) for various quantities of union services.

Equilibrium in such a setting can be determined by the preferences of the median voter, in this case worker 3. The model predicts that U^*, the preferred quantity of union services of worker 3 at cost C_1/n, will be the observed outcome of majority voting. No alternative level of union services would be a stable outcome since U^* would be preferred by a majority, whereas once U^* is achieved no alternative level would displace it. The median voter model also provides a framework for predicting the existence of union representation. If, as with C_2/n, the per unit cost of union services is greater than d_3 at every level of U, the median voter and a majority of workers would oppose union representation. This outcome is particularly likely if there are high fixed costs of union services such that per unit costs are high for small levels of union services. Likewise, if unions are willing (or able) to provide only some minimum quantity of union services, and that quantity constraint is substantially greater than the level preferred by the median voter, U^*, then a majority would again oppose representation.[7]

It is worth noting that the equilibrium outcome predicted by the median voter model is in general not economically efficient. Economic efficiency for a collective good requires that output be at the point where the sum of the marginal valuations equals the marginal cost of the good (Samuelson, 1955). This can be seen in Figure 2.5, where D, the aggregate demand curve, is equal to Σd_i over all individuals at each quantity (the vertical sum). There is no presumption that the efficient output, U_E, will in general be equal to the equilibrium output, U^*, predicted by the median voter model. Thus, even if the market 'fails', as suggested by the collective voice view, it does not follow that unionism necessarily improves efficiency in the workplace. Apart from worker mobility, whereby workers choose jobs where union representation and services correspond closely to their preferences, there is no mechanism that ensures economic efficiency.

A final point is that, in general, only the median voter or voters with similar preferences will be satisfied with the collective outcome determined by majority rule, assuming that all workers pay the same price. As seen in Figures 2.4 and 2.5, at a cost C/n equal numbers of workers prefer more and less than U^*. Alternatively, each worker might in principle be levied a cost equal to his marginal valuation. An example of this outcome is the Lindahl equilibrium, shown in Figure 2.5, where

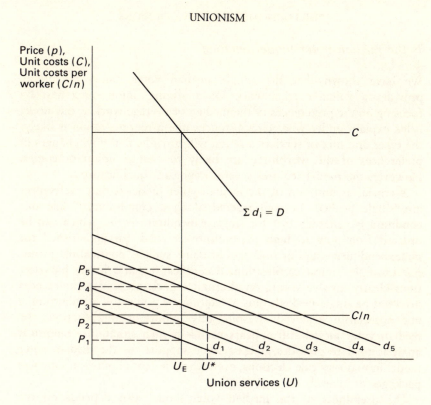

Figure 2.5 Efficient output of the union collective good

workers 1–5 face prices p_1 to p_5 respectively. In this case, the collectively determined outcome is equivalent to each worker's preferred outcome. However, such differential pricing for union representation does not appear feasible and is not observed in practice in unionized firms.

An interesting implication of the median voter model, given that workers face a similar price and that outcomes conform closely only to workers with preferences near those of the median voter, is that the *distribution* of worker preferences around those of the median voter is important (Hirsch, 1982; Farber and Saks, 1980). Unions are more likely to be politically stable and to provide a package of services that on balance provides benefits to more workers when worker preferences are relatively homogeneous. The relationship between unionism, the distribution of earnings, and the dispersion in worker characteristics is examined in Chapter 6.

Is the median voter model tenable?

We have shown that the simple median voter model potentially provides a valuable framework for analyzing union outcomes. By focusing on the preferences of the median or average worker, the model helps explain under what circumstances union representation is likely, the types and mix of services a union will provide, and how changes in preferences of the workforce are likely to change union outcomes. However, the model requires several important qualifications.

A crucial assumption of the median voter model is that preferences are 'single peaked' or well-ordered along a continuum. While this condition is generally met for single expenditure items, which can be ordered from low to high expenditure, it need not be satisfied for nonexpenditure issues or packages of issues such as political platforms. For example, union certification, decertification, and leadership elections clearly involve voting on alternative packages where preferences need not be single peaked; thus a determinate and stable equilibrium is not necessarily achieved. Despite this important qualification, the median voter model still appears useful in such situations. Empirical analysis to date provides at least some support for the median voter model in majority rule elections, even where potential outcomes involve packages of issues.[8]

The usefulness of the median voter model also depends on the responsiveness of union leaders to the demands of current and potential members. Union leaders are faced with periodic votes by the rank and file and also confront some probability of decertification and takeover. Thus, it is unlikely that the union leadership will knowingly venture too far from the preferences of the median voter. However, to the extent that the union leadership can affect the voting agenda and limit the available alternatives open to the membership, there is likely to be some divergence between what unions do and worker preferences (Romer and Rosenthal, 1978, 1979). This is reinforced by institutional and legal arrangements that favor incumbents in their bid for reelection. In particular, 'exclusive jurisdiction' agreements among unions, coupled with 'union security' clauses that mandate payment of dues, lessen competition in the provision of union services. Finally, the nonproprietary nature of most unions may allow union leaders significant discretion in representing the rank and file, subject to the constraint of remaining in office (Martin, 1980). And because both union leaders and members have time-limited non-transferable ownership claims to potential economic rents, labor is likely to exhibit a more myopic perspective than management (i.e. have a higher time rate of discount).

Empirical evidence is broadly consistent with the median voter model in that most of what unions do in the economic and political spheres is clearly in the interests of their average members. However, this is obviously a weak test of the model that is unlikely to discriminate between the median voter model and other plausible explanations of union behavior. Unfortunately, few specific empirical applications of the median voter model are available (a notable exception is work by Farber, 1978b, c, but even here the median voter model is assumed and not tested against an alternative).

While the caveats entered above warn against any dogmatic adherence to a pure agent–principal model whereby union leaders perfectly represent the preferences of members with median preferences, we believe the median voter model is the most useful initial approach for analyzing union determination and outcomes. At a minimum, the model suggests that unionized labor markets will weigh relatively heavily the preferences of 'average' and 'inframarginal' workers who are relatively senior and immobile. Nonunion labor markets, by contrast, will be more responsive to the preferences of younger, more marginal, and relatively more mobile workers.

2.5   The Demand for and Supply of Unionism

In the previous section we have argued that, within the workplace, union representation, bargaining goals, and the types of union services are likely to be determined approximately by the preferences of the median worker. Moreover, once collective bargaining coverage and other collective good characteristics of a work environment are determined across jobs, workers maximize utility by selecting jobs whose characteristics conform most closely to their preferences, all other aspects of the jobs being equal. For these reasons, formal development of a model of the demand for unionism can help in understanding the large differences in union representation over time and across industries, workers, and geographic areas. However, because the costs of organizing and providing union services are likely to vary substantially across jobs, the supply of unionism will also be an important determinant of union status. In this section, we outline a model of the demand for and supply of union services.

Beginning with an early paper by Berkowitz (1954), and subsequent studies by Pencavel (1971), Ashenfelter and Johnson (1972), and Ashenfelter and Pencavel (1969), labor economists have analyzed union determination within a conventional demand and supply framework, which views unionism as an asset that provides a flow of services to utility-maximizing workers. These services are both private and collective goods. And, because many services that unions provide are realized over time (e.g. seniority systems, grievance procedures), the decision to join a union or accept a unionized job can be treated in part as an investment as well as a consumption good purchase. The greater the sum of the union compensation advantage and the value of union-induced nonpecuniary changes in the work environment relative to the costs, the more likely an individual is to prefer a union or union job.

Demand for union services

Following standard theory, demand for union representation (U^d) can be specified to depend on the relative price or cost of union services, p; permanent income or wealth, y; the union–nonunion compensation differential, *diff*; the price of substitutes for union services, s; any net nonpecuniary benefits from a unionized work environment, z; and tastes toward unionism, t. Or, following the median voter model, (p, y, *diff*, s, z, t) pertain specifically to the median worker. In equation form, demand for union representation is given by

$$U^d = f(p, y, diff, s, z, t), \qquad (2.2)$$

where

$$U_p' < 0 \text{ and } U_y', U_{diff}', U_s', U_z' > 0.$$

The price p represents the cost of membership (comprising initiation fees and dues) relative to the price of other assets and goods. In cross-sectional analyses workers face similar prices for alternative assets and so only differences in union fees and dues are relevant. In time-series analyses, however, it is appropriate to account for changes over time in the price and rate of return on alternative assets (yet data on union dues or membership costs are rarely available). Evidence about the rationing function of dues is circumstantial at best (for an exception, see Raisian, 1983b). It is generally argued that there is excess demand for union jobs at current (non-clearing) prices. Thus attention is given to the selection of members by the union (Becker, 1959) or of workers from the union queue by firms (Abowd and Farber, 1982).

If union services are a normal good, then demand for union representation should increase with wealth or permanent income. There is some disagreement whether or not an income variable belongs in the union demand function (or alternatively, whether union services are in fact a normal good). Duncan and Stafford (1980) have suggested that union status is a response to job characteristics that are measured in part by the wage rate. However, they in fact find a positive union membership–wage relationship despite the inclusion of work quality variables. The negative simple correlation between unionism and wages over time and across occupations should at a minimum make one cautious in accepting the hypothesis that union services are a normal good. This is ultimately an empirical question, and, as seen in the next chapter, such a relationship must be estimated using simultaneous equations methods because unionism affects wages and wages affect unionism.

The proposition that union representation is most likely where the relative union–nonunion compensation differential is largest is widely accepted. The relative gain is generally measured by the proportional wage differential, $(W_u - W_n)/W_n$, or the log differential, $\ln(W_u) - \ln(W_n)$, where W_u represents the union wage, W_n represents the nonunion wage, and ln is the natural logarithm. The union wage effect should be measured by the *expected* wage differential at the time a decision on union status is made (Bloch, 1982a). Moreover, it should measure the wage effect attributable solely to unionism; or, in other words, compare workers truly similar other than in union status. As will be seen in Chapters 3 and 5, because wages and union status are determined simultaneously, and because union and nonunion workers with identical *measured* characteristics are not likely to be truly similar, estimation of the union status–wage differential relationship is difficult.

Because the relative wage differential cannot in general be measured directly, studies typically examine the relationship of unionism with personal and industry characteristics, which serve as proxies for the expected benefits of union representation. For instance, potential union gains may be larger where demand is more inelastic. Because firm demand is more inelastic within highly concentrated industries owing to a lower elasticity of product demand, one should expect to observe higher levels of unionism in more concentrated industries (high concentration will also lower organizing costs). Likewise, capital intensity may be associated with lower demand elasticities and larger potential benefits from union voice (for an elaboration, see Hirsch and Berger, 1984, and Chapter 3). A related point, not generally noted in the union membership literature, is that conditions such as high industry concentration that may make possible above-competitive rents need not substantially increase relative wage gains from union organizing. What is a potential gain for workers is a potential loss for firms; thus, management's willingness to expend resources to resist union organizing attempts may be larger in such firms.

Several personal characteristics are believed to be related to potential union compensation gains. For instance, younger or less experienced union workers typically gain relatively more in wage benefits and less in job security than more senior union workers, who, by contrast, may gain more in nonpecuniary benefits, particularly from seniority plans, pension benefits, and grievance procedures, and may be preferred by unionized employers. Similarly, differences in expected wage benefits may vary with such factors as sex, race, region, and skill level. While each of these relationships will require elaboration and discussion (see Chapter 3), the essential point is that workers with personal and industry characteristics that suggest larger potential union compensation gains are more likely to be union members or employed in covered jobs.

Demand for union services should be less, the lower the cost of substitute services, s – for example, government provision (at low user cost) of many social welfare benefits, tax advantages for self-financed pensions, and the like (Neumann and Rissman, 1984). On the other hand, demand for union representation is expected to be higher in jobs where a unionized work environment will yield positive net non-pecuniary benefits, z. While such benefits can rarely be measured directly, it is believed that variables such as firm size, capital intensity, accident risk, and expected strike activity serve as proxies for some of the potential benefits or costs (Duncan and Stafford, 1980; Hirsch and Berger, 1984). The benefits of union services – particularly institutionalized work, reward, and grievance procedures – may be greater in larger firms where monitoring and worker–management communication may be more difficult. Unionism is also more likely in firms with capital-intensive continuous process activities if unions provide a means to schedule work in ways that more fully utilize the capital stock and lessen public good and free-rider problems resulting from worker effort complementarities. In short, unions are more likely to arise in those firms where formalization of the work environment provides the largest benefits.

Finally, an individual's taste for unionism, t, affects the demand for union representation. While preferences and attitudes toward unions vary significantly, much of this variation is likely to stem from differences in the expected wage and nonwage benefits of unionism across workers and jobs, and is therefore measured in part by personal and industry characteristics. Variables representing region, urbanization, and the presence of right-to-work laws, however, are also believed to capture, albeit imperfectly, differences in attitudes toward unionism.

Supply of union services

The supply of union services, U^s, can be expressed as a function of the relative price, p, the costs of union organizing, CO, the costs of providing and maintaining services to existing members, CS, and union goals, G. Symbolically:

$$U^s = g(p, CO, CS, G), \qquad (2.3)$$

where

$$U'_p > 0 \text{ and } U'_{CO}, U'_{CS} < 0.$$

The association between the supply of union services and price and costs is in part related to union goals. The usual price-theoretic relationship between quantity supplied, product price, and factor costs derives from the assumption of profit maximization; that is, maximization of the difference between revenues and opportunity costs. Because a union can be regarded as an agent for workers with incomplete proprietary or ownership rights to residual revenues, profit maximization cannot be ascribed directly to unions. However, unions can be considered to face a binding budget constraint in that they must fully fund union organizing, services, strike payments, pensions, and the like.[9] Even in the absence of net revenue or profit maximization, a binding budget constraint will result in a positive relationship between U^s and p, and a negative relationship of U^s with CO and CS. For example, the goal of membership maximization would lead to the prediction that unions organize where the marginal organizing costs are lowest.[10]

It is useful to separate costs into organizing and servicing costs. Organizing involves a substantial fixed-cost component and exhibits sizeable economies of scale. National unions can set up the machinery, procedures, and expertise to organize at a number of plants or firms, more effectively spreading overhead costs than could individual local unions. Since per unit organizing costs are typically lower in units with greater numbers of employees, one would predict greater union coverage among larger firms, *ceteris paribus*. Likewise, workers in more highly concentrated industries may be less costly to organize in that the number of nonunion firms may typically be small. Finally, note that much of the cost of organizing new workers is borne by existing members. However, existing members also gain increased bargaining power the greater the extent of industry coverage (Voos, 1983, provides estimates of organizing costs and benefits to existing members).

Servicing costs are also likely to have a significant fixed-cost component. Thus, collective bargaining over wage and nonwage compensation, work conditions, and grievance procedures – as well as the collection, interpretation, and dissemination of information and preferences – is likely to have decreasing unit costs with respect to membership over a fairly large range. Unionism is therefore less likely in very small firms or bargaining units, unless workers are organized by craft or skill group across firms or, alternatively, unless union services are linked to collective bargaining services and outcomes in other firms or units.

Costs of organizing and servicing will also be affected by the employer's attitude toward union organizing and collective bargaining. The degree of resistance by firms will in large part be determined by economic considerations. For example, firms selling products with an elastic demand in a highly competitive industry and with low industry-wide union coverage will have little discretion or flexibility with respect to compensation. Such firms may exhibit substantial resistance, despite the absence of economic rents with which to fight union representation. Union organizing costs may be high in such circumstances, and, even if organized, such a union would have difficulty in substantially changing compensation and the work environment from a competitive outcome. In addition, employer attitudes toward unions probably differ substantially across firms and regions, independent of economic considerations.

Finally, organizing costs will be influenced significantly by the legal structure within which unions must operate (see Weiler, 1983, for a comparison of the US and Canadian representation processes). The clearest evidence of this is the enormous increase in the US in private sector unionism following passage of the Wagner Act in 1935 and in public sector unionism following legal changes in the 1960s and early 1970s. Of course legal rules and judicial interpretation of existing labor laws are not exogenous; rather, they are heavily influenced by prevailing attitudes and the actual extent of unionization.[11]

The equilibrium level of unionism

In the simple market-clearing model presented above, the equilibrium level of unionism, U, will be determined by the interaction of demand and supply so that

$$U = U^d = U^s. \tag{2.4}$$

In a reduced form, U and p are functions of all of the other variables within the system, the unionism equation being

$$U = h(y, \textit{diff}, s, z, t, CO, CS, G) \tag{2.5}$$

where, as above, y is wealth or permanent income, $\textit{diff}$ is the relative union compensation gain, s is the cost of substitutes for union services, z are the net nonpecuniary benefits of a union work environment, t are worker tastes toward unions, CO are organizing costs, CS are servicing costs, and G are union goals. Because none of these determinants enter both the structural demand and supply equations, the sign on each in the reduced-form equation is unambiguous. In practice, however, because we seldom measure these factors directly, many proxy variables are likely to affect unionism through more than one channel. Worker age or seniority, for example, may indicate a lower relative wage gain but be associated with larger nonwage benefits from union voice, expected pension benefits, and the like. In addition to affecting equilibrium U through its effect on compensation, age is likely to be associated with lower costs in organizing owing to lessened mobility.

Empirical studies generally estimate some variant of the reduced-form equation. We know of no study that specifies and estimates structural demand and supply equations. The absence of such a study reflects the paucity of data measuring directly the factors specified in equations *(2.2)* and *(2.3)*. In addition, the quantity of union services, U, is not directly observed. However, if the level of union services is proportional to the level of unionization across jobs, direct measures of union membership status or collective bargaining coverage can be used to estimate U. In practice, aggregate studies use data for industry, occupation, state, or Standard Metropolitan Statistical Area (SMSA) on either the percentage of union members or the percentage covered by collective bargaining agreements. Studies using individual data employ a dichotomous variable indicating that the worker either is or is not a union member or, alternatively, employed in a job covered by a collective bargaining agreement.

Theoretically, it is not clear whether union membership or coverage is the more appropriate variable to consider. The framework developed above treats union services as a choice variable. In states where the open shop exists, as a result of the passage of right-to-work (RTW) laws (currently 20 states), individuals need not join the union despite being covered by a collective bargaining agreement. While free-rider problems are not believed to be large (Reynolds, 1980b; Bennett and Johnson, 1979), at least some workers who would choose to join the union if exclusion from union services was possible will choose not to join a union under the open shop. Likewise, under a union shop (in non-RTW states) some covered workers will be members even though union benefits are for them less than the cost. Even in RTW states, peer pressure in many job settings may effectively necessitate joining a union as a condition of employment. Thus we will observe some union members for whom union benefits are less than costs and some nonmembers for whom union benefits are greater than costs. A collective bargaining coverage variable allows a more straightforward interpretation than the membership variable. Since an individual's job is a choice variable, a coverage variable measures whether an individual chooses to work in a covered job or not. Because union representation is only one component of job choice, however, coverage data are also an imperfect measure of desired union services.[12]

An important issue relating to the demand–supply framework outlined above is the appropriateness of the market-clearing assumption by which we set $U = U^d = U^s$. As pointed out by Abowd and Farber (1982), the market-clearing assumption, while appropriate for the determination of union coverage across jobs and the size of the union sector, is less appropriate for determining the union status of individual workers. Since the major costs of unionization are incurred when a bargaining unit is organized, union coverage can be expected to develop as long as marginal benefits are greater than marginal costs. However, once coverage is determined, there may be a queue of workers seeking existing union jobs, as long as the benefits from unionism are not completely capitalized in initiation fees and dues. In this case, the union status of *individuals* is determined by the joint probability of their desiring to work in a covered job (the probability of being in the union queue) and, if in the queue, the likelihood that employers will select them for employment. Some personal characteristics may thus have ambiguous effects on union status. For example, individual experience may be related inversely to the probability of being in the union queue (since, for experienced workers, relative union wage effects may be smaller and the opportunity costs from tenure in nonunion jobs greater), but positively affect the probability of employment once in the queue.

The Abowd and Farber argument suggests that considerable caution be exercised in interpreting empirical results from union choice models. In the next chapter, we summarize this empirical literature and argue that union membership models might best be specified and interpreted as explaining the existence of union and nonunion jobs, rather than the union status of individuals.

The demand–supply model presented above provides a comprehensive framework for explaining differences in union membership and coverage by reference to benefits and costs. Embedded in this approach is some final economy-wide equilibrium level of unionization whose properties are not made explicit, except that, in equilibrium, the marginal benefits to the union of increased unionization will just equal the marginal organizing and servicing costs. Several papers have recently developed models of the equilibrium level of unionism that explicitly address the question of a determinate equilibrium (Lazear, 1983a, b; Farber, 1984c; see also Wessels, 1984). These models have elucidated possible answers to the often-asked question: if unions raise wages, how can a unionized firm survive in an industry with free entry? (We ignore, for the moment, the possibility of positive union productivity effects.) In other words, can there be a 'competitively' determined level of monopoly unionism?

In two related papers, Lazear presents a model that assumes utility maximization by workers and profit maximization by firms. Labor markets clear such that all qualified workers can claim nonunion jobs, while at the same time there is a queue for union jobs. The union must take into account the effect of its wage choice on nonunion wages. Lazear assumes that a higher union wage implies not only a higher probability of employment in the nonunion sector, but also *lower* nonunion wages. (At a high enough union wage, all firms are nonunion so that the nonunion and competitive wages are identical.) That is, spillover effects are assumed to outweigh threat effects. (For empirical evidence on this issue, see Chapters 5 and 6.)

Firms must bear a cost to prevent unionization and will pay more to resist, the higher the union wage. It is the *distribution* of these costs (similar to those costs discussed previously) that generates a well-defined equilibrium. Because these costs differ among firms, union and nonunion firms can coexist in the same competitive industry with the marginal union and nonunion firms having the same profit levels. The higher cost of labor to the union firm is just offset by the cost of preventing the union in the nonunion firm.

Although we are primarily interested in Lazear's explanation of a determinate and stable equilibrium, several other implications of his model are also worth noting: (1) a higher likelihood of unionization the lower is the elasticity of product demand; (2) inelasticity of labor demand need not increase union membership or the wage differential (since inelastic labor demand in the nonunion sector is a disadvantage to the union); (3) the increased costs of union organizing and servicing decrease the likelihood of unionism, but increase the wage differential; (4) featherbedding can be efficient, while unions that can simultaneously select wages and employment will select the preunion employment level; (5) union workers take a greater share of their compensation in fringes; (6) union workers are older and older union workers receive more of the benefits, yet younger workers have no incentive to leave and observed age–earnings profiles are flatter in unionized firms (this discourages firms from hiring younger workers); and (7) union wage differentials move countercyclically.

Whereas Lazear assumes a competitive market structure and a dominant spillover effect, Farber (1984c) assumes that unions exploit monopoly elements in the labor market and that threat effects dominate (i.e. unions raise nonunion wages). An exogenously determined decline in unionism is assumed to bring about an associated decline in nonunion benefits, owing to lessened threat effects, and increase the union–nonunion wage differential. The increased differential increases the demand for unionism by nonunion workers, which limits the decrease in the extent of unionization. (An exogenous increase in unionism has exactly the opposite effects.) Implicit in the process is a new equilibrium extent of unionization where, at the margin, the threat of unionization to the nonunion employer provides just the incentive to discourage further unionization.

While we are uncomfortable with specific assumptions in both the Lazear and Farber models, both point to an important conclusion: union and nonunion firms can and do exist alongside each other in the same product market. Whether as a result of differences in worker tastes, cost or other special advantages among firms, or market imperfections, some degree of industry unionization can survive in long-run equilibrium. Perceived from the union side, marginal benefits from increased coverage or membership will just equal marginal organizing and servicing costs. Viewed from the perspective of marginal firms, the marginal cost of preventing union representation will just equal the marginal benefits of nonunion status. Marginal union and nonunion firms should realize equivalent profits.

Yet another explanation (Brown and Medoff, 1978) for the coexistence of union and nonunion firms in the same industry is that unions raise productivity by amounts sufficient to offset union cost increases. This possibility is explored in detail in Chapter 7.

2.6 Unionism in the Public Sector

The most rapidly growing area of union membership during the past 20 years in the US has been the public sector. While much of our discussion and analysis up to this point applies to the public as well as to the private sector, there are a number of fundamental differences between unionism in the two sectors in the US.[13]

Unlike workers in the private sector, federal employees were not provided with the right to organize and bargain collectively until 1962, and even now cannot generally bargain over wages (postal workers are a notable exception). During the 1960s and 1970s, many but not all states adopted legislation allowing collective bargaining over wages and work conditions for state and local employees. Even in states where there are no provisions for collective bargaining, public sector workers have the legal right to join a union.

Possibly the most fundamental difference between unionism in the two sectors is that public sector workers generally do not possess the right to strike, even in those situations where bargaining over wages is possible. While some strikes occur even where illegal, the power of the strike weapon clearly is attenuated in the public sector (although some public employee strikes do create quite substantial costs). A number of states possess mandatory arbitration procedures to deal with impasses in bargaining (these are discussed in some detail in Chapter 4). In the UK and many other developed countries, by contrast, public sector workers can and do strike.

Because public sector unions typically have attenuated rights with respect to the strike weapon and because compensation and work conditions are determined in the political marketplace, political lobbying and voting activity are more important than for private sector unions. A related point is that incomplete ownership rights in the public sector are likely to affect labor market outcomes. We previously argued that, in the private sector, nonproprietary unions are likely to possess a shorter time perspective (a higher discount rate) than profit-maximizing firms. In the not-for-profit public sector, however, politicians, whose length in office is typically not long, are likely to display shorter time perspectives. For instance, unless forced by informed voters fully to take into account future tax liabilities, politicians are likely to prefer increases in pension payments to equivalent present value increases in wages. The union, by contrast, may take a longer time perspective than would a private sector union since employment longevity in the public sector is typically greater.

Despite these differences between the private and public sectors, the demand and supply analysis presented earlier is still useful in analyzing public sector unionism (Ehrenberg and Smith, 1985; and Ehrenberg and Goldstein, 1975). Demand for union labor in the public sector is likely to be downward sloping with respect to wages or compensation, even in the absence of profit-maximizing behavior. Labor supply will be upward sloping (or, in the extreme, perfectly elastic) at compensation levels equal to and greater than these available in the private sector (net of any differences in job characteristics). Public sector wages are typically set in part on the basis of 'comparability' with private sector wages, but a preferable measure of compensation differentials may in fact be relative differences in turnover rates and the length of queues of qualified job seekers.

As in the private sector, public sector unions seem likely to be more effective in acquiring wage and employment gains the more inelastic is labor demand and the larger is demand for the final product (public services). Thus unions are expected to fare best when budgets are large and growing, where substitution by citizens (for schooling, law enforcement, postal services, etc.) is difficult, where substitution of private sector services or nonunion for union labor is costly, and where labor accounts for a small share of the total budget.[14]

In our opinion, demand analysis, coupled with an understanding of public sector labor law, takes us a long way toward understanding union wage and employment determination in the public sector. While it is frequently argued that demand for state and local employees is highly inelastic, empirical studies do not find large differences between private and public demand elasticities (these estimates are summarized in Ehrenberg and Smith, 1985, pp. 421, 100). It is also clear that union membership and wages are affected heavily by voter attitudes and budget size. Just as public employee unions flourished in the 1960s and 1970s following changes in labor laws and during a period of rapid budget growth, they are likely to have much weaker power as federal, state, and local budget growth markedly slows (but see Chapter 9).

Our discussion of public sector unionism in this chapter has been intentionally brief. In subsequent sections of the book, we analyze public sector union membership determination (Chapter 3), public sector strikes and compulsory arbitration (Chapter 4), union–nonunion compensation differentials in the public sector (Chapter 5), and the role of unions in the political marketplace (Chapter 9).

2.7 Summary

Labor unions are associations of employees that seek to further the interests of their members through organizing, collective bargaining, and politicial activity. Unions seek increases both in compensation and in employment; thus, the level and elasticity of labor demand greatly affect unions' ability to organize and achieve benefits for their members. Relatively little progress has been made in discovering unions' objective functions so that no simple answer can yet be given to the question of what it is unions maximize. Such considerations are complicated by the fact that union wage–employment settlements may occur both on and off labor demand curves. While much of what unions do is inefficient and leads to results divergent from perfectly competitive outcomes, unions also provide a collective voice for their members and facilitate changes in the work environment consistent with economic efficiency.

Observed unionization is the outcome of both individual choice, in that workers choose utility-maximizing job paths, and collective choice, since union representation within any job is determined by past and present workers. Because union representation is determined by majority rule and because most collective bargaining outcomes have public good characteristics – nonrivalry in consumption and costly exclusion – the median voter model is a useful framework for analyzing labor market outcomes, even though it is unlikely to apply strictly in any single instance. Workers with preferences close to those of the median voter will heavily influence both the union status of a work unit, as well as the bargaining goals and services associated with the union.

Empirical studies examining the size of the union sector, interindustry and interarea differences in the extent of unionism, the union status of individual workers, and changes over time in unionization have tended to interpret their results within a demand–supply framework. Individual demand for union services is determined by price, income, relative wage and nonwage benefits, the price of substitutes, nonpecuniary job characteristics, and tastes. Union supply is determined by price, organizing costs, servicing costs, and union goals. Some long-run equilibrium level of industry unionism exists wherein marginal workers (or the union) and firms are just indifferent between union and nonunion status. In the following chapter, we examine empirical studies analyzing the determination of union membership and coverage.

Notes

1   Rather than characterizing unionism on the basis of whether or not it leads to efficient outcomes, Lazear (1983a, b) develops a competitive theory of monopoly unionism in which, at the margin, the cost to firms of preventing union representation just equals the benefits. This model is discussed in Section 2.5.
2   There is a large literature on union goals and behavior. Among the best-known treatments are Dunlop (1944), Fellner (1947), Ross (1948), Berkowitz (1954), Cartter (1959) and, more recently, Atherton (1973), Farber (1978b, c), Martin (1980), Dertouzos and Pencavel (1981), Oswald (1982), Faith and Reid (1983), and Pencavel (1984). For a recent survey see Farber (1984b).
3   This can be shown as follows:

$$\{\max\ [(W-\gamma)^{\theta}\ (L-\delta)^{1-\theta}]\ |\ \theta = 0.5,\ \gamma = \delta = 0\} = \{\max\ (WL)^{0.5}\}.$$

Maximization of this last term implies maximization of the wage bill since $(WL)^{0.5}$ is a monotonic transformation of WL.
4   Condition (3), commonly referred to as the 'importance of being unimportant', assumes that scale (output) effects resulting from union wage and subsequent price increases are large relative to the substitution effect in production. By contrast, if scale effects are small (i.e. consumers show little sensitivity to price increases) relative to the substitution effect, condition (3) is reversed.
5   McDonald and Solow (1981) provide assumptions necessary so that the contract curve originates at the lower point C.
6   A number of recent papers have challenged the generality of the Tiebout mechanism. For such a critique, see Stiglitz (1982). Epple, Zelenitz, and Visscher (1978) outline the difficulties in providing empirical tests of the Tiebout model.
7   The minimum quantity constraint must be sufficiently greater than U^* such that no consumer surplus exists for the worker with median preferences.
8   See, for example, Holcombe (1980). However, Romer and Rosenthal (1979) argue that most tests of the median voter model are weak and

provide little support for the model. Recently, Blair and Crawford (1984) and Black and Parker (1984, 1985) have developed theoretical models of union behavior based on majority rule voting, while Kaufman and Martinez-Vazquez (1984) provide an empirical test of a median voter model.

9 This constraint is binding not on a yearly basis but over the lifetime of the union, with the qualification that public pension guarantees and bankruptcy provisions may allow avoidance of the constraint under some circumstances.

10 This assumes p and CS are fixed. In a dynamic context, the union must simultaneously take into account p, CO, and CS in maximizing membership.

11 For such evidence on the passage of state right-to-work laws, see Moore, Newman, and Thomas (1974) and Moore and Newman (1975). See also Chapter 3.

12 As will be seen in Chapter 3, several studies examine the expressed preferences for union membership by nonunion workers.

13 For an excellent introduction to the literature on unions in the public sector see Ehrenberg and Schwarz (1983). In addition, see the collection of papers in Aaron *et al.* (1979) and Hamermesh (1975).

14 For a qualification of the last condition, see the discussion earlier in this chapter. While total salaries account for a large proportion of most municipal budgets, the share for most employee groups, (teachers and police excepted) is small. However, if settlements for one employee group set a pattern for other groups, labor demand will be more elastic.

CHAPTER 3

Union Membership and Growth

3.1 Introduction

There are substantial differences in the extent of union membership and collective bargaining coverage over time and across industries, occupations and regions. In order to understand the wage and nonwage effects of unions in the workplace more clearly, it is essential that we first explain the determination of union status. In this chapter, we summarize available data on union membership and coverage along various dimensions and evaluate the growing empirical literature seeking to explain the determination of union status within the demand and supply framework developed in Chapter 2. Finally, we provide a tentative appraisal of future union growth in light of the theory and evidence presented.

3.2 Data Sources, Membership, and Growth

Data sources

In most countries, detailed data on union membership and collective bargaining coverage are limited. In the US, there are no unionization questions in either the Census of Manufactures or the decennial Census of Population; hence, researchers must rely on alternative sources. The *Directory of National Unions and Employee Associations* (formerly the *Directory of National and International Labor Unions in the United States*) had been published biennially until being discontinued recently by the Bureau of Labor Statistics (BLS). Troy and Sheflin (1985) have taken over tabulation of this survey and, in addition to providing key historical time series in a single volume, plan to publish survey results annually.[1] The membership data in these surveys are self-reported by unions and allow aggregation by union, state, and large industry groupings. Although extremely valuable, these data have many disadvantages due, in particular, to differences in reporting accuracy and definition of membership across unions (Lewis, 1963, pp. 262–4; Freeman and Medoff, 1979a, p. 144; Troy and Sheflin, 1985).

A source for relatively recent data on union coverage is the Expenditures for Employee Compensation (EEC) establishment surveys, conducted by BLS. These surveys provide data on the number of office (nonproduction) and nonoffice (production) workers by establishment, and whether more than 50 percent of each are covered by collective bargaining agreements. They thus provide the best available detailed data on coverage for production and nonproduction workers in the private sector. Freeman and Medoff (1979a) have merged the 1968, 1970, and 1972 surveys and provided percentage covered estimates for production and nonproduction workers by three-digit industry (both Census and SIC coding). The primary disadvantages of the EEC coverage data are their failure to measure precisely situations where a significant minority of workers have coverage status different from the majority, and the absence of detailed data on personal characteristics, occupation, and location.

The most comprehensive survey data available on individual union membership are from the May Current Population Survey (CPS), beginning in 1973. The CPS contains detailed information on worker characteristics and location, but not establishment or coverage information. Freeman and Medoff (1979a), using the 1973–5 May CPS tapes, have calculated union membership data for production and non-production workers, three-digit Census industries, three-digit occupations, 29 state groups, and the 98 largest Standard Metropolitan Statistical Areas (SMSAs). Kokkelenberg and Sockell (1985) have provided similar data for the entire 1973–81 period.

Like the CPS, the National Longitudinal Surveys (NLS) and Michigan Panel Study of Income Dynamics (PSID) provide individual data on union membership and detailed personal characteristics. In addition, they provide separate data on collective bargaining coverage and allow longitudinal analyses of union membership and union impacts on wage and nonwage outcomes. Unlike the CPS, however, sample sizes in the NLS and PSID do not allow precise estimates of union membership or coverage by detailed industry, occupation, state, or SMSA. While self-reported union status data from the CPS, PSID, and NLS are believed to be more accurate than data from alternative sources, such survey data still contain substantial reporting error.[2]

The union data summarized above provide the sources for most recent empirical studies; however, several earlier works give estimates of union membership and coverage. Perhaps most notable is H. Gregg Lewis's pathbreaking 1963 book, *Unionism and Relative Wages in the United States*, in which Lewis meticulously summarizes and constructs alternative union membership and coverage data. Readers interested in historical union data should consult Wolman (1936), Lewis (1963), Troy (1965), and Troy and Sheflin (1985).

While membership and coverage data provide evidence on the existing *stock* of unionized workers and jobs, data on the *flow* into and out of the union sector are also of interest. Of course figures on the net flow of unionism can be obtained simply by examining changes in the stock of union members or coverage between time periods. Such evidence does not, however, provide information on the various sources of these changes. We are unaware of publicly available data that directly measure lost union jobs or new union jobs (but see below our discussion of Dickens and Leonard, 1985). Data are available, however, on increases or decreases in unionism resulting from union certification and decertification elections conducted by the National Labor Relations Board (see NLRB, *Annual Reports*, by year).

In Britain, statistics on aggregate trade union membership are compiled by the Department of Employment and published in the *Department of Employment Gazette*. A brief time series of these data is provided annually in *British Labour Statistics: Year Book*, while *British Labour Statistics: Historical Abstract 1886–1968* provides earlier historical data. Individual union data are even more limited in the UK than in the US. The annual General Household Survey provides detailed individual data for a wide range of variables, but not information on union membership or coverage. The New Earnings Survey provides detailed coverage data by industry, but not for individuals. The only microdata set of which we are aware containing data on individual union membership is the National Training Survey, conducted in late 1975 (see Stewart, 1983), but unfortunately this survey used grouped earnings data.

An overview of union membership

Evidence on union membership in the US during early periods of this century is rather fragmentary. Despite differences among available time series, the overall temporal pattern is fairly clear. As seen in Table 3.1, unionism, as measured by membership as a proportion of the labor force, increased rapidly during the late 1930s and continued increasing through the mid-1950s. Since about 1970 there has been a gradual but steady decline in union density. By 1984, union membership accounted for less than one-fifth of the labor force.

Union density in the UK is significantly greater than in the US and has not shown the same long-run decline evident in the US. Table 3.1 shows that, except for sizeable increases during the 1970s, followed by declines during the 1980s, density in the UK has been remarkably steady for most of the post-war period.

45

Table 3.1   *Union density in the US and Britain, 1900–84*

Year	US membership/ civ. labor force	US membership/ nonagric. labor force	British membership/ net labor force[a]
1900	3.3	6.5	12.7
1901	4.1	7.8	12.6
1902	5.1	9.3	12.4
1903	6.3	11.4	12.1
1904	6.4	12.0	11.9
1905	6.0	10.8	11.9
1906	5.8	10.1	13.1
1907	6.0	10.5	14.7
1908	5.9	10.9	14.4
1909	5.6	9.9	14.2
1910	5.9	10.3	14.6
1911	6.2	10.9	17.7
1912	6.6	11.1	19.1
1913	6.9	11.7	23.1
1914	6.6	11.7	23.0
1915	6.6	11.5	24.1
1916	6.9	11.2	25.6
1917	7.7	12.1	30.2
1918	9.1	13.9	37.7
1919	10.7	15.7	43.1
1920	11.7	17.6	45.2
1921	10.5	18.0	35.8
1922	8.8	14.5	31.6
1923	8.0	12.2	30.2
1924	7.7	12.2	30.6
1925	8.2	12.8	30.1
1926	8.2	12.5	28.3
1927	8.3	12.8	26.4
1928	8.0	12.6	25.6
1929	7.6	12.0	25.7
1930	7.5	12.7	25.4
1931	7.1	13.4	24.0
1932	6.7	14.4	23.0
1933	6.8	14.7	22.6
1934	7.7	15.4	23.5
1935	6.9	13.5	24.9
1936	7.7	14.2	26.9
1937	10.6	18.4	29.6
1938	10.9	20.4	30.5
1939	11.8	21.2	31.6
1940	13.1	22.5	33.1
1941	15.6	23.9	35.7
1942	18.1	25.4	39.0
1943	21.0	27.5	40.4
1944	22.2	29.0	39.8
1945	22.8	30.4	38.6

Table 3.1 *continued*

Year	US membership/ civ. labor force	US membership/ nonagric. labor force	British membership/ net labor force[a]
1946	22.5	31.1	43.0
1947	23.7	32.1	44.5
1948	23.5	31.8	45.2
1949	22.7	31.9	44.8
1950	23.0	31.6	44.1
1951	24.4	31.7	45.0
1952	25.2	32.0	45.1
1953	25.9	32.5	44.6
1954	24.8	32.3	44.2
1955	24.8	31.8	44.5
1956	24.7	31.4	44.1
1957	24.6	31.2	44.0
1958	23.0	30.3	43.2
1959	22.6	29.0	44.0
1960	22.3	28.6	44.2
1961	21.9	28.5	44.0
1962	23.9	30.4	43.8
1963	23.9	30.2	43.7
1964	24.1	30.2	44.1
1965	24.5	30.1	44.2
1966	25.0	29.6	43.6
1967	25.4	29.9	43.7
1968	25.4	29.5	44.0
1969	25.0	28.7	45.3
1970	25.4	29.6	48.5
1971	24.5	29.1	48.7
1972	24.4	28.8	49.5
1973	24.5	28.5	49.3
1974	24.1	28.3	50.4
1975	23.7	28.9	51.0
1976	23.0	27.9	51.9
1977	21.8	26.2	53.4
1978	21.3	25.1	54.2
1979	21.0	24.5	54.3
1980	19.6	23.2	52.8
1981	19.0	22.6	50.2
1982	17.8	21.9	48.0
1983	16.6	20.7	—
1984	16.1 est.	19.5 est.	—

Note [a] excludes military, employers, and self-employed.
Sources: Cols 1 and 2 – provided by Leo Troy; taken from Troy and Sheflin (1985, Appendix); Col. 3 – based on data and calculations from *British Labour Statistics: Historical Abstract 1816–1968* (London: HMSO, 1971); George Sayers Bain and Robert Price, *Profiles of Union Growth: A Comparative Statistical Portrait of Eight Countries* (Oxford: Basil Blackwell, 1980); and *Department of Employment Gazette*, various issues.

In the US, differences across regions in the level of unionization are large: the industrial mideast regions have particularly high union density, while the south and western mountain regions have very low union density. Unionization is significantly lower in states with right-to-work laws, a topic to which we return later in this chapter. Unionization also differs significantly within states and regions, not only between urban and rural areas but also among metropolitan areas. Data on union membership by state are provided by Troy and Sheflin (1985), while state and SMSA data are provided in Freeman and Medoff (1979a) and Kokkelenberg and Sockell (1985).

Differences in union coverage across industries are particularly large, density being highest in transportation, communications, utilities, and in much of the manufacturing sector. Within such highly aggregated industrial groupings, there is significant variation in density across detailed industries. Among occupations, blue-collar (craftsmen and operatives) production workers are more likely to be members than nonproduction workers. The most detailed industrial and occupational data available, derived from the May CPS, are presented by Freeman and Medoff and by Kokkelenberg and Sockell.

We should note that data on union membership and coverage can differ significantly. Freeman and Medoff (1979a, Table 9, p. 169) estimate that 23.7 percent of all workers and 36.3 percent of production workers were union *members* during 1973–5. These figures compare to 29.8 percent of all workers and 45.0 percent of production workers being *covered* by collective bargaining agreements in 1968–72. While these figures would suggest that approximately 80 percent of covered workers are union members (23.7/29.8 or 36.3/45.0), this figure is probably too low, since the 1973–5 membership figures are lower than the 1968–72 coverage figures in part because of overall declines in unionism between these periods.[3] Using the Michigan PSID for 1976, Freeman and Medoff (1979a, Table 8, p. 171) find that about 91 percent of covered workers are members. Covered women, however, are less likely to be members than men (85 versus 93 percent) and covered workers in the south are less likely to be members than nonsoutherners (80 versus 94 percent).

An 'accounting' of membership changes

While data are available on total changes in US union membership over time, there is little evidence accounting for the specific channels through which these changes took place. Changes in union coverage or density derive from a number of sources. Gains in union membership occur following the organization of new bargaining units (although successful organization does not always lead to a collective bargaining agreement),

Table 3.2 Components of union growth: five-year averages, 1950–79

Period	Percent union[a]	Organizing rate[b]	Success rate[c]	Decertification rate[d]	Decertification success rate[e]	Labor force growth rate[f]	Union membership growth rate	Net growth due to representation elections[g]	Net growth due to economic causes[h]
								Components	
1950–54	34.4	2.59	76	.07	52	2.1	3.7	3.6	0.1
1955–59	34.6	1.53	62	.09	49	1.3	0.0	1.6	−1.6
1960–64	31.2	1.56	55	.12	49	1.6	−0.7	1.6	−2.3
1965–69	29.0	1.46	55	.10	42	3.7	2.2	1.8	0.4
1970–74	27.2	1.25	46	.14	48	1.9	0.6	1.3	−0.7
1975–79	23.8	.97	37	.23	54	3.0	−1.0	.9	−1.9

Notes

a the percentage of all private nonagricultural nonconstruction employees who are members of national labor unions or local affiliates of national labor unions;

b the percentage of all previously unorganized private nonagricultural employees who were eligible to vote in NLRB certification elections in a given year;

c the number of eligible voters in units choosing union representation as a percentage of total eligible voters in all election units;

d the percentage of all workers eligible to vote in decertification elections divided by total union membership;

e the number of eligible voters in units that choose to decertify as a percentage of total eligible voters in such elections;

f the growth rate of the private nonagricultural nonconstruction labor force;

g the difference between new members added through elections and old members lost through decertifications divided by total union membership;

h the residual found by subtracting net growth in membership due to representation elections from total growth or decline in membership.

Source: Dickens and Leonard (1985), Table 1, p. 326.

when union contracts are extended to cover workers in new plants, and when employment increases in organized plants. Losses in union membership occur as a result of decertification elections, layoffs, attrition and plant closings. Finally, changes in union density are brought about not only by changes in membership (the numerator), but also by changes in total employment (the denominator).

By combining BLS 'stock' data on membership with NLRB 'flow' data on certification elections, Dickens and Leonard (1985) have recently provided an accounting of changes in US union membership from 1950 to 1979, a period characterized by a decline in density. Table 3.2 (taken from their Table 1) provides summary data in five-year averages on the factors that account for union growth (their density figures differ from those in Troy and Sheflin, 1985). Column 1 shows the decline in union density, measured by the percentage of private nonagricultural wage and salary workers who are union members. This decline is accounted for by a combination of factors. First, there were declines in the organizing rate – defined as the percentage of currently unorganized workers taking part in certification elections – and in the success rate – defined as the ratio of the number of workers in units choosing representation to the total number of eligible voters involved in such elections. There was a sharp increase in the decertification rate during this period; however, the numbers involved in such elections were so small that it explains virtually none of the decline in union density. On the basis of these data and a series of assumptions regarding 'leakages' (resulting from the fact that not all covered workers become union members in right-to-work states, and that many newly certified bargaining units fail to negotiate a contract), Dickens and Leonard calculate the average net growth due to representation elections. In short, the 1970s showed a sharp decline in growth due to successful organizing, particularly as compared to the early 1950s (discussed later in the chapter is evidence from Voos, 1984, on expenditures by unions on new organizing).

Dickens and Leonard then estimate the growth rate in union membership due to 'economic' causes by taking the difference between total membership growth (or loss) and the net growth from representation elections. Of particular interest here is the finding that a significant loss in membership from economic causes is not restricted to recent years, but rather was also significant during the late 1950s and early 1960s (however, successful organizing was much higher during the earlier periods).

Because no one factor can explain the decline in unionization, Dickens and Leonard outline several counterfactual paths in order to assess each factor's relative importance. Based on their data, union density was 33 percent in 1950 and decreased to 21 percent by 1980.

Had the organizing rate, success rate, and economic growth rates held at their 1950 values, union density would have instead grown to 41 percent by 1980. If just the organizing and success rates had held constant, union density would have remained almost unchanged at 34 percent; if just the economic growth rate had held constant, density would have fallen to 28 percent; if just the organizing rate had held constant, density would have fallen to 27 percent; and if just the success rate had held constant, density would have fallen to 25 percent (Dickens and Leonard, 1985, Figure 1).

Whereas Dickens and Leonard provide evidence on what union density would have become had organizing, success, and economic growth rates remained constant, Freeman (1983c) asks what union density might become if current rates are maintained. Changes in unionism over time are summarized by a stock–flow equation (see also Ellwood and Fine, forthcoming). Letting P represent union density (measured by the proportion of the workforce who are union members) and $GAINS$ the new members from NLRB representation elections divided by the workforce:

$$\Delta P = GAINS - \lambda \ (P_{t-1}), \qquad (3.1)$$

where λ is the *net* attrition rate. That is, λ shows the rate at which union density will decrease (when $\lambda > 0$) in the absence of new members from NLRB elections (λ includes losses from decertification elections). For example, if we begin with union density equal to 0.25 and have a 4 percent attrition rate, union density declines by 0.01 (i.e. 0.04×0.25) to 0.24, assuming $GAINS = 0$.

The net attrition rate, λ, is determined primarily by cyclical and secular changes in both union and nonunion employment. Each year there will be employment changes and plant shutdowns and openings in both the union and nonunion sectors. Freeman calculates the rate of attrition among private sector workers at about 3 percent a year. With $P = 0.20$ and $\lambda = 0.03$, unions would have to organize 0.6 percent of the workforce each year to maintain 20 percent union density. While new union organizing during the 1960s was about that rate, new organizing by the late 1970s was only half as large, about 0.3 percent. If $GAINS$ remain at about 0.003, this implies continuing decreases in unionism until a steady-state level of union density is reached at approximately 10 percent of the private nonagricultural workforce $[\Delta P = 0 = 0.003 - 0.03 \ (0.10)]$.

While the analyses by Dickens and Leonard and by Freeman help *account* for changes in union density over time, they do not *explain* the determinants of these changes. In the following sections, we examine time-series and cross-sectional models that seek to explain unionization.

3.3   Time-Series Models of Union Growth

Despite widespread acceptance by economists of a theoretical framework viewing unionism as the outcome of demand and supply forces,
extant time-series studies do not closely test such an approach. An early
study by Ashenfelter and Pencavel (1969), examining American trade
union growth between 1900 and 1960, has received considerable
attention and serves as the basis for much subsequent analysis.

Ashenfelter and Pencavel (A–P) specify and provide estimates of the
following time-series model ($|t|$ in parentheses):

$$\dot{T}_t = -10.584 + .673\dot{P}_t + .367 \sum_{i=0}^{3} \dot{E}_{t-i} + .249U^{Pt} \qquad (3.2)$$
$$\quad\;\;(4.22)\qquad (5.26)\qquad\;\; (2.34)\qquad\qquad (2.59)$$

$$-.063(T/E)_{t-1} + .222\,D_t \qquad R^2 = .749 \qquad D.W. = 1.66$$
$$(2.33)\qquad\qquad (3.96)$$

(2

where $\dot{T}^t$ is the percentage change in union membership,

$\dot{P}^t$ is the percentage change in the consumer price index,

$\sum_{i=0}^{3} \dot{E}_{t-i}$ measures the percentage change in employment in highly
unionized sectors during the current and three previous years
(manufacturing, mining, construction, and transportation
and utilities),

U^{Pt} is the unemployment rate at the pit of the preceding
recession, allowed to 'decay' as t becomes farther from the
pit,

$(T/E)_{t-1}$ is the proportion of employment that was previously
unionized in the more unionized sectors, and

D_t is the percentage of Democrats in the House of Representatives.

Ashenfelter and Pencavel, as well as others, interpret these results in
terms of expected benefits and costs of union membership.[4] The
positive relationship between union membership growth and price
inflation, found consistently by A–P and others, has been interpreted as
reflecting the demand for union membership as a vehicle for catching up
with previous inflation and the attendant decrease in real wages.
Alternatively, organizing costs may be lower owing to reduced
management resistance in an inflationary environment in which cost

increases are more easily shifted forward to consumers. Implicit in these interpretations are the assumptions that inflation is not completely anticipated and that, following an inflationary period, workers expect unions to be better able to catch up and achieve real wage increases. Of course, it need not follow that unanticipated inflation is greater the larger the rate of price increase, or that the benefits of unionism are greater following high inflation.[5] Some membership studies have examined the extent to which the rate of price inflation serves as a proxy for profits or wages; however, the price variable remains empirically robust after controlling for these other factors.

Although union membership growth has in the past been positively related to price inflation, the absence of a good understanding of the reasons for the relationship makes us wary of placing undue emphasis on it. Indeed, the continuing decline of unionism following the rapid inflation of the late 1970s and early 1980s may suggest that there is little causal relationship between past inflation and current union growth, although it is of course possible that the effects of inflation have been offset by other factors.

The A–P model also indicates, not surprisingly, that membership growth is positively related to recent employment growth in highly unionized industries. A–P argue that, during periods of increasing employment and a tight labor market, union organizing funds and activity are greater and that employers' retaliation efforts are less. A simple alternative interpretation is of course that employment growth in those industries where expected benefits from union membership are large relative to organizing costs will lead to higher union growth.[6] Likewise, recent declines of employment growth in manufacturing and other high-density industries are an important explanation for declining unionism.

While the relationship of $\dot{T}$ with $\dot{P}$ and $\dot{E}$ indicates that union membership growth is procyclical, A–P also suggest that labor's grievances and existing pro-union sentiment are in part a function of the past severity in unemployment. They find empirical support for this proposition, obtaining a positive coefficient on U^{P}, the unemployment rate during the previous trough, allowed to decay with time. Implicit in this relationship is the assumption that workers expect unions to *increase* job security, particularly over the business cycle. It is doubtful whether most *unorganized* workers, comprising the pool of potential union members, believe this to be the case.

The variable $(T/E)_{t-1}$ is included in the A–P model to test the saturationist thesis that membership growth slows as union coverage increases. There is empirical support for this view, reflecting the fact that marginal organizing costs increase with coverage; in other words, industries and workers with the lowest organizing costs are most likely

53

to already be members. This finding is consistent with results obtained long ago by Hines (1964), who found the rate of British union growth to be negatively related to the growth rate in membership during the previous period. An offsetting factor might be that, within industries, the benefits from union membership, particularly the expected union wage gain, typically increase as industry coverage increases (Rosen, 1969; Freeman and Medoff, 1981).

Finally, A–P find that the percentage of Democrats in the House, D_t, a measure of union sentiment, is positively related to union growth. Pro-union sentiment should lead to a greater demand for union representation by unorganized workers, less resistance from management, and more favorable legislation and legal interpretations from the NLRB and the courts. Surprisingly, A–P do not allow for any shifts or structural changes in their model following the Wagner Act or other major pieces of labor legislation.

The A–P model has not gone uncontested. Recently, Sheflin, Troy, and Koeller (1981), using revised and corrected US union membership data extended through 1975, have reestimated the A–P model, as well as a similar model developed by Bain and Elsheikh (1976) for the UK. They find that there was a significant 'break' in the structure of the model around 1937, shortly after passage of the Wagner Act. Moreover, during the 1937–75 period the variable D_t is no longer statistically significant, while U^P has the 'wrong' sign. These findings are consistent with those presented by Moore and Pearce (1976), who find the A–P model to be a poor predictor for 1961–9, and Fiorito (1982), who detects a significant structural change in the Bain–Elsheikh model.

Abbott (1982) has provided a detailed econometric investigation of several variants of the A–P model applied to Canadian union membership data. He finds that the A–P model does a good job in 'explaining' trade union growth in Canada between 1925 and 1966. Union growth is found to be positively and significantly related to (1) current inflation, but at a decreasing rate (a positive coefficient on $\dot{P}_t$ and a negative one on $\dot{P}^2$), (2) current and past rates of growth in potential unionizable employment, (3) worker discontent, as proxied by the severity of past business cycle contractions, and (4) the rate of change in US union membership. Union growth is negatively related to union density, consistent with the saturationist hypothesis. While Abbott's results are robust for the 1929–66 period, he finds the A–P type model does a poor job of predicting post-sample union growth during the 1967–72 period.

Because of temporal instability, poor predictive power, and the inability of available explanatory variables to measure expected benefits and costs of unionism directly, we believe the A–P type time-series models provide a fairly limited basis for understanding past unionization or for predicting future membership growth. Unfortunately, no clearly superior models have been developed that lend themselves to time-series estimation.

Rather than analyzing the growth in total union membership, several time-series studies have examined some measure of union success in NLRB certification elections (among others, see Roomkin and Juris, 1978; Ellwood and Fine, forthcoming; and Freeman, 1983c). Interestingly, all of these studies stress the importance of public policy factors on union organizing success through representation elections. Roomkin and Juris include variables measuring Democratic control of the NLRB, passage of the Landrum–Griffin Act, NLRB 'regionalization', and election procedure delays. Freeman argues that the marked increase in unfair labor practices during recent years has been a major cause for unions' poor showing in NLRB elections, while Ellwood and Fine show that both unfair labor practices and right-to-work laws have had significant effects (the Ellwood–Fine paper is discussed more fully in the next section).

The time-series studies examining union organizing have not provided a conclusive explanation for the decline in union membership. Structural change in employment and industrial composition is clearly a major part of any such explanation, but is not a sufficient explanation (Dickens and Leonard, 1985). Cross-sectional studies examined below suggest that demographic and regional changes have been important, yet the time-series studies do not account for these factors. The emphasis by Freeman (1983c) and Ellwood and Fine (forthcoming) on the role of the legal structure and unfair labor practices may well be appropriate. However, the law, as well as its interpretation and enforcement, is clearly endogenous; thus, researchers must explain the determination of the legal structure, as well as its resulting effect on union organizing. Increasingly effective management resistance to union organizing, evidenced in part by the increase in unfair labor practices, is most likely the consequence of greater latitude on the part of the NLRB (Weiler, 1983) and increased pressure on profits. This pressure on profits arises from increased foreign competition, from deregulation of industries with significant union strength (e.g. transportation and communications), and, as suggested by Freeman, from an increasing union–nonunion wage differential (but, as seen in Chapter 5, the evidence here is not clear-cut).

A final factor that may explain some of the decline in union organizing success is union expenditures on organizing. Voos (1984) has collected data on the organizing expenditures of 20 major US unions from 1953 to 1974. Interestingly, total expenditures (in constant dollars) and expenditures per union member have actually shown a small increase during this period, while expenditures per *nonunion* production worker have exhibited a small decline. While real expenditures have shown only modest change over the 1953–74 period, Voos (1983) has argued elsewhere that the marginal benefits to existing union members from organizing substantially exceed the marginal costs of organizing.[7] However, we doubt whether unions have been able to maintain real organizing expenditures during the early 1980s in the face of decreases in employment of and dues from their members. Coupled with large increases in nonunion employment, real organizing expenditures per nonunion worker may be falling sharply. Moreover, as unions (e.g. Teamsters) attempt to organize workers outside their traditional area, some of the funds for union organizing are spent competing with other unions for the same groups of workers.

In addition to studies examining union growth, a few studies have analyzed determinants of the trend in decertification elections.[8] Anderson, O'Reilly, and Busman (1980) attempt to explain decertification within the context of the A–P model. Although they hypothesize a model identical with the A–P union growth model (i.e. one whose coefficients are opposite in sign), their results are generally inconsistent with their hypotheses. Elliott and Hawkins (1982) use a first-difference equation model and find changes in the relative frequency of successful decertification elections to be cyclical – declining during business expansions, increasing with increases in inflation, and decreasing with increases in unemployment. They also find that decertification increases as the extent of union organizing activities increases, suggesting that unions face a tradeoff between new organizing and maintenance of services for existing members. An alternative explanation for this result is that causation also runs the other way – increased decertification efforts lead to greater new organizing activity.

Before turning to a summary appraisal of the time-series studies, we should reiterate a point made earlier. Workers (jobs) involved in certification (or decertification) elections are not likely to be representative of either existing union or nonunion workers (jobs). Thus, much care must be exercised in comparing results from different types of studies and in generalizing the inferences drawn from any given study.

We believe the lacuna of the time-series studies investigating union growth is their inability to relate membership changes explicitly to expected benefits and organizing costs.[9] The studies rarely have direct measures of organizing or membership costs, although it is likely that the previous proportion unionized, political climate proxies, and labor legislation variables primarily affect membership via their effects on costs. While one would like to measure the expected wage and nonwage gains to existing and potential union members, the existing studies at best proxy these gains by including cyclical variables such as the rate of change in prices and money wages or measures of unemployment.

Although it is true that union membership growth has varied over the business cycle, such a theoretical relationship generally relies on the untenable assumption of persistent price illusion or nonrational expectations. Not surprisingly, the empirical relationship between union growth and price inflation and unemployment is not particularly stable.

Possibly a more fruitful approach in the time-series analyses would be to use models that incorporate the personal and industry characteristics variables utilized in cross-sectional studies, variables believed to systematically proxy the benefits and costs of unionism. Variables measuring the proportion of women in the labor force, the age structure, the proportion of blue-collar employment, race, regional and urban location, capital intensity, and average firm size, for example, could be incorporated partially into a time-series model without prohibitive difficulty (see, for example, Ellwood and Fine, forthcoming). On the basis of the results from cross-sectional studies, reviewed below, it is possible that such factors could explain some significant portion of the change in union membership over time. Moreover, these relationships could be interpreted more easily within the economic framework presented in Chapter 2.

3.4 Cross-Sectional Models of Union Status Determination

Cross-sectional studies of union determination constitute a larger, more varied, and richer literature than do the time-series studies. Models examining the union status of workers have used individuals, two- and three-digit industries, NLRB bargaining units, states, and SMSAs as their unit of observation.[10] Unionism equations from these studies can best be interpreted as reduced-form membership equations deriving from the demand–supply framework presented in Chapter 2. That is, union representation is estimated as a function of independent right-hand-side variables affecting either the benefits or costs of unionization. We shall examine the effects of personal, industry, and labor market characteristics; attitudes and the legal environment; and the wage rate and the union wage differential.

Estimation and interpretation of such models involve several difficulties. A fundamental problem is the existence of simultaneity between unionism and key explanatory variables, particularly the wage rate and the union wage differential. In addition, several explanatory variables affect both the benefits and costs of unionism, making a straightforward interpretation of results difficult. We briefly discuss such problems when they are encountered.

Personal characteristics

Union membership has been found to be systematically related to a number of personal characteristics. One of the more interesting determinants is age or, more appropriately, years of experience. At first glance, the empirical evidence seems ambiguous: some studies find unionism to increase with age (e.g. Antos, Chandler, and Mellow, 1980), some find the likelihood of voting for a union to decrease with age (e.g. Farber and Saks, 1980), while others obtain insignificant results (e.g. Hirsch, 1982). Duncan and Stafford (1980) and Hirsch and Berger (1984), *inter alia*, find a concave union–experience relationship – a positive coefficient on experience and a negative coefficient on experience squared. Hirsch and Berger estimate the effect of experience on unionism to peak at 34 years among production workers in manufacturing, while Duncan and Stafford find a peak at about 28 years among all production workers (based on estimates reported in Duncan and Stafford, 1980, Table 1). In an interesting paper, Farber (1983b) finds both union membership and the preference for union membership among nonunion members to exhibit a concave relationship with respect to both experience and job seniority.

These somewhat ambiguous results can be interpreted within the framework discussed in Chapter 2. On the one hand, older workers are likely to exhibit less mobility and greater firm attachment, and to value relatively more highly union-generated health and pension benefits and structured pay scales emphasizing seniority. On the other hand, if unionism tends to flatten earnings–experience profiles and provides the largest wage (but not nonwage) advantages to the youngest workers (such evidence is summarized in Chapters 5 and 6), older workers may be relatively less likely to support unions.

A median voter model of union objectives provides perhaps the simplest explanation for the observed concave relationship between union membership and experience. If worker preferences vary with experience (age), individuals' support of unions should first strengthen and subsequently weaken as experience increases. Another explanation for some of the apparently disparate results is that studies finding a positive or concave relationship are using union membership status as a dependent variable, while studies finding a negative relationship with age are generally using data from NLRB representation elections or on preferences for union membership by nonunion workers. Thus, whereas older workers may be increasingly likely to be union members owing to past optimizing decisions (and the historical context in which unionization developed), older *nonunion* workers may be less likely to vote to join a union. Or, as Abowd and Farber (1982) have argued, age may make workers less likely to be in the union queue (to prefer a union job), but, up to some age, more likely to be chosen by employers once in the queue.

Women are significantly less likely to be union members than men (see, among others, Antos, Chandler, and Mellow, 1980). Much of this difference stems from differences in job structure – women being less likely than men to choose or be employed in the covered sector. For example, union coverage is less likely in job settings with less permanent labor force attachment or where part-time or more flexible work schedules are present.[11] However, even among production workers in manufacturing, Hirsch and Berger (1984) find women significantly less likely to be union members. Moreover, Freeman and Medoff (1979a) show that among workers covered by a collective bargaining agreement women are less likely than men to be union members, and Farber and Saks (1980) find that women are less likely to vote for a union in NLRB representation elections. However, Farber (1983a, b), who separately analyzes the likelihood of married and single women being union members and being willing to vote for a union if nonunion, obtains largely inconclusive results. Such inclusive results are consistent with the finding (reviewed in Chapter 5) that union–nonunion wage differentials are similar between men and women. We believe the overall evidence regarding women and union membership, while not conclusive, suggests that increased labor force participation by married women explains at least some of the secular decline in union density.

Production or blue-collar workers have consistently been found more likely to be union members. Such workers are likely to have less identification with management, not to be self-employed, and to have relatively more homogeneous preferences and working conditions. For these reasons, organizing costs are likely to be lower and unions can more likely devise an agenda that will satisfy a majority of workers. Production jobs are also more likely to be characterized by less flexible work conditions, greater worker–machine complementarity, and team production, characteristics that Duncan and Stafford (1980, 1982) have shown make unionism more likely (for conflicting evidence see D. Leigh, 1981).

Other personal characteristics are not related so consistently to the likelihood of unionism. Most studies report that nonwhites are more likely to be union members or to vote for unions in representation elections. This might best be explained by the fact that estimated relative union wage gains are generally (but not always) larger for nonwhites; alternatively, many nonwhites may believe they fare better in a work environment with highly structured work rules, seniority provisions, and so forth. Although union membership is significantly less likely among those with more than a high school education, most studies do not find education to be a significant determinant of union membership after controlling for other characteristics. We can think of few important reasons why education *per se* should affect the demand for or supply of union services, except perhaps that education makes workers more mobile and less dependent on internal union voice.

Finally, several studies examining voting in representation elections find that perceptions regarding management and unions play an important role in determining election outcomes (see, for example, Farber and Saks, 1980). Workers who are dissatisfied with the current work environment and who believe that unions help improve work conditions and fairness are significantly more likely to vote for a union. This evidence is consistent with the importance that management consultants place on improving communication channels and providing outlets for grievances as means of decreasing the probability of union representation.

Industry characteristics

There is relatively little empirical work examining the relationship between unionism and industry characteristics and, due to data limitations, the little evidence that is available is restricted almost exclusively to the manufacturing sector. This very limited evidence, however, strongly supports the view that industry characteristics significantly affect the benefits and costs associated with unionism. In this section we examine the evidence concerning industry concentration, capital intensity, establishment size, and job hazards.

Workers in highly concentrated industries are more likely to be unionized for several reasons. Labor demand elasticities in concentrated industries are likely to be lower, at least for the largest firms which will face downward sloping product demand schedules. Thus a union's ability to organize and subsequently acquire wage gains may be greater. Higher industry concentration may also indicate the possibility of maintaining economic rents over a longer time period, and unionization may provide a mechanism for capturing some portion of these rents (see Chapter 7 for evidence on this point). Of course, the existence of such rents may also increase the investment by management in resisting organizing. Finally, an industry with a higher concentration of sales is also likely to have a higher (less dispersed) concentration of workers so that organizing costs will be lower.

Ashenfelter and Johnson (1972), using aggregate data, find union membership positively and significantly related to industry concentration, while Kahn (1979) finds no significant relationship. Hirsch (1982) and B. Miller (1984) find a significant relationship before, but not after, controlling for average firm sales. Both Lee (1978) and Hirsch and Berger (1984), bridging three-digit industry concentration to individual data, find a positive and significant relationship. We believe the evidence available to date thus allows one to conclude that greater industrial concentration increases at least moderately the likelihood of unionization, although the channels by which it most affects union status are not known.

It is commonly believed that greater capital intensity also leads to greater unionization, although the evidence is sparse. A higher capital to labor ratio implies that labor comprises a smaller share of total costs (holding constant the wage), hence leading to a more inelastic labor demand schedule – assuming the elasticity of substitution is less than the price elasticity of demand. More capital intensive firms are also likely to be less mobile due to high fixed costs, leading to a more inelastic short-run labor demand and possibly lower organizing costs. And Duncan and Stafford (1980, p. 361) have hypothesized that "unions will be more prevalent in capital-intensive continuous process activities which give rise to worker effort complementarities, corresponding public goods problems, and incentives to schedule work in a way that will more fully utilize the capital stock."

The only studies of which we are aware that examine capital intensity and union membership are those by Hirsch and Berger (1984) and B. Miller (1984). Hirsch and Berger match four-digit SIC-coded capital to labor ratios (measured by the log of industry gross book value of plant and equipment divided by employment) from the Census of Manufactures to three-digit Census coding for individual workers from the 1971 March CPS. They find that capital intensity significantly increases the likelihood of union membership for both production and nonproduction workers in manufacturing. Miller obtains similar (although less conclusive) results using industry data. While the unionization–capital relationship clearly requires further study, the results to date lead us to believe that future work will support the existence of a significant positive effect of capital intensity on unionization.[12]

Relatively more evidence exists on the relationship between firm or establishment size and unionization. A priori, this relationship is ambiguous. On the one hand, larger establishments are likely to involve substantially lower organizing costs for a union, leading to a positive membership–size relationship. In addition, the benefits from formalized work, reward, and grievance procedures may be valued most highly in large units where worker–management communication and monitoring are generally more difficult. On the other hand, larger nonunion establishments may be able to provide much of the same formalization more easily than can smaller nonunion establishments (Foulkes, 1980). Moreover, to the extent that union resistance activities involve substantial fixed costs for management, larger establishments may choose to pursue more of these activities.

Available evidence, while limited, shows clearly that existing unionism is significantly more prevalent in industries with larger firms. Hirsch (1982) finds the level of unionization in manufacturing industries increases with average firm sales in the industry, while B. Miller (1984) obtains the same result using average number of employees. Likewise, Bain and Elsheikh (1979), for an admittedly small sample of British industries, find unionization to be positively related to average establishment size, measured by the number of employees. Hirsch and Berger (1984), too, find individual union membership in manufacturing to be more likely the larger is average establishment size in workers' industry of employment.

While the evidence concerning firm size and *existing* unionization is unambiguous, that concerning *new* membership is not. Most studies examining NLRB election outcomes find that union success in winning certification *decreases* as unit size increases. For example, Rose (1972) and Sandver (1982), using all-industry samples, and Becker and Miller (1981), examining outcomes in the hospital industry, find an inverse relationship. Delaney (1981), however, also using data from the hospital industry, finds union victories negatively related to election unit size, but positively related to total number of employees. This interesting finding suggests that election unit size may be a poor measure of establishment size. Voos (1983), in an attempt to estimate the marginal benefits and costs to existing union members from union organizing, finds that organizing success in an industry (measured by the proportion of previously unorganized workers who become members) increases with size.

In summary, the available evidence to date shows that unionism is significantly more likely in industries with larger establishments, probably owing to significantly lower organizing costs. Similarly, it may also be the case that unions can better organize new members within industries with larger establishments. However, success in winning representation elections is greater when relatively smaller bargaining units are involved.[13]

Although the findings with respect to the union–size relationship may appear confusing, it is worth noting that existing union membership is not directly comparable to certification election outcomes. Existing unionism has resulted from past membership and job choice decisions and provides good evidence on the 'average' or typical relationship between union or nonunion status and characteristics. Data from representation elections, on the other hand, while allowing us to observe explicitly individual choices on representation, provide evidence only on work units that are relatively new or where the representation decision is a marginal one. These studies may not provide reliable information on more typical work units where nonmarginal preferences are predominantly pro-union or anti-union.

A final industry characteristic for which little evidence exists is job risk or safety. J. P. Leigh (1982) finds that unionism is positively correlated with the probability of injury and several measures of job hazards, while Hirsch and Berger (1984) find individual union membership more likely, other things equal, in more dangerous industries. Although the evidence regarding the nature of this relationship is not conclusive, a plausible explanation is that demand for union representation is greater in more dangerous work environments. That is, unionism may provide a means for formalizing work and safety rules and may make possible an effective collective voice in the determination of the job safety and compensation mix.

The effects of industry characteristics on unionism have not been studied nearly as thoroughly as the effects of personal characteristics. The available evidence nevertheless indicates that industry characteristics are important determinants of the benefits and costs associated with unionism. Despite serious data limitations, we would expect that future research will pay increased attention to industry characteristics.

Labor market characteristics

Significant differences in unionization exist across labor markets. While some of these differences are accounted for by differences in personal characteristics of the labor force, much of the variation also stems from important differences in industry structure and other characteristics across areas. In particular, areas with high proportions of employment in transportation, communication, utilities, and manufacturing, or a low proportion in agriculture, tend to have significantly higher levels of unionization (Hirsch, 1980). This relationship is explained in part by the fact that transportation, communication, and utility industries are typically publicly regulated, highly concentrated within individual labor markets, and capital intensive – all of which lead to low labor demand elasticities, large expected benefits from union representation, and low organizing costs. Likewise, deregulation of the airline, trucking, and other industries in the US has significantly lessened union membership and wage gains in this sector.

Unionization is found to be more likely among workers in SMSAs than in non-urban areas, and somewhat more likely in larger than in smaller SMSAs (Lee, 1978). While this relationship probably reflects differences in attitudes toward or in costs and benefits associated with union representation (but not captured by other variables), we have little confidence in any single explanation. As is well known, regional differences in unionization are quite large. In particular, unionism is much less prevalent in the south and large portions of the western region than in the north–central region. Regional differences are believed to reflect both differences in personal characteristics and job structure not accounted for elsewhere by other variables, and also systematic differences in attitudes toward unionism held by employees and employers. However, there is no general agreement about the importance of region *per se* on unionism. Empirical studies using individual data consistently find that regional dummy variables are among the most significant explanatory variables. On the other hand, studies using aggregated data obtain much weaker results. For instance, Hirsch (1980) finds that, among SMSAs, regional dummy variables are not jointly significant determinants of unionism, after accounting for personal characteristics, industry structure, and the existence of a right-to-work law. Likewise, Hirsch (1982) does not find variables measuring percentages of employment by region to be jointly significant determinants of interindustry differences in unionism.

These apparently conflicting results are not explained easily. In the aggregate studies, it may simply be that other explanatory variables capture (or are correlated with) regional differences that affect unionism, whereas in the individual studies they do not. Our guess is that *most* interarea differences in unionism result from differences in personal, industry, or labor market characteristics, but that regional differences in attitudes do in fact make some difference. One possible explanation for large regional differences in unionism is historical differences in the time frame of rapid industrialization. The south was highly agrarian and had relatively little manufacturing during the period of rapid unionization in the US. To the extent that current unionism reflects past as well as current worker (and employer) preferences, some of the south's low level of unionism reflects its later economic development. While southern workers are less likely to be union workers, *nonunion* southern workers may have preferences toward union representation only slightly less favorable than those of non-southern nonunion workers (Sandver, 1982; Farber, 1983a, b).

Right-to-work laws and the legal structure

There is widespread agreement that the legal rules and environment surrounding the union representation process are an important determinant of unionism. This can be seen most readily in the US by the rapid increases in private sector unionism following the Wagner Act and by the increase in public sector unionism attendant upon legal changes in the early 1960s. As is generally acknowledged, however, laws themselves are not determined independently of those forces affecting union membership. For this reason, empirical estimation of the effects of the legal structure on union status is rarely straightforward.

Because most US labor law concerning collective bargaining is federal, there are few differences in legal structure among units of observation in a cross section. The major exception is the existence of right-to-work (RTW) laws. Section 14-B of the Taft–Hartley Act of 1947 gave states the right to pass RTW laws that make the 'union shop' illegal. Whereas in non-RTW states the union shop is predominant (employers in covered establishments are free to hire whomever they want, but workers must join the union within a given time period), RTW states have 'open shops' in which mandatory union membership or dues collection is illegal. Twenty states, primarily in the southern and western mountain regions, currently have RTW laws. On average, these RTW states have much lower levels of unionization than do non-RTW states.

Repeal of Section 14-B has been a long-standing goal of labor unions. Although the likelihood of repeal in the near future is small, heated battles have occurred at the state level over proposals either to adopt or repeal RTW laws. The intensity of conflict over RTW indicates that both the proponents and opponents of organized labor believe the issue is one of substantial importance. However, apart from a couple of recent studies, most estimates indicate that the effects of RTW laws on union membership are not statistically significant.

Studies using cross-sectional state data by Lumsden and Petersen (1975) and Moore and Newman (1975) cast considerable doubt on the conventional wisdom that RTW laws significantly decrease unionization. Lumsden and Petersen estimate state union membership regressions for 1939, 1953, and 1968. Each includes an RTW dummy variable equal to 1 for states that *would adopt* RTW by 1968, and 0 otherwise. In each year, the RTW variable is negative and statistically significant, indicating that 3.5–4.5 percent fewer of the nonagricultural labor force are union members in RTW states, *ceteris paribus*. However, Taft–Hartley was not passed until 1947; thus, *no* states had RTW laws in 1939! Consequently, Lumsden and Petersen conclude that the lower unionism found in RTW states results not from RTW *per se*, but rather because of tastes and preferences in RTW states which are less favorable toward unionism. Indeed, the coefficient on the RTW variable is most negative in the 1939 regression, whereas just the reverse should be the case if RTW laws in fact have an independent impact on union membership.

Moore and Newman (1975), using state data for 1950, 1960, and 1970, also find a negative and significant coefficient on the RTW variable for their ordinary least squares (OLS) equations. However, because states with a lower proportion of union members are more likely to pass RTW laws, a simultaneous equation approach accounting for the endogeneity of RTW is more appropriate. Using two-stage least squares (2SLS), they no longer find that RTW laws significantly decrease union membership (though 2SLS is not without statistical problems here since the RTW equation has a dichotomous dependent variable). That is, the large negative correlation between RTW and unionism exists primarily because highly unionized states are least likely to pass RTW laws, and not because RTW laws significantly decrease unionization.

Several more recent studies have reexamined the RTW issue. Hirsch (1980) uses 1970 SMSA data and argues that a state RTW law might be regarded as largely exogenous to any SMSA within a state (though some simultaneity is still likely to exist). He suggests that RTW is likely to have a differential effect on collective bargaining coverage and union membership. Workers in RTW states enjoy the same legal protection and bargaining rights as do workers in non-RTW states, apart from the inclusion of compulsory dues or membership clauses in labor contracts. While RTW may discourage organizing efforts or lessen bargaining power, the overall effects on contract coverage are likely to be small. On the other hand, the free-rider problem – all members of a bargaining unit receive benefits from collective bargaining regardless of membership – should lead RTW laws to have a more substantial impact on membership (most analysts do not, however, believe free-rider problems are substantial). Consistent with these arguments, Hirsch finds that RTW laws have no significant impact on coverage, but do decrease union membership by approximately 3–5 percent.

Results from other studies are conflicting. Warren and Strauss (1979) use a mixed logit model that simultaneously estimates the effects of RTW on union membership and membership on RTW. They conclude that RTW significantly decreases membership. However, the number of variables in their model is small and questions have arisen regarding econometric problems with the mixed logit model first used by Schmidt and Strauss (1976).[14] Wessels (1981), using econometric methods developed by Lee (1978) and Heckman (1976) which account for simultaneity and selectivity bias within a system of equations containing continuous and limited dependent variables, concludes that RTW laws do not significantly affect union membership. Moore (1980), using individual data from the PSID, also concludes that state RTW laws have no effect on union membership. Farber (1984a), using data from the CPS and the Quality of Employment Survey (which measures the preference for unionism among nonunion workers), finds the demand by workers for representation to be significantly lower in RTW states. He concludes that his evidence is most consistent with the hypothesis that RTW laws mirror preexisting preferences and have little direct impact on union membership.

In contrast to the above studies, which analyze the impact of RTW laws on *levels* of union membership, Ellwood and Fine (forthcoming) examine the effect of RTW laws on union *organizing*. Using state-by-year data, they find large decreases in organizing directly after the passage of RTW laws. The decline in new membership results primarily from decreases in the number of certification elections and in the size of newly organized units, rather than from changes in the union success rate. The decrease in union organizing found by Ellwood and Fine is consistent with a reduction in the *level* of union coverage of 1–3 percentage points in most states.[15] Interestingly, this is well within the range of most prior estimates on the effects of RTW on union levels; however, previous studies have had large standard errors surrounding their estimates.

Ellwood and Fine also examine directly whether or not RTW laws mirror preexisting preferences. Using data on seven RTW states where sufficient data are available before and after the passage of RTW laws, Ellwood and Fine do not detect evidence of a decrease in union organizing in the five years *prior* to the passage of RTW (indeed, organizing is estimated to be higher, but not significantly so). If RTW simply mirrored preexisting conditions, union organizing might be expected to have decreased even before the passage of RTW. On the basis of these findings, Ellwood and Fine conclude that the estimated effects of RTW laws are real and substantial.

While most empirical work relating union membership to differences in legal structure has focused on RTW laws, additional evidence suggests that the legal framework is important. The most convincing evidence of this is the sharp increase in private sector unionism following passage of the Wagner Act and in public sector unionism following the establishment of a similar legal framework in the federal government. Reid and Kurth (1983, 1984) provide further evidence from the public sector, finding that unionism among teachers during the 1970s was significantly influenced by laws enhancing union security agreements (the absence of RTW, exclusive representation, and optional and mandatory dues checkoff).

Ellwood and Fine (forthcoming) and Freeman (1983c) detect that union organizing over time is affected adversely by the number of unfair labor practices found by the NLRB. Their rather robust findings are consistent with the view that legal rules, or, more generally, any factors significantly affecting the marginal costs of union organizing, are important determinants of unionism. Intense political lobbying over labor law legislation may well reflect the fact that the effects of the legal structure are as much substantive as symbolic. Relatedly, Dickens (1983) and others have shown recently that company campaigns against unions significantly affect how workers vote in certification elections.

Union status, wages, and the wage differential

Many of the empirical studies containing union membership equations have been concerned primarily with the effect of unions on wage rates. Because union status is not determined independently of the wage rate, simultaneous equation models including both union status and wage equations have been estimated. Several studies find unionism to be positively related to the wage rate (or earnings) and to the union–nonunion wage differential. Unfortunately, there is little consensus regarding either the theoretical or empirical validity of these results.

Ashenfelter and Johnson (1972), in an important and frequently cited paper, specify a three-equation model in which wage rates, union membership, and labor quality (education) are endogenous. The model is estimated using aggregated two-digit industry data from manufacturing. The proportion unionized is found to be positively and significantly related to the industry wage level using OLS, 2SLS, and 3SLS regression techniques. Indeed, the effect of wages on unionism is statistically more significant than the effect of unions on wage rates. A similar relationship between unionism and wages (or earnings) has subsequently been reported for three-digit manufacturing industries (Kahn, 1979; Hirsch, 1982), SMSAs (Hirsch, 1980), individual workers across occupations (Schmidt and Strauss, 1976), and blue-collar workers (Duncan and Stafford, 1980). While the result appears robust for production workers in the manufacturing sector, no sizeable or significant relationship is found for three-digit nonmanufacturing industries (Hirsch, 1982).

One possible explanation for the apparently positive impact of wages and earnings on unionization is that union services are a normal good (i.e. they have a positive income elasticity). However, the facts that union membership is particularly unlikely for high-income workers, that it has decreased during a period of generally rising income, and that the positive relationship may be restricted to production workers in manufacturing make us cautious in accepting this interpretation. The positive unionism–wage relationship may instead result from the fact that the wage rate is a proxy for other factors that increase expected benefits and/or lower costs of union representation. Alternatively, as argued by Duncan and Stafford (1980), a higher wage rate may be in part an intervening factor associated with both less flexible working conditions and a higher probability of unionism. In summary, there is general disagreement regarding the appropriateness of including a wage or earnings variable in the unionism equation, and hence no consensus regarding interpretation of the positive income elasticity found in existing studies.

A stronger theoretical argument can be made for including the potential relative union wage differential in a union status equation since this variable may measure much of the benefit associated with representation. However, because union wage effects are themselves difficult to measure, their inclusion in the unionism equation is not straightforward. Studies using individual data by Lee (1978), Duncan and Leigh (1980), Farber (1983c), and Hirsch and Berger (1984) have estimated the following type of model:

$$\ln W_u = \beta_{u0} + \beta_{u1}X_u + \varepsilon_u \qquad (3.3)$$

$$\ln W_n = \beta_{n0} + \beta_{n1}X_n + \varepsilon_n \qquad (3.4)$$

$$U = \alpha_0 + \alpha_1 Z + \gamma (\ln W_u - \ln W_n) + \varepsilon \qquad (3.5)$$

where W_u and W_n represent the union and nonunion wage respectively, U is a dichotomous variable indicating union status, X is a vector of characteristics affecting union and nonunion wages, Z is a vector of characteristics affecting union status (X and Z have most elements in common), and ε_u, ε_n, and ε are disturbance terms. The variable $(\ln W_u - \ln W_n)$ measures the union–nonunion wage differential (see Chapter 5) for each individual and is expected to make union membership more likely.

Actual estimation of such a model is not straightforward. Because the union variable is dichotomous, estimation of equation (3.5) by OLS is inappropriate since it leads to inefficient estimates, biased standard errors resulting from heteroskedasticity, and predicted values outside the [0,1] range. Moreover, a simultaneous equation procedure is necessary since unionism affects the relative wage and vice versa. Finally, because the error terms across equations are likely to be correlated, it is inappropriate simply to include an instrument for $(\ln W_u - \ln W_n)$ in (3.5) obtained from direct OLS estimation of (3.3) and (3.4). This problem can be thought of as a sample selection bias, resulting from the fact that the samples of union and nonunion workers are not drawn randomly from the population. In other words, union and nonunion workers *with similar characteristics* are likely to be different. A statistical solution to this problem was developed by Lee (1978), based in part on work by Heckman (1976).[16] It involves first estimating a union equation by probit analysis, including all exogenous variables (the vectors X and Z), but not $(\ln W_u - \ln W_n)$. From this equation 'selectivity variables' are obtained (the inverse Mills ratio) to be included in the wage equations (3.3) and (3.4). From the wage equations one obtains predicted values of $(\ln W_u - \ln W_n)$ for each worker. The value $(\ln W_u - \ln W_n)$ serves as an estimate of the union wage effect and is then included in the estimation of equation (3.5).

Lee (1978), Duncan and Leigh (1980), and Hirsch and Berger (1984), using three diverse samples, find the likelihood of union membership to increase with the union wage differential, though Hirsch and Berger obtain a weak relationship that is highly sensitive to alternative specifications. Farber (1983b), using alternative estimation techniques, also obtains positive but insignificant coefficients on his wage differential variables.

Estimation of the relationship between union status and the wage differential entails additional problems. The wage differential variable should measure the expected potential differential at the time the decision on union status is made, and not the observed union wage differential after union status is determined (Bloch, 1982a). Moreover, a large union wage differential will not only increase the demand for membership by workers, but also stiffen the resistance of firms to unionism. It seems likely that these opposing effects have been entangled statistically in the models estimated to date. Thus, while there is good theoretical reason for believing that the potential union wage gain is an important determinant of union status, precise estimation of this relationship must still await more precise estimation of the wage effects of unionism and the underlying structural union status demand and supply model.

Finally, Hirsch (1982) has argued that union membership and collective bargaining coverage should also be affected by the *distribution* of earnings and worker characteristics within an industry or bargaining unit. Similarly, Farber and Saks (1980) have shown that workers' position in the wage distribution will affect their votes in certification elections. Despite the paucity of statistical evidence in this area, we believe future research may prove quite important; we therefore provide a separate discussion of unionism and the distribution of earnings in Chapter 6.

3.5 Conclusions and Prospects for the Future

In this chapter, we have seen that a considerable body of evidence has developed on the determination of unionism over time and across persons, industries, and labor markets. Although our knowledge remains imperfect, considerable progress has been made in establishing a relationship between unionism and a number of personal, industry, and labor market characteristics. The various models employed in these studies have been somewhat *ad hoc*, but most of the observed empirical relationships can be interpreted within the context of the demand–supply framework presented in Chapter 2.

The principal weakness of the union determination literature, in particular the time-series studies, has been the inability to estimate structural demand and supply equations for union services. The reasons for this failure are numerous. Much of the literature on union demand is couched in terms of individual worker choice, whereas what we generally observe is whether or not a worker is a union member or in a covered job. Union status encompasses not only individual choices on union membership, but also the collective choices of past workers, the job choices of individuals, and hiring decisions by employers. Moreover, the costs of unionism are in large part organizing costs occurring prior to representation. Viewed from the perspective of current members, a significant portion of their dues is used to finance the organizing of currently uncovered workers.

The inability to estimate demand and supply equations directly also stems from data limitations. Price generally plays the crucial role in equilibrating quantities demanded and supplied. Although most labor economists do not believe that price (most notably union dues) is a major factor in organizing and membership decisions, the paucity of data on dues severely limits our ability to examine this question. Where such data are available – in Pencavel's (1971) time-series study of British membership and Dworkin and Extejt's (1979) cross-sectional study of US decertification elections – the dues variables are statistically significant.[17]

While some progress has been made in incorporating the expected union wage differential into the union status equation, we know of only one study that explicitly measures and estimates the impact of organizing costs on union membership (as opposed to including variables believed to be proxies for costs, such as establishment size). Voos (1983) examines new union membership between 1964 and 1977 and attempts to estimate the marginal costs and marginal benefits to *current* union members associated with union organizing. She finds that the proportion of potentially organizable workers for whom unions win representation is positively and significantly related to the actual organizing expenditures by unions. Yet she is not able to examine directly the hypothesis that the level of membership or coverage is inversely related to the marginal costs of winning representation.

Despite the shortcomings of the literature summarized in this chapter, we believe the demand–supply framework has proven a useful approach. Substantial progress has been made in understanding how various factors affect the benefits or costs of unionism and the subsequent membership and coverage outcomes. However, because of the methodological and data problems summarized earlier, we believe this literature can best be interpreted as explaining the determination of the union status of jobs, rather than the current union choice decisions made by workers.

On the basis of the research summarized in this chapter, what can be said about future prospects for union membership growth in the US? Will the secular decline in the proportion of the labor force who are union members continue? Will labor unions remain an important force in US labor markets? Unfortunately, the time-series studies available to date tell us very little. For example, rates of inflation, unemployment, and employment growth tend to be cyclical and cannot be predicted with much accuracy. More fundamentally, the theoretical under-pinnings for such relationships are, in our opinion, rather weak and not closely related to economic explanations for unionism based on expected benefits and costs. It is not surprising that these models have not proven structurally stable over time. Accordingly, we have little faith in the reliability of membership forecasts based on available parameter estimates from time-series models.

Results from the cross-sectional studies, on the other hand, do permit reasoned speculation as to union prospects (for a different view, see Freeman, 1983c). These results suggest that the decline in the extent of unionism since the mid-1950s is in large part a consequence of significant employment shifts into industries and regions where unionism is less prevalent, of a declining share of production jobs, of increased foreign competition, of increases in female labor force participation, of a younger and more mobile labor force, and of changing attitudes and a legal environment decreasingly conducive to union organizing. Clearly, deregulation and increased competition in transportation (i.e. airlines, trucking, buses, and railroads), communi-cations, and other industries have significantly weakened union strength in these areas. We suspect that overall changes in industry concentra-tion, firm size, and capital intensity over this period have had little effect, however, although we are unaware of any study examining their role over time.[18]

It appears likely that decreases in employment among production workers in several major manufacturing industries will continue. Although changes in industry job structure are likely to decrease further the overall proportion of union members, other factors should not continue to have such a negative effect. Labor force participation by women may continue to increase, but it will not increase at as rapid a rate as in the past. Moreover, as women become increasingly attached to the labor market and achieve a job structure more similar to that of men, their preferences for unions and union jobs may come to approach more closely those of men. While employment may continue to shift toward less unionized regions, it is unlikely that such movements will be rapid. Moreover, a changed regional structure of the population is likely to lead to smaller interarea differences in unionization. In addition, as the labor force ages and the share of youth employment decreases, attachment to the labor force and unionism may increase.

A further factor, examined in detail in Chapter 7, is the long-run relationship between unionism, productivity, and profitability. Much casual evidence, along with an increasing number of empirical analyses, suggests that unionism may be associated with lower profitability, investment, and growth. For industries subject to intense domestic and foreign competition, we are likely to see a continued weakening in union bargaining power and membership.

The discussion above indicates that, while a changing industry and employment structure is likely to bring about further declines in unionism, these declines may not be precipitous. Of course the future will be determined in part by the ability of unions and management to adapt to change in a dynamic economic environment and by changes in the legal environment in which the parties operate. For the foreseeable future, we believe labor unions will continue to play an important role in the economy.

Notes

1   The Bureau of National Affairs in Washington, DC, has also published union membership figures for 1980 and 1982.
2   For a discussion of response error in the CPS, PSID, and NLS, see Mellow and Sider (1983), Mincer (1983), and Jones (1982), respectively.
3   Estimates in the 80 percent range were earlier made by Lewis (1963) and Troy (1965).
4   For surveys providing references to later time-series studies, see Fiorito and Greer (1982) and Heneman and Sandver (1983).
5   In earlier times unions typically fared more poorly during inflationary periods. See Lewis (1963) and the discussion in Chapter 5.
6   And, as Mancke (1971) notes, the positive relationship between T and E is true arithmetically.
7   The estimated benefits to existing workers result from the higher union wage gains made possible by increased union density (see Freeman and Medoff, 1981). The estimates by Voos (1983) suggest that unions do not optimize in organizing. If instead one assumes optimizing behavior on the part of unions, this implies that her estimates of marginal benefits are too high or marginal costs too low.
8   Following the Taft–Hartley Act of 1947, decertification elections have been possible where 30 percent or more of the employees in a unit indicate an interest in decertification. Such elections currently constitute only about 10 percent of all representation elections and are not an important factor in the decline in membership (Dickens and Leonard, 1985). However, decertification activity has shown a significant upward time trend. Unions lose certification in about 75 percent of these elections. For a summary of such data, see Dworkin and Extejt (1979).
9   The closest thing to an exception may be Pencavel (1971), who finds British unionization to be negatively related to union dues and fees, while

positively related to income (though price and income elasticities were low).

10 Fiorito and Greer (1982) and Heneman and Sandver (1983) survey many of these studies.

11 For evidence on unions and work flexibility, see Duncan and Stafford (1980) and Allen (1984b).

12 There are two opposing statistical biases in the Hirsch–Berger estimates. On the one hand, capital intensity and unionism are determined simultaneously, which is likely to lead to a positive bias on the capital coefficient. Not only does capital intensity increase the likelihood of unionism, but also union wage increases may lead to greater capital intensity. On the other hand, measurement error in the capital variable (the industry average is not likely to measure accurately the capital intensity in an individual's bargaining or potential election unit) will lead to an underestimate of the effects of capital on unionism.

13 Dworkin and Extejt (1979) find unions to be less successful in preventing *decertification* in smaller units.

14 Olsen (1978) has argued that such a model is not properly identified. Identification of their statistical model results from nonlinearities in the system.

15 Reduction in union *membership* resulting from RTW laws should be larger than reductions in *coverage* owing to free-rider problems (Hirsch, 1980).

16 However, several recent papers find the Heckman–Lee method not to be robust when the normality assumption is violated. Estimates are highly sensitive to specification and data source. See Chapter 5 for fuller discussion.

17 Union dues average about 1.25 percent of weekly earnings. For an analysis examining the relationship between union dues and the wage differential, see Raisian (1983b).

18 However, changes in technology and in the nature of the workplace may be having a significant impact on union density.

CHAPTER 4

Unions, Bargaining, and Strikes

4.1 Introduction

Unions achieve wage gains for their members and affect nonwage aspects of the workplace primarily, although not exclusively, through the process of collective bargaining. An important source of union bargaining power is the strike threat weapon. The ability of the union to impose costs on the firm through a withdrawal of labor and, likewise, the ability of management to sustain a strike and force workers to bear costs, underpin the bargaining power of the parties and the eventual settlements that occur. The fact that aggregate output losses from strikes are rarely substantial in no way lessens the importance of the strike weapon. Indeed, it is the large *potential* cost of strikes to the participating parties that drives bargaining and ensures that the vast majority of contract negotiations are settled without work stoppages.

Economists typically treat union–management negotiations as a bilateral monopoly situation in which the final settlement is, in the absence of simplifying assumptions, indeterminate. The typical case is where the union's minimum acceptable offer is less than management's maximum acceptable offer so that there is some range of potential settlements – a contract zone – that both parties prefer to a strike. The existence of a contract zone is a necessary but not sufficient condition for a negotiated settlement since strikes may still occur as 'accidents' of the negotiation process. When the union's minimum acceptable offer exceeds management's maximum acceptable offer, no contract zone exists and an impasse will necessarily result. If striking is illegal and there is a mechanism for third-party settlement determination (e.g. mandatory arbitration), a settlement is imposed on the parties. In the absence of these conditions, a strike occurs and a negotiated settlement is conditional on the parties' acceptable offers adjusting sufficiently to generate a contract zone.

In this chapter, we first examine the impact of strikes on output and employment. We then discuss the factors affecting union and management bargaining positions and hence the range of settlements that result from collective bargaining.[1] Alternative theoretical models of strike activity are examined next. These are grouped into four general classes: Pareto optimal accident models, which generally assume rational maximizing behavior by both parties; bargaining models that posit strategic interaction between the parties as central to bargaining outcomes; 'political' models that assume either nonmaximizing behavior or divergence between the preferences of union members and their bargaining representatives; and sociological–institutional–political models, which tend to be multidisciplinary and are rarely grounded in economic theory. We attempt to assess these alternative models in light of the empirical evidence. Finally, we examine the issue of strikes in the public sector and review theory and evidence on conventional and final-offer arbitration procedures used increasingly in the US.

4.2 Strike Activity and the Costs of Strikes

The frequency and duration of strike activity varies significantly across industries, within countries over time, and between countries. Total days lost from a strike equal:

$$DAYS\ LOST = STRIKES \cdot SIZE \cdot DURATION, \qquad (4.1)$$

where STRIKES is the number of work stoppages (this typically includes both strikes and lockouts), SIZE measures the average number of workers involved, and DURATION is the average length of work stoppages. For purposes of comparison across industries, time, or countries, DAYS LOST is divided by population or total employment so as to provide a per capita measure.

Since the mid-1930s, the number of annual work stoppages in the US has varied between about 2,500 and 6,000, about 1–3 million workers have been involved each year, and the estimated percentage of working time lost has ranged from about 0.1 to 0.5 percent (excepting 1946) (US Department of Labor, Bureau of Labor Statistics, 1983, Table 128). There appears to have been little trend in US strike frequency since the late 1950s, apart from a temporary increase or 'bubble' from about 1967 through the early 1970s, and a decrease after 1980 which may or may not prove to be permanent.

Comparison of strike behavior across countries is made difficult because of criteria differences as to the minimum conflict size and duration necessary before statistical agencies categorize a conflict as an official work stoppage. A variety of analysts (e.g. Ross and Hartman, 1960; Hibbs, 1976; Paldam and Pedersen, 1982) have classified countries into groupings on the basis of the degree to which bargaining is centralized (i.e. plant versus industry-wide versus economy-wide bargaining). For example, Paldam and Pedersen (1982, Appendix 2) group OECD countries into two broad categories. The 'centralized' low-conflict group (consisting of Austria, Denmark, West Germany, the Netherlands, Norway, and Sweden) have a low general level of conflict (strikes and duration) but relatively large 'peaks' with occasional economy-wide conflicts. The 'decentralized' high-conflict group (consisting of Australia, Canada, France, Italy, New Zealand, the UK, and the US) have relatively high average levels of conflict, but relatively smaller 'peaks' and few economy-wide conflicts. Whereas strikes in countries with decentralized systems generally are economically oriented and operate within the industrial relations legal framework, strikes in countries with centralized bargaining systems at times may seek to challenge the political and industrial relations systems in those countries.

The cost of strikes can be examined at an economy-wide level or at the level of the participants. As noted earlier, it is the cost of strikes to participants that affects the parties' bargaining positions and the resultant strike probability and final settlement. Hence, participant costs play a crucial role in models of strike activity. Economy-wide costs are relevant in assessing total union effects on the economy and in evaluating the appropriateness of labor law and administrative implementation of legal rulings that affect strike behavior.

A conventional measure of economy-wide losses is the percentage of total work time directly lost as a result of strikes, a figure that is always a small fraction of 1 percent. This measure is inadequate for a number of reasons. It overstates strike losses to the extent that forgone production can be replaced in struck firms through intertemporal substitution of production (i.e. rescheduling of production to periods prior to and following strikes) and by non-struck firms. Economy-wide losses from strikes will thus be lower to the extent that strikes are anticipated (for stock market evidence on the predictability of strikes, see Neumann, 1980), if inventory accumulation and decumulation can easily offset production variability, if substitution in consumption is relatively easy (due, for instance, to foreign competition), if production can continue during a strike, and to the extent that there are slack resources so that the opportunity cost of shifts in production is low. For example, losses from a strike in the manufacturing sector are likely to be lower than in, say, commuter transportation, since intertemporal and locational shifts in production and consumption are extraordinarily difficult in the latter case. Simple measures of direct strike (employment) losses can also understate losses since they fail to measure spillover costs to other sectors, such as forgone output in the steel industry due to strikes in the automobile industry.

Conceptually, one would like to measure the aggregate losses in consumer and producer (factor) surpluses resulting from strikes (for a fuller exposition, see Neumann and Reder, 1984), yet no such measures exist. The most recent and novel analysis of strike losses is the study by Neumann and Reder (1984), which estimates losses from strikes between 1958 and 1977 in all sectors of US manufacturing (divided into 63 industry groupings). For each grouping, they first estimate vector autoregressions of output on strikes and of strikes on output. They find that in only 25 of the industries do strikes predict, or are causally prior to, output and thus involve a cost at the industry level. A few industries exhibit causality running from output to strikes or two-way feedback, while in 29 industries there is statistical independence between strikes and output. Using the parameter estimates from the autoregressions and data on strike activity, Neumann and Reder estimate the percentage of annual output loss due to strikes in those 25 industries where strikes unambiguously reduce output. In only one case is the loss estimate greater than a fraction of a percent (1.5 percent in ordnance). Their findings reinforce those of much earlier studies (for useful references, see Neumann and Reder) that *industry* losses from strikes are quite small. At least for US manufacturing, then, shifts in production across time and among firms offset virtually all of the output losses due to strikes.

While industry- and economy-wide costs of strikes may be small, *participant* costs will be higher and indeed serve as a principal motivating force in collective bargaining negotiations. Unfortunately, the discussion of strike costs in the empirical literature on strikes has largely been *ad hoc*. On theoretical grounds, we believe it is most appropriate to treat strike activity as a joint maximization problem (Kennan, 1980; Reder and Neumann, 1980). Thus, the frequency and duration of strikes are inversely related to the *joint* strike cost – the sum of costs to workers and the firm. For instance, in settings where joint strike costs are low – owing, say, to the ability easily to replace strike-lost output with increased pre- and post-strike production – the parties have less incentive to negotiate, develop improved bargaining procedures, or acquire costly information as means of avoiding a strike.

Whereas strike activity by this view is related to joint costs, the *distribution* of costs between the parties will affect primarily the location of the contract zone and hence the bargaining settlement. Thus, a factor that increases relative strike costs to the union (holding joint costs constant) will decrease the expected wage settlement but not necessarily affect expected strike activity. Note that implicit in the above discussion are important assumptions regarding optimizing behavior by both parties, the symmetrical distribution of information, relative risk aversion of the parties, speeds of adjustment to new information, and the role of union leaders. These assumptions and varying perspectives on the determination of strike activity will be elaborated on in the discussion of alternative strike models.

The major participant costs are clearly related to the value of output forgone as a result of a strike; or, more precisely, the present value of wages and profits associated with the forgone output. These costs will be smaller the greater the ability to shift production intertemporally. This is in turn determined by such things as inventory costs, product perishability, consumers' willingness to make intertemporal shifts in consumption of the struck firm's product, and consumers' willingness to shift to the products of domestic and foreign competitors. Additional determinants of participant costs include the firm's ability to continue operations while struck, the business cycle (via its effects on both demand for the firm's product and alternative employment opportunities for workers), the degree of uncertainty (assuming risk aversion), and the availability of alternative income to strikers from sources such as union strike funds, unemployment insurance, savings, and alternative employment prospects for workers and other family members. Empirical studies of strike activity, reviewed in Section 4.4, include variables that measure, albeit quite imperfectly, some of these costs.

4.3 Models of Strike Activity

Economists have long agonized over the strikes phenomenon because, at least on the surface, a strike appears to represent an inefficient outcome of negotiations. Given that strikes impose costs, both parties presumably would be better off agreeing to the post-strike settlement before embarking on a strike. Hence, strikes have been viewed as resulting from faulty negotiations or accidents. It has been argued (albeit incorrectly) that such a view would point to a random pattern of strikes; yet, we observe systematic patterns in strike activity. Theoretical models have therefore incorporated such factors as incomplete or asymmetric information, miscalculation, time (since strikes may affect future bargaining power), and a divergence between union member and leader preferences to explain why strikes may occur. It has proved more elusive to discover empirical proxies for those conditions that make bargaining failures or strikes most likely. In what follows, we examine various accident, political, and bargaining theories of strike activity in some detail and then turn briefly to a number of largely noneconomic theories.

Pareto optimal accident theories

Here we consider three related models: the famous Hicks model and some recent extensions; an approach that rests on an analogy between strikes and road accidents; and a bargaining protocols model that focuses on the costs of avoiding strikes relative to their expected costs. The hallmark of all three models is their adoption of a maximizing cost–benefit approach to the strike.

The usual starting point for any discussion of the accident model of strikes is Sir John Hicks' (1963, Chapter 7) celebrated treatment, first published in 1932. Hicks argued that the employer's tendency to make concessions in wage bargaining and the union's resistance to making concessions are, respectively, directly and inversely related to the expected duration of a strike. The model is depicted in Figure 4.1. The curve labeled *EC* denotes the employer's concession curve, namely the *maximum* wages he would be prepared to pay to avoid strikes of given durations. At each wage on curve *EC*, the expected cost of a stoppage just equals the expected cost of concession. (0Z gives the wage the employer would pay in the absence of a union.) The curve labeled *UR* gives the union resistance schedule, namely the *minimum* wages workers would accept to avoid strikes of given durations. Hicks argued that if both parties are equally well informed about the other's concession curve there will be no strike and at least implied that a determinate solution will be reached at the wage *W** where the two curves intersect.

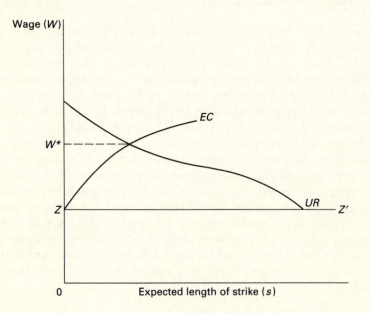

Figure 4.1 The Hicks model

That a strike is not optimal can be seen easily by restating slightly the Hicks model along the lines suggested by Comay and Subotnik (1977). In Figure 4.2 let the set of curves π_i^u represent the union's indifference curves such that $\delta\pi^u/\delta W > 0$ and $\delta\pi^u/\delta s < 0$, where π^u equals the utility to the union (or the median union worker), W equals the wage, and s the expected length of strike. The set π_i^m represents management's isoprofit curves, where, letting π^m equal the firm's profit, $\delta\pi^m/\delta W < 0$ and $\delta\pi^m/\delta s < 0$. The union and firm will seek to achieve their highest π_i^u and π_i^m, respectively. Note that any point to the right of the vertical axis (say, point B) is not optimal since either party can be better off without harm to the other. That is, any no-strike wage settlement between W_1 and W_2 is preferred to point B. Thus, any no-strike settlement along the vertical axis represents a Pareto optimum.

The existence of strikes in this static model is attributed to incomplete or asymmetric information and hence miscalculation on the part of either or both sides as to the location and shape of the other's concession curve. This might arise were each side to use different variables from the other to draw up its concession schedule (for example, see Mauro, 1982). Similarly, one side may overestimate its opponent's rate of concession, thus making a strike more likely. For Hicks, the majority of actual strikes are the result of an accident or faulty negotiation. He recognized, however, that within a long-run model of repeated bargaining rounds strikes (and presumably lockouts) are sometimes required to establish the credibility of the strike threat. Hicks (1963, p. 146) writes: "The most able Trade Union leadership will embark on strikes occasionally, not so much to secure greater gains upon that occasion (which are not very likely to result) but in order to keep their weapon burnished for future use, and to keep employers thoroughly conscious of the Union's power."

Although Hicks did not address in detail how the parties would go about arriving at the wage W^*, a large literature on bargaining models has developed (see note 1). While a review of these models is not attempted here, suffice it to say that the nature of the negotiating process is important if we are to understand fully why strikes occur, or, stated alternatively, why the bargaining process on occasion fails. The Hicks model also illustrates that the location and slopes (or concession rates) of curves EC and UR in Figure 4.1 are the primary determinants of the negotiated settlement. Factors that raise or flatten UR will tend to raise the negotiated wage, while factors lowering or flattening EC will tend to lower the wage settlement.

The position of the curves is, of course, most importantly affected by demand–supply conditions in the relevant markets. It is customary to point to the Marshall–Hicks laws of derived demand as important determinants of union bargaining power. That is, the more difficult is

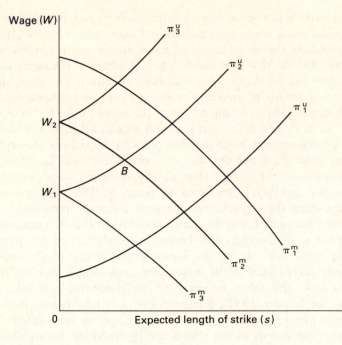

Figure 4.2 Union indifference and management isoprofit curves

substitution in production and consumption, the more inelastic is demand for union labor, and the greater the ability of unions to acquire wage gains with small employment losses. Because the union values employment as well as the wage, implicit in the location of its concession curve will be the underlying demand elasticity. Likewise, the magnitude of scale and substitution effects (determining the demand elasticity) will affect the location of the firm's offer curve. The concession rates of the curves are determined by the change in costs with respect to duration of the strike, the primary cost being the lost value of output (wages to workers and returns to the firm). Additional factors affecting concession rates include bargaining costs, damage to equipment through idleness, availability of strike or other funds, future impacts on bargaining power, and the state of the labor and product markets. As stated earlier, the size and distribution of participant strike costs will affect the parties' relative rates of concession and thus the expected settlement. However, in the absence of some further assumption, the relative distribution of costs should not affect the probability of a strike. Rather, it is increasing joint strike costs that make the avoidance of strikes more likely.

Subsequent papers have built upon the Hicks framework in an attempt to explain why strikes (or accidents) might occur. We believe papers by Siebert and Addison (1981), Kennan (1980), Reder and Neumann (1980), and Mauro (1982) are particularly helpful in this regard. Siebert and Addison exploit the Hicksian argument that imperfect information causes strikes, but incorporate into the model probabilistic elements as in Zeuthen (1930) and time costs as in Cross (1965). Risk elements enter the model because claims are made in the knowledge that there is a certain risk of negotiations breaking down. The introduction of time costs is equally fundamental: the reason the parties are not perfectly informed is that time is costly. Negotiations are time limited and the shorter the period of bargaining, the less perfect will be information and the greater the chance of miscalculation. That is, their model assumes an exogenously determined tradeoff between the negotiation period and strike probability (on which more below).

Siebert and Addison argue that strikes may be likened to road accidents in the sense that, although any single accident is unforeseen, the probability of having an accident is foreseen and is a consequence of rational choice. The idea, then, is that people 'demand' accident avoidance (or safety) and the demand varies inversely with time costs (Peltzman, 1975). Automobile drivers are viewed as choosing some nonzero probability of having an accident so as to maximize their income net of expected losses from accidents. Accidents are seen as voluntary and maximizing in the round, although any particular accident will be involuntary and the result of some mistake. In the same way, Siebert and Addison argue, one can visualize negotiations as selecting a negotiation period and with it expected wage increases and strike probabilities so as to maximize income net of negotiators' costs and expected strike losses. Strikes or bargaining failures will occur on occasion because information is costly and the parties will not negotiate indefinitely, yet such failures or accidents should be less frequent in their model where strike costs are highest. Moreover, higher strike losses have to affect *both* parties if they are to negotiate for a longer period and hence reduce strike probability. On this view strikes do not 'pay' but are instead a hazard of collective bargaining.

The exogeneously determined tradeoff between strike probability and negotiation period is assumed to depend on the ease of communication between the two sides. The experience of the bargaining parties will be a factor here in that less experienced bargaining pairs will confront a less favorable tradeoff. Moreover, the tradeoff may be expected to worsen when it becomes more difficult for either side to assess the other's position and signal its own. Thus, for example, if the parties are suddenly confronted with an entirely new situation, new learning must occur and new conventions must develop. Less stable industries and time periods should have a less favorable tradeoff than more stable industries and time periods, although it is difficult to measure the stability of the conditions facing the parties. In sum, strike probability will reflect not merely factors causing the parties to move up or down an existing tradeoff (in response to the joint cost of disagreement), but also factors such as the skill of the bargaining parties and the instability of their circumstances, which determine the position of the tradeoff itself.

The view that increasing joint strike costs reduce the probability of a strike is developed most explicitly in papers by Kennan (1980) and Reder and Neumann (1980). As Kennan states:

The major theoretical defect in earlier work is the implicit assumption that either workers or firms behave systematically in an irrational way. Attempts to eliminate this defect have led to complex bargaining models with virtually no refutable predictions. The approach taken here, on the other hand, is to impound the bargaining process in a 'black box', and make an assumption about the outcome of this process, based on a natural extension of the postulate of rational behavior. This approach yields useful empirical predictions, which may be summarized by the statement that the probability of settling a strike over a given period of time depends on the total cost of the strike to *both* parties over that period. (Kennan, 1980, p. 92)

Whereas Siebert and Addison suggest that bargainers lessen the strike probability by choosing a longer negotiating period in the face of higher strike costs, Reder and Neumann (1980) posit a model wherein 'bargaining protocols' develop in response to high strike costs. The basic idea behind their model is straightforward: strikes are not avoided by the bargaining parties when the cost of avoiding them is prohibitive relative to the cost of strikes. The costs of strikes are a function of output losses during a strike net of increases in output during the periods preceding and following the strike. Strike avoidance has a price, too, in terms of the costs of designing complex contingent contracts applicable to a multitude of circumstances.

Reder and Neumann are primarily concerned with experienced bargaining pairs that are able to set up bargaining protocols. The latter are conventions that guide subsequent bargaining behavior and facilitate the interpretation of bargaining signals. Such protocols necessarily place limitations upon a bargainer's behavior so that each party "limits his own behavior in any specified situation to what is compatible with the established behavior pattern already learned by the 'bargaining partner'" (Reder and Neumann, 1980, p. 869). If both parties are to accept limitations that may lead them to accept a lower payoff, then this must be more than offset by the savings in expected costs of strike activity over the entire bargaining relationship.

Strikes are said to reflect differences in the bargaining protocols of experienced bargainers, each alternative protocol having an expected cost of strike activity over its life. Parties choose the protocol that minimizes the *sum* of present and future strike costs plus the costs of specifying the protocol. If there were no specification costs, then protocols would be chosen that covered all possible contingencies, thus preempting strikes or bargaining failures. However, the costs of protocols rise with their complexity, so bargainers balance the cost reduction from reduced strike activity against the measured cost of a more complex protocol. In short, bargaining pairs with high joint strike costs develop more detailed protocols that yield a smaller expected quantity of strikes (by reducing the number of items that have to be considered afresh at each contact renegotiation) than pairs faced with low strike costs.

A recent paper by Mauro (1982) also models the relationship between strikes and imperfect information, yet in a manner more faithful to Hicks' original presentation. Whereas Reder and Neumann posit that high strike costs (relative to the cost of avoiding them) lead to the development of procedures that in turn reduce strike activity, Mauro takes a somewhat different view of causation: strikes or bargaining errors are most likely to occur where information is most costly to obtain. Indeed, a valid criticism of Reder and Neumann is the lack of attention given to differences across units (industries) in the cost of designing protocols (which presumably varies with the cost of information), in sharp contrast to their detailed examination of interindustry differences in strike costs. We view these papers as complementary: costly strikes should clearly improve information flows (as in Reder and Neumann) and costly information should make strikes more likely (as stressed by Mauro).

Following Mauro, the effect of imperfect information can be shown easily within the Hicks framework. Figure 4.3 shows the *actual* union and employer concession curves, UC and EC respectively, and *incorrect* concession curves perceived by the opposite parties, $UCperc_E$ being the employer's perception of UC and $ECperc_U$ being the union's perception of EC. In this case, each party is overly optimistic regarding the other party's concession curve. (In Mauro's specific example, imperfect information results because the firm considers the product price in determining labor demand while the union considers the price level in determining the real wage and labor supply.) As a result, the employer expects a wage settlement equal to W_E whereas the union expects the higher wage W_U. If, as seems reasonable, the likelihood of a strike is positively related to $(W_U - W_E)$, then imperfect information

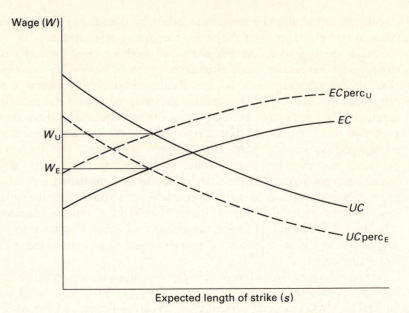

Figure 4.3 Strikes as a result of incorrect perceptions

leading to misperceptions and overly optimistic expectations can be expected to increase strike probability. While we are sympathetic to this view, it is not altogether clear why one party, in constructing its estimate of the opponent's concession curve, should use information different from that employed by the opponent himself. Our unease is heightened by the fact that both sides apparently purchase the same or similar data from commercial forecasters (see, for example, Kaufman and Woglom, 1984, p. 425).

Siebert and Addison (1981), Kennan (1980), Reder and Neumann (1980), and Mauro (1982), along with others, have thus shown how strikes or bargaining failures will occur even among optimizing parties, as long as information is scarce. And because information gathering, the negotiation process, and the specification of protocols are costly activities, strikes are most likely to result where such costs are high relative to the costs of a strike. Thus, these models provide two clear, testable hypotheses. Strike frequency should be least among those bargaining pairs with the highest joint strike costs and where the protocol or information costs are lowest. We evaluate empirical studies attempting to test such relationships in Section 4.4.

An interactive bargaining model

A difficulty with the Pareto optimal accident models is that they do not explicitly model key elements of the bargaining process itself. Many analysts (e.g. Kaufman, 1981) contend that strategic interaction between interdependent parties must be central to any bargaining model. This is similar to the problem facing oligopoly theory, where theorists have constructed reaction functions of firms that trace out a convergence to equilibrium. Likewise, bargaining models can be constructed where, in the face of limited information, strategic interaction during the bargaining process is a *necessary* condition for convergence of the parties' concession–reaction schedules. That is, actual negotiations must occur in order for the parties to become well informed about each other's concession schedule (negotiations play a similar role in Siebert and Addison, 1981).

Kaufman (1981) develops a bargaining model of strikes (based in part on an earlier model by Cross, 1965) that posits concessions by both the union and the firm resulting from the bargaining process. The initial demands of each party are higher, the lower are direct bargaining costs and the higher the expected rate of concession by the other party. The process of bargaining provides information and acts to reduce the overly high expectations of the parties. This downward revision of expectations leads to a gradual convergence in the bargaining demands of the parties. If the convergence occurs prior to contract expiration, a negotiated settlement is reached. If convergence is not reached by that point, the possibility of an immediate strike significantly increases the costs to the parties of continued negotiations (i.e. a continued failure to settle), and both parties moderate their demands. If a positive contract zone still fails to materialize, a strike results and will last until the concession curves converge.

In short, Kaufman contends that, with imperfect information regarding the other party's concession schedule, strikes can occur despite rational behavior by both parties. If either party moved too quickly toward the eventual settlement, it would cause the other side to increase its demand.

The nature of the concession process is such that both parties must approach the settlement point incrementally lest one take the other's concessions to be a sign of weakness or lack of commitment to its announced point of resistance. Seen in this light, strikes are not, as sometimes claimed, irrational events but rather arise out of the imperfect information and strategic interaction inherent in the bargaining process. (Kaufman, 1981, p. 340)

While the Kaufman model has the advantage of treating interdependent behavior and the bargaining process explicitly, it still requires the assumption of myopic behavior on the part of at least one of the parties (Kaufman, 1981, p. 338n). Why should *experienced* bargaining partners come to the table with overly optimistic expectations? Kaufman suggests that 'demand exaggeration' by bargainers is an inherent part of the negotiation process, even where both parties have an accurate estimate of the actual agreement. Alternatively, one can simply argue that strikes are most likely to occur where at least one of the parties is overly optimistic and that such misinformation is more likely to result where there is an immature bargaining relationship or a change in the economic environment (which increases uncertainty).

Kaufman uses his bargaining model as a basis for explaining the variation in US strike activity over the business cycle and with respect to inflation. Employing reasoning similar to that of Friedman's 'natural rate' hypothesis and the expectations Phillips curve (see Chapter 8), Kaufman outlines how a short-run strike cycle will emerge, yet, in the long run, strikes will return to a 'normal' level. The strike cycle tends to lag the inflation cycle – the lag length depending in part on whether adaptive or rational expectations obtains. Following an upswing in unanticipated inflation, strikes will become more likely as workers attempt to restore their real wage. If inflation is later lessened to a rate below workers' expectations, wage demands should fall (owing to the higher than anticipated real wage) and strike activity will decrease below its normal rate. In the long run (when actual and anticipated inflation are equal), strike activity is predicted to return to its normal level.

The prediction Kaufman derives from his model is that strike activity will be directly related to past price increases and inversely related to past wage increases. (As we shall see later in the chapter, numerous empirical studies support these propositions.) Such a relationship, however, does not follow in any obvious manner from the Pareto optimal accident theories, where strike frequency is predicted to be inversely related to joint strike costs and positively related to strike avoidance costs.

The Ashenfelter–Johnson 'political' model

A principal alternative to accident models of the strike process is the well-known political model of strikes advanced by Ashenfelter and Johnson (hereafter A–J) (1969). The A–J model exploits the notion that strikes play an important role in the learning process by motivating modifications of what were initially mutually inconsistent offers. It obtains its 'political' tag by exploiting the argument of Ross (1948) that there are not two but three parties involved in collective bargaining:

management, union leadership, and the rank-and-file membership. The objectives of and information possessed by the union leadership and membership differ. The union leadership or agent pursues its own objectives subject to providing some acceptable level of benefits to its members or principals. The leadership is assumed to assess the bargaining possibilities more accurately than the rank and file. Yet, since it cannot risk the threat to its tenure implied by signing an agreement that is less than the membership expects, the preferred alternative may be to incur a strike. It is assumed that the unrealistically high wage aspirations of the membership will be eroded by the loss of wage income attendant on a strike. As the strike proceeds, workers lower their wage aspirations; the strike thus functions as an equilibrating mechanism to square up the union membership's wage expectations with what the firm is prepared to pay.

The firm, for its part, seeks to maximize the present value of its profit stream: it will choose the optimum tradeoff between forgone profits during the strike and increased costs after a strike subject to the union concession curve. There results a determinate wage and strike length outcome. Note, then, that this is not a bargaining model but simply one postulating profit maximization by the firm subject to a given union concession curve constraint.

The basic elements in the A–J model are presented in Figure 4.4. The Y_A function represents the union concession curve facing the firm. The dashed Y^* line indicates the minimum wage increase acceptable to the union after a strike of infinite duration, while Y_0 shows the minimum acceptable wage increase without striking. Accordingly, the union concession curve can be written $Y_A = Y^* + (Y_0 - Y^*)e^{-as}$, where a is the rate at which Y_A decays during a strike. The π functions shown in the figure are the employer's isoprofit curves, indicating the tradeoff between wage offer, Y_g, and length of strike, s, for any given present value of the firm.[2] The employer seeks to reach the isoprofit curve that corresponds to the highest present value of the firm (forgone profits during a strike minus increased labor costs after a strike) or, alternatively put, to get as close to the origin in Figure 4.4 as possible. In this endeavor, the employer is of course constrained by the union concession curve.

Panel (a) of the figure depicts a no-strike outcome, in which the wage increase that the employer is prepared to pay to avoid a strike, Y_g, is greater than or equal to the union's minimally acceptable wage increase without a strike, Y_0. Here, the firm will maximize profits by settling at a wage increase of Y_0. In panel (b), however, $Y_0 > Y_g$, and the firm will maximize profits by taking a strike of length s_1, with an ultimate settlement of Y_1, yielding a profit of π_1, which is higher than the profit, π_0, obtainable without the strike.

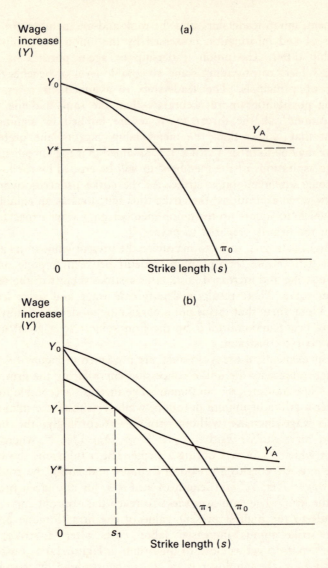

Figure 4.4 The Ashenfelter–Johnson model

The A–J model implies that strikes in some sense are caused by the union side alone. Even though strikes are never in the interests of the (ignorant) membership, the union leadership, while more acutely aware of the bargaining possibilities, nevertheless goes along with the membership to avert any challenge to its continued tenure in office. Conceivably the leadership might even promote a strike if that raises their political stock among the rank and file, although this possibility is not aired by A–J.

Ashenfelter and Johnson, and subsequently Farber (1978a), focus on differences in unions' Y_A schedules as determining strikes and not on differences in the slopes of firms' isoprofit schedules. Their models show, *inter alia*, that a strike is more likely, the higher is the union's minimum acceptable percentage wage increase (Y_0) and the higher is its rate of concession (since it will then 'pay' the firm to take a strike). A strike is less likely, the greater the union's discount rate (the rate they discount future relative to present consumption) and the higher the minimum acceptable wage increase after a strike of infinite length (the higher Y^* the less the firm has to gain by taking an infinitely long strike). The effect of labor's share (and profits) is indeterminate in the A–J model (for a discussion of this issue, see Farber, 1978a, p. 267).

Arguments in the A–J strike model do not have obvious empirical counterparts. A–J suggest a specification in which the probability of a strike depends directly on the magnitude of Y_0, which is conjectured to be a negative function of the unemployment rate and the past rate of real wage change. (Farber focuses on the determinants of the union concession rate, a, and the minimum wage increase acceptable to the union after a strike of infinite length.)[3]

The A–J treatment has been highly influential, reflecting both its 'accessibility' in a literature of highly abstract bargaining models (most of which do not have a direct bearing on strikes) and also its attempt to provide a model of union behavior. Recently, however, the model has been subjected to searching criticism (for an extensive critique, see Shalev, 1980). The main difficulty with the A–J model lies in its failure to consider the bargaining process by which the parties *jointly* concede; it assumes that one side maximizes subject to given behavior by the other. In this respect a model such as Kaufman's (1981) is preferable. Why should the blame for strikes be unilaterally attributed to the union side? One can, for example, construct a model employing the opposite assumption (see Eaton, 1972; Rabinovitch and Swary, 1976; Siebert, Bertrand, and Addison, 1985). Another criticism concerns the theoretical pedigree of the A–J model: it is not obvious that this treatment should be labeled a political model in the spirit of Ross (1948). We return to both points below.

Intentionally or not, the main hallmark of the A–J model would appear to be its reliance on the assumption of asymmetric information, a topic that has proved an important argument in modern contract theory (see Chapter 8). Here, asymmetric information means that the bargaining parties have unequal access to the same information, as opposed to the parties using different information to construct estimates of the other's concession curve (as in Mauro, 1982). Recently, Hayes (1984) has attempted to explain strikes and a declining schedule in wages (which figures centrally in the A–J model) as necessary concomitants of optimal contracts. In a world of perfect information strikes do not occur. With asymmetric information, however, this first-best solution may not be available.

Assume that the union determines the wage and the firm then selects the employment level. However, the union proposes a wage schedule dependent upon its expectation of the firm's labor demand schedule, but only the firm knows the true state of nature (i.e. the firm's demand for labor is determined in part by its profit position, complete information on which is effectively denied the union, even in the presence of disclosure laws). The firm may not have the incentive to reveal the true state; indeed, it may be expected to cheat or misrepresent the state of nature on profit-maximizing grounds. The task facing the union, therefore, is to discover a wage offer schedule that maximizes its expected utility subject to the firm's maximizing response. It thus offers a schedule in which wages decline through time; in effect, offering the firm a set of wage–strike combinations. Strikes in this model are used to achieve 'incentive compatibility', or, in other words, ensure that the firm selects the wage the union desires for the appropriate state. Strikes thus have the important function of providing the union with information about the true state.

An important contribution of the Hayes paper is the strict derivation of a downward-sloping wage–strike length offer curve based on the assumption of asymmetric information but without assuming, as do A–J, differences between union leadership and its rank and file. An implication of Hayes' theoretical model is that empirical strike analysis should focus on performance of the firm relative to that of the general economy. Hayes notes that the procyclical nature of strikes may result in part from a difference between the profitability of the firm and the performance of the economy at large. The union observes the general economy to be doing well and therefore expects the firm to be profitable.[4] If it is not, strikes may result. She concludes that tests of the model should involve data on the profitability of firms and uncertainty of the firm relative to performance in the general economy.

Finally, let us return to the statement made earlier that the A–J model is not really a political model at all in the spirit of Ross (1948). Despite the authors' discussion pointing to a dissonance between the goals of the leadership and the rank and file, the A–J model is in fact a two-party model involving management profit maximization subject to the union constraint. Once an offer is made that will satisfy members, the union settles. Union leaders do not pursue their own special interests independent of their members' preferences; indeed, they act as perfect agents for their (irrational) principals. This results from the model's failure to specify the objective function of what the authors assert to be a self-serving leadership. A more authentic political model has been provided by Swint and Nelson (1978, 1980), who allow union leaders actively to pursue their own interests at the expense of the members' interests, subject to some minimum gain below which leaders are voted out of office. In their model, union members can gain from a strike and strikes can result even where negotiations are faultless. However, empirical implications of their model differ little from those of the A–J model.

Sociological–institutional–political approaches

While our discussion to this point has centered on economic explanations for strikes, a number of analysts have analyzed strikes in primarily noneconomic terms. One (macrosociological) approach, employing the notion of 'pluralistic industrialism', relates strike behavior to the degree of societal cohesion and the institutionalization of conflict through mature collective bargaining (on this view, see Dahrendorf, 1959; Ross and Hartman, 1960). This approach views strike activity as merely a transitory phenomenon which 'withers away' with the maturation of the union movement and with the development of the collective bargaining apparatus and the institutions of political democracy. In support of this view, Ross and Hartman and others cite cross-country data showing a gradual decrease in strike activity over time. (We return to this empirical evidence in the next section.) We might add that there is at least some similarity between this view, which focuses on economy-wide industrial relations, and that of Reder and Neumann (1980), who emphasize the prerequisite of repeated inter-action to the establishment of bargaining protocols. And, as noted earlier, Siebert and Addison (1981) view the maturity of the bargaining relationship as one determinant of the position of the tradeoff between strike probability and negotiation length/intensity.

An often cited set of papers by Snyder (1975, 1977) has emphasized the importance of the development of political and economic organiz-ations that allow the expression of grievances. Snyder criticizes economists for the emphasis on short-run economic determinants of strikes while ignoring the role of long-run institutional changes. In particular, he stresses the need to examine the determination of union membership as a necessary precondition for the expression of discontent via strikes. Snyder contends that economic variables have become the dominant determinant of strikes during the postwar years only because of the stability of union membership during this period.[5]

While Snyder's major point clearly has much validity (organizational–political institutions do matter), his work lacks the balance necessary for an objective appraisal of comparative approaches (for one such attempt, see Kaufman, 1982, and the discussion below).

Corporatist models (e.g. Korpi and Shalev, 1979; Crouch, 1980) challenge the notion that institutional development in the industrial relations machinery ensures industrial peace. The basic idea of the corporatist view is that the real potential for institutional development to lessen industrial conflict exists only in those societies where labor has a real share in political power. The crucial issue in this class-based conflict model is the distribution of power resources. Until labor obtains substantive political influence, the beneficial features commonly attributed to centralized and coordinated union movements may actually exacerbate the strike problem if the economy retains an essentially free market form. Substantive political influence is indexed by the ability of parties linked to labor to hold political office.

The political scientist Hibbs (1976) has also viewed strikes as a manifestation of class-based conflict over the distribution of the national product. Hibbs argues that the long-term decline in strike activity, where it is observed, has resulted from a shift in the locus of bargaining from the marketplace to the electoral arena. Within welfare state economies, class-centered competition over distribution has increasingly adopted the polity route over the market route. This shift was facilitated by the success of labor and social democratic parties within a number of European nations in the postwar period. Unions have allocated an increasing portion of their scarce organizational resources to activity in the political arena where they are likely to enjoy greater success. Hibbs also argues that many workers prefer to take their rewards in the form of public goods and the 'social wage', in part because of the high and progressive tax structure of welfare states (on this point, see also Neumann and Rissman, 1984). His model is thus very much a hybrid of the economic, noneconomic, and organizational–political approaches, yet narrower in scope than the corporatist model (for a critical analysis of Hibbs' model and the corporatist view, see Addison, 1984).

A final, 'microsociological' theory of strikes is Kerr and Siegel's (1954) isolated-mass theory. Kerr and Siegel report a considerable degree of consistency between nations in the relative strike proneness of industries. They offer an explanation of such patterns based on the concept of labor's locational position in society, determined by the intersection of two continua, described as 'individual–mass' and 'isolation–integration'. The first continuum locates the extent to which members of a community or occupation are homogeneous, while the second continuum measures the degree of integration enjoyed by this

94

group with the rest of society. It is predicted that the most highly strike-prone workers are those forming a homogeneous, occupationally undifferentiated community capable of sustaining internal cohesion, yet relatively isolated from the rest of society. Hence the isolated-mass theory of industrial conflict. While a critique of Kerr and Siegel's theory is not made here (but see Edwards, 1977), we note that our preference is to view interindustry differences in strike propensity in terms of the costs and benefits of such action. Unfortunately, Kerr and Siegel conspicuously fail to consider how these costs and benefits might relate systematically to their classification.

4.4   Empirical Evidence: A Testing of the Models

As is evident from the preceding discussion, there are substantial differences among analysts in their view of strikes. The empirical evidence might therefore be expected to play an important role in appraising the relative merits of the alternative theoretical approaches. Unfortunately, tests that would allow us to discriminate clearly between competing views have not been developed. Empirical testing of the strike models has proved difficult for several reasons. The most obvious problem is that the theoretical determinants of strikes have no clear-cut empirical counterparts. Data sets providing information on the actual offers and rates of concession of the bargaining parties are generally unavailable and, even where they exist, empirical tests of specific models are difficult (Hamermesh, 1973; Svejnar, 1980). Empirical studies are unable to measure directly the relative perceptions and expectations of the bargaining parties as well as any differences between union leadership and the rank and file, even though these factors play a crucial role in bargaining theory. Even strike costs, which play a critical role in the theories reviewed above, must be inferred from rather indirect proxies.

A fundamental weakness in many, although not all, of the empirical models is a confusion between the determinants of bargaining power on the one hand and the determinants of strikes on the other hand. Studies that focus on the union as the initiator of strikes generally contend that any factor strengthening labor's position (e.g. a low unemployment rate) will increase strike frequency. Yet the Pareto optimal accident view of strikes suggests that changes in relative bargaining power, while affecting the wage settlement, will affect strike probability if and only if the joint costs of strikes are also affected. Few studies make this distinction between the determinants of strikes and wage settlements, and even fewer estimate such relationships within an appropriate simultaneous framework (for two such attempts, however, see Blejer, 1981, and Geroski, Hamlin, and Knight, 1982).

Following Kaufman (1982), we believe it is important to recognize that strikes vary over time or across observational units because of differences both in strike propensity among given groups of workers, and in strike opportunity, holding worker propensity constant. The opportunity to strike will of course fluctuate – most importantly with the extent of union coverage, as well as with the number of contract expirations for a given time period. Therefore, empirical tests that purport to explain strike propensity rather than opportunity should statistically control for (or estimate within a simultaneous framework) the number of units with contract expirations and the number of workers in those units.

The choice of which strike measure to employ as the dependent variable is not obvious (on this issue, see Stern, 1978). Should one measure the number of strikes, strike duration, strike incidence, the number of striking workers, total working days lost, or what?[6] Most authors implicity or explicitly assume that variables measuring strike frequency, size, and duration reflect similar information, yet continue to provide estimates using these alternative measures.

Empirical tests of the accident theories

Perhaps the most direct test of a specific theoretical model is Reder and Neumann's (1980) empirical analysis of their protocols model. Using two- and three-year moving averages of strike activity in 14 manufacturing industries during 1953–73, they relate three measures of strikes (number or frequency, mean duration, and man-days lost per employee) to variables that measure (albeit indirectly) the joint costs of strikes. Because their dependent variables are measured as deviations from industry means, their model in fact explains intertemporal changes in strike activity, after accounting for industry-specific differences (fixed effects), rather than interindustry differences in strike activity.

Reder and Neumann contend that the direct costs of strikes vary inversely with the intraindustry variation in inventories of finished goods and directly with the variation in shipments. The rationale for the expected sign on the former variable is that intrayear variability in inventories (holding shipments constant) proxies the ability of the industry to substitute production intertemporally in anticipation of, and as a subsequent response to, a strike (Neumann, 1980, uses stock market evidence to show that strikes are to some extent predictable). Thus, joint strike losses are limited by the intertemporal substitution of production and labor inputs. The intrayear variation in shipments, holding constant the variation in inventories, is hypothesized to proxy the premium placed on timely deliveries. Because the costs of producing and delivering a given stream of output will be lower the steadier the rate of delivery, strike costs are expected to be positively related to the variability in shipments. In addition, a relative wage variable (wage in industry i divided by the all-industry wage) is included to proxy differences in relative value added per worker.

Reder and Neumann find, as predicted, that all measures of strike activity are greater, the greater the variability in inventories and the lower the variability in shipments (although the latter results are not always statistically significant). Strikes also vary inversely with the relative wage (proxied by value added).[7] Such results, they argue, provide rather strong evidence for the hypothesis that strike activity is inversely related to the joint costs of the strike. While these results provide support for the Pareto optimal accident model – whereby protocols, extended negotiations, or improved information to avoid strikes develop in situations where strike/accident costs are highest – they are not necessarily inconsistent with other models of strike activity and therefore do not provide a discriminating test of the alternative theories.

Cousineau and Lacroix (1983) attempt to provide a test of the Siebert–Addison (1981) accident model, which views strikes as most likely to result where information costs are high (due, in particular, to uncertainty) and strike costs are low. They employ data on 2,511 wage agreements (527 involving a strike) in Canadian manufacturing for the period 1967–82. Unlike Reder and Neumann, they do not find strike probabilities significantly related to joint strike costs, proxied by the coefficient of variation of the ratio of inventories to sales in the firm's industry (although we believe the ratio of the coefficients of variation of inventories to sales would have been a preferable measure of strike costs and more consistent with Reder and Neumann). Cousineau and Lacroix do find strikes to increase significantly with uncertainty, as measured by the coefficients of variation in capacity utilization (which may in fact measure, as in Reder and Neumann, the scope for intertemporal substitution in production), the retail price index, and job vacancies. Although we do not find their particular specification appealing, on the whole these results provide support for the accident model.

One of the more sophisticated tests of the Hicks accident model is that of Mauro (1982), who also focuses on imperfect and costly information as a source of strikes. Mauro estimates a maximum-likelihood fixed-effects probit model using a 30-year wage chronology series on 14 US bargaining pairs. Mauro finds strikes to be less likely where the potential for misperceptions is least, as proxied by pattern bargaining and COLA (cost-of-living adjustment clauses) dummy variables (such variables may also proxy strike costs). Quite interestingly, when using a fixed-effects model (but not otherwise), he finds strikes are significantly less likely if a strike occurred at the expiration of the previous contract. Such a result is consistent with both the hypothesis that prior strike activity provides information and with Hicks' 'rusty weapon' argument that strikes are used occasionally to establish credibility. Additionally, Mauro reports that the strike outcome is less likely the smaller are the changes in shipments in the two months prior to contract expiration, the greater the increase in real wages over the existing contract, the larger are firm profits, the larger the growth in labor productivity, and the higher the unemployment rate. Several of these latter findings complement empirical research testing variants of the A–J model and examining the cyclical nature of strike activity. These results will be discussed below.

In summary, we find the Pareto optimal accident models of strike activity rather appealing on *a priori* grounds. And the limited empirical evidence that does exist suggests that strikes are most likely where joint strike costs are low and information–negotiation costs are high. However, such evidence is quite limited and almost always indirect. Moreover, the accident models do not provide an immediately obvious explanation for a number of other empirical regularities in the literature.

The A–J model and the cyclical nature of strikes

Although the A–J strikes model has been widely criticized, the underlying empirical approach they employ has formed the basis for much subsequent research examining cyclical strike activity. As shown in the previous section, the A–J model is fundamentally a non-Pareto optimal model of firm profit maximization subject to a union wage–strike concession schedule. That is, firms face a tradeoff between granting a minimum acceptable wage increase, Y_0, in order to avoid a strike, or bearing a strike of length s so as to lower the wage increase. Strikes are on occasion necessary to bring the demands of the rank and file in line with settlements that are obtainable. As noted earlier, Y_0 does not have an obvious empirical counterpart and is conjectured to depend negatively on the unemployment rate and prior real wage changes.

A–J estimate a time-series model using quarterly data from 1952(I) through 1967(II). They find the number of strikes – crudely adjusted for strike opportunity by means of seasonal dummies but not union membership or contract expiration information – is greater, the lower the unemployment rate and the lower past real wage increases (or, separating real wage change into its component parts, inversely related to nominal wage increases and positively related to price increases). In addition, they find a negative time trend and an increase in strike activity following the Landrum–Griffen Act in 1959, but no systematic relationship between strikes and past firm profits. They interpret these findings as supporting their model: the union rank and file base their initial wage demands and presumably rates of concession on past changes in real wages and on alternative employment opportunities, rather than adjusting their expectations quickly to the actual employer concession curve they face. Thus, 'inefficient' strikes will occur systematically over the business cycle as a means of squaring the preferences of union members with those of the leadership and management.

Farber (1978a) has provided a more sophisticated test of the A–J model using microdata on 80 wage settlements (21 involving strikes) for ten large manufacturing firms from 1954 to 1970. Using maximum-likelihood estimation, Farber explicitly models the determination of the union concession rate, a, and minimum acceptable wage increase after a strike of infinite length (Y^*) as part of the strike determination process. It is argued that factors that increase union militancy or bargaining power imply a lower concession rate and therefore decrease the likelihood of the firm taking a strike (as shown in Figure 4.4, a flatter Y_A schedule increases the chances of a no-strike corner solution). Both the unemployment rate and the prior change in real wages are hypothesized to be positively related to the union's rate of concession and therefore *positively* related to the probability of a strike. (Note that, although the predicted sign on unemployment is the exact opposite of that suggested by A–J, unemployment works in the opposite direction via its effects on Y^*.) While Farber's findings provide some support for the A–J model, most of his results are statistically insignificant and, in some cases, counterintuitive. Possibly more destructive of the model, however, is the finding of Siebert, Bertrand, and Addison (1985) that the model performs almost as well when turned on its head, namely by assuming optimal worker adjustment in response to the concession curve of an ignorant or intransigent management.

Moreover, the A–J model has not proved stable over time and is a poor predictor of strike activity beyond its sample period (Moore and Pearce, 1982). In addition, its results are fairly sensitive to empirical specification and sample period (see, in particular, Shalev, 1980). Most economists are simply uncomfortable with a model that on the one hand does not permit bargaining and relies on the assumption of systematic worker ignorance and nonmaximizing behavior, while on the other hand assumes perfect knowledge and maximizing behavior by management.

Despite these criticisms, the A–J findings of procyclical strike activity (an inverse relationship with the unemployment rate) and of an inverse relationship with prior real wage increases have been replicated in various forms in a number of studies using postwar (and, in a few cases, prewar) US data (see, for example, Kaufman, 1981, 1982, 1983; Mauro, 1982), but not always with data from other countries (Paldam and Pedersen, 1982). The US results generally support the A–J view that union rank and file in certain situations systematically overestimate the potential settlement and that only an uneconomical (for members, though not employers) strike will bring their demands back into line. However, we believe that the intertemporal instability of the model, combined with its rather unappealing theoretical content, should make analysts cautious in accepting in its entirety the A–J explanation for strike activity.

Finally, let us consider explicitly the positive relationship between inflation and strike frequency. This result, while consistent with the A–J model, is at first blush difficult to square with the accident model. Might we not expect that wage offers and demands would increase proportionately at a rate equal to expected inflation? The issue is, however, more complicated than this for a number of reasons. In the first place, few studies have modeled inflationary expectations. Use of a direct measure of price expectations does not reveal any systematic relationship between changes in expected price inflation and strikes (Kaufman, 1981). The possibility nonetheless remains that the two sides will have different expectations of the other's position during inflationary episodes, not necessarily because the two sides are using different information in constructing estimates of the other's concession curves, but simply because higher rates of inflation typically involve a greater variance or degree of uncertainty. If the relation of the product price to the general price index changes in an unpredictable manner with the inflation rate then it might reasonably be expected that the deterioration in the quality of information at such times produces higher strike frequency.

Second, and relatedly, it has been reported that past inflation has less impact on strikes if the contract contains an escalator clause (Kaufman, 1981). Such clauses may be expected to figure more prominently the greater the costs of strike activity (Reder and Neumann, 1980). But the more variable the inflation rate, the greater the risk of incorporating a *mean* rate escalator into the contract. Accordingly, interpretation of a positive relation between inflation and strikes is rather more difficult than it appears at first sight. Third, studies using the inflation rate as an argument generally have entered the variable in some distributed lag form. The meaning of the variable is less than clear-cut. Is it a measure of price expectations or, holding wage change constant, a measure of militancy or catch-up pressures?

We would place emphasis upon the signal extraction problems attendant upon a high and variable inflation rate. Another possibility, although as yet untested for the US, is that higher inflation reduces contract length. Few studies of which we are aware link the frequency of wage change to inflation or inflation variability (see Chapter 8), but the issue of contract endogeneity is of great potential interest from the perspective of strikes, since a greater number of bargaining pairs, even with the probability of strikes held constant, should increase strike frequency.

Sociological–institutional–political evidence

Few economists would disagree that institutional and political factors are relevant in analyzing strike activity or that the economics literature on strikes has been overly narrow in its focus. Yet, the theories and evidence offered in support of noneconomic approaches are generally *ad hoc*, often contradictory, and in the end unconvincing.

An influential study by Snyder (1977) contends that, although economic variables were important in the US during the postwar period owing to the stability of union membership and the industrial relations regime, they cannot explain strike activity during earlier periods. Snyder argues correctly that empirical strike studies must account for the level of union organization or, more precisely, strike opportunity. Yet most recent studies hold union membership and/or the number of contract expirations constant, and, in some cases, explicitly model the simultaneous determination of membership and strikes. Also, many studies have tried to account for changes in the industrial relations regime through the use of dummy variables (to account for Landrum–Griffen, price controls, and the like), although none have been able to estimate models accounting for the endogeneity of the legal structure. Most important, subsequent studies of the early US strike experience (Edwards, 1978; Skeels, 1982; Kaufman, 1982) report that economic variables *do* matter and soundly reject Snyder's contention.

While the empirical finding for the US that strike activity is inversely related to unemployment and prior real wage growth is relatively robust (although parameter values are not particularly stable), these findings cannot be replicated for most other countries. Studies by Davies (1981) and Paldam and Pedersen (1982), providing bewilderingly diverse evidence for a large number of western countries, are able to find the US pattern in but a few countries. Because the theoretical underpinnings for these relationships are rather opaque to begin with (not least the notion of a 'target' real wage), the lack of consistent cross-country evidence increases our unease with the A–J model's explanation of strike activity.

Well-known papers explicitly examining the role of institutions, class, or politics include Korpi and Shalev (1979), Hibbs (1976), and Crouch (1980). Korpi and Shalev anticipate a withering away of the strike where the working class is highly organized politically and industrially with direct influence over the polity, and where the union movement is centralized, coordinated, and engages in collective bargaining with employers and in public policy bargaining with the state. These conditions are broadly met in the cases of Sweden, Norway, and Austria – countries in which, at least over the sample period, the strike had indeed withered away. The experiences of Ireland, Canada, and the US also fit into the Korpi–Shalev predictive frame. In these strike-prone countries the working class as such has not played a significant role in national politics. Conflicts are, so the argument runs, largely confined to pecuniary markets and labor is weak both industrially and politically. A third type of outcome is where the 'left' is not only isolated from the polity but is alienated from it. Countries of this type are said to be France, Italy, and Japan. It is hypothesized that, lacking the institutional preconditions for political exchange (i.e. control of government and strong unions), the existence of a significant left presence in politics serves to increase the level of industrial conflict. The authors note the unfavorable relationship of vote shares to cabinet shares of the left in Finland, Australia, and New Zealand, and point specifically to the relevance of a frustration thesis in these countries. Having explained to their own satisfaction the position of 12 of their 18-country sample, Korpi and Shalev face the difficult task of explaining the anomalous long-run strike performances of Belgium, Denmark, Britain, West Germany, Switzerland, and the Netherlands. Various rationalizations of the data are offered for each country. However, once it is admitted that 'political exchange' can take place even where working-class based parties are weak, little appears to be left of the model.

Crouch (1980), in an analysis of 17 industrial nations covering the period 1965–77, examines the relationship between strikes and, separately, four measures of industrial relations corporatism and two measures of social democratic corporatism (i.e. the tendency for the state to share decision making with private interest groups).[8] Separate regressions of strikes on each corporatist measure are estimated and then used to predict the strike behavior of the individual countries and to identify (and subsequently rationalize) 'deviants'. He concludes that strong corporatist elements significantly reduce strike activity. Unfortunately, his statistical procedures are flawed and the policy implications drawn do not necessarily follow (see Addison, 1984).

Finally, Hibbs (1976) offers an interesting dynamic analysis of strike activity in 10 advanced nations during the period 1950–69. Unlike the above models, Hibbs employs a mix of economic and political variables. His economic model basically comprises a real wage hypothesis, where the expectation–achievement function is one of long-run expectations with a polynomial distributed lag after A–J, coupled with an unemployment term and a variable measuring the rate of change in the ratio of aggregate profits to employee compensation. Hibbs finds strong support for this economic component of his model, with significantly negative coefficients on the unemployment and real wage change terms, and a little over half of the variation in strike volume explained. We do not discuss this further except to say that Hibbs, in contrast to Davies (1981) and Paldam and Pedersen (1982), shows that the slope parameters of the model do *not* vary significantly by country. (Hibbs allows different intercepts for each country which capture the net effects of nation-specific, structural–historical factors that are not modeled explicitly.)

To his basic economic model, Hibbs adds three political variables: an index summarizing the incentive of labor/socialist parties to dampen industrial conflict in the hope of attracting the middle-class votes necessary to achieve reelection; a labor/socialist government dummy; and a measure of communist party influence so constructed as to pick up the supposedly deleterious effect of that party on strikes once membership attains a certain critical mass or threshold. Of all the political variables, only communist party membership emerges as significant. In short, during the postwar interval, left-wing governments have been no more successful than their center or right-wing counterparts in discouraging short-run upward movements in strikes, notwithstanding their electoral ties to the working class.

This, then, is a very mixed bag of results, offering, we believe, only the most marginal support for corporatist notions. The studies reported above advance us little along the road to understanding the differences between countries in strike experience. We interpret the studies by Paldam and Pedersen and by Davies as indicating just how easy it is to run unsuccessful strike equations. We see little theoretical rationale for many of the empirical arguments employed in these studies, and therefore are not surprised by the plethora of conflicting evidence.

The more sociologically based arguments perhaps confront even greater difficulties, based as they are on inductive propositions about past events. The models quickly degenerate into explanations of 'special cases' when the generality of the model is threatened by apparent deviant behavior. Their general failure to model economic variables is another apparent conspicuous lacuna, as is their failure to analyze abrupt changes in terms of the endogeneity of systems. Moreover, since there is no suggestion that systems can be transferred from one country to another and since there is evidence that the institutions themselves have not always operated in the hypothesized manner, one can only speculate as to what one is left with at the level of theory at the end of the day.

Nevertheless, all the analyses rightly draw our attention to differences between countries in strikes and alert us to the possible role of institutions in moderating industrial conflict. Despite the fact that our economic models of strikes take the institutional environment as a datum, the road accident model, stressing the role of uncertainty, seems helpful in explaining the reduced strike frequency of economies with centralized and coordinated collective bargaining, while the 'openness' of such economies may further contribute to stability. This does not discharge us from the responsibility of penetrating the institutional façade, even though empirical research in this area, still less theoretical work, is in its infancy.

A summing up

Despite substantial theoretical and empirical work on strikes, we are ultimately left in a state of unease. The empirical evidence lends some support to each of the theories – Pareto optimal accident models, interactive bargaining and business cycle models, A–J-type political models, and the sociological–institutional–political approaches.

On theoretical grounds, we prefer the Pareto optimal accident theory view of strike activity, which posits that strike probabilities vary inversely with the joint costs of strikes and directly with the costs of negotiation, of establishing protocols, and of acquiring information. Factors that affect relative bargaining power, holding these costs constant, will affect negotiated wage settlements but *not* the likelihood of strikes. Limited evidence to date, albeit indirect, generally supports the accident model of strikes. Yet much more evidence and direct testing of these models are required.

What the accident models fail to explain easily is the procyclical nature of strike activity long evident in the US and in at least some other countries. Indeed, joint strike costs seem likely to increase with the level of economic activity (although expected costs to workers will be lower with lower unemployment), leading to the incorrect prediction of countercyclical strike activity. Hayes' (1984) suggestion that we examine how individual firms are faring relative to the general economy is relevant here, but in and of itself does not provide a convincing explanation for the time-series findings.

Accepting the accident model, the observed cyclical pattern of strikes presumably has to do with factors that affect, over the business cycle, the number of bargaining pairs and/or the difficulty confronting each side in assessing the other's position and signaling its own. High unemployment, for example, may be argued to reduce unrealistic bargaining demands and increase the likelihood of a positive contract zone, principally by making the parties more certain of where they stand (i.e. a large change from the current contract is less likely). The fact that high inflation typically implies more variable inflation (and hence uncertainty) possibly provides a more potent explanation for the procyclical nature of strike frequency than any effects of inflation *per se*. In both cases it may be argued that the information costs of accurately locating the contract zone move procyclically. However, the role of unemployment/inflation in influencing the number of bargaining pairs is opaque at this stage.

The A–J model may provide a more obvious explanation for procyclical strike activity, but it does not follow in any obvious manner from theory that procyclical increases in bargaining power and militancy should lead to increased strike activity. It is probably incorrect to view the real wage variable in the A–J model as a cyclical factor, since there is apparently no clear-cut cyclical behavior of the real wage. A number of problems attach to this variable, most notably concerning the determination of labor's long-run expectations. While there is no place for this variable in the accident model, its theoretical role is less than transparent in the A–J model. Without further theoretical elaboration, high past real wage increases seem just as likely to cause divergence as convergence in the two sides' expectations. Though we see little theoretical justification for this variable, its empirical robustness, at least for the US, requires some explanation.

There probably is *some* truth in the contention that union rank and file on occasion overestimate the wage increase that is obtainable and that strikes ensue as a means of moderating these demands. However, we remain uncomfortable with a model that assumes nonoptimizing behavior by workers coupled with profit maximization by firms, and fails to allow any role for bargaining. Here, we are more comfortable with other nonmaximizing models (e.g. Kaufman, 1981) that explicitly model bargaining and strikes as necessary ingredients for concessionary behavior that makes mutually acceptable wage settlements possible.

The sociological–institutional–political literature, in and of itself, is not particularly helpful in understanding and explaining strike activity. What it has shown is the diversity of international evidence and the importance of political, legal, and institutional factors that affect industrial relations. Future theoretical and empirical analyses of strike activity will increasingly need to incorporate into models the endogenous determination of the political and industrial relations systems and their effects on strike activity and wage determination.

4.5   Impasse Resolution in the Public Sector

Public sector strikes

Public sector strikes in the US are illegal in all but a handful of states (US Department of Labor, 1981). Despite this, strike activity in the public sector increased dramatically during the 1960s and 1970s, averaging 463 work stoppages per year during the 1977–81 period (US Department of Labor, 1983, Table 132), most of these being at the local level. Compared to private sector strikes, those in the public sector have a mean duration about half as long but involve slightly more workers per strike (Freeman, 1984b).

There is substantial disagreement about whether public sector workers should be allowed to strike (Wellington and Winter, 1969; Burton and Krider, 1970). The argument against permitting strikes centers on the contention that the monopoly power of government implies highly inelastic demand schedules and hence unacceptable bargaining power for public employees. Although this contention is no doubt true for some unions in some localities, we do not believe it is the general case. Short-run budget (revenue) constraints in the public sector need not be any less binding than in the private sector, while, in the long run, citizen and business mobility constrains localities' ability to increase revenues (Freeman, 1984b). Most important, empirical evidence does not indicate more inelastic demand in the public sector (for a summary of such evidence, see Ehrenberg and Schwarz, 1983). And where public sector workers are deemed essential (e.g. police and firefighters), strikes can be (and typically are) made illegal.

There is little empirical work examining the intertemporal pattern of public sector strike activity. Nelson, Stone, and Swint (1981) use quarterly work stoppages data from 1953 to 1973 and conclude that, unlike private sector strikes, public sector strikes are countercyclical, based on the coefficient on a 'state of the economy' dummy variable. (As in private sector studies, however, they obtain a negative coefficient on the unemployment rate.) While we are reluctant to place undue emphasis on their result, the suggestion is that, during a downturn, public revenues contract more significantly than do workers' expectations. Future research comparing cyclical strike activity in the public and private sectors is clearly warranted.

There has been much more extensive examination, mostly with cross-section data, of the effects of public sector laws and sanctions on strike frequency. As summarized by Freeman (1984b), the general finding is that weak or noncomprehensive labor relations laws do not deter (and may encourage) strikes, relative to states with blanket prohibition by law or by the courts. However, states with compulsory arbitration laws clearly have fewer strikes. We now turn our attention to this method of impasse resolution.

Compulsory arbitration

As an alternative to strikes, many states have adopted some form of compulsory arbitration as a means of dispute resolution, particularly for police and firefighters where strikes are regarded as particularly costly.[9] Such techniques have attracted considerable theoretical and empirical attention from researchers in economics and industrial relations.

Compulsory arbitration takes two major forms. Most common is conventional arbitration, whereby an arbitrator fashions a settlement of his choice, based loosely on mandated guidelines but not restricted by the stated preferences or offers of the parties. A second form is final-offer arbitration (FOA), sometimes referred to as pendulum arbitration in the UK, whereby the arbitrator must choose between the parties' final offers. Variants of this technique are issue-by-issue FOA, in which an arbitrator constructs his own settlement from the individual components of the parties' final offers, and multiple-offer FOA, where arbitrators select from among several offers. In addition to those procedures currently in use, researchers have not been reluctant to suggest some imaginative variations on existing techniques (e.g. Donn, 1977).

Typically, arbitration procedures are evaluated in terms of three (sometimes conflicting) criteria (see Crawford, 1981; Hirsch and Donn, 1982). First, it is felt that the arbitration technique should provide incentives for the parties to negotiate a settlement themselves, rather than encouraging reliance on third-party awards. In short, a good procedure is believed to be one that is rarely used. Indeed, an important focus in the research literature is whether or not particular procedures 'chill' bargaining and lead to undue reliance on third-party settlements, and whether such procedures create 'narcotic' effects evidenced by repeated usage by the same parties.

A second criterion is that the procedure should be 'neutral' and not distort settlements relative to what would occur in its absence. Several caveats attach to this hypothetical. First, one cannot directly observe outcomes that would have occurred in the absence of the procedure. (And is the benchmark outcome the one that would occur with or without the strike weapon?) More importantly, the existence of any procedure will affect not only arbitrated outcomes, but also bargainers' expectations and hence the outcomes of *negotiated* settlements. Finally, impasse procedures may be adopted by a state or locality not as a means of providing neutrality but, rather, as a means of 'tilting' outcomes in favor of one side or the other.

A third criterion is the efficiency or quality of both negotiated and arbitrated settlements engendered by a procedure. It is believed that a 'high-quality' settlement requires a procedure that allows both parties to weight and accurately express (implicitly or explicitly) preferences and tradeoffs regarding various components of any compensation package (on this issue, see Crawford, 1979; and Donn, 1977). However, the most frequently used models of conventional arbitration (e.g. Farber and Katz, 1979) and final-offer arbitration (e.g. Farber, 1980a) assume a fixed pie, such that settlements are by definition Pareto optimal. In these models, bargaining power, the parties' expectations and preferences, the arbitrator's preferences, and uncertainty surrounding an arbitration procedure affect the distribution but not the size of the pie. However, most models that explicitly consider the quality of the settlement (e.g. Crawford, 1979) are unable to incorporate the uncertainty surrounding the arbitrator's preferences. As we show below, it is this uncertainty that plays a key role in the Farber–Katz and Farber models (for an alternative treatment of arbitral risk, see Crawford, 1982a).

The best-known model of conventional compulsory arbitration is that of Farber and Katz (1979).[10] Each utility-maximizing party forms expectations about the mean and variance (or uncertainty) of the arbitrator's award. Let Y_A and Y_B represent the prior expectations of parties A and B as to A's share of a fixed pie, with σ_A^2 and σ_B^2 representing the variance of these expectations.

Assuming that the parties are risk averse, and letting δ_A and δ_B measure the absolute risk aversion of the respective parties (risk aversion implies $\delta < 0$), Farber and Katz derive the certainty awards that each party would prefer to a risky arbitrated outcome. Party A's *minimum* certainty award that is preferred to arbitration is $Y_A + (1/2)\sigma_A^2 \delta_A$, while party B's *maximum* certainty award to party A is $Y_B - (1/2)\sigma_B^2\delta_B$. Thus a contract zone, Δ, is defined as the range of potential settlements lying between A's minimum and B's maximum acceptable certainty awards. That is:

$$\Delta = (Y_B - Y_A) - (1/2)(\sigma_A^2\delta_A + \sigma_B^2\delta_B). \qquad (4.2)$$

If $\Delta > 0$, a contract zone exists and it is assumed that the larger the zone the more likely will be a negotiated settlement.[11] If $\Delta < 0$, no contract zone exists and recourse to arbitration must be made. Note that risk aversion implies that the far-right term of (4.2) in parentheses will be negative, thus increasing the value of Δ.

Equation (4.2) shows that the likelihood of a negotiated settlement is greater (i.e. the contract zone is larger) the relatively more pessimistic are the parties about the arbitrator's award (the larger is $Y_B - Y_A$); the greater the uncertainty surrounding these expectations (the higher are σ_A^2 and σ_B^2); and the more risk averse the parties.

Farber and Katz, as well as others, have emphasized the role of uncertainty within this model. Indeed, they assume that the parties' expectations about the mean and variance converge to common values ($Y_A = Y_B$; $\sigma_A^2 = \sigma_B^2 = \sigma^2$), producing a contract zone of:

$$\Delta = -(1/2)\sigma^2(\delta_A + \delta_B). \qquad (4.3)$$

For the contract zone to be positive in this case, there must be uncertainty surrounding arbitrator behavior (i.e. $\sigma^2 > 0$). Thus, Farber and Katz conclude that: (1) as uncertainty decreases over time, owing to experience with particular arbitrators or procedures, there will be increased use of arbitration; and (2) the terms of both negotiated and arbitrated settlements will converge to the expected award or preferences of arbitrators.

The latter implication is particularly important in light of the proposed arbitration criteria itemized above. While negotiated settlements and neutrality may be desirable outcomes, negotiated settlements will necessarily be affected by the preferences of arbitrators. And, as Farber (1981) has shown elsewhere, both parties are likely rationally to position their final offer around the expected arbitrator's award, with the relatively more risk averse party positioning its offer somewhat closer. Thus, empirical tests of whether arbitrators 'split the difference' between the parties in conventional arbitration and of 'who wins' in arbitration are difficult to interpret. Evidence that arbitrators split the difference may simply imply that both parties position their offers symmetrically around the expected arbitrator's award, and *not* that the arbitrator was influenced by the parties' offers and then split the difference. Similarly, evidence that an arbitrated outcome is closer to, say, the union's final offer need not imply that the union won, but rather that the union is the more risk averse party and accordingly positioned itself closer to the arbitrator's expected award.

In contrast to Farber and Katz, Hirsch and Donn (1982) contend that experience with a compulsory arbitration scheme can best be viewed as creating opposing effects on the frequency of use. While decreased uncertainty does reduce the incentive to bargain, the convergence of expectations Y_A and Y_B can work either to increase or to decrease arbitration usage over time. If the parties begin as relative optimists ($Y_A > Y_B$), so that party A expects to receive a higher award from an arbitrator than party B expects A to receive, experience with an arbitration procedure (leading to a convergence of expectations Y_A and Y_B) will decrease reliance on arbitration.

Hirsch and Donn suggest that such optimism is frequently present in collective bargaining and that the narrowing of unrealistic expectations through experience with an arbitration procedure may more than offset the decrease in the size of the contract zone from reduced uncertainty. They hypothesize a scenario in which, owing to a large reduction in uncertainty, arbitration usage initially increases after implementation of a new procedure, yet eventually declines as unrealistically optimistic expectations about arbitral awards are reduced (for evidence along these lines, see Butler and Ehrenberg, 1981, and the discussion below).

An additional factor enlarging the contract zone and hence encouraging a negotiated settlement is the cost associated with the use of an arbitration procedure. Such costs can easily be incorporated into the Farber and Katz model (Bloom, 1981; Hirsch and Donn, 1982). Arbitration costs are clearly less important than are legal fees in civil cases (which serve to ensure that most cases get settled out of court), but they are nonetheless nontrivial, at least in some instances (Hirsch and Donn, 1982, provide some imprecise estimates), and states or localities might choose to discourage the use of arbitration by imposing larger fees. Kochan *et al.* (1979), Hirsch and Donn (1982), and Donn and Hirsch (1983) discuss the relative merits and effects of imposing arbitration costs on the parties and proffer alternative policy proposals (in which, for example, costs vary with unit size and with the divergence in the final offers).

Final-offer arbitration (FOA), whereby an arbitrator selects one of the parties' final offers without compromise, was long ago suggested as an alternative to conventional arbitration (Stevens, 1966), and currently is used in a number of states to settle certain public sector labor disputes (as well as in major league baseball). Under conventional arbitration, the parties may have relatively little incentive to provide useful information once it appears likely that the apparatus may be used. Indeed, if arbitrators are perceived to 'split the difference' (although we do not accept this premise), then the bargaining parties' offers are likely to diverge since neither party wants to prejudice the arbitrator's decision against itself. Final-offer arbitration is intended to make both parties more reasonable and thus encourage more serious negotiating. And by introducing greater risk into the arbitration process, it is hoped there will be decreased reliance on the procedure itself (although for disagreement on this point, see Farber, 1980b).

Farber (1980a), and subsequently Ashenfelter and Bloom (1984), have modeled the FOA process. Their models show that the more risk averse party will submit a more reasonable final offer, and that, the greater the uncertainty surrounding the arbitrator's preferences, the greater the divergence between the parties' offers. Implications of the FOA model are in many ways similar to those of the Farber–Katz model of conventional arbitration. Again, one cannot judge who 'wins' from the procedure on the basis of an arbitrator's award, since the decision depends in large part on where the bargainers position their final offers relative to the arbitrator's preferences. For example, the more risk averse party should 'win' most of the time under FOA since its final offers will be most reasonable. Also, as with conventional arbitration, the preferences of arbitrators affect not only arbitrated outcomes but the offers and outcomes of negotiated settlements as well.[12]

Empirical evidence on arbitration procedures is varied. Most studies have focused on one of two areas of interest: first, usage rates and the 'chilling' effects of arbitration procedures; and, second, the question of who 'wins' under arbitration and how compensation is affected (for a summary of such evidence, see Ehrenberg and Schwarz, 1983).

A number of studies have found that arbitration usage increases after passage of an arbitration procedure, providing some support for the argument that arbitration 'chills' or discourages bargaining and for the Farber–Katz view that decreased uncertainty over time makes use of arbitration more palatable (for a summary of evidence, also see Hirsch and Donn, 1982). There is also some evidence that FOA leads to a reduction in the number of issues taken to arbitration relative to conventional arbitration.

A related empirical question is whether arbitration has a 'narcotic' effect, whereby once a party uses an arbitration procedure it is more likely to rely on it in the future. Kochan and Baderschneider (1978) find such tendencies among New York police and firefighters following adoption of compulsory arbitration. However, Butler and Ehrenberg (1981), using the same data but superior econometric techniques (namely, fixed effects models), find that, after an initial increase in usage, the effect of having gone to impasse in the past for any given party was to *reduce* the chance of again reaching an impasse. This finding is consistent with the Hirsch and Donn (1982) interpretation of the Farber–Katz model, whereby the narrowing of expectations by 'optimistic' parties over time increases the size of the contract zone and makes arbitral usage less likely.

The second major empirical issue concerns the actual effects of the availability and usage of arbitration procedures. Evidence on FOA awards in New Jersey, Michigan, and Massachusetts shows that unions 'win' well over half of all awards. For example, in New Jersey over the 1978–80 period, unions 'won' 69 percent of the cases (calculated from Ashenfelter and Bloom, 1984, Table 1). However, the FOA awards were generally *lower* and less dispersed than those resulting from conventional arbitration. Thus, Ashenfelter and Bloom contend that the evidence shows not that unions fare well under FOA, but rather that they are the relatively more risk averse party and moderate their

111

demands accordingly.[13] Evidence on who 'wins' in *negotiated* settlements is in interesting contrast. Hamermesh (1973) and Bowlby and Schriver (1978) find that negotiated awards are on average closer to management's initial offer than to the union's initial demand. While such evidence suggests that unions have greater scope or willingness (or necessity?) than does management for bluffing in negotiations, FOA eliminates such opportunity and moderates most substantially the final offer of the more risk averse party.[14]

Several studies have attempted to measure the effects that the availability and usage of an arbitration procedure have on wage levels (e.g. C. Olson, 1980; Delaney, 1983; Kochan *et al.*, 1979). While the evidence is not clear-cut, it appears that such procedures have little effect on wages, except when accompanied by the right to strike. Ehrenberg and Schwarz (1983) have reviewed this literature and conclude that methodological problems prevent any clear inferences. In particular, they emphasize the need to treat the availability and use of arbitration procedures as endogenous and within the context of budgetary and other governmental issues. We concur.

Finally, there are a limited number of experimental studies examining the impact of alternative impasse procedures (e.g. Magenau, 1983; Subbarao, 1978). However, results here are no more conclusive than in the non-experimental studies. In perhaps the most careful experimental study, Magenau (1983) finds that FOA is more effective than conventional arbitration in encouraging the parties to narrow their differences, but only after impasse has been reached (for further qualifications, see Magenau, 1983).

4.6 Conclusions

We have seen that the strikes literature is in a somewhat unsettled state. There is no widely accepted theoretical framework for analyzing strike behavior, although analysts are turning increasingly to models that posit rational maximizing behavior on the part of both parties. Possibly the most fundamental difficulty in the literature has been the inability to implement direct empirical tests of the various models. This failure reflects the fact that the theoretical determinants of strikes rarely are observed directly or have close empirical counterparts. And so, while our knowledge regarding strike activity has increased markedly in recent years, no single theoretical model as yet appears capable of explaining the diverse array of statistical evidence.

Given the current state of play, the time appears ripe for a major breakthrough. Such a breakthrough would have to provide a testable theoretical model that assumed rational maximizing behavior and would have to be able to explain both interindustry and cyclical patterns of strike behavior. Our guess is that the most promising avenue for future research will involve micro-level game-theoretic bargaining models that can be tested with firm-level or experimental data (for such an attempt, see Fudenberg, Levine, and Ruud, 1983). It seems likely therefore that the strikes literature will become more closely integrated with the growing theoretical and experimental literature on game theory and prisoner's dilemma (see, for example, Axelrod, 1984).

Much of the literature surveyed in this chapter has dealt with the determination of strike activity. Yet the wider relevance of this literature may have less to do with the determinants of strikes than with the effects of bargaining power on both wage and nonwage outcomes in the workplace. Even though strikes are the exception rather than the rule in bargaining outcomes, and rarely involve substantial costs to society, they involve significant costs to participants. Accordingly, strike threat power may be expected to have an important impact on negotiated settlements.[15] However, with the exception of a paper by Reder (1984), who finds that union–nonunion wage differentials are larger in industries where strike costs are higher, we have little evidence relating strike costs and bargaining power to wage and nonwage outcomes.

Notes

1 However, we largely ignore the many papers that provide bargaining models examining the *process* by which parties arrive at a settlement. Frequently cited works in this area include Zeuthen (1930), Nash (1950), Harsanyi (1956), Schelling (1963), Bishop (1964), Cross (1965), and Walton and McKersie (1965).

2 Following Farber (1978a), the present value of the firm may be written

$$v = \int_{s}^{\infty} [PQ - LW(1 + Y_g)]e^{-rt}dt - \int_{0}^{\infty} He^{-rt}dt,$$

where PQ is total revenue, LW is the prestrike wage bill, Y_g is the proportional wage increase offered by the employer, H are fixed costs, r is the rate of discount, and s is strike length (this formulation assumes the firm ceases operation during the strike). Integrating this equation and solving for Y_g yields:

$$Y_g = \frac{PQ}{LW} - \frac{(vr+H)}{LW} e^{rs} - 1,$$

indicating that, for any given present value of the firm, the firm faces a tradeoff between Y_g and s. This formulation underpins the π curves shown in Figure 4.4.

3   Specifically, Farber argues that the union rate of concession will be higher, and hence strike probability will be greater, the higher is unemployment, the lower are union fund balances per member, the lower are past profit rates, in the presence of pay restraint, the higher is labor's share, and the higher are past real wage increases. The Y^* variable is said to be a function of unemployment (lower unemployment increasing Y^* and strike probability), together with a set of firm dummies. Thus, the unemployment rate has an indeterminate effect on the strike probability. Note that this specification is in many respects arbitrary (see Siebert, Bertrand, and Addison, 1985).

4   We do not find this explanation totally convincing. If workers have accurate information about the state of the general economy, then, on average, individual firms are just as likely to be performing above as below the average, regardless of the position of the business cycle. And, if workers' perception of the cycle lags the true state of the economy (owing, for example, to a reporting lag on national statistics), a *countercyclical* pattern of strike activity is possible.

5   In the prewar period, Snyder argues, unionism was poorly established and unstable, while its political power was uncertain. In these circumstances, strikes fluctuated primarily in response to labor's organizational strength and political changes. The political element enters insofar as periods of political change increased the effectiveness of the strike weapon, government being allegedly more responsive/vulnerable to the demands of organized labor at these times.

6   Kennan (1980) argues persuasively that strike models should employ *settlement* rates as the dependent variable.

7   Strikes are also found to be related positively to the number of NLRB elections within the industry during the time period. It is hypothesized that industries with a large number of elections are less likely to have established or maintained effective protocols.

8   Crouch's four industrial relations corporatist variables, proxying what he terms 'concertative' institutions, are: the degree of centralization of the union movement, the degree of employer coordination, the presence of work councils, and the absence of shop floor autonomy. The two measures of social democratic corporatism are: the percentage of parliamentary seats held by labor parties and government revenues as a proportion of GNP less defense spending.

9   As of May 1981, 20 states and the District of Columbia had some form of mandatory arbitration (US Department of Labor, 1981).

10 The determination of whether bargaining will result in negotiated settlement or go to arbitration is similar in many respects to the determination of whether legal disputes will be settled out of court or go to trial (on this, see Gould, 1973).

11 The parties need not reach a settlement when a positive contract zone exists; rather, it is assumed that the probability of reaching a settlement increases with the size of the contract zone (Hirsch and Donn, 1982, p. 58, point out an ambiguity in the Farber and Katz paper on this point). Crawford (1982b), building on work by Schelling (1963), shows that the probability of settlement need not increase with the size of the contract zone.

12 Bazerman and Farber (forthcoming) provide an interesting analysis of the determinants of arbitrator decision making. They reject the simple split-

the-difference view of arbitrator behavior, but do find that arbitrators' awards are affected by the parties' offers as well as by the facts of the case. However, as the 'quality' of the offers decreases (as they become further apart), the facts are weighted more heavily. But in an analysis of Canadian wage settlements between 1966 and 1975, Auld *et al.* (1981) find that labor market conditions, measured by a vacancy rate, have little effect on arbitrated wage settlements.

13 Within a different context, Farber (1978b) finds that members of the UMW exhibit highly risk averse behavior.

14 Such initial bluffing seems more consistent with the Ashenfelter–Johnson (1969) political model, which envisions a divergence between the preferences of the rank and file and the (more realistic) position of union leaders, than with the Pareto optimal accident models, which posit rational behavior for both bargaining parties.

15 There is little theoretical reason for believing that strikes (as opposed to strike threat power) and wages should be positively correlated, despite the frequent assertion to the contrary. For discussion and evidence on this issue, see Lacroix (1983).

CHAPTER 5

Union Effects on Relative Wages

5.1 Introduction

The aspect of labor unions most extensively studied by economists has been their effect on relative wages. The pathbreaking book by H. Gregg Lewis, *Unionism and Relative Wages in the United States*, published in 1963, set the tone and agenda for much of the subsequent research. Despite numerous studies on union wage effects since that time, a consensus does not exist as to the magnitude of these effects. In recent years particularly, a plethora of studies have attempted to measure union wage effects. Much of this renewed interest has stemmed from the availability of new microdata sets, coupled with lower computing costs and the development of econometric techniques better designed to measure union wage effects with these data. Despite significant improvements in data and econometric techniques, however, such studies have produced a range of estimates that are sensitive to specification, sample, and estimation procedure and that are unrealistically high or low in a large number of cases (for an extensive review of recent evidence, see Lewis, forthcoming).

In this chapter we first briefly examine theory regarding union effects on the compensation of union and nonunion workers and then discuss conceptual and empirical issues involved in the measurement of union–nonunion wage differentials. We then review recent empirical studies that quantify union wage and nonwage effects and, finally, provide an appraisal of this evidence.

5.2 Union Wage Effects: Theory

Direct and indirect wage effects

Unions in the long run cannot markedly increase the wages of union members relative to otherwise similar nonunion workers unless either there are monopoly returns, Ricardian rents accruing as a result of special cost advantages, or unions are organized across most firms in an industry. If unions successfully increase the wages for workers in some but not most firms within a competitive industry, those firms are not likely to survive if they continue to bear higher costs than their competitors. However, union wage gains will create an excess supply of workers to covered jobs. Because profit-maximizing firms will select the relatively most productive workers from this queue, in the (very) long run union–nonunion wage differentials between similar workers (or labor efficiency units) may be small (for a related discussion, see Kalachek and Raines, 1980). Much of the wage gain associated with unionism would thus accrue to inframarginal workers.

Although movement and selection of higher-skill workers into union jobs in the long run will mitigate wage differentials for truly similar workers, union–nonunion differentials are not likely to be eliminated. Because most firms have substantial fixed costs over reasonably long time periods and because replacing an existing labor force in a unionized setting with strict seniority provisions takes many years, observed relative wage differentials between similar union and non-union workers can be substantial. Above-competitive wages can be maintained for a long time where unions have organized most firms in an industry, particularly in those that are publicly regulated, face little foreign competition, or have an inelastic product demand. In such noncompetitive market environments, unionism may be seen as a way of redistributing a portion of existing economic rents from owners of capital to labor (see Chapters 6 and 7). Even where there is free entry into an industry, differences among firms in the costs of resisting unionism – due, say, to differences in worker tastes – will allow unions to acquire and maintain wage differentials (Lazear, 1983a, b).

The reasoning above suggests several important points regarding union wage effects. First, unionism may significantly alter the *structure* of wages in an economy, yet in the long run have little measurable impact on relative union–nonunion wage differentials. That is, although unionism may change relative wages by skill type, worker mobility and employer selection will in the long run mitigate wage differentials between truly similar workers. An alternative way of stating this point is that unionism's unobservable effect on wage rates relative to what would exist in the absence of unionism (a 'wage gain') is quite distinct from the relative wage differential (a 'wage gap') between similar union and nonunion workers, given the presence of unionism in the labor market. This important distinction will be shown more precisely in the subsequent section on measurement. We might note at this point, however, that, while we can provide reasonable measures of union–nonunion relative wage differentials (gaps) given existing levels of unionism, we generally are unable to measure wage gains or the overall effect of unionism on the wage structure.[1]

The preceding discussion suggests, secondly, that union wage effects are likely to vary over time, by industry, occupation, and region, and with worker and job characteristics. More precisely, any direct effects of labor unions on wages and the workplace will in turn generate indirect effects or responses by firms and workers. Estimated union wage effects are likely to be sensitive to the stage of the process at which the differential is measured and to the extent to which the researcher can control for these secondary or indirect responses to union organizing and collective bargaining.

Much of the existing empirical literature estimating union wage effects has not sufficiently addressed many of these issues. However, some recent econometric studies attempt to measure union–nonunion wage differentials, after controlling for the extent of unionism in the industry or labor market. This may help prevent a confounding of the specific effects of union membership or coverage on the wage differential with the effects of industry-wide union density on the wage structure.[2] Much of the recent literature in this area has been concerned with controlling for unmeasured differences in worker quality between union and nonunion workers in order to obtain better measures of the relative wage differential. These studies, employing new techniques (e.g. correcting for 'selectivity' bias or estimating 'fixed effects' models) and new data sets (e.g. longitudinal panel data), are reviewed in Section 5.3.

Union effects on union and nonunion wages

There is a large literature by institutional labor economists and industrial relations analysts outlining the conditions under which unions have the greatest bargaining power and can obtain the largest wage gains. Economists have generally approached the bargaining power issue in terms of the demand for and supply of union labor. Anything that increases labor demand will allow increases in union wages and employment, while restrictions on labor supply allow wage gains. As discussed in Chapter 2, potential union wage gains are largest where demand for union (but not nonunion) labor is least elastic. It thus follows from Marshall's laws of derived demand that union wage effects should be largest where substitution by firms in production and by consumers in consumption is most difficult. Because labor demand (and supply) conditions vary considerably across industries, geographic areas, and over time it is not surprising that union wage effects exhibit similar variability. Although limited evidence is available on the wage effects of factors affecting demand elasticities (for example, union density, firm size, concentration, and capital intensity), empirical studies generally have not controlled for these factors.

Unions affect not only union wages but also those in the nonunion sector. Most discussion of these effects has centered on what are referred to as labor spillover, threat, and demand effects. The labor spillover effect causes equilibrium wages in the nonunion sector to decline if there is a movement of employment out of the union sector, owing to union-induced wage increases, into the nonunion sector.[3] If labor shifts costlessly and completely from the union to the nonunion sector, no unemployment need result from union-induced wage increases. However, it is rational for some workers to queue for covered jobs or in highly unionized labor markets as long as the discounted present value of the expected earnings advantage from acquiring a union job, times the probability of obtaining such a job during future time periods, is greater than the costs of not accepting a noncovered job (we are ignoring risk aversion). Thus unemployment is typically higher within highly unionized labor markets (for an argument along these lines, see Hall, 1970). While econometric studies are able to measure wage differentials between union and nonunion workers, direct estimation of the labor spillover effect is not generally possible.

Unionism can also increase nonunion wages as a result of so-called 'threat' effects. The existence of a legal framework (i.e. the National Labor Relations Board election process) that makes union organizing possible provides an incentive to employers to increase the wages of nonunion labor as a means of discouraging unionism. The same reasoning applies to such nonwage outcomes as seniority systems, grievance procedures, and pension and health benefits. Both employers and employees may prefer a nonunion work environment to a union outcome with equivalent compensation, since costs arising from such things as union dues, strikes, and less flexible work rules might be avoided. It thus seems likely that unionism increases wage rates of nonunion workers in industries where unions are prevalent or most likely to organize and in potentially organizable jobs where similarly skilled workers in the same labor market are highly organized. As is the case with labor spillover effects, separate measurement of threat effects, as opposed to the relative wage differential at given levels of unionism, generally cannot be obtained in any straightforward manner.

Finally, demand effects may result from a shift of demand away from now more costly products produced in the union sector (assuming unionism raises prices) to the relatively less costly products from the nonunion sector. As long as labor supplies to the nonunion sector are not perfectly elastic, demand effects will put upward pressure on wages in the nonunion sector. Of course, in the long run, equilibrium price differentials between union and nonunion firms competing in the same product market cannot exist.

As previously mentioned, union wage effects are likely to vary systematically with union density; that is, with the extent of coverage or organization within the particular industry or labor market. Union density is likely to affect union wage effects due primarily to its impact on the elasticity of demand for union labor (Freeman and Medoff, 1981). Increased union coverage in a sector will lower product demand elasticity since substitution to a reduced number of nonunion firms is more difficult. Consequently, labor demand elasticity will be lower and union wage gains potentially higher. An alternative explanation of the positive relationship between union wage effects and union density is that unions are most likely both to organize and to acquire wage gains in sectors with low demand elasticities. Studies by Lee (1978), Kahn (1978a), Freeman and Medoff (1981), Mellow (1983), and Holzer (1982) provide evidence on the net effects of union coverage on the wages of nonunion workers. These studies will be examined subsequently, but we note here that the overall effect of unions on *nonunion* wages is estimated to be positive in most studies.

Because union coverage within an industry or labor market is likely to affect the union–nonunion wage differential, it is important that empirical estimates of the wage differential control for differences in union density. As Lewis (forthcoming) documents, most available estimates of union wage effects do not, and thus entangle to some degree the effect of union membership *per se* with that of density.

5.3 Econometric Specification

Measurement of the differential

Let W_{0i} be the (unobserved) competitive wage rate for individual i in the absence of unionism in an economy. Introducing unionism, and letting subscripts 'u' and 'n' designate union and nonunion status, the proportionate effects of unionism on union and nonunion wages are:

$$D_{ui} = (W_{ui} - W_{0i})/W_{0i}, \qquad (5.1)$$

$$D_{ni} = (W_{ni} - W_{0i})W_{0i}. \qquad (5.2)$$

We have strong priors regarding the sign of D_{ui}, believing it to be positive for most union members and certainly positive on average. The effect of unionism on nonunion wages, D_{ni}, may be positive or negative depending on the relative strengths of the labor spillover, threat, and demand effects discussed previously.

Because W_{0i}, the wage rate that would exist in the absence of unionism, is not observed, we are unable to estimate D_{ui} or D_{ni} in any reliable fashion. What can be estimated, however, is the proportionate union–nonunion wage differential:

$$D_i = (W_{ui} - W_{ni})/W_{ni}. \qquad (5.3)$$

Or, letting bars represent means:

$$\bar{D} = (\bar{W}_u - \bar{W}_n)/\bar{W}_n. \qquad (5.4)$$

Most of the empirical literature on union wage effects has been directed at obtaining estimates of $\bar{D}$, the mean proportionate wage differential between otherwise similar union and nonunion workers.

In practice, most studies estimate some version of a semi-logarithmic wage equation in which the dependent variable is the natural logarithm of the wage and right-hand variables include schooling, age or experience, and other wage determinants.[4] From these studies, estimates of the mean logarithmic wage differential, $\bar{d}$ (where $\bar{d} = \overline{\ln W}_u - \overline{\ln W}_n$), are obtained. For small values of $\bar{d}$ (less than about 0.15) the log differential approximates the proportionate differential. The log differential typically is converted to the proportionate differential by:

$$\bar{D} = e^{\bar{d}} - 1, \qquad (5.5)$$

or to a percentage differential by multiplying by 100.[5]

Aggregate cross-section estimation

Until the last ten years or so, virtually all estimates of union wage effects were based on aggregate or grouped data. Data were typically aggregated by industry, although some studies used states or SMSAs as the unit of observation. Grouped data have numerous shortcomings, the most serious of which is the absence of separate data on W_u or W_n, wages for union and nonunion workers (for an exception, see Killingsworth, 1983).

Given that data are available on average wages only for *all* workers, how might the researcher estimate union wage effects? Starting with the identity that the log of the *geometric mean* wage in industry k is a weighted average of the logs of the geometric means of union and nonunion wages (or, equivalently, the mean log wage is a weighted average of mean log wages for union and nonunion workers), we can write:

$$\overline{\ln W}_k = P_k \overline{\ln W}_{uk} + (1 - P_k)\overline{\ln W}_{nk}, \qquad (5.6)$$

121

where P is the proportion unionized in industry k. Note that the relative wage differential, D_k, can be rearranged such that:

$$D_k = (W_{uk} - W_{nk})/W_{nk} = (W_{uk}/W_{nk}) - 1, \qquad (5.7)$$

and

$$1 + D_k = W_{uk}/W_{nk}. \qquad (5.8)$$

Taking logs and then means yields:

$$\overline{\ln W_{uk}} = \overline{\ln W_{nk}} + \ln(1 + D_k). \qquad (5.9)$$

Substituting for $\overline{\ln W_{uk}}$ in the identity (5.6), canceling terms, and assuming D does not vary by group or with P, yields:

$$\overline{\ln W_k} = \overline{\ln W_{nk}} + P_k \ln(1 + D). \qquad (5.10)$$

In order to put such an equation into a form that can be estimated, the standard procedure is to postulate a vector C of j observable worker and industry characteristics that determine nonunion wages. That is:

$$\overline{\ln W_{nk}} = f(C_{kj}). \qquad (5.11)$$

The wage equation can then be estimated in the following form:

$$\overline{\ln W_k} = f(C_{kj}) + P_k \ln(1 + D) + e_k, \qquad (5.12)$$

where e_k is the error term and an estimate of $\bar{D}$ is obtained from the regression coefficient $\hat{d}$ on P_k by $\bar{D} = e^{\hat{d}} - 1$.

A large number of studies have obtained estimates of union wage effects from such an equation. Yet this approach is replete with problems. While theory calls for use of the natural log of the geometric mean wage (or, equivalently, the mean of the log wage), virtually all studies in fact use the log of the arithmetic mean or median wage since these are available in published form. Hirsch (1981) estimates such an equation using all three measures and finds that estimated union wage effects are in fact quite sensitive to the choice of the dependent variable.

Estimation using ordinary least squares (OLS) is dependent on unionism and all variables in D_j being exogenous. Yet, as is clear from our discussion in Chapters 2 and 3, this assumption is breached since union membership is not in fact exogenous. Unfortunately, aggregate estimates obtained using two stage least squares (2SLS) and three stage least squares (3SLS) are highly erratic and very sensitive to specification of the wage and union equations. Ashenfelter and Johnson (1972) find that estimated union wage effects in manufacturing decline and become insignificant as one moves from OLS to 2SLS or 3SLS. Kahn (1979) obtains exactly the opposite result. As an illustration of such sensitivity, Hirsch (1982) obtains coefficient estimates of the average log differential, $\bar{d}$, in manufacturing of 0.03, 0.10, and 0.17 using OLS, 2SLS, and 3SLS, respectively, while in nonmanufacturing the comparable figures are 0.17, 0.07, and 0.02. All these estimates have large standard errors.

OLS estimates of $\bar{d}$ are also likely to be biased and inconsistent if $\bar{d}$ is correlated with P or any variable in C_j. Each of these cases is likely. As first shown in Rosen (1969), and subsequently emphasized in later work, union wage effects are likely to increase with union density. Likewise, union wage effects are likely to differ across demographic groups (i.e. by age, race, sex, etc.) and with industry characteristics. A fundamental problem is that the entire wage structures within the union and nonunion sectors are different, thus necessitating separate estimation of wage equations by union status. Yet this is generally impossible with available grouped data. Moreover, as previously discussed, grouped data do not allow the separation of two distinct effects: first, that of union density on the structure of union and nonunion wages; and, second, that of union membership (coverage) on relative wages given union density. Lewis (1983) has argued convincingly that aggregate equations such as those above confound the two effects and that there is no reliable way to extract estimates of $\bar{d}$ from such equations. Fortunately, preferable alternatives to aggregate wage equations are now readily available.

Micro cross-section estimation

Most empirical studies now use large microdata sets to estimate union wage effects. Such studies became commonplace in the US during the mid-1970s along with and as a part of a large empirical literature estimating multiple regression wage and earnings equations within a human capital type framework. Micro cross-section studies are now common in Britain and other countries as well.

Initially, studies estimated the following simple but highly restrictive form of the earnings function:

$$\ln W_i = \sum_{j=0}^{m} \beta_j X_{ij} + \alpha U_i + e_i, \qquad (5.13)$$

where $\ln W_i$ equals the natural log of the wage of individual i, X_j is a

123

vector of m earnings-determining characteristics (and $X_0 = 1$ so that β_0 is the constant), U_i is a dummy variable equal to 1 if individual i is a union member (or in a covered job) and 0 otherwise, e_i is the error term, and α, the coefficient on U_i, is an estimate of the average log differential $\bar{d}$. A large number of union wage estimates are available from such studies, many of which include U_i merely as a control variable in the examination of some other aspect of wage determination. Estimates of $\bar{d}$ from these studies are significantly less variable than are estimates from the aggregate studies. A large proportion of these estimates fall within the range 0.05–0.30, depending on data set, sample coverage, specification, and year.

However, estimation by such a method has several major short-comings. First, the functional form is overly restrictive, not allowing the structure of earnings (the vector of coefficients) to differ between the union and nonunion sectors. Second, union status is treated as exogenous, leading to the possibility of simultaneity bias. (Duncan and Leigh, 1985, explicity test and reject the hypothesis of exogenous union status.) Third, unmeasurable quality differences between union and nonunion members with similar measured characteristics – differences believed probably to be due to selective hiring and optimal job matching – cannot be taken into account within such a framework. Finally, the estimating equation does not hold constant the extent of unionism or coverage density within the appropriate labor market or industry, leading to possible bias from an omitted variable.

A preferable approach (see, for instance, Bloch and Kuskin, 1978), which allows for differences in earnings structure, is the separate estimation of union and nonunion wage equations (or, equivalently, a single equation allowing union interactions with all right-hand variables):

$$\ln W_{ui} = \sum_{j=0}^{m} \beta_{uj} X_{uij} + e_{ui}, \qquad (5.14)$$

$$\ln W_{ni} = \sum_{j=0}^{m} \beta_{nj} X_{nij} + e_{ni}. \qquad (5.15)$$

The mean logarithmic union–nonunion wage differential is thus estimated as:

$$\bar{d} = \overline{\ln W_u} - \overline{\ln W_n} = \sum_{j=0}^{m} (\beta_{uj} - \beta_{nj}) \bar{X}_j, \qquad (5.16)$$

124

where $\bar{X}_j$ can represent either union means, nonunion means, or all-worker means. Use of, say, all-worker means, $P\bar{X}_{uj} + (1-P)\bar{X}_{nj}$, corresponds to asking the question: for a worker with average characteristics, what is the predicted wage differential between his working in the union and nonunion sectors?[6]

It is worth noting the correspondence of this measure of the log differential with an alternative statement of the conceptual experiment. Ignoring sigma and the j subscript, consider the following expressions:

$$(\overline{\ln W_u} - \overline{\ln W_n}) - \beta_u(\bar{X}_u - \bar{X}_n), \qquad (5.17)$$

$$(\overline{\ln W_u} - \overline{\ln W_n}) - \beta_n(\bar{X}_u - \bar{X}_n). \qquad (5.18)$$

Expression *(5.17)* shows the part of the log wage differential that is *not* accounted for by differences in characteristics, assuming the union wage structure. Expression *(5.18)* provides the same calculation assuming the nonunion wage structure. But by least squares, $\overline{\ln W_u} = \beta_u\bar{X}_u$ and $\overline{\ln W_n} = \beta_n\bar{X}_n$. Substituting into *(5.17)* and *(5.18)* and canceling terms yields:

$$(\beta_u - \beta_n)\bar{X}_n \qquad (5.19)$$

$$(\beta_u - \beta_n)\bar{X}_u. \qquad (5.20)$$

Thus, measure *(5.17)*, measuring the differential assuming the *union* wage structure (β_u), corresponds exactly to *(5.19)*, which evaluates the differential using *nonunion* mean characteristics. Likewise, measure *(5.18)* corresponds exactly to *(5.20)*. In order to obtain the measure based on all worker means (equation *5.16*), one takes a weighted average of either pair, using the proportion union, P, to weight *(5.18)* or *(5.20)*, and $(1-P)$ to weight *(5.17)* or *(5.19)*. Unfortunately, no single one of these measures is conceptually superior and the three estimates can vary considerably.

Bloch and Kuskin (1978), using data on white males from the May 1973 Current Population Survey (CPS), evaluate the log differential using measures *(5.17)* and *(5.18)*. We convert their calculations to a weighted average using $(1-P)$ and P as weights to provide estimates based on all worker means. Their results imply an estimate of $\bar{d} = 0.11$ for their entire sample, as compared to an estimate of 0.15 obtained by simply including a union dummy variable in a single regression equation. They also find, as have similar studies, significantly flatter earnings profiles with respect to schooling and experience. That is, once in the union sector, additional years of schooling add less to earnings than for workers in the nonunion sector, and union workers exhibit earnings–experience profiles that are less concave. These interesting findings from cross-sectional studies will be examined further in the next section and in Chapter 6 where we turn to unions and their effect on earnings dispersion.

More recent studies (e.g. Lee, 1978; Duncan and Leigh, 1980; Leigh, 1980) not only have estimated separate union and nonunion equations, but also have treated union status as endogenous and attempted to adjust for selectivity bias (or, alternatively stated, omitted variable bias) resulting from unmeasured differences between union and nonunion workers. As seen in Chapter 3, such a model includes a union status equation, in which union membership is affected by the relative log wage differential, and a wage function for each sector:

$$U_i \;\; = \sum_{h=0}^{r} \beta_h Z_{ih} + \delta\,(\ln W_u - \ln W_n)_i + e_i, \qquad (5.21)$$

$$\ln W_{ui} = \sum_{j=0}^{m} \beta_{uj} X_{uij} + e_{ui}, \qquad (5.22)$$

$$\ln W_{ni} = \sum_{j=0}^{m} \beta_{nj} X_{nij} + e_{ni}. \qquad (5.23)$$

Estimation of this model has proceeded by first estimating with probit analysis a reduced-form union status equation, including all independent variables in Z and X on the right-hand side. From the probit union equation one derives 'selectivity variables' for each individual measured by the inverse Mills ratio (the standard normal density function divided by the cumulative distribution of the standard normal). These selectivity variables are then included in the estimation of the wage equations in order to obtain unbiased estimates of the union and nonunion wage function parameters. The predicted mean log wage differential ($\ln W_u - \ln W_n$) can then be obtained as in the Bloch–Kuskin type studies reviewed above, or, alternatively, by taking the mean of the wage differential variable subsequently included in final estimation of the union status equation (5.21).[7]

Lee (1978), using a sample of full-time operatives in 1967, obtained estimates of $\bar{d}$, the wage differential, of 0.14 using OLS (the Bloch–Kuskin method) and 0.12 after adjusting for selectivity. Duncan and Leigh (1980) obtained corresponding estimates of 0.13 and 0.30 with a sample of older white men from the 1969 National Longitudinal Survey (NLS) and somewhat higher estimates from the 1971 NLS. Hirsch and Berger (1984) report estimates of 0.11 and 0.53 using a 1971 sample of blue-collar workers in manufacturing. A full survey of such studies is available in Lewis (forthcoming) and indicates even wider fluctuations than in the estimates summarized above. Estimates appear quite sensitive to violations of the error normality assumption. We concur with the strong conclusions reached by Freeman and Medoff (1983), Cain *et al.* (1981), and Lewis (forthcoming) that estimates obtained by this selectivity adjusted approach are so highly variable and sensitive to sample and specification that they cannot be regarded as reliable (for an alternative view, see Duncan, 1983).

Not included in most of the extant studies is the variable P, measuring the union density or extent of coverage over the appropriate labor or industrial market. Evidence indicates that the size of the union wage differential increases with industry coverage (Rosen, 1969; Lee, 1978; Freeman and Medoff, 1981; Mellow, 1983) and Lewis argues convincingly that P should be included as a control variable in estimating union wage effects. Holzer (1982) examines the effect of *labor market* density (i.e. the percentage unionized in workers' SMSA) on union and nonunion wages of young male blue-collar workers. The union–nonunion differential is found to widen with density, particularly among blacks. Interestingly, Holzer finds the net effect of SMSA density on *nonunion* wages to be positive for whites and negative for blacks.

By way of summary, researchers attempting to estimate d from cross-sectional microdata at this point face the dilemma between choosing a single equation estimation technique (OLS) known to produce results that are biased, yet often plausible and relatively robust, or employing recent econometric techniques designed to overcome the shortcomings of OLS, but whose results are often neither robust nor plausible. Although new estimation techniques continue to be developed, it is still too soon to know how satisfactory they will be.[8]

Estimation with longitudinal data

A promising new approach to the estimation of union wage effects has involved the use of longitudinal data. The primary advantage of longitudinal data is that they allow the researcher to control for unmeasured person-specific quality differences. Because one is observing person-specific *changes* in wages, union status, and other wage determinants, unmeasured quality differences 'fall out' as long as these effects are fixed across periods. Thus, longitudinal wage change models do not suffer from the sort of selectivity or omitted variable bias that has plagued cross-section studies. However, because estimation of union wage effects with longitudinal data relies on the existence of union status changes (union joiners and leavers) over the sample period, another type of selectivity bias may arise since workers who change status may have different (unmeasured) attributes from those who do not change status. Even more important may be the existence of substantial measurement error in the union status variable from major surveys and the apparent sensitivity of estimated union wage effects to the measurement error (Freeman, 1984a).

The approach taken by Mellow (1981) and Mincer (1983) can be illustrated below (for a more extensive analysis, see Chamberlain, 1982; Lewis, forthcoming; Freeman, 1984a). Let $U00$ = not a union member in years 1 or 2 (never union), $U01$ = not a member in year 1 but a member in 2 (a union joiner), $U10$ = a member in year 1 but not in 2 (a union leaver), and $U11$ = a member in years 1 and 2 (always union). An individual wage change equation of a form similar to the following can be estimated (we delete subscript i):

$$\ln W_2 - \ln W_1 = \sum_{j=0}^{m} \beta_j(X_{j2} - X_{j1}) + d_{11}U11 + d_{01}U01 + \quad (5.24)$$
$$d_{10}U10 + (e_2 - e_1).$$

Any person-specific component of the error term in each year that is fixed across years 1 and 2 falls out of the model. Thus one is controlling for unmeasured quality differences (fixed effects) across workers. The omitted reference group is $U00$ (never union). The coefficient d_{11} is interpreted as the change in d (the mean union–nonunion wage differential) between years 1 and 2. The coefficients d_{01} and $-d_{10}$ provide alternative measures of union wage effects based on union joiners and union leavers, respectively.

Mellow uses two samples of year pairs, 1974–5 and 1977–8, from the May CPS.[9] The coefficient d_{11}, measuring changes in d over time, was small (0.00 and -0.02 in the respective samples), as might be expected for a large sample from two adjacent years. In both years, Mellow obtains estimates of union wage effects of about 0.07 or 0.08, and, quite interestingly, finds similar magnitudes for union joiners (d_{01}) and leavers $(-d_{10})$. These estimates are significantly lower than his cross-sectional single equation estimates. For comparison, Mellow provides a union wage effect estimate of 0.19 for the same sample using conventional cross-sectional analysis. These results seemingly imply that about half of the union wage premium observed in cross-sectional analyses may result from unmeasured quality differences among union and nonunion workers (but see below). Union joiners $(U01=1)$ are observed to have somewhat higher wages than those never in a union $(U00=1)$ *prior* to joining a union, while union leavers $(U10=1)$ have lower wages than union stayers $(U11=0)$ *prior* to leaving the union. The wage change model, by allowing worker-specific fixed effects to fall out, appears at first glance to provide reasonable estimates of both union wage effects and the significant selectivity bias resulting from unmeasured quality differences in conventional cross-section estimates.

Mellow also finds, consistent with other studies, a significantly higher union wage premium for younger workers (age ≤ 25), and moderately higher for males than females. In sharp contrast to previous studies detecting larger union wage effects for blacks, Mellow finds evidence of a smaller wage premium. His results suggest that black union members are of relatively higher quality and would earn more than nonunion blacks with similar *measured* characteristics even in the absence of unionism.

The study by Mincer (1983) utilizes data from the NLS Young Men and Older Men Surveys and the Michigan Panel Study of Income Dynamics (PSID). It differs from the Mellow study in that Mincer distinguishes between those changing employers and those not (referred to as movers and stayers, respectively), as well as identifying changes in union status. In the NLS samples, Mincer also distinguishes between union membership and collective bargaining coverage. Of interest is the fact that, in both samples, union joiners ($U01$) are *more* likely to be stayers than movers. This totally implausible finding almost certainly indicates substantial misreporting in the union status variables.

Although the results of the Mincer study are more varied than those in Mellow, the overall findings are similar. Mincer also finds much smaller estimates of $\bar{d}$ after controlling for fixed effects than with typical cross-sectional estimates. Most, but not all, of his estimates show larger wage gains for young workers. In addition, Mincer obtains substantially higher estimates of union wage effects for job movers than for stayers. This may result in part from measurement error in the union status variables for job stayers. In addition, it is likely that the greatest gains from change into union status result when there is an employer change. In fact, it is probably impossible with these data to separate the effect of union status change from employment change. Mellow as well found that substantial wage gains among union joiners existed only for those changing occupation or industry.

The longitudinal studies appear to show conclusively, as economic theory would suggest, that a part of the observed cross-sectional wage differential between union and nonunion workers with similar observable characteristics is in fact due to significant quality differences. The fixed effects wage change models appear to account for the omitted variable (selectivity) bias, which has not been handled satisfactorily in the cross-sectional studies previously reviewed. Although overall estimates of the union wage differentials from longitudinal studies do differ, most are close to 0.10, significantly less than in corresponding cross-sectional wage estimates, but more in line with the magnitude one plausibly might believe could survive in a reasonably competitive environment.

The longitudinal studies have added significantly to our understanding of union wage effects, but they are not without shortcomings. Sample sizes of union joiners and leavers are generally quite small, particularly with the NLS and PSID and among particular groups (by race, sex, age, industry, occupation, etc.). For example, Mellow (1981) reports that about 5 percent of the CPS sample were measured as union joiners and 4 percent as leavers over the 1977–8 period, while Freeman (1984a) reports 3 percent joiners and 3 percent leavers in the CPS between 1974–5. Of course, a larger proportion change union status the longer the time period measured in any longitudinal data set.

Possibly the most important problem with longitudinal analyses of union–nonunion wage differentials is the substantial measurement error in the union status variables (Freeman, 1984a; Mincer, 1983; Lewis, forthcoming). Freeman first estimates the degree of measurement error in major surveys, on the basis of data from two surveys that allow a matching of union status information for the same individual. He estimates that about 10 percent of all workers have their union status misclassified, most of the error being among union workers. Freeman then shows that measurement error of this magnitude causes a significant *downward* bias in the estimated union wage effect relative to the 'true' effect. Freeman concludes that this downward bias in longitudinal estimates may be roughly similar in size to the upward bias in estimates from cross-sectional data (due to unmeasured quality differences). Thus, under some circumstances, longitudinal and cross-sectional estimates may provide reasonable lower and upper bounds on the 'true' union–nonunion wage differential.

An additional problem with longitudinal estimates is that changes in union status often result from changes in jobs and possibly in occupation or industry. As long as union jobs have different characteristics from nonunion jobs, some of the wage change associated with changes in union status may in fact be compensating differentials for job characteristics. Because union jobs are on average relatively less flexible and entail greater risk, it is likely that this bias leads to an overestimate of the union wage effect. The same bias is of course also found in cross-sectional studies unable to control for job characteristics (on this point, see Duncan and Stafford, 1980). A related problem is that union status and changes in union status are endogenous. Stated alternatively, one faces a selectivity problem in that a union joiner, for example, is likely to differ from a union leaver or those recording no change in status, even if measured characteristics are identical. Unfortunately, accounting for the simultaneous determination of union status and wages within a longitudinal framework would not only prove complex, but also doubtless produce estimates exhibiting the same large variation as cross-sectional estimates using simultaneous equation methods.

5.4 Variation in the Union–Nonunion Wage Differential

The effect of unionism varies considerably across labor markets, industries, occupations, and demographic groups. Indeed, it would be rather surprising if it did not, given that elasticities of demand and supply vary significantly across wage determination units. In this section we review briefly the evidence on the variation in union wage effects (Lewis, forthcoming, provides an extensive survey). Unfortunately, studies that may best estimate average (full sample) union wage effects are unable to provide reliable estimates of variation in the differential by group. For example, the longitudinal studies by Mellow (1981) and Mincer (1983) are plagued by small sample sizes of union joiners and leavers and cannot provide precise estimates for particular groups. In fact, considerable variation in union wage effects by group suggest that longitudinal estimates may be fairly sensitive to the representativeness of the relatively small group that has changed union status.

Demographic characteristics, occupation, and region

Most studies estimating union wage effects do not provide separate estimates by age group, but those that do generally find the largest gains for younger workers. Mellow (1981), for example, obtains estimates of $\bar{d}$ of about 0.13 for workers aged 25 years or less, compared to 0.06 for those older than 25. Mincer (1983), who presents more varied estimates, finds the same pattern in almost all cases.[10] Larger union wage effects for young workers imply that unions not only raise but also flatten and make less concave the age–earnings profile. This is exactly the pattern reported in cross-sectional studies. As summarized in Lewis (forthcoming), wage equations estimated with a quadratic experience (or age) term suggest a U-shaped relationship between the wage differential and experience. The initially large union–nonunion differential first decreases with experience, reaching a minimum at about 30 years of experience, and then widens for older workers. If fringe benefits are included in the compensation measure, however, the union–nonunion differential does not vary as much by age (Freeman, 1984b; Freeman and Medoff, 1984, Chapter 8). In addition, a study by Robinson and Tomes (1984) using Canadian data, while finding a flatter union experience profile, reports a significantly *larger* return to union members from tenure (seniority) on the current job. There is some question as to *why* unions in fact have or would choose to have particular effects on the wage structure. In addition, the typical cross-sectional finding could result because unions organize in job settings with flatter earnings profiles; that is, causation could run in both directions (Hirsch, 1982; Hutchins and Polachek, 1981). These issues are addressed in Chapter 6.

Table 5.1 *Union–nonunion log wage differentials by race and sex, 1967, 1973, and 1975*

| | All workers | Male workers | | Female workers | |
		White	Black	White	Black
1967	0.12	0.10	0.22	0.14	0.06
1973	0.15	0.16	0.23	0.13	0.13
1975	0.17	0.16	0.23	0.17	0.17

Source: Ashenfelter (1978), Table 2.1, p. 33.

A number of studies have found relatively larger union wage effects for blacks than for whites, at least among males (the most frequently cited study is Ashenfelter, 1972). Differences between males and females, on the other hand, have rarely been found to be sizeable. In Table 5.1 we present summary union–nonunion log wage differential estimates from a later study by Ashenfelter (1978). Ashenfelter uses CPS microdata on nonfarm wage and salary workers for the years 1967, 1973, and 1975 and estimates four separate OLS cross-sectional log wage equations by race and sex. He does not estimate separate wage functions by union status (as in Bloch–Kuskin and other studies), but he does allow differential union effects (i.e. union interaction terms) by one-digit occupation and industry. Although such cross-sectional estimates do not account for the simultaneous determination of unionism and wages, or control for unmeasured quality differences between union and nonunion workers (and thus are significantly higher than the estimates produced from wage change models using longitudinal data), it is possible that *relative* differences among different groups are estimated accurately. This should hold true to the extent that selectivity bias or the union determination process do not differ significantly across region, industries, or occupation, or by race, sex, or age.

As seen in Table 5.1, black males appear to gain more from union membership or coverage than do white males. This is not a universal finding, however, and may result from an entangling of race with other unmeasured wage determinants. If blacks do realize a larger wage advantage, it is unlikely to result from preferential treatment of blacks

132

in the union sector but, rather, from particularly poor wage opportunities for black males in the nonunion sector. It is also likely to reflect, as Mellow's (1981) results suggest, the fact that black union members are of relatively higher quality and would earn higher wages than nonunion black workers with similar *measured* characteristics even in the absence of unionism. The existence of relatively larger black wage gains is consistent with the finding of many of the studies reviewed in Chapter 3 that blacks are more likely, *ceteris paribus*, to be union members and vote for union representation.

From the results presented in Table 5.1 and elsewhere it can be seen that, apart from the possibly higher union wage advantage for black males, differences among females and between white males and females appear quite small. To the extent that women on average have less permanent labor force attachment than men, they may have a lower present value of *lifetime* wage gains from unionism even if the union–nonunion differential is equal for men and women. This might help explain women's lower likelihood of choosing union representation even within the same job, although much of the lower coverage among women is due to differences in job structure.

Significant differences exist in union–nonunion wage differentials across occupations and industries. Table 5.2 summarizes evidence from Ashenfelter for estimated union wage effects for white males in various occupations and industries. Among nonproduction workers, unions produce positive and significant wage differentials among service

Table 5.2 *Union–nonunion log wage differentials for white males by occupation and industry, 1975*

Professional	0.07	Operatives in:	
Managerial	0.04	Construction	0.51
Clerical	0.09	Durable manufacturing	0.19
Sales	0.01	Nondurable manufacturing	0.16
Service	0.14	Transportation, communication, utilities	0.24
Craftsmen in:		Laborers in:	
Construction	0.40	Construction	0.48
Durable manufacturing	0.06	Durable manufacturing	0.22
Nondurable manufacturing	0.07	Nondurable manufacturing	0.15
Transportation, communication, utilities	0.08	Transportation, communication, utilities	0.25

Source: Ashenfelter (1978), Table B.1, pp. 49–50.

workers (0.14), not just for 1975 (as shown), but also in the 1967 and 1973 samples (Ashenfelter, 1978, Table B.1, pp. 49–50). Estimates for professional, managerial, clerical, and sales are not consistently positive, significant, or stable across the 1967, 1973, and 1975 samples.

Among production workers, consistently positive union–nonunion wage differentials are found for craftsmen, operatives, and laborers in all industries. Table 5.2 presents 1975 estimates for production workers in the most highly unionized sectors. In construction, unionized craftsmen, operatives, and laborers are estimated to realize an extremely large wage premium (for similar recent evidence, see Perloff and Sickles, 1983). This almost certainly implies significant productivity and quality differences among union and nonunion construction workers, exactly what Allen (1984d) has found. In manufacturing and in transportation, communication, and utilities, union wage differentials are estimated to be about 0.15–0.25 for operatives and laborers. Wage gains appear somewhat higher in transportation, communication and utilities than in manufacturing, possibly because of its publicly regulated and highly concentrated nature. Evidence for the 1980s should show a decrease in the union differential among workers in recently deregulated industries within this sector. The relatively low union wage gain for craftsmen, other than in construction, suggests that unions tend to narrow skill differentials significantly and benefit the most skilled relatively least. Note that the most obvious distinction between construction and the other sectors is that unions in construction tend to be organized along craft lines, whereas in other sectors organization is primarily along industrial lines. Since each craft is a small proportion of total cost and workers striking one firm can be employed elsewhere, bargaining power is enhanced within construction. Moreover craft unions have limited ability and incentive to narrow wage differentials between high and low skilled workers, in contrast to industrial unions.

Hamermesh (1971), Oaxaca (1975), Bloch and Kuskin (1978), Duncan and Leigh (1980), and others present similar evidence on union wage differentials by occupation (not cross-classified by industry). For instance, Bloch and Kuskin, using May 1973 CPS data, estimate an overall log differential of 0.11. They find the largest differentials for laborers and transport equipment operatives (0.39 and 0.32 respectively), differentials of 0.16–0.19 for craftsmen, non-transport operatives, and service workers, and differentials close to zero for nonproduction (white-collar) occupations. Using more recent data, Antos (1983) finds a wage differential of 0.04 and a compensation (wages plus fringes) differential of 0.07 among white-collar workers, compared to differentials of about 0.15 among blue-collar workers. In short, the literature to date indicates that the union wage differential by occupation is significantly larger among blue-collar than among white-collar workers. Across industries, wage differentials are largest in construction, and smaller in manufacturing than in nonmanufacturing.

The union–nonunion wage differential has also been found to differ across regions, even after accounting for differences in the workforce, occupation, and industry structure. This is not surprising given the strong attempt by unions to standardize wages, in part by lowering wage differences between members across areas. Thus one would expect to see the largest union–nonunion differences in the south and in non-urban labor markets since wage levels here are relatively lower. Extant evidence is consistent with both predictions (Lewis, forthcoming). For example, Kiefer and Smith (1977) have provided separate estimates of the log wage differential, estimated from the May 1973 CPS, for the northeast, border states (and Washington DC), and the deep south (excluded from their analysis are the north central and west regions). Their results are summarized in Table 5.3. As can be seen, union wage effects are significantly larger in the south and border states than in the northeast.[11] Union membership appears particularly attractive for nonwhite males in the south, reflecting the relatively poorer wage opportunities for nonunion nonwhites in that region.

Table 5.3   *Union–nonunion log wage differentials by region, race, and sex, 1973*

	Males	Females
Whites:		
Northeast	0.18	0.13
Border	0.37	0.31
Deep south	0.31	0.28
Nonwhites:		
Northeast	0.15	0.10
Border	0.24	0.21
Deep south	0.49	0.23

Source: Kiefer and Smith (1977), Table 4, p. 530.

By way of summary, there are significant differences in union wage effects among demographic groups and across regions. Union–nonunion wage differentials vary significantly by industry and appear larger for young and old than for prime-age workers, for production (blue-collar) than for nonproduction (white-collar) workers, for less skilled than for more skilled production workers, and for southern and rural than for nonsouthern and urban workers. Estimated differences by sex and race are relatively small or are not systematic. Although we are confident that *relative* differences by group and region have been estimated reasonably accurately in cross-sectional studies, we have little confidence in the *level* of the wage differentials reported in these studies.

Industry and job characteristics

There is relatively little empirical work examining differences in union wage effects by industry and job characteristics. Because microdata sets containing detailed information on individual worker characteristics (wages, union status, age, schooling, sex, race, etc.) generally do not provide information on industry and job characteristics, aggregate data must be bridged to individual data. What has been studied most extensively to date is the effect and interaction of unionism with industry concentration and firm size. More recently, several studies have been able to examine the relationship between unionism, wages, and several nonpecuniary job characteristics.

A frequently cited study by Weiss (1966) matched industry data on concentration and unionization to individual data from the 1960 Census of Population for male operatives and kindred workers in manufacturing, mining, and construction (for regressions with alternative sample definitions, see Weiss). Below, let E represent dollar wage and salary earnings in 1959, P the percentage of workers covered by collective bargaining agreements in an individual's industry of employment, and CCR a corrected (a scaling up of national concentration ratios for industries with strong regional or local product markets) concentration ratio (bounded 0–100) calculated for the worker's three-digit census industry. In the absence of 'control' variables, Weiss obtains ($|t|$ ratios in parentheses):

$$E = 1936 + 23.74P + 53.47CCR - .4426P{\cdot}CCR. \quad \bar{R}^2 = .040 \quad (5.25)$$
$$ (5.71) \quad\quad (6.85) \quad\quad\quad\quad (4.30)$$

These results, indicating that unionism has *smaller* wage effects the more highly concentrated an industry, are qualitatively identical to those obtained earlier by Lewis, (1963, pp. 161, 178).

The theoretical explanation for a negative coefficient on $P{\cdot}CCR$ is suspect. Weiss suggests that high wages will occur in highly concentrated but unorganized industries owing primarily to the threat of unionism, while unions are able to achieve high wages in both less and more concentrated industries. In a sense, Weiss argues, unionism and concentration 'represent the same force' so that their combined effect is less than the sum of their separate effects. Of course, one could argue exactly the opposite. Concentration decreases the labor demand elasticity and may allow economic profits to be sustained. If unionism is a means by which rents are shifted from owners of capital to labor one might expect a positive rather than a negative interaction coefficient. Indeed, if unions are more likely to capture profits in concentrated industries (Chapter 7 summarizes this evidence), then union wage effects might be expected to be larger in more concentrated industries.

When Weiss adds detailed personal, labor market, and other industry characteristics, not only does the coefficient on $P \cdot CCR$ become insignificant, but so do those on CCR and P. With detailed control variables included, Weiss obtains ($|t|$ ratios in parentheses):

$$E = -156 + 6.17P + .29CCR + .0687P \cdot CCR. \qquad \bar{R}^2 = .342 \qquad (5.26)$$
$$ (1.44) \quad (.04) \qquad (.62)$$

These results suggest that wages for workers with similar characteristics do not differ markedly with concentration in the industry of employment (a result consistent with cost-minimizing behavior by firms and competitive labor markets). As pointed out by Weiss, these results are also consistent with the expectation that union members and workers in highly concentrated industries not only have higher wages but also are of higher quality (again, as theory would predict).

A large number of studies since Weiss have examined differences in union effects with respect to concentration. Although overall results are inconclusive, studies that do not control in detail for personal characteristics find a positive coefficient on CCR and a negative one on $P \cdot CCR$ (e.g. Hendricks, 1981), while studies using detailed controls generally do not find that concentration significantly affects wages (for exceptions, see Hendricks, 1977; Dalton and Ford, 1977) or the union wage differential. For example, Bloch and Kuskin (1978), estimating separate wage functions for union and nonunion workers in manufacturing from the 1973 May CPS, find small negative effects of industry concentration in both the union and nonunion sectors, this effect being just significant ($|t| = 1.98$) in the union sector. Similarly, Freeman and Medoff (1981) estimate separate union and nonunion wage equations using the 1973–5 May CPS (they also include the variable P to measure the effects of union density, as opposed to union membership). Concentration is not found to affect wages significantly in either sector; a small negative coefficient is obtained in the union sector and a small positive coefficient in the nonunion sector. Similar models, estimated by Freeman and Medoff with 1968–72 Expenditures for Employee Compensation (EEC) data for both wages and total compensation (including fringes), again indicate no significant effects of concentration.

A recent study by Long and Link (1983), using the Older Men's Sample of the NLS, finds a positive effect of concentration on wages that decreases with unionism (the Weiss results without controls) even with the inclusion of control variables, but exactly the opposite effect of unionism with respect to fringes (pension and insurance payments). They argue that, as concentration increases, union *wage* effects decrease, but *nonwage* effects increase. However, the Freeman and Medoff finding of no significant effects of concentration on wage or total compensation (and little difference in regression results between the two measures) makes us question the applicability and robustness of the Long and Link findings to a larger and more representative sample than the Older Men's NLS. In sum, we believe the extant evidence suggests no significant difference in union wage effects between high and low concentration industries (for a similar conclusion, see Lewis, forthcoming).

Wages and the union–nonunion differential do differ with firm size. A large literature has found higher wages in larger firms or plants (Mellow, 1983; Kwoka, 1983) within the manufacturing sector, even after accounting for measured worker quality differences, and several studies find the effects of size to be larger in nonunion firms than in union firms. For example, Freeman and Medoff (1981) report that average firm size (measured by the value of shipments) in an individual's industry of employment positively affects wages for union and nonunion workers. However, the coefficient in their nonunion wage equation is 80 percent larger than that in the union equation. Bloch and Kuskin (1978), using a similar framework, find a positive effect of size on wages in the nonunion sector, but no significant effect in the union sector. And, in perhaps the best study in this area, Mellow (1983) finds that the union differential is much larger in small firms and that flatter union earnings profiles with respect to schooling and experience are restricted to workers in large firms.

Explanations for a positive firm size–wage relationship are numerous but rarely compelling. They include the argument that firm size proxies market power and, in turn, higher wages. Yet neither wages nor firm size are highly correlated with concentration, which some contend measures market power more directly. Others have argued that larger firms choose to pay more in order to hire more able workers owing, for instance, to greater capital intensity and skill requirements. Alternatively, large firms might *have* to pay more and thus will select higher-quality workers. No convincing evidence exists regarding either of these hypotheses. Large firms may have greater disamenities, such as rigid work schedules and a poor communication environment, and thus have to pay more. However, the observed lower turnover in larger firms suggests that real compensation is in fact higher. Consistent with high wages and low turnover would be the provision of more firm-specific job training in large firms. This should lead not only to lower turnover, but also to a steeper earnings–experience profile. Finally, Garen (1985) argues that higher wages in large firms result from hierarchical loss of control; large firms have higher costs in evaluating workers and pay everyone a higher wage in order to increase the probability of retaining the most able workers.

Although these explanations may help explain higher wages in larger firms, they do not directly explain the weaker relationship (or absence of a relationship) in the union sector. One possible explanation is the threat effect. Since larger firms are more likely to be organized, large firms may be willing to pay somewhat higher wages in order to deter unionism. Once unionized, however, there is no longer an incentive to pay a deterrence premium! An additional explanation may be union attempts at wage standardization that lower wage differences across similar workers in different-sized firms. Such standardization would produce a larger union wage effect for smaller firms. A further possible explanation – alluded to by Lazear (1981) and in line with Garen's hypothesis that the firm size premium results from more costly monitoring in large firms – is that unionism serves as a substitute for costly monitoring and thus lowers the wage premium paid by large firms. However, we know of no direct evidence on this point.

Unionism and union–nonunion wage differentials also appear to be related systematically to working conditions on the job. J. Paul Leigh (1982) shows that unionized production jobs are significantly more hazardous than nonunion production jobs.[12] Duncan and Stafford (1980), using the Michigan 1975–6 Time Use Survey and PSID data for 1968–71, provide evidence indicating that in some cases as much as two-fifths of the observed wage difference is a compensating differential for certain work conditions; in particular, a structured work environment, inflexible hours, employer-determined overtime, and a faster work pace. However, they are unable to distinguish between two hypothesized explanations for the observed relationship. On the one hand, unionism may be most likely to occur within work settings with these characteristics. Discussion and evidence in Chapters 2 and 3 support this direction of causation. On the other hand, less attractive work conditions may *result* to some extent from unionism, as employers rationally respond to union-induced wage increases.

Duncan and Stafford provide cross-sectional and longitudinal evidence supporting the existence of compensating wage differentials. Variables from the Time Use Survey measuring whether the individual works most of the time with a machine, whether it is easy to get a couple of hours off from work for personal business, and a scale variable measuring intensity of work effort on the job (relative to watching TV) are found to affect both wages and union membership positively. Further, within a log wage equation, the coefficient on union status falls from 0.27 with the work condition variables excluded, to

0.19 when these variables are included. As additional support for their argument, Duncan and Stafford examine longitudinal data in the Michigan PSID. They find that union joiners had significant declines in two work-quality variables.

In a critique of their longitudinal analysis, Duane Leigh (1981) provides similar information tabulated from the Young Men's NLS between 1971 and 1976. He contends that cross-sectional evidence on the relationship between working conditions and wage differentials is inappropriate because of heterogeneous tastes among workers regarding job characteristics. On the other hand, longitudinal analysis controls for this problem by looking at changes by the same workers. Leigh, however, finds little supporting evidence for the compensating differential hypothesis. Examining worker attitudes regarding the *change* in job pressure, the ability to keep up with job pace, and level of fatigue, Leigh finds few differences between the 113 union joiners and 96 union leavers. In a subsequent reply, Duncan and Stafford (1982) provide further evidence supporting their contention that union–nonunion wage differentials result in part from job disamenities.

Thus, from the evidence to date we know that union jobs do have significantly different working conditions than nonunion jobs, and that cross-section estimates of the union wage premium are significantly reduced after accounting for these job characteristics. Longitudinal evidence from the PSID and Young Men's NLS is less conclusive. We suspect that the seeming inconsistency between Leigh's results and those of Duncan and Stafford arises not so much from the inherent problems with cross-sectional analysis as from the small sample size and possible lack of representativeness among the NLS Young Men who changed union status.

Although we believe that a significant portion of the union–nonunion differential may be a compensating differential for worker-quality differences or job disamenities, we continue to believe that much of the differential reflects non-competitive rents. As evidence on this point, Raisian (1983b) shows that union dues and the wage premium are positively correlated. On the assumption that there are no rents among workers with the lowest dues (i.e. in the lowest decile) but that higher dues reflect payment for rents, Raisian calculates that 44 percent of the wage premium for union workers with average dues represents a noncompetitive rent.

5.5 Unionism and Fringe Benefits[13]

Most of the empirical literature on union–nonunion differentials has focused exclusively on money wages or earnings. However, unionism is also likely to affect nonpecuniary fringe benefits in two ways: first, the *share* of fringes in the total compensation package may differ between union and nonunion establishments and, second, union-induced increases in the *level* of total compensation will increase fringes as long as there is a positive income elasticity for fringes. Empirical studies to date – the most comprehensive being by Freeman (1981) – find that unions significantly increase fringe benefits in both of the above ways. Moreover, estimates of the union–nonunion *wage* differential are found to understate the total compensation differential.

There are a number of reasons why unions are expected to increase the share of fringe benefits in the compensation package. As suggested by Freeman (and discussed in Chapter 2), unions are likely to give greatest weight to the preferences of average workers or those with preferences near the median union voter, in contrast to a competitive market in which more mobile marginal workers have the most influence. Because inframarginal or average workers are likely to be older, more permanent, and have greater demand for fringes than their younger, more mobile counterparts, unionism should increase the share of fringes. Older workers appear to prefer greater amounts of pension benefits, health and other insurance, and any seniority-linked benefits such as vacation time. A related argument advanced by Freeman (1976) is that unions may elicit more accurate information about worker preferences than employers gain through individual bargaining, and that, in the absence of a collective bargaining framework, employers may estimate too low a desire for fringes among workers.

Unionism will also increase the relative demand for fringes as a result of its role in increasing job tenure and decreasing quit rates, since tenure increases the probability that workers will receive deferred fringes such as life insurance and any nonvested portion of pensions. In sectors where firms are typically not large and where workers are more attached to occupations than to firms (e.g. construction, trucking), unions might provide a structure for instituting multi-employer plans that are vested across employers. A union also provides a mechanism whereby information is processed so that evaluation and monitoring of current and future fringes can be done at a relatively lower cost than if done individually by workers. These lower information costs lower the relative price and risks of fringes and thus increase the quantity demanded by workers. Freeman also believes that, because fringes are a mandatory bargaining topic given current labor law, the more serious attention and discussion given to this area may encourage relatively more fringes in the compensation mix.

Of course unionism is not the only or even the primary determinant of fringes. Fringes will tend to increase with the level of total compensation and, if the income elasticity is greater than unity, the fringe *share* will also increase. In addition, because many fringes are either untaxed (e.g. health insurance) or tax deferred (e.g. pensions), the relative attractiveness of fringes increases as marginal tax rates increase. Larger firms are also more likely to have greater fringes since there are substantial economies of scale with pensions (Mitchell and Andrews, 1981) and other fringes, and because tenure is longer in firms that allow intrafirm mobility. Firms providing substantial firm-specific human capital will also have higher fringes since there are lower quits and thus greater worker demand, and as a means for employers to discourage quits. Finally, demographic characteristics are likely to be correlated with fringes. In particular, older workers and males tend to have a greater demand for health and pension plans.

Freeman (1981), in his statistical analysis, attempts to control for each of the above factors, as well as including detailed industry dummies and several other control variables. Using establishment data primarily from the Expenditures for Employee Compensation (EEC), Freeman finds that unionism significantly increases the total level and share of fringes among production workers. Table 5.4 provides descriptive data from Freeman's analysis. Voluntary fringes account for 16.2 percent of total compensation of production workers in union establishments (19.1 in manufacturing alone) as compared to 10.6 percent in nonunion establishments (13.3 in manufacturing). In particular, unionized establishments provide significantly larger amounts of insurance and pension benefits than do nonunionized establishments.

Freeman's further statistical analysis attempts to isolate the effects of unionism *per se* on the fringe package. He finds that unionism increases fringes significantly both through an increasing fringe share and through an increased level of compensation (coupled with a positive income elasticity of fringes with respect to compensation slightly greater than unity). He also obtains evidence suggesting that fringes paid to *nonproduction* workers increase in establishments with covered production workers. Union effects on fringes are found to be relatively larger in low-wage and small firms. While the magnitudes of Freeman's estimates do show sensitivity to underlying assumptions and the method of estimation, his 'best' estimate (p. 508) is that unionism increases fringes by 0.18–0.20 log points in all private industry and 0.10–0.13 in manufacturing. Indeed, Freeman's estimate of the union fringe effect is somewhat greater than corresponding union wage effect estimates. Freeman's analysis indicates that previous estimates of the union wage differential understate the union compensation differential by about 0.02, a fairly sizeable amount relative to the level of d, but small relative to the large variation observed in empirical estimates of d.

Table 5.4 Dollars spent per hour on total compensation and on the components of compensation, and the share of dollars spent; production workers in union and nonunion establishments, 1967–72

| Compensation per hour paid for | Manufacturing (n=4074) | | | | All private nonfarm (n=10,088) | | | |
| | Union (n=2580) | | Nonunion (n=1494) | | Union (n=4973) | | Nonunion (n=5115) | |
	$	Share %	$	Share %	$	Share %	$	Share %
Total	3.66	100.0	2.81	100.0	4.33	100.0	2.73	100.0
Straight-time pay	2.75	75.0	2.26	80.4	3.35	77.3	2.25	82.6
All fringes	0.91	25.0	0.55	19.6	0.99	22.7	0.47	17.4
Legally required fringes	0.22	5.9	0.18	6.3	0.28	6.5	0.18	6.7
Voluntary fringes	0.70	19.1	0.37	13.3	0.70	16.2	0.29	10.6
Life, accident, health insurance	0.15	4.1	0.07	2.3	0.16	3.6	0.05	1.7
Vacation	0.15	4.1	0.07	2.6	0.11	2.5	0.06	2.1
Overtime premiums	0.12	3.3	0.09	3.2	0.13	3.1	0.07	2.6
Pensions	0.12	3.3	0.05	1.7	0.15	3.5	0.04	1.3
Holidays	0.09	2.4	0.05	1.8	0.07	1.5	0.04	1.4
Shift premiums	0.03	0.7	0.01	0.4	0.02	0.4	0.01	0.2
Sick leave	0.01	0.3	0.01	0.3	0.01	0.3	0.01	0.4
Bonuses[a]	0.01	0.3	0.02	0.8	0.01	0.3	0.02	0.7
Other[b]	0.03	0.7	0.01	0.2	0.04	1.0	0.01	0.2

Notes:
[a] Lump-sum payments under profit-sharing plans or seasonal bonuses.
[b] Leave benefits, severance, vacation and holiday funds, supplemental unemployment benefits, savings plans, and other private welfare benefits.
Source: Freeman (1981), Table 1, p. 496. All figures are in 1967 labor cost units, obtained by deflating 1968–72 figures by the ratio of average hourly earnings in the private sector in each year to average hourly earnings in the private sector in 1967.
Calculated from the US Bureau of Labor Statistics, Expenditures for Employee Compensation Survey, tapes 1967–8, 1969–70, and 1971–2. Shares are based on dollars carried to additional decimal places. Column sums do not always add to the correct total due to rounding.

5.6 Union Wage Effects: Membership versus Coverage

Most empirical studies utilize one of two alternative measures of unionism: a union *coverage* variable or a union membership variable. Coverage and membership variables differ because (i) many covered workers are not union members, (ii) some union members are not currently covered by collective bargaining agreements, and (iii) available data sources contain substantial response error. The first of these reasons is probably the most important. On the basis of evidence from the Michigan PSID, Freeman and Medoff (1979a, p. 171) report that about 9 percent of all covered workers are not members (the corresponding figures for men and women are 7 and 15 percent, respectively). In the south, however, where right-to-work laws are most prevalent, approximately 20 percent of all covered workers are not members. Jones (1982), using eight age–sex–race panels of the NLS for 1971, finds 13 percent of all covered workers are not members.

What effect should the choice of union variable have on estimates of the union–nonunion wage differential? First assume that it is union coverage and not membership that affects compensation. Then, covered union members and nonmembers should have the same wage, as should noncovered members and nonmembers. As pointed out by Jones (1982), use of a union membership variable will in this case *understate* the true coverage–noncoverage differential.[14]

However, extant evidence finds exactly the opposite result. Estimates of union–nonunion differentials using a union membership variable are generally *larger* than estimates with a coverage variable. Jones (1982, p. 281) obtains this result in seven of her eight NLS panels, although these differences are generally small.[15] Hirsch (1982) and Christensen and Maki (1983), using aggregate industry data, also find larger union wage effects with a proportion membership variable than with a proportion covered variable.

Why does union membership have a larger impact on wages than does coverage? Although there is little direct evidence on this point, we can offer several possible explanations. Christensen and Maki contend that it is compulsory union membership that provides unions with greater bargaining power, since nonmembers typically do not contribute to dues and are more likely to work during a strike. An alternative explanation not noted by Christensen and Maki is that, with the aggregate union data obtained from Freeman and Medoff (1979a), the coverage variable may be measured with larger error than is the membership variable, thus biasing the former's coefficient toward zero.

Jones examines several factors that could cause covered nonmembers to have lower wage gains from bargaining than members. She concludes that much of the difference is explained by the facts that covered nonmembers are more likely to be in public or white-collar employment, where union wage differentials tend to be smaller, and that many workers in the NLS coded as covered nonmembers may in fact have been uncovered, as evidenced by their inability to name their covering union.

Depending on the reasons for the disparate results between studies using union coverage and membership variables, the issue is potentially of some importance. First, empirical estimates of the union differential can be sensitive to the type of union status variable employed. Second, if membership does in fact increase bargaining power within covered establishments, the issue of right-to-work laws and compulsory membership assumes increased importance.

5.7 Union Wage Effects in the Public Sector

There is less evidence available on union–nonunion wage differentials in the public sector than in the private sector. As with the private sector, there is likely to be large variability in public sector union wage effects. Union bargaining power is likely to differ between the federal, state, and local sectors, and by agency or bargaining unit, occupation, region, and municipality. In addition, the rights of unions to bargain over compensation and the right to strike differ between the public and private sectors and within the public sector. Moreover, the nature of public sector wage determination implies that unions become an integral part of the political process whereby compensation is determined. Finally, the difficulties inherent in determining compensation via prevailing wage or job comparability criteria, and the lesser sensitivity of government pay systems to market forces, make it likely that union wage effects are not identical in the public and private sectors.

A frequently cited study by Smith (1977) is representative of work in this area (Ehrenberg and Schwarz, 1983, and Freeman, 1984b, provide surveys of this literature). Using May 1973 CPS data, she finds a sizeable wage advantage for federal, but not for state or local, workers relative to private sector workers with similar characteristics. However, union relative wage effects are estimated to be less than half as large among public sector as compared to private sector workers (about 10 percent as compared to 20–25 percent). The union–nonunion differential is approximately the same for men and women and in the federal, state, and local sectors. Indeed, after surveying a large number of studies in this area, Ehrenberg and Schwarz (1983) find the most striking result to be the small size of most estimates of union wage effects in the public sector.

Let us accept for the moment the finding of a significant federal/private pay differential coupled with smaller union wage effects in the federal (and other public) sector than in the private sector. One interpretation of this finding is that public sector unions have weaker power than do private sector unions, owing perhaps to attenuated bargaining and strike rights. An alternative interpretation is that unions increase wages via the political process for *both* union and nonunion public employees. Thus, some of the union effect is measured by the public–private rather than the union–nonunion compensation differential. Available evidence strongly suggests that positive geographic and occupational wage spillovers from unions exist in the public sector (Ehrenberg and Schwarz, 1983).

The apparently lower union wage in the public than in the private sector is not a universal finding. Edwards and Edwards (1982), in a study of the less than glamorous municipal sanitation collection industry, find large and significant union wage effects in the public sector, compared with small and insignificant effects in the private sector. In a study of Canadian workers, Robinson and Tomes (1984) find large differentials among private *and* public sector workers. Moreover, available evidence suggests that nonwage benefits – fringes, working conditions, and employment security – are greater in the public than in the private sector (Bellante and Long, 1981; Quinn, 1979). Unions in the public sector are likely to have an even greater impact on nonwage than on wage benefits (particularly pension benefits if taxpayers do not take fully into account future tax liabilities), thus rendering comparisons of wage differentials less meaningful (for limited evidence on union nonwage effects, see Bartel and Lewin, 1981).

We have argued that comparisons between public and private compensation should take into account pension, job security, and other nonwage benefits. Some analysts (see, for example, Hartman, 1983) contend also that comparison of wages among similar *jobs* rather than workers (as in Smith) is the more appropriate comparison because of unmeasured ability differences among workers with identical schooling and age. Hartman, while acknowledging overpayment of some groups of federal workers (particularly postal and clerical), makes the case that many federal workers are underpaid, particularly in the top grades. And Borjas (1980) has shown that wages do vary significantly across federal agencies, again making us wary of generalizations. And of course, an alternative (and possibly preferable) way to examine the issue of relative public–private compensation is to compare job queues and turnover rates (Long, 1982), although the large size of government as employer leads in some cases to monopsonistic situations where such comparisons are less meaningful.

Freeman (1984b) has argued that the conclusion that unions have smaller wage effects in the public sector is premature for a number of reasons. In particular, he notes that much public sector unionization is concentrated among white-collar and service occupations, where private sector unions also provide relatively small wage gains. Freeman also contends that a particularly important role for public sector unions is their use of the political process to increase demand for public expenditures and employment (on this point, see Chapter 9). Finally, note that most available evidence is from the early and mid-1970s. Since that time, federal pay has grown more slowly than pay in the private sector (Hartman, 1983, p. 23) and all levels of government have faced serious budgetary constraints. Before accepting any previous conclusions regarding public–private differentials and union effects in the public sector, it is essential that we obtain evidence for the 1980s.

5.8   Changes in the Union–Nonunion Differential over Time

It has long been argued that there is relative wage rigidity in the union sector owing to the collective bargaining process. Long-term contracts, lags in bargaining, and the reluctance to accept wage cuts cause the union–nonunion wage differential to move countercyclically, widening during recessions and narrowing during upturns. More precisely, the union sector is expected to respond more slowly to transitory changes in product and labor markets. Note, however, that union contracts can provide an explicit mechanism for responding to inflation outcomes. For example, cost-of-living adjustment clauses (COLAs) allow automatic adjustment of wages over the contract period (Chapter 8 provides an analysis of COLAs).

Lewis (1963), using aggregate wage and union density data for high-union and low-union sectors of the economy, estimated the union wage differential for the 1920–58 period. Pencavel and Hartsog (1984), using a similar methodology, provide a careful reestimation of aggregate union wage effects for this period, with an extension to 1980, while Johnson (1984) provides an admittedly crude extension of the Lewis analysis from 1958 to 1979. The Pencavel–Hartsog results are broadly consistent with Lewis' estimates: union wage effects are apparently countercyclical, enormous during the first half of the 1930s, very small (close to zero) during the 1940s, and about 0.15–0.20 during the 1950s.

For the post-1958 period, however, the Pencavel–Hartsog results differ from Johnson's estimates and from those from recent micro studies. Whereas Pencavel–Hartsog estimate d at approximately

0.20–0.25 during the 1960s, they find a sharp subsequent reduction, particularly in the late 1970s (where d is not significantly different from zero). In marked contrast, Johnson's 'crude extension' (1984, p. 5) of the log differential shows a sharp increase in d from 0.17 in 1970–4 to 0.26 in 1975–9.

What do we make of these estimates? We agree with Pencavel–Hartsog (who are also puzzled by these divergent results) that the findings from recent micro studies are more reliable than those from aggregate studies. Fortunately, Lewis (forthcoming) has provided a painstakingly careful survey of the micro studies and drawn from them estimates of the wage differential from 1967 to 1979. Table 5.5 presents Lewis' estimates. In order to provide approximate comparability, all estimates have been adjusted for differences in estimation technique, specification, measurement of key variables, and sample. Lewis prefers estimates in column 5 over column 3 because these give greater weight to studies he deems of higher quality. Estimates in column 5 are viewed as upper bounds because Lewis believes micro cross-sectional OLS results are biased upward owing to the inevitable omission of right-hand variables correlated with union status.

The results presented in Table 5.5 suggest an overall union–nonunion differential of about 0.15 over the 1967–79 period. They also suggest a moderate increase in d during the late 1970s (at least through 1978) from

Table 5.5 *Estimated union–nonunion log wage differentials by year*

Year (1)	No. of studies (2)	Mean estimate (3)	Standard dev. of estimates (4)	Lewis bound estimate (5)
1967	20	0.14	0.04	0.11
1968	4	0.15	0.07	0.11
1969	20	0.13	0.04	0.11
1970	8	0.13	0.05	0.12
1971	18	0.14	0.04	0.15
1972	7	0.14	0.03	0.12
1973	24	0.15	0.03	0.15
1974	7	0.15	0.04	0.14
1975	11	0.17	0.04	0.16
1976	7	0.16	0.05	0.18
1977	8	0.19	0.05	0.17
1978	7	0.17	0.04	0.17
1979	2	0.12	—	0.13
1967–79	143	0.15	0.04	0.14

Source: Lewis (forthcoming), Chapter 9, Table 9.7.

about 0.12 during the 1967–72 period to about 0.16 in 1973–8. It is worth noting that year-to-year changes are much smaller than would be suggested by comparing across small numbers of dissimilar studies or year-to-year differentials from a single study (e.g. Moore and Raisian, 1980).

Particularly interesting would be an extension of Lewis' micro estimates for the post-1979 period and a careful analysis of the relationship between these differentials and macroeconomic events since 1967. Moore and Raisian (1983) have related the union wage premium from 1967 to 1977 (calculated from the PSID) to economic conditions. They conclude that the more rapid growth in union than in nonunion wages during this period was due primarily to the greater sensitivity of nonunion wages to increased unemployment. Union wage rates, by contrast, exhibited less variability over the business cycle.

5.9 Union Wage Effects in the UK and Canada

Our attention up to this point has focused primarily on union wage effects in the US. Of course, the bargaining power and wage impacts of unionism are likely to vary substantially across countries owing to differences in labor law, trade union organization, worker and employer attitudes, the industrial–occupational structure, labor force characteristics, and the degree of competitiveness in the economy resulting from exposure to international trade, government regulations, and the like. In this section we review recent evidence on union–nonunion wage differentials in the UK and Canada, not only because this evidence is of interest in its own right, but also to discover similarities and differences between the US and these countries.

Until recently, all of the UK evidence was based on studies using aggregate industry or occupation data. These studies are subject to the same serious criticisms, discussed previously in this chapter, as are the US studies of this type. One of the best-known studies is by Pencavel (1974), who uses data from 29 industries in 1964. Such a small sample size of course prevents him from drawing strong inferences. However, his results suggest a relatively small overall union–nonunion wage differential of 0–10 percent. Union membership appears to have no effect in industries without industry-wide wage bargaining or where hourly earnings are typically no different from those determined by industry-wide agreements. In the seven industries where earnings are substantially higher than the industry-wide agreements, however, he finds a differential of approximately 15 percent. In contrast to Pencavel's study, a later study by Mulvey (1976), using data on 77 industries for 1973, finds a union–nonunion wage differential in excess of 25 percent, a finding replicated in subsequent studies.

Recently, however, a paper by Geroski and Stewart (1982) subjects these aggregate industry findings to very careful scrutiny. It is found that there is such substantial interindustry variation in the differential that any average is seriously misleading. In particular, purging from the sample three industries where data are inconsistent causes the estimate of the wage differential to fall from about 25 to 11 percent and the R^2 of the wage equation to double (the Railway Carriage industry is the primary outlier). Like Pencavel, they find large wage differentials among a small group of industries (accounting for about 10 percent of employment) – those dominated by the closed shop and where local bargaining supplements national agreements – and a large number of industries where union wage effects are at most very small. Statistical problems are so serious, however, that Geroski and Stewart conclude that any inferences based on industry studies must be carefully hedged. We concur.

In an excellent paper, Stewart (1983) provides the first UK analysis that measures union–nonunion differentials with individual data. He estimates separate union and nonunion equations in a fashion similar to Bloch and Kuskin (1978) and Freeman and Medoff (1981). Based on a sample of 5,352 full-time manual male employees from the 1975 National Training Survey, Stewart finds an average union–nonunion log wage differential of only 0.076, compared to a raw differential (unadjusted for region, worker characteristics, plant size, industry concentration, and union density) of 0.183. The large difference between the adjusted and unadjusted differentials indicates the importance of including adequate control variables and that employers upgrade hiring in response to union wage gains (that is, unionized manual workers are on average more productive than similar nonunion workers). More recently, Shah (1984) has found a log wage differential of about 0.10 using UK microdata. While we are reluctant to conclude too much on the basis of two studies, these results suggest a somewhat smaller UK average union wage differential than in US manufacturing.

Stewart emphasizes that the union differential varies significantly by personal characteristics, region, and industry. Interestingly, many of his findings correspond closely with the US evidence. Larger wage differentials are found for younger (10 years of experience) than for older (40 years) workers; the largest differential is found in the region with lowest earnings (Wales); the differential declines with industry concentration; and the differential increases with union density (density increases union wages but has little net effect on nonunion wages). He also finds a U-shaped relationship between the wage differential and firm size, a result not directly comparable with US findings.

Estimates of the union–nonunion differential by two-digit industry exhibit large variability. The major pattern evident in these differences,

Stewart notes, is that the differential is larger the lower an industry's average nonunion wage. This evidence, along with that previously presented regarding wage effects by experience and region, is consistent with the hypothesis that unions tend to standardize wages and decrease earnings dispersion. Similar evidence for the US is presented in Chapter 6.

There is less evidence on the union–nonunion differential in Canada than for the US or the UK. Extant studies, using primarily aggregate data, indicate an overall log differential of 0.10–0.20, although a recent study by MacDonald (1983) suggests a somewhat larger value. The most detailed Canadian study using microdata (the Social Change in Canada Survey for 1979) is by Robinson and Tomes (1984); however, even this study is plagued by small sample sizes and the possible unrepresentativeness of their sample (hourly workers only). Using a method similar to that of Bloch and Kuskin (1978) – the estimation of separate OLS union and nonunion wage functions – Robinson and Tomes (1984, Table 4) obtain estimates of $\bar{d}$ of 0.23 in the private and 0.21 in the public sector. They obtain somewhat larger estimates after the inclusion of a selectivity variable (as in Lee, 1978): 0.30 in the private and 0.24 in the public sector. They note, however, that their estimates of the differential are lower when their sample is not restricted to workers reporting an hourly wage (for an analysis of this issue with US data, see Lewis, forthcoming). Robinson and Tomes obtain many findings similar to those of the US micro studies – higher differentials for lower-skill workers, flatter experience (but steeper tenure) profiles for union workers, and a (weakly) positive union density wage effect. Unlike the US studies, they find little difference between the sectors in the return to schooling or in regional wage differentials (this is correct for the OLS results only; regional differences are large when selectivity variables are included).

Evidence on union–nonunion wage differentials in the UK and Canada is still far too limited to draw strong conclusions. Yet, despite the substantial differences between these countries and the US in their legal, economic, and social landscape, extant evidence shows many similarities in union wage effects.

5.10 Union Effects on Relative Compensation: An Appraisal

There is no question that the extensive recent literature reviewed in this chapter has significantly furthered our understanding of union wage effects. While much of this progress has resulted from the increased availability of microdata sets and lowered computing costs, improved econometric techniques have sharpened our awareness of the many problems inherent in measuring union–nonunion differentials. Possibly the most important lesson learned is that union wage effects are not uniform over time, across industries, occupations, regions, age groups, race, and sex, or with respect to other personal or job characteristics. Although the search for improved estimates of the *average* union–nonunion differential remains interesting, and perhaps irresistible, no single estimate or narrow range of estimates can provide information that is particularly useful. In addition, empirical studies can at best measure accurately union–nonunion wage differentials given existing levels of union coverage. Estimates do not directly measure the effect of unionism on the overall skill structure of wages. Finally, the sensitivity of these estimates to estimation technique, specification, and data source, even where sample coverages are similar, makes us cautious in attaching much weight to any single estimate.

The evidence presented in this chapter indicates that the use of aggregated industry data, which formed the basis for most of the earlier studies of unionism, is now generally unacceptable owing to the absence of separate data on union and nonunion wages and characteristics and because of the sensitivity of the estimated differentials obtained with these data. Cross-section microdata are now used for most studies on union wage effects. OLS estimates from such studies are relatively stable and regarded by many as reasonable, but no completely satisfactory approach has been found that treats for the known simultaneous determination of union status and wages, and for the selectivity bias resulting from unmeasured differences between union and nonunion workers with similar characteristics. Because estimates obtained using simultaneous equation and selectivity adjusted techniques are rarely robust and often implausible, we are reluctant to place much credence in them.

A more promising approach to the estimation of union wage differentials is the use of longitudinal panel data. 'Fixed effects' wage change models appear to provide a more appropriate correction for selectivity bias. As expected, estimates of the log differential based on longitudinal data are substantially lower than comparable cross-section estimates – about 0.10 compared to 0.15–0.20. Despite the substantial advantages of longitudinal data, several potentially serious problems attach to such studies. Sample sizes of union joiners and leavers are small, separate analysis of narrow industrial, occupational, or demographic groups is not possible, substantial misclassification appears to exist, and the endogeneity of union status changes cannot be easily modeled. Moreover, the effects of changing union status cannot readily be separated from the effects of changing industry, occupation, or job. Future research using panel data will provide much-needed evidence on the robustness of the findings in this area.

Finally, two major factors not addressed in most union wage studies appear to bias estimates in opposite directions. On the one hand, unions appear to increase total compensation more than wages, since unionism leads to a larger fringe benefit share in the compensation package. Estimates by Freeman (1981) suggest the downward bias in wage studies is of the order of 0.02 log points. On the other hand, evidence by Duncan and Stafford (1980) and others indicates that a significant portion of the union wage differential is in fact a compensating differential for numerous job disamenities. It appears that this latter bias fully or more than fully offsets the bias resulting from ignoring fringes.

What then is our best estimate of the union compensation differential? While we are reluctant to provide yet another estimate of the average differential, for the reasons stated previously, we shall plunge ahead in the name of reader interest. On the basis of what we regard as the most defensible empirical evidence summarized in this chapter, and a reasonably strong set of priors, we believe the *average* log compensation differential between otherwise similar union and nonunion workers is about 0.10–0.15. Interestingly enough, this is about the range Lewis (1963) suggested on the basis of much cruder data and econometric analyses. We do not conclude that the enormous amount of current research has added little to our knowledge since Lewis' pathbreaking book. On the contrary, we believe recent research has provided substantial improvements in our understanding of unionism. Other analysts reviewing the same literature might reasonably conclude that union wage differentials are either smaller or larger than 0.10–0.15. However, a differential of this size is consistent not only with empirical evidence, but with our prior expectations. It is large enough to support the common-sense notion that union effects are in fact substantial, yet not so large as to conflict with the expectation that, in the long run, competitive forces limit to a large extent the size of differences in compensation that can exist between similar workers.

Notes

1 See Lewis (1983) for a fuller discussion regarding wage gaps and wage gains. For an attempt at estimating the effects of unionism on the wage structure within a general equilibrium framework, see Pettengill (1980).

2 For a thorough discussion of this point, see Lewis (forthcoming). For estimates of union wage effects that control for the extent of industry unionism, see Lee (1978), Freeman and Medoff (1981), and Mellow (1983).

3 Johnson and Mieszkowski (1970) and DeFina (1985) provide general equilibrium analyses of union effects on the wage distribution (see Chapter

6). A two-sector framework is also used to analyze the effects of minimum wage laws (Mincer, 1976).

4   The semi-log wage equation can be derived from a simple human capital model (Mincer, 1974) and, on the basis of a Box–Cox test for functional form, appears superior to alternative specifications (Heckman and Polachek, 1974).

5   See Halvorsen and Palmquist (1980). Kennedy (1981) provides a more precise measure.

6   The methodology employed in measuring union–nonunion differentials is similar to that used in measuring race or sex differentials. Of course, one obvious (and important) difference is that union status is in part a choice variable whereas race and sex are not.

7   There is disagreement whether the selectivity variable should be excluded or included in calculating the wage differential from the corrected wage equation. On this point see Lewis (forthcoming) and Duncan and Leigh (1980). Results are often sensitive to the treatment of the selectivity variable.

8   For alternative estimation methods not adopted widely, see Farber (1983c), Schmidt and Strauss (1976), Schmidt (1978), Duncan and Leigh (1985) and the discussion by Duncan (1983).

9   Mellow's actual specification is slightly different from that shown above, but his results can be interpreted identically. A primary advantage of the CPS is its large sample size. However, it cannot in general be used as longitudinal panel data except for adjacent years (one-half the sample continues from May to May).

10 The exceptions are when a collective bargaining coverage rather than union membership variable is used with the NLS data, and among union joiners in the PSID who had quit their previous job.

11 However, union effects on the overall south/non-south wage differential are relatively small since the proportion unionized in the south is small.

12 Leigh uses Michigan's 1977 Quality of Employment Survey which contained 13 questions relating to job hazards. Union workers indicated more hazardous conditions than nonunion workers in each of the 13 categories.

13 This section relies heavily on the discussion and evidence in Freeman (1981). More recently, Freeman (1983b) examines the effect of unions on pensions within the framework of the 'two faces' model of unionism.

14 A numerical example may be useful. Assume that 100 covered workers have a wage of $10, while 100 noncovered nonmember workers have a wage of $8. In addition, suppose that 20 of the covered workers are nonmembers. One then obtains a *coverage* differential of 25 percent ($8 versus $10), compared to a *membership* differential of 20 percent ($8.33 versus $10).

15 The largest difference is obtained for black males aged 19–29, where Jones finds $\bar{d} = 0.215$ using a membership variable, compared with $\bar{d} = 0.174$ using a coverage variable.

CHAPTER 6

Unions, Wage Dispersion, and the Distribution of Income

6.1 Introduction

Much of the empirical research by economists has focused on union–nonunion wage differentials between otherwise similar workers. The existence of significant union wage differentials suggests that trade unions are likely to affect the overall distribution of earnings. Thus, a logical extension of Chapter 5 is the examination of union effects on wage dispersion within and across establishments, industries, and labor markets, as well as effects on the functional and size distributions of income. As before, it is worth pointing out that at best we are able to observe union–nonunion differences in wage and earnings dispersion, given existing levels of unionism, and are unable to say with much confidence what the earnings distribution would look like in the absence of unionism.

There are a number of routes through which labor unions can influence the earnings distribution. We first examine the possible ways in which unions might affect wage dispersion. Next, we investigate *why* unions choose to affect wages in the manner that they do, examining in particular the standardization of rates of pay within and across establishments. Empirical evidence on the distribution of wages – much of it showing that unions significantly lessen dispersion – is then reviewed. Some attention is paid to the simultaneity issue; that is, we present theory and evidence suggesting not only that unions affect dispersion, but also that the distribution of earnings affects the likelihood of unionism. We then examine theory and evidence relating specifically to union effects on the slopes of earnings–experience profiles and the distribution of union gains among its members. Finally, the economy-wide impact of unionism on the functional distribution of income is considered.

6.2   Union Effects on Wage Dispersion: Potential Routes[1]

There are several ways in which unionism can either increase or decrease wage dispersion. Assuming that the primary effect of unions is to increase the wage rates of their members, unionism will tend to decrease wage dispersion within establishments (or industries, occupations, and labor markets) if members have below-average wages, and increase dispersion if members have above-average wages. Of course, union wage increases may have differential effects on dispersion according to whether our focus is upon establishments or individual labor markets. For example, a union wage increase affecting workers with below average wages in high-wage establishments may decrease intraestablishment dispersion, yet increase dispersion within the labor market.

To the extent that unionism creates wage differentials between otherwise similar workers, unions will increase overall wage dispersion; but to the extent that unions standardize rates of pay within the union sector, wage dispersion is reduced. Standardized rates of pay reduce dispersion by permitting less individual variation in wages for workers with, say, similar years of seniority than would exist in the absence of unionism. Moreover, collective bargaining agreements act to limit the number of job (pay) categories and lessen the ability of firms to differentiate among workers. A wage rate or range of rates is established for given *jobs*, rather than for *individuals*. Thus, unionized establishments generally place greater weight on factors such as seniority, while relying less on differentiated individual evaluations based on merit. Because the number of job and pay classifications that can reasonably be defined within a collective bargaining contract typically is less than the number employers would make based on individual evaluations in a nonunion setting, unionism will tend to lessen the dispersion in wages. As will be seen below, union standardization of wage rates both across and within establishments appears to be the dominant vehicle whereby unions affect wage dispersion.

An important way in which unions standardize wages is by lowering the return or wage differential associated with characteristics that augment human capital. For example, a lower return to schooling or general experience in the union sector than in the nonunion sector would be consistent with reduced dispersion. Of course, a lower return to general human capital (such as schooling or transferable on-the-job training) may result less from unionism *per se* than from the nature of the job. Job settings where firm-specific on-the-job training is more important will not only place increased emphasis on seniority relative to schooling and general experience, but may also be more likely to be unionized. And of course wage premiums and reduced turnover within the union sector will tend to increase firm-specific investments. It also is worth noting that unionism may be associated with lower dispersion either by flattening the average earnings–experience profile, or by lessening variation in wages around earnings profiles of a given slope. We return to this point in Section 6.6.

While unions may decrease wage dispersion within and across union establishments, it does not necessarily follow that overall wage dispersion within and across industries, labor markets, and the economy is decreased. Higher but less-dispersed union wages could increase intraindustry wage dispersion if the nonunion sector is large. A more likely result is an increase in interindustry wage dispersion because of wage differentials between workers in predominantly unionized and nonunionized industries. Within a labor market, unionism may decrease dispersion in the union sector yet increase overall wage dispersion if union members tend to have above-average wages. Likewise, wage dispersion across highly and lowly unionized labor markets may either increase or decrease depending on the relative impact of union wage effects. The overall effect of unionism on wage dispersion in an economy is clearly indeterminate *a priori* and warrants thorough empirical study.

Optimally, we would like to estimate the effects of trade unionism on wage dispersion relative to what would exist in the absence of unions. Such estimation would be possible if there were no union effects on nonunion wages. However, unionism will affect both union and nonunion wages, as well as altering the skill structure of wages. As discussed in Chapter 5, although unionism can alter relative wages by skill type, in the long run there may be little observed wage difference between similarly skilled union and nonunion workers owing to selective hiring and optimal job matching. For these reasons, empirical studies examining the dispersion in wages will typically measure union–nonunion differences in dispersion, given extant levels of unionism.

6.3 Unions and the Incentives for Rate Standardization

A long-standing policy of trade unions has been pursuit of the 'standard rate', defined by Freeman (1980c) and others as a limited number of impersonal rates or ranges of rates within establishments and uniform rates among comparable workers across establishments. Standardization of rates within establishments generally involves the creation of job rates rather than personal rates of pay, with a limited number of job classifications. Each job classification typically involves many diverse activities, yet rate differentiation within job categories is small. Within a job category there will often be a small number of wage steps, typically based on seniority. Often the top step or pay category is such that a large proportion of workers within a job category will have reached it, leading to little wage dispersion among workers in that category.[2]

There are a number of reasons why unions pursue the goal of rate standardization. Evidence supplied by Farber and Saks (1980) and others strongly suggests that perceived inequities in compensation, combined with the belief that unions will produce a more equitable environment, are an important determinant of worker demand for union membership. Rather than having wages depend principally on personal characteristics and individual merit, as determined by foremen or other supervisors, wage rates are determined by job and step category. Of course, a reduction in wage dispersion resulting from decreased reliance on supervisors' performance evaluations may decrease equity as perceived by some workers. Workers who are relatively more productive and recognized as such in a nonunion work environment are most likely to oppose a unionized work setting in which the wage differential between more and less productive workers is narrowed.[3]

Returning to the simple median voter model analyzed in Chapter 2, the tendency for unions to pursue policies more in line with the preferences of average (or median) workers than with those of marginal workers may help explain the demand for rate standardization within a unionized establishment. A majority of workers can always improve their welfare by the adoption of a wage structure that 'taxes' the minority. Coalitions can form in many different ways, but Freeman (1980c) contends that a 50+ percent majority seems most likely to form at the lower end of the wage distribution since a larger amount of income can be redistributed from high-wage to low-wage workers than can be redistributed with any other coalition. While public choice theory does not provide an unambiguous prediction of where a majority coalition will form (except under fairly stringent assumptions), we believe it is more likely to represent the interests of relatively senior workers.[4]

It is important to note that potential demands for wage leveling are limited by lower-wage (younger) workers' knowledge that they will in the future be higher-wage (older) workers. Moreover, disincentive effects from 'inefficient' wage leveling, which will reduce the size of the wage pie, should generate increasing resistance from employers. Finally, considerations of equity eventually may limit redistribution, since few would regard equality of wages as equitable.

In contrast with the public sector, where individuals cannot easily leave (move) if they are harmed by collective choices of the majority, higher-wage workers in unionized jobs are free to leave (quit), thus placing additional limits on the amount of redistribution. We are not likely to see much quitting in response to union rate standardization, however, since presumably all or most workers gain relative to the nonunion wage, and because more senior workers are likely to be less mobile owing to age, nontransferable seniority, and firm-specific human capital.

A desire (or the necessity) for solidarity in union establishments might also result in demand to limit wage differentials (Freeman, 1980c). Likewise, risk aversion by workers may increase their demand for small wage differentials if their place in the distribution is not known with certainty. Each of these factors is likely to be more important where monitoring of workers' productivity is difficult or where merit evaluations by supervisors are regarded as unfair and arbitrary.

Union wage policies also attempt to standardize wages among comparable workers across establishments, thus lowering dispersion among comparable union workers within the same industry or product market. The economic rationale for such standardization is that it partially removes wages from interfirm competition. The existence of similar wages among firms competing in the same product market also reduces the probability that business downturns will force down wages. Standardization of union wages across establishments is most in the interest of relatively low-paid employees and high-wage firms, while opposition to such policies comes primarily from highly paid workers and employers with lower wage costs. For example, standardization of rates across similar plants in the south and non-south might most benefit southern workers and non-south employers.

Of course, union wage policies affect employment as well as compensation. Rate standardization lessens the incentive for union plants to locate in low-wage areas, thus slowing employment loss in high-wage areas and employment gains in low-wage areas. Indeed, where plant costs cannot be equalized, multiplant bargaining agreements on occasion specifically limit the firm's ability to shift production from high- to low-cost plants. While rate standardization across establishments is a goal of unions, it is limited by market conditions. Exceptions to standardized rates are likely to arise where particular firms or plants risk closure, where firms face significant local competition from nonunion firms, and where underlying product demand or labor supply conditions differ markedly.

The existence of multiplant and multiemployer contracts both facilitates, and provides evidence for, across-establishment wage standardization. Hendricks and Kahn (1982, p. 186) find that 66.6 percent of the bargaining contracts for production workers in manufacturing on file with the Bureau of Labor Statistics (BLS) for

1975 were single-employer and multiplant while 12.7 percent were multiemployer. Only 20.7 percent were single-employer and single-plant.

6.4 Union Effects on Wage Dispersion: Empirical Evidence

Two papers by Richard Freeman (1980c, 1982) provide the most comprehensive evidence to date on unions and the dispersion in wages. Both show convincingly that unionism is associated with lower wage dispersion. In his earlier paper, Freeman first presents summary data on wage dispersion among union and nonunion male workers in the manufacturing and nonmanufacturing sectors, calculated from the May 1973–5 Current Population Surveys (CPS) and the 1968–72 Expenditures for Employee Compensation (EEC) surveys. Freeman uses the standard deviation of the log wage, $\sigma(\ln W)$, as a measure of dispersion. This commonly used measure allows dispersion to be measured in relative rather than absolute terms, corresponds closely to the semi-log earnings generating function, and is most appropriate where earnings are approximately lognormally distributed.

Figure 6.1 illustrates the differences found by Freeman in log wage distributions between union and nonunion male production workers. In both the manufacturing and nonmanufacturing sectors, the distribution of union wages lies to the right (i.e. has a higher mean wage) and is more peaked (i.e. less dispersed) than the distribution of nonunion wages. The standard deviations of the log wage are 0.29 and 0.35

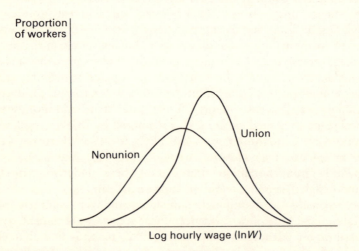

Figure 6.1 Comparison of wage distributions among union and nonunion male production workers

among union workers in manufacturing and nonmanufacturing, respectively, compared with 0.40 and 0.45 among nonunion workers. Freeman (1980c, Table 2) then compares union and nonunion dispersion within two-digit industries, three-digit industries, two-digit occupations, state groups, schooling categories, age categories, and SMSA-by-size groups. The difference between nonunion and union dispersion, $\sigma(\ln W)_n - \sigma(\ln W)_u$, is found to be positive and significant in most cases. In no case is it negative and significant. Thus, even within relatively narrow groups, union wages are significantly less dispersed than are nonunion wages.

Differences in wage dispersion between the union and nonunion sectors are attributable to three sources: differences in characteristics between union and nonunion workers; differences in earnings function parameters between the union and nonunion sectors; and differences in the variation of the residual in the two sectors. Using a standard regression approach in which separate union and nonunion log earnings functions (with detailed control variables) are estimated, Freeman finds that each of these factors contributes significantly to lower union wage dispersion.

First, wage dispersion is calculated after correcting for differences in characteristics. It is shown that workers with nonunion characteristics would exhibit significantly less dispersion if compensated according to the parameters of the union wage equation than they in fact exhibit in the nonunion sector; likewise, workers with union characteristics would exhibit significantly greater dispersion if compensated according to the nonunion wage equation parameters. After appropriate adjustments for differences in characteristics, the difference in dispersion between union and nonunion workers is 17–36 percent less than the unadjusted difference. Thus, a 'moderate' but not major amount of the lower dispersion of union wages can be attributed to less dispersion in wage-generating characteristics among union members.

Freeman finds the two other sources of the union–nonunion difference in dispersion to be more important. Much of the difference is attributed to differences in wage function parameters. That is, workers with either union or nonunion characteristics would have significantly less dispersion if compensated according to the union function rather than the nonunion function. Alternatively put, the coefficients in the union wage equation on such variables as schooling, experience, and race are lower than in the nonunion equation, and the sets of coefficients on industry, occupation, and other dummy variables are less dispersed. In short, the earnings-generating process in the union sector produces a less dispersed distribution of wages than it does in the nonunion sector for any set of characteristics.

The third source of difference between wage dispersion in the two sectors results from differences in the residual variation. The standard error of the equation estimate (SEE $= \sqrt{\Sigma e^2/(n-k)}$, where e is the equation residual and $(n-k)$ are degrees of freedom) in the union wage equation is significantly smaller than the SEE in the nonunion equation. In other words, given the set of characteristics and parameters in each sector, there is greater error in predicting nonunion wages. This finding probably reflects the existence of substantial wage standardization in the union sector, as compared to relatively greater discretion and individual wage determination in the nonunion sector. An alternative explanation is that standard earnings function variables measure true productivity less well for nonunion than for union workers. We do not find this explanation compelling.

Freeman (1980c) provides a similar analysis using establishment data from the EEC, matched with some grouped data from the CPS which provide control variables. This analysis uses total compensation rather than wages, and measures union coverage rather than union membership. Findings are similar, although results in the nonmanufacturing sector are not as clear-cut as with the CPS data. Overall, Freeman's analysis provides strong evidence that unionism acts to decrease wage dispersion significantly among production workers in manufacturing and nonmanufacturing owing to smaller impacts on earnings from wage-determining factors and smaller residual variation among comparable workers.

Freeman also examines the effect of unionism on the relative wage differential between white-collar (nonproduction) and blue-collar (production) workers. Because unionism occurs primarily among production workers, and, within establishments, production workers earn relatively less than nonproduction workers, it is likely that unionism lessens wage dispersion by lowering the white-collar/blue-collar differential. To examine this question, Freeman estimates the following equation:

$$\ln(W_W/W_B)_i = a_0 + a_1 X_{Wi} + a_2 X_{Bi} + a_3 U_i + e_i, \qquad (6.1)$$

where $(W_W/W_B)_i$ is the ratio of white-collar to blue-collar wages within establishment i, U_i is a dummy variable equal to 1 if a majority of blue-collar workers are covered by collective bargaining, X_{Wi} and X_{Bi} are vectors of characteristics in establishment i for white-collar and blue-collar workers respectively. The coefficient a_3 is negative and significant in both manufacturing ($a_3 = -.12$) and nonmanufacturing ($a_3 = -.14$). In manufacturing, an average differential of 0.40 (which implies $W_W/W_B = 1.5$) is reduced to 0.28 (implying $W_W/W_B = 1.3$) while in nonmanufacturing the respective reduction is from 0.27 (implying $W_W/W_B = 1.3$) to 0.13 (implying $W_W/W_B = 1.1$). It thus appears that unions significantly decrease the white-collar/blue-collar differential within establishments.

While unionism seems unambiguously to decrease wage dispersion among male production workers and within establishments, it will increase dispersion, *ceteris paribus*, by creating a wage differential between comparable workers and possibly through increasing earnings dispersion *across* industries. Freeman attempts to measure the overall effects of unionism on the earnings of male workers, taking into account the dispersion-decreasing effects of wage standardization and the reduced white-collar/blue-collar differential, coupled with the dispersion-increasing effects of the union–nonunion wage differential. He concludes that the net effect of unionism is to decrease significantly the dispersion of earnings in manufacturing, whereas the overall effect in nonmanufacturing is quite small. Unionism appears to decrease moderately the dispersion in wages between manufacturing and nonmanufacturing. (Union wage effects are larger in nonmanufacturing but coverage is lower, the net effect being to decrease dispersion by lowering the relative manufacturing wage advantage.)

Despite the extensive and detailed examination by Freeman of unions and wage dispersion, we again return to the point that these estimates do *not* isolate the effects of unionism on wage dispersion relative to that obtaining in the absence of unionism. Because there is no precise way to measure the effects of unionism on nonunion wages or on the skill structure of wages, the overall effect of unionism is still an open question.[5] The study by Freeman does nonetheless show conclusively that, given existing levels of unionism, wage dispersion among union members and within union establishments is significantly lower than among nonunion workers and within nonunion establishments.

While the Freeman (1980c) paper is the most comprehensive to date, several other studies examining unionism and dispersion warrant mention. In a subsequent study, Freeman (1982) examines union wage practices and wage dispersion within establishments among nine three- and four-digit industries. Data are from the BLS Industry Wage Surveys and include nearly 3,000 establishments, approximately half of which are organized, and about 500,000 individuals. Freeman finds that organized establishments have lower dispersion in wages than otherwise comparable establishments in the same industry, before and after controlling for establishment size, region, and detailed occupational structure. Much although not all of the lower dispersion appears to result from explicit wage practices in organized establishments that lessen dispersion: organized establishments are more likely to have single rate or automatic progression modes of payment whereas unorganized establishments are more likely to rely on individual wage determination and explicit merit review procedures.

Table 6.1 *Differences between union and nonunion establishments in standard deviations of within-establishment log wages*

Industry	No. of estab-lishments (percentage union)	Mean of within establishment[a]		Differences in means	Union coefficient (standard errors)
		Union	Nonunion		
Paints & Varnishes	291 (62%)	0.0887	0.1276	−0.0389*	−.0251 (.0075)
Textile Dyeing & Finishing	148 (49%)	0.1122	0.1275	−0.0153	−.0098 (.0118)
Cotton, Manmade Fiber Textiles	306 (14%)	0.1374	0.1385	−0.0011	−.0106 (.0044)
Wool Textiles	56 (34%)	0.1031	0.1301	−0.0270*	−.0220 (.0101)
Industrial Chemicals	269 (74%)	0.0727	0.1087	−0.0360*	−.0360 (.0057)
Wood Household Furniture	330 (42%)	0.1098	0.1251	−0.0153	−.0178 (.0074)
Miscellaneous Plastic Products	875 (45%)	0.1402	0.1776	−0.0374*	−.0340 (.0049)
Fabricated Structural Steel	331 (71%)	0.0851	0.1407	−0.0556*	−.0561 (.0062)
Non-ferrous Foundries	363 (49%)	0.1270	0.1686	−0.0416*	−.0492 (.0064)

*Significant at better than the 1 percent level in a one-tailed test.

Note:

[a] The union and nonunion means for the standard deviations of wages are calculated from the means of the standard deviations of the log wages for each firm. The *t*-test is the standard test of the difference between two means, assuming unequal variances of the union and nonunion distribution. Also included in the regressions are size and region and, for the overall firm equation, occupation controls. In the detailed occupations, firms with only one worker listed under one occupation are deleted.

Source: Freeman (1982), pp. 7, 21.

Table 6.1 provides a summary of some of the results from the Freeman (1982) study. Column 1 provides the number of establishments in each industry and, in brackets, the proportion organized. Columns 2 and 3 give the means of the standard deviation of log wages, $\overline{\sigma(\ln W)}$, within the organized and unorganized establishments. In every case, wage dispersion is less in the union sector than in the nonunion sector of the same industry. Column 4 shows the difference in means, $\overline{\sigma(\ln W)}_u - \overline{\sigma(\ln W)}_n$, and whether the difference is statistically significant. Column 5 presents the regression coefficient and standard error on the union dummy variable (equal to 1 if an organized establishment) from regressions with $\sigma(\ln W)$ as the dependent variable and with size, region, and occupation as control variables. It can be seen that unionism is associated with less intraestablishment wage dispersion in all nine industries. Of interest is the finding, not discussed by Freeman, that the differences are smallest and least significant in those industries with the smallest proportion unionized – textile dyeing, cotton and manmade textiles, wool textiles, and wood household furniture. A possible interpretation of this result is that union wage practices that lessen wage dispersion are suboptimal, acting to decrease economic efficiency, and are less likely significantly to alter compensation patterns in the most competitive industries with the greatest nonunion competition. An alternative explanation would be that threat effects are most significant in *less* unionized industries; thus, unionism lessens wage dispersion similarly in organized and unorganized establishments. We do not find this to be a plausible explanation. If anything, we would expect threat effects to increase (at least initially) with union density in an industry.

Although unions clearly narrow dispersion within and to a lesser degree across organized establishments, union wage effects increase intraindustry dispersion by creating wage differentials for otherwise similar workers. Freeman calculates that the net effect of unionism is to lessen blue-collar wage dispersion within six of the nine industries. In all nine industries, however, unionism decreases wage dispersion among *all* workers, since raising the wages of blue-collar relative to white-collar workers lessens dispersion.

A recent study by Hirsch (1982) finds that unionism significantly decreases intraindustry (three-digit Census) male earnings dispersion in the manufacturing and nonmanufacturing sectors. In this study, unionism is treated as endogenous, and alternative measures of earnings dispersion ($\sigma^2(\ln E)$ and the Gini coefficient) and unionism (the proportion union members and proportion covered by collective bargaining agreements) are used. Interestingly, results using 2SLS and 3SLS, which account for the endogeneity of unionism, show a larger and more significant equalizing effect of unionism than do OLS results, which treat unionism as exogenous. Results using the Gini coefficient as an inequality measure are relatively larger and more significant than those using the variance of log earnings. This is most likely because $\sigma^2(\ln E)$ weighs dispersion in the lower end of the distribution more heavily than in the upper end, as compared to the Gini coefficient. Hirsch (1982, Table 4) shows that unionism acts to increase most significantly the proportion of workers in the upper middle of the earnings distribution.

Hyclak (1979) has examined the effects of unionism on earnings inequality, measured by the Gini coefficient, within Standard Metropolitan Statistical Areas (SMSAs) (Hyclak, 1980, provides a similar analysis for states). He finds an equalizing effect of unionism on all-male and black male earnings, but no significant effect on all-female or black female earnings. Hyclak fails to offer a plausible explanation for these differential effects, but the findings are not surprising. Among males, unionism acts to decrease dispersion within and most likely across establishments via rate standardization policies previously discussed. Union wage differentials probably have few offsetting effects on dispersion since most male union members have approximately average earnings. Among females, on the other hand, it seems likely that union members will have wage and salary earnings well above average, and therefore union wage increases act to increase inequality and offset the equalizing effects of wage standardization. On balance, unionism thus appears slightly to equalize male earnings in labor markets (the elasticity of dispersion with respect to unionism is quite small) and to have no measurable impact on the dispersion of female earnings. Although these conclusions appear reasonable, we are reluctant to place undue weight on Hyclak's results, in part because of the absence of detailed control variables, and also because of the inherent problems with aggregate data. Quan (1984) also concludes that unions have an equalizing effect on the size distribution of earnings, although the estimated magnitude of the effect appears to be small. His estimates are based on a calculation of union density by earnings class and the assumption of equal union wage effects across earnings classes.

The overall effect of unionism on wage dispersion within labor markets is of course related not only to union wage effects within the organized sector, but also to the strength of threat and labor spillover effects in the nonunion sector. Research attempting to measure threat and spillover effects is limited, but a recent study by Holzer (1982) provides an interesting and detailed analysis of these topics (see also Kahn, 1978b, 1980). Overall, the proportion organized in a labor market (SMSA) acts to increase wages for nonunion workers, suggesting that threat effects are dominant. A clear exception to this finding, however, is for young (aged 16–24) black males, whose wages are significantly lower in highly unionized labor markets. Unionization also acts to sharply and significantly decrease *employment* for both white and black young nonunion males, this finding being qualitatively similar to that in Kahn (1978b). Holzer's results suggest that, while unions tend to raise medium- and high-skill wage rates in a labor market, young blacks are least likely to be hired for these jobs and thus suffer wage and employment losses.

Unions can be expected to have a smaller impact on the distribution of family income than on individual earnings. Podgursky (1983) concludes that the overall impact of unions on poverty and the size distribution of income is negligible, primarily because middle-income families reap the largest gains from collective bargaining.

6.5 The Simultaneous Determination of Unionism and Earnings Dispersion

A possible objection to the conclusion that unions significantly decrease wage dispersion is that unions are likely to organize in firms or industries with lower wage dispersion. Therefore, causation may run from wage dispersion to unionism rather than the converse.

Freeman (1982) contends that there is little, if any, evidence in support of this argument, citing results reported in Farber and Saks (1980) showing that the likelihood of voting for union representation is positively related to the firm's standard deviation in wages; evidence from the 1977 Quality of Employment Survey (QES) showing that there is no difference in earnings dispersion between nonunion blue-collar workers who would and would not vote for union representation; and evidence from the Panel Study of Income Dynamics (PSID) and Young Men's NLS showing decreases in wage dispersion among union joiners and increases in dispersion among union leavers. Freeman's response to the simultaneity criticism is not compelling. Evidence in Farber and Saks and from the QES are for union certification votes or membership preferences. As seen in Chapter 3, the determinants of union status are likely to differ, possibly substantially, between workers in 'marginal' election units and those who are inframarginal union or nonunion workers. In addition, evidence from the QES, PSID, and NLS comparing overall dispersion among union joiners, leavers, or nonunion workers wanting or not wanting a union does not provide direct evidence on dispersion within establishments or industries.

Recently, Hirsch (1982) has suggested a number of reasons why earnings dispersion is likely to affect unionism. In addition, he provides estimates within a simultaneous framework examining the effect of dispersion on industry unionization and of unionism on industry earnings dispersion. As discussed in Chapter 2, unionism has important public good characteristics and the equilibrium (but not economically efficient) level of a public good can be treated as if determined by the preferences of the median voter. Many of the services that unions provide or propose to provide for unorganized workers are nonrival, and exclusion from these services is difficult. For example, all workers within a bargaining unit are covered by a single contract so that workers in similar circumstances receive roughly similar treatment and are not excluded from contract provisions. Of course, other types of union services, such as assistance in carrying out grievance procedures, may have less of these public good aspects, in spite of labor law provisions that require unions to service all covered workers. Union coverage then can be treated as offering workers a single package of expected services, which, for workers with preferences near those of the median voter, are likely to be close to their preferred package, whereas for workers with preferences far from the median, the expected benefits of the offered package are likely to be small (or negative).

Hirsch then argues that the lower is earnings dispersion within a firm, the more homogeneous are workers in their characteristics and preferences. If this is correct then it is likely that, other things equal, union coverage is more likely in firms with smaller earnings dispersion. For any package of services a union can offer close to the preferences of the median voter, support for the union will be greater the more highly concentrated are preferences around the median. Stated differently, for a given level of demand for union services, a union can more easily construct a package that will satisfy a majority the less dispersed are preferences around the median. Thus unionization should be more likely, more effective, and politically more stable the more homogeneous are workers.

The benefits and costs of unionism may also be related directly to the dispersion in worker preferences (which is probably related to the dispersion in worker characteristics). Similar workers are more easily substitutable and are more likely to face an elastic demand and be in a relatively weak individual bargaining position. Thus, they may value collective bargaining more highly. We should also expect lower costs the more homogeneous are workers due to economies of scale in both the provision of union services (grievance procedures, institutionalized work rules, etc.) and negotiations with management. Management may also find there are economies of scale in bargaining with a union the greater the commonality in voice among its employees.

All the above arguments imply a negative relationship between unionism and earnings dispersion. However, other factors point to a positive relationship. As discussed previously, workers may demand unions as a means of reducing some elements of risk or to decrease dispersion in compensation, both across and within job categories. Because unions tend to represent the average or median worker – whereas the 'market' will more closely represent the marginal worker – differences in preferences between average and marginal workers (for example, between existing and new workers) may affect the likelihood of unionism. If it is true that relatively larger differences exist between average and marginal workers in those work settings where earnings dispersion is greater, then demand for union-induced wage equalization would be greater, leading to a positive relationship between unionism and earnings dispersion. Where differences between average and marginal workers are small, worker demand for altering the market-determined compensation structure should be less. For example, if all workers were identical, union wage standardization would bring about little change from the existing wage distribution.

In addition, Farber and Saks and others have found that individuals are significantly more likely to vote for union representation if they believe that employees have been treated unfairly and that unions ensure greater fairness. If these sentiments are more likely the greater the dispersion in earnings, then a positive unionism–dispersion relationship is again possible. Therefore, where worker demand for union-induced wage equalization is large (and union election campaign literature suggests it frequently is), then this may offset the negative unionism–earnings dispersion relationship outlined above.

Based on the above discussion, the relationship between unionism and the dispersion in earnings is *a priori* indeterminate and poses an interesting empirical question. At issue is not only whether and how earnings dispersion affects unionization, but also whether (after accounting for their simultaneous determination) the estimated equalizing effects of unions on earnings dispersion are less or greater than single-equation estimates might suggest.

Hirsch (1982) estimates a simultaneous model consisting of earnings, earnings dispersion, and unionism equations. Grouped three-digit industry data for 1970 are used and all equations are estimated separately for the manufacturing and nonmanufacturing sectors (union coverage data at the firm level, while preferable, are not available). As previously mentioned, his results provide strong support for the expectation that unionism significantly decreases earnings dispersion within industries, even after accounting for the simultaneous determination of unionism and dispersion. If anything, the estimated equalizing effects of unions on dispersion are larger using 2SLS and 3SLS estimation techniques in which unionism is endogenous. Hirsch also models the effect of (endogenous) unionism on the distribution of workers across eight earnings classes and finds that unionism increases the proportion in the upper middle classes, while decreasing the proportions in the lower and highest classes.

The estimated effects of earnings dispersion on unionism, the primary focus of the Hirsch study, are somewhat ambiguous. In the nonmanufacturing sector, results clearly show that industry levels of unionism are higher the *less* dispersed are earnings, regardless of the measure of unionism or dispersion. Hirsch interprets these findings as indicating that the homogeneity of worker preferences and characteristics – or, alternatively, a narrow dispersion of preferences around those of the median worker – makes unionism in the workplace more likely. For manufacturing, however, the relationship between unionism and earnings dispersion is ambiguous. Depending on estimation technique and the variables used to measure unionism and earnings dispersion, the estimated relation ranges from negative and significant to positive and significant. The inconclusive results for the manufacturing sector do not allow any clear-cut inferences. It appears likely, however, that in manufacturing worker demand for union-induced wage standardization may be particularly strong in industries (or firms and plants) where dispersion is large. This effect may offset to a large extent the opposing effect whereby unionism is more likely in a workplace with less dispersion in characteristics and preferences around the median.

In summary, we have reasonably strong priors that unionism acts not only to narrow wage and earnings dispersion within and across establishments and within narrowly defined industries, but also that the likelihood of unionism is affected by the distribution of worker characteristics and preferences. Given that union representation status is determined by collective choice within a majority-rule framework, it would be surprising if unionism and dispersion were not determined simultaneously. While research findings to date are suggestive, it is hoped that future studies can increase understanding of the complex relationship between unionism, wage dispersion, and the distribution of worker preferences and characteristics.

6.6 Unions and the Earnings–Experience Profile

There is a fairly strong consensus that unions act to decrease the slope of the log earnings–experience profile. This conclusion is based primarily although not exclusively on cross-sectional evidence showing flatter and less concave earnings and wage profiles among union members, and a larger union–nonunion wage differential for younger workers. A flattening of the earnings or wage profile with respect to age or experience is simply one way in which unions may narrow dispersion. It is *not*, however, a necessary condition for a decrease in dispersion. Even if earnings growth rates (measured by the slope of the longitudinal earnings–experience profile) were identical among union and nonunion jobs, unionism would act to lessen dispersion by decreasing variation in earnings among workers in each experience cell. For example, a strict union seniority system might significantly decrease overall earnings dispersion by lessening management discretion in compensation, and yet dictate an earnings growth rate as fast or faster than would occur in a nonunion environment.

Despite the apparent consensus that unions flatten earnings profiles, a number of recent theoretical and empirical contributions to the literature on unions make us question the appropriateness and relevance of this finding. Specifically, if one considers earnings growth with respect to tenure (seniority) as well as experience, union impact on pensions and other nonpecuniary forms of compensation, and the decreased risk of layoff as seniority rises, the conclusion that unions provide the relatively largest benefits to young workers no longer appears to hold. Moreover, the theoretical arguments that attach to such empirical evidence are in some instances rather ambiguous. We elaborate on these points below.

Although wage growth with respect to general experience typically is slower among union than nonunion workers, recent evidence suggests that wage growth with respect to tenure or seniority is not slower. For example, Mincer (1983), using the 1968–78 PSID, obtains similar coefficient estimates on tenure variables for union and nonunion workers in both wage level and wage growth equations. He concludes that union workers invest significantly less in general on-the-job training (OJT) than do nonunion workers (as evidenced by a flatter experience profile), but investments in firm-specific OJT are similar (as evidenced by similar tenure profiles).[6] Robinson and Tomes (1984), examining the wages of public and private sector workers in Canada, find flatter experience profiles but *steeper* tenure profiles among union workers. And, in an analysis of the determinants of promotion, Olson and Berger (1983) find that seniority *per se* is significant for union workers, but has little effect for nonunion workers. We believe the results from these studies suggest the importance of using data sets that have separate measures of general experience and tenure.

Although the union–nonunion *wage* differential may be largest among young workers, older workers benefit relatively more from non-pecuniary benefits – pensions, vacation pay, health benefits, life insurance, and increased employment security associated with seniority. Freeman and Medoff (1984, Chapter 8) provide a summary of their unpublished work in which union–nonunion compensation differentials by age group are estimated after accounting for these factors (for a detailed analysis of pensions, see Freeman, 1983b). They report the *largest* relative gain for older workers, aged 56–65. Even though they continue to find a U-shaped pattern of the differential with respect to age, the pattern is a relatively weak one and young workers are no longer found to receive the largest relative gains. We also note that the finding that unions decrease quit rates more among older than younger workers (e.g. Blau and Kahn, 1983) supports the finding that union rents are relatively larger for older workers.

How might we explain why union and nonunion compensation profiles differ with respect to age or experience? We are unable to provide a clear-cut answer to this question, but three theoretical approaches appear most promising: the median voter model; a human capital model of OJT; and an 'incentive' model based on the assumption of implicit long-term contracts.

The median voter model does not provide unambiguous predictions of the distribution of rents among union members. First, the existence and uniqueness of the median voter equilibrium is not guaranteed (for a presentation of the necessary and sufficient conditions for such an equilibrium, see Blair and Crawford, 1984). Even where an equilibrium exists, the identity of the median voter and the makeup of the coalition that forms the majority generally are not determinate. However, let us assume that preferences can be ordered by age and that outcomes maximize the utility of the median-age union member. One then might expect the largest wage gains for median-age workers, with relatively smaller gains for younger and older workers. While there is some evidence of this type of outcome in specific cases (White, 1982), extant evidence generally shows exactly the opposite result.

Of course, since median-age workers will someday become senior workers, we might not expect outcomes that redistribute rents away from older workers. Indeed, Grossman (1983) and Black and Parker (1984, 1985) have developed voting models whereby a majority coalition favors senior workers in regard to wages, seniority, and layoff provisions. Yet such models do not explain in any obvious fashion the relatively large wage gains for young workers.[7] While we believe the median voter model is a useful tool for understanding union outcomes, it does not appear sufficient to explain union–nonunion differences in the age–compensation profile.

Lazear (1979, 1981) has developed an 'incentive' model that attempts to explain the slope of the earnings profile in terms of optimal incentives and monitoring costs. It is commonly observed that wage differentials between young and old are greater than differences in value of marginal products (VMP) would dictate (e.g. Medoff and Abraham, 1980, 1981). Lazear suggests that it is optimal to have age–earnings profiles steeper than VMP profiles if holding out payments until late in an individual's career provides an incentive to increase work effort. This reasoning assumes that monitoring of workers (agents) by employers (principals) is costly and that both parties prefer a lifetime contract whereby reduced 'shirking' or increased effort will increase the probability of continued employment, accompanied by a relatively large reward. Lazear notes that such a scheme may achieve efficiency at the effort margin, but not on the hours margin since wages and marginal products diverge. Thus, such compensation patterns will be accompanied by hours restrictions such as a fixed work week and mandatory retirement.

Lazear contends that unions may act as a substitute for such an upward-sloping earnings profile by monitoring and regulating the workforce at a lower cost. Just how unions would achieve this is uncertain. Lazear believes it might occur through peer pressure or direct supervision. Alternatively, unions may achieve this monitoring function by allowing less flexibility and discretion on the job, as evidenced in

Duncan and Stafford (1980, 1982). Thus, unions may act to both raise and flatten the earnings profile by lessening shirking among younger workers and decreasing the need for the incentives generated by a steeper profile. Although this explanation is consistent with evidence of a *flatter* union wage profile, it does not explain *larger* union–nonunion compensation differentials among the most senior workers (but see Kuhn, 1982, who attempts to explain the U-shaped differential using a long-term contracts model). Supporting the belief that senior workers are receiving the largest rents is Leigh's (1984b) finding that union workers are significantly more likely to face a mandatory retirement provision. Even if one accepts the prevailing view of a flatter union wage profile, extant evidence does not make clear whether unions flatten the profile by inducing such monitoring and inflexible work conditions, or, alternatively, whether unions are most likely to organize in types of jobs with such working conditions and methods of monitoring.

An alternative way to explain differences between union and nonunion workers in the shape of earnings–experience profiles is the use of conventional human capital theory. The steepness of the profile is viewed by human capital theorists as representing some combination of the intensity, time span, and rate of return of investments in on-the-job training (Mincer, 1974). Investments in OJT act to steepen the profile by depressing earnings in early years when investment intensity is greater, and increasing earnings in later years as one receives a return on one's investments or skills (but earnings increase at a decreasing rate due to decreasing growth in investment intensity and human capital depreciation). Within this context, one could argue that, on average, union jobs involve less total OJT, thus leading to lower differentials in productivity between young and old workers and a flatter profile.

It should be noted that the above reasoning does not identify causation. If the human capital explanation for differential profiles is correct, it seems likely that the correlation between unionism and flatter wage profiles may arise as much from unions organizing where wage (productivity) profiles are flatter as from any direct effect of unions on productivity by age. However, as noted earlier, there is no convincing econometric evidence sorting out the simultaneous relationship between unionism and wage profiles.

One can also infer from the slope of the earnings profile the intensity of firm-specific or non-transferable OJT relative to general or transferable OJT. For a given *total* amount of OJT, workers with more firm-specific and less general training will have *flatter* profiles, since workers with specific training are initially paid more and subsequently paid less than the value of their marginal products (exactly the opposite of the pattern in Lazear's model). Unfortunately, specific and general

OJT can rarely be directly measured and must be inferred from the observed pattern of earnings.

Mincer (1983) makes inferences regarding the relative amounts of union and nonunion OJT based on his estimated experience and tenure profiles. He suggests that the flatter experience profile of union workers implies relatively less general OJT, while similarly shaped union and nonunion tenure profiles suggest similar amounts of firm-specific OJT. Thus, union workers are believed to invest less heavily in total OJT and have a higher ratio of firm-specific to general OJT than do nonunion workers. This latter result is not surprising. Because unionism reduces quits – owing, among other things, to the union wage differential and collective voice mechanism – firms (and workers) will invest more heavily in specific OJT. Causality may work in the opposite direction as well. Unions may be more effective in organizing firms with a relatively larger amount of specific OJT if it acts to increase worker attachment to the job and lessens mobility.

While the human capital model appears to be consistent with both lower quit rates and initially flatter earnings profiles among union workers, it does not provide a ready answer as to why the most senior workers receive the largest premium (i.e. why union wage growth slows less rapidly with age than the nonunion profile). A possible explanation is that union seniority and wage provisions, supported by senior workers, allow union firms relatively less discretion in the awarding of merit-based pay. Although older workers in general may be paid more than their marginal products (as in Lazear's incentive model), the gap may be even wider for union than for nonunion workers. That is, wage growth in the more merit-based nonunion sector is more likely to slow along with worker productivity. Thus, the union–nonunion compensation differential will be largest among the most senior workers (see Freeman and Medoff, 1984) and mandatory retirement provisions will be more likely in union firms (see Leigh, 1984b).

Leigh (1984b) summarizes a specific training model proposed by Alan Blinder whereby a worker's wage exceeds the VMP during early and late periods of a worker's tenure. As in the traditional specific-training model the wage profile is initially flatter, but like the Lazear incentive model (but for a different reason) the wage profile steepens in later years relative to VMP. The logic is that the promise of a high wage in later years will help retain employees during those prime years in which a return on investment accrues to the firm. As in the Lazear model, mandatory retirement is more likely since the wage exceeds VMP for older workers. If the Blinder model of specific training is correct and union jobs do entail a higher ratio of specific to general training, the prediction is that a U-shaped union–nonunion wage differential with respect to age will exist. This is exactly what we observe.

In summary, differences between union and nonunion workers in the shapes of their earnings profiles are not fully understood at this time. We do know that it is important to compare not only money wages, but also fringes and employment security benefits resulting from seniority. In addition, we must compare earnings growth not only with respect to general experience but also with respect to tenure. Alternative frameworks – the median voter, incentive, and human capital models – have been provided in order to explain differences between union and nonunion compensation profiles. No single one of these models is necessarily sufficient to explain all observed differences. Of course the models are not mutually exclusive, yet separating the individual explanatory power of these models may prove difficult.

6.7 Unions and the Functional Distribution of Income

How does unionism affect the shares of aggregate income going to labor and capital? The conventional wisdom is that unions have little if any effect on aggregate shares. As stated by Milton and Rose Friedman, ' . . . the gains that strong unions win for their members are primarily at the expense of other workers. . . . Union leaders always talk about getting higher wages at the expense of profits. That is impossible: profits simply aren't big enough' (Friedman and Friedman, 1980, pp. 233–4). The logic of the Friedmans' argument is straightforward. Assuming union wage settlements on the demand curve (see Chapter 2) and mobility of labor between the union and nonunion sectors, higher wages and decreased employment in the union sector act to decrease wages and increase employment in the nonunion sector. Corporate profits typically account for only about 10 percent of national income and, at the margin, rates of return to investment must be similar in both sectors.

Multisector general equilibrium models provide a mechanism wherein the effects of unions can be simulated. DeFina (1985) provides perhaps the most detailed model and obtains results similar to those of earlier studies (Johnson and Mieszkowski, 1970; Diewert, 1974; Ballentine and Thirsk, 1977). DeFina solves a numerically specified general equilibrium model, with and without a 15 percent union wage differential. The model is disaggregated into 12 sectors on the production side and incorporates interindustry commodity flows. Under a variety of assumptions, DeFina finds that virtually all the gains by union labor come at the expense of nonunion labor, while income to capital is decreased only slightly.

Despite the seemingly clear-cut results from such simulations, we are reluctant to accept the conclusion that unions do not measurably affect the income shares going to labor and capital. Higher union wages need not imply lower nonunion wages (Holzer, 1982, provides a thorough discussion). In the several studies that estimate the impact of industry and SMSA union density on the wages of *nonunion* workers, virtually all find a *positive* and occasionally significant impact. The notable exception is young black males, for whom Holzer (1982) finds the nonunion wage decreasing with SMSA union density. But young black males account for only a small proportion of the labor force. If unions decrease nonunion wages so significantly, as the conventional view suggests, should not such a relationship be transparent in regression estimates of nonunion wage functions?

It certainly is correct that, because profits account for a small proportion of total income and marginal rates of return to investors between union and nonunion firms must be similar, the ability of unions to capture rents at the expense of capital has limits. However, studies to be reviewed in Chapter 7 show that unions decrease firm and industry profitability. Indeed, a rough estimate by Voos and Mishel (1985) suggests that the decrease in profits associated with unionism is similar in magnitude to the increased wage bill due to union wage effects. In short, the empirical evidence showing that unionism decreases profits, coupled with an absence of evidence that unions decrease nonunion wages, makes us reluctant to accept the conventional wisdom that unions have no effect on income shares to labor and capital.

Surprisingly, there is little direct evidence of union effects on income shares, and that which exists is dated. There is even disagreement about the existence and direction of a time trend in labor's share (Solow, 1958; Gujarati, 1969; Close and Shulenburger, 1971), largely because of measurement differences among data sources. Likewise, there is disagreement about whether unions affect labor's share. For example, Levinson (1954) contends that unions increase labor's share, while Denison (1954) and Simler (1961) argue that unions have no significant effect. A recent study by Kalleberg, Wallace, and Raffalovich (1984) finds that unionism increased labor's share in the printing industry between 1946 and 1978; however, the union effect decreased significantly over time. Of course, results from a single industry do not allow inferences to be drawn as to unionism's economy-wide effect.

As seen above, the impact of unions on the functional distribution of income has been a neglected area of research, owing, no doubt, to the widespread belief that unions have little effect on the aggregate shares of income to labor and capital. Recent econometric evidence of union effects on profits and nonunion wages casts considerable doubt on the conventional wisdom. We feel certain this topic will not remain neglected.

6.8   A Summing Up

This chapter provides strong evidence that trade unions not only increase wage levels for their members, but also affect significantly the distribution of wages. Wage standardization appears to be the dominant union effect on wage dispersion. Unions seek to establish job rather than individual rates of pay within establishments and to acquire a similar wage structure across establishments. This goal apparently derives from the union's representational nature — survival requires that it responds more to the interests of average workers and majority coalitions than to marginal workers — coupled with its rational attempt to lessen wage competition across establishments.

Evidence by Richard Freeman and others shows that unions act to decrease wage dispersion significantly within and across establishments, within industries, and, to a lesser extent, within labor markets (among males). Evidence relating to union effects on interindustry and economy-wide earnings dispersion is less conclusive, but suggests that the overall impact is small. As pointed out in the chapter, although we are able to analyze how wage dispersion varies with union coverage, we are unable to estimate directly the effect of unionism on the overall structure of wages relative to what would exist in the absence of unionism. Union effects on the size distribution of family income are clearly quite small, while the impact of unionism on the functional distribution of income requires further study.

Despite substantial evidence that unions decrease wage dispersion, there is little consensus as to the importance of dispersion as a determinant of unionism. Although evidence in this area is meager, we believe not only that unionism affects wage dispersion, but also that the dispersion in worker characteristics and preferences affects the likelihood of union coverage. On the one hand, a narrow dispersion of preferences around those of the median worker will increase the likelihood of a union producing a package of services that can obtain and maintain strong support. On the other hand, a large dispersion in wages may increase demand for union-induced rate standardization to the extent that the inequality of wages is perceived as unfair and workers believe unions can in fact significantly alter the wage structure.

Finally, there is disagreement about the effects of unions on the slope of the earnings–experience profile. Extensive cross-sectional evidence indicates that union wage profiles are flatter and less concave than nonunion profiles. However, the union–nonunion compensation differential appears to be weakly U-shaped with respect to age, with the largest benefits accruing to older workers. This latter conclusion follows only after accounting for fringe benefits and the reduced employment risk associated with seniority. Differences between union and nonunion compensation profiles lend themselves to several explanations that are not mutually exclusive. We have explored explanations based on, alternatively, human capital theory, an 'incentive' model, and a public choice model based on policy determination within unions.

What are the implications of the empirical evidence on the appraisal of the equity and efficiency aspects of unionism? Although there are no universally accepted principles of equity or fairness, if one perceives any decrease in wage inequality as equitable then presumably it can be argued that unionism at a minimum enhances equity within and across establishments, if not for the economy as a whole. On the other hand, to the extent that unions lessen wage differentials based on individual merit and effort, these effects may be perceived by many as inequitable. Likewise, union-generated wage differentials among otherwise similar workers conflict with most people's standard of equity.

The efficiency of union wage standardization depends crucially on one's interpretation of both the theory and evidence presented in this chapter. To the extent that unions are a response to public good aspects of the workplace (job risks, complementarities in production, and the like) and provide a collective voice that accurately transmits through bargaining the preferences of the average worker, then unions may increase efficiency in the workplace. A wage compensation schedule based strictly on seniority, then, might improve efficiency by increasing cooperative behavior and facilitating the training of junior workers by senior workers. Likewise, if rate standardization lessens some wage differentials that are arbitrary or discriminatory (i.e. differential pay for similarly productive workers), efficiency in the labor market might be enhanced.

While such efficiency-enhancing aspects of wage equalization are possible, we would not expect them to be dominant. Rather, wage standardization seems more likely to decrease efficiency and to produce consequences that in fact limit its adoption in more competitive markets. To the extent that market-determined wage differentials reflect productivity differences and the market mechanism of wage determination provides optimal incentives to workers, union wage policies seem likely to decrease efficiency. The key question in this area is the extent to which collective bargaining facilitates, or produces outcomes consistent with, efficient internal labor market contracts. The overall impact of unions on economic performance – efficiency, productivity, profitability, and growth – has become an important area of theoretical and empirical research by labor economists. We turn to this topic next.

Notes

1 This section relies heavily on the important paper by Richard Freeman (1980c). Also see the discussion in Freeman (1982) and Hirsch (1982).

2 Of course, a similar formalization of job- and pay-step classifications will be likely in large nonunionized firms or public agencies. Bloch (1982b) provides a comparison of formalization and collectivization (i.e. unionism), while the idiosyncratic exchange literature (e.g. Williamson, Wachter, and Harris, 1975) provides a rationale for such formalization.

3 Farber and Saks (1980) find that nonunion workers further up in an election unit's wage distribution are less likely to vote for union representation.

4 Stigler (1970) and Tullock (1971) apparently believe redistribution toward the middle and away from both tails is most likely. White's (1982) findings on faculty union salary bargaining goals support this belief. See also Black and Parker (1984, 1985), Blair and Crawford (1984), and Section 6.6 below.

5 Pettengill (1980), however, claims to have measured the effects of unionism on the skill structure of earnings within a general equilibrium framework. He concludes that unionism significantly increases earnings dispersion relative to what would exist in the absence of unionism.

6 Hutchins and Polachek (1981) question whether unions do in fact flatten earnings profiles. Using Michigan PSID data for 1968–76, they examine the wage growth of 63 union joiners and 117 union leavers. Consistent with previous cross-section results, they find a steeper profile for union joiners *prior* to joining and for leavers *after* leaving. However, they do *not* find a slower rate of wage growth for union joiners (after joining) than for union leavers (after leaving). If anything, their results suggest faster growth (a steeper earnings–experience profile) for union joiners than for leavers. While specifically applicable only to their small sample of union status changers, their results show that unions do not always flatten the earnings profile. Moreover, they suggest that previous results may best be explained by concluding that unions do not flatten profiles, but, rather, organize where earnings profiles are relatively flat.

7 Lazear provides a possible explanation for large union wage gains to young workers. He assumes that the union wants benefits to accrue primarily to *senior* workers; however, the firm and not the union does the hiring. 'A way by which the union can discourage the firm from hiring young workers is to overprice them relative to more experienced workers. This provides the union firm with incentives to hire the workers which the union would have selected' (Lazear, 1983a, p. 641).

179

CHAPTER 7

Unions and Economic Performance:

Productivity, Productivity Growth, and Profitability

7.1 Introduction

After several decades of comparative neglect, the issue of union impact on economic performance is once again the subject of intense scrutiny and no small controversy.[1] Much of the contemporary discussion has centered on a remarkable series of studies emanating from Harvard which have argued forcefully that trade unions frequently raise productivity, even after accounting for the predictable microeconomic responses of firms when confronted with higher wages. The scale of the union productivity differential reported in some of these studies seems to be of sufficient magnitude to offset the increase in compensation brought about by the union. Thus, it has been concluded that higher-paying unionized plants can after all compete with their unorganized counterparts in the same markets. The orthodox view of unions as monopolies pure and simple has been somewhat shaken by this literature, despite the acknowledged allocative inefficiencies that still attach to unionism owing to the distortion of factor prices.

In this chapter we evaluate the impact of unions on economic performance and efficiency along a number of dimensions. We begin with a statement of the orthodox view of unions as monopolies, before turning to examine the theoretical basis of modern approaches to the union, including the unions-raise-productivity thesis. The balance of our discussion addresses empirical analyses of union impact on productivity, productivity growth, and profitability. Discussion of unionism's impact on economic performance via its operation in nonpecuniary markets is remitted to Chapter 9.

7.2 Unions as Monopolies – The Orthodox View

It is conventional to view unions as monopolies that impose allocative costs by distorting the wage structure. In addition, the job regulatory or nonwage effects of unions are viewed as a more or less pervasive source of technical inefficiency. It is sometimes further argued that the strikes associated with unions constitute an additional source of output loss. Let us consider each source of inefficiency in turn.

Unions and allocative efficiency

Orthodox theory suggests that union wage effects cause a misallocation of resources, redirecting higher-quality workers and capital from higher to lower marginal product uses. As a result there will be economy-wide inefficiencies in production and consumption even though each firm may be operating on its production frontier. Economy-wide allocative efficiency requires that *identical* inputs be allocated in such a way that their marginal products are equalized across firms and industries. The union wage premium clearly interferes with any such equalization by distorting factor prices and usage. This in turn will reduce efficiency in consumption if cost increases are pushed forward so that the relative prices consumers face no longer reflect social opportunity costs. The private cost of union labor will exceed its social opportunity cost and thus the prices of goods produced by the union sector exceed their social opportunity costs. In short, too few workers/goods will be employed/produced in the union sector, and conversely for the nonunion sector.

The allocative costs of unionism are demonstrated in Figure 7.1. The curve MC_L denotes the labor supply curve to the industry under perfectly competitive conditions. In this union-free regime, the wage is W^* and employment is L^*. After the industry is partially unionized, assume the wage in the union sector increases above labor's social cost to, say, W_u, while employment is cut back to L_u (we ignore here the possibility of outcomes off the demand curve, but see Chapter 2). Triangle abc provides a measure of the welfare loss in the union sector, while rectangle $W_u ab W^*$ is the union transfer effect. Up to this point it is assumed that labor shed from the union sector, $L_u L^*$, can costlessly find employment elsewhere, so that bcL^*L_u represents the earnings and productivity of the surplus labor. In fact, nonunion wages and productivity may fall below labor's true social cost. Assume that the nonunion wage falls to W_n, redesignating VMP_L as the demand for labor in the nonunion sector. In this case, the absorption of the excess labor in the nonunion sector causes overproduction of sectoral output and hence an additional welfare loss of triangle ced. And, of course, the

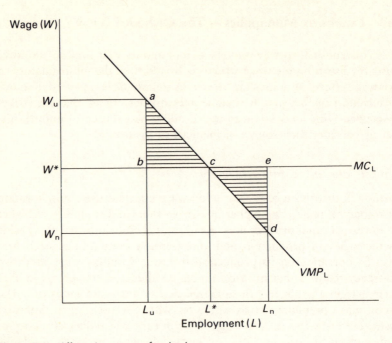

Figure 7.1 Allocative costs of unionism

output losses will be considerably higher if the union effect on the union and nonunion wage structure causes increased unemployment (i.e. if surplus labor is not absorbed).

In this model, the efficiency-detracting effects of unionism, which raises the wage above labor's social opportunity cost and induces firms to substitute toward capital and higher-quality labor, are unequivocal. At issue is the precise magnitude of the welfare loss. The size of the distortion or welfare loss associated with any given wage increase rises with the price elasticity of demand in the union sector and with the elasticity of substitution between labor and other inputs, although unionism is of course less likely when these elasticities are high (see Chapter 3).

Conventional estimates of the efficiency loss, using the Harberger (1954) method, are very modest. Rees (1963), assuming a 15 percent union relative wage effect and equal elasticities of demand for labor in both sectors, arrives at an estimate of the output loss for the 1957 US economy of only 0.14 percent of GNP. Recently, in a general equilibrium analysis that allows for distortions elsewhere in the system, DeFina (1983) arrives at an even lower estimate of the efficiency change from a removal of the union premium. His model comprises 12 industries, several primary factors, and commodity flows between industries. The specific distortion allowed for by DeFina is that associated with corporate income taxes, which reduce the rate of return on capital. His first task is to compute the market clearing adjustments of prices and output introduced by the elimination of the union wage premium. These price and quantity effects are derived from a set of production functions and demand schedules for the 12 industries. The next step is the computation of the net effect of the observed changes in prices and quantities on economic efficiency – note that the presence of taxes on capital (which decreases capital intensity) may mean that economic efficiency is not impaired by the union wage premium (which increases capital intensity). DeFina calculates the total efficiency change using the construct of Hicksian equivalent variation, namely the lump sum payment which, if given to individuals in the presence of the wage premium, would allow the attainment of the same level of utility resulting from the removal of the premium. He reports that although efficiency is improved by eliminating the union wage differential the magnitude of the gain is tiny. It ranges from 0.2 percent (of prechange income) in the case of an unrealistically high 25 percent wage differential, down to only 0.02 percent for a 7.5 percent differential.

Before we jump to the conclusion that the allocative costs of unionism are indeed trivial, a number of limitations attaching to such estimates should be noted. First, as previously mentioned, they ignore any unemployment effects of unionism arising from wage rigidities in the system or from the queuing by workers for union jobs. Second, they are conducted in a static framework. The problem here is not simply that measured welfare losses, although apparently tiny, persist, but also that unions may impact on profitability, investment, and growth, while themselves using resources to establish and maintain the labor cartel. We shall investigate the profitability and growth issue later. Focusing for the moment on the costs of cartelization, therefore, we note that the conventional estimates assume that the additional earnings received by union members are obtained by a costless transfer of purchasing power from the rest of the economy. Yet we know that resources are involved in establishing and maintaining monopoly prices or rents.[2] We do not know the exact proportion of the union wage premium that is true rent and that which is competed away. Clearly, if all potential union gains are expended to obtain rents then the true efficiency loss will be significantly greater, namely by the product of the union wage differential and the quantity of employment in the union sector (i.e. the transfer effect). Although this extreme case is implausible, it does indicate the need for caution in drawing firm conclusions on the basis of the allocative cost estimates cited above.

It was noted earlier that reduced substitutability between labor and other factors would serve to reduce estimates of the welfare loss. Thus, conventional estimates of the welfare loss may also contain an upward bias since labor demand is significantly less elastic in the union sector (Freeman and Medoff, 1982). Lower demand elasticities in the union sector reflect not only the tendency for unions to organize and obtain wage gains in such jobs but also the possibility that unions reduce substitutability between union labor and other factors. This latter effect is perhaps best viewed as part of the union-induced output loss.

The analysis up to now has assumed that collective bargaining outcomes occur on the demand curve. As developed in some detail in Chapter 2, such outcomes are unlikely to be Pareto optimal since there are points off the demand curve, with lower wages and greater employment, preferred by both the union and the firm. If the union and management can bargain simultaneously over wages and employment, settlements off the demand curve can occur. The implication of this analysis is that featherbedding or other union work rules may in fact increase efficiency, relative to an outcome on the demand curve at a higher wage. And, in the case of a vertical contract curve, no static inefficiency results since the nonunion output and factor mix obtain. As we shall see below, however, such an outcome will reduce the rate of return on capital and may impact adversely on investment behavior and long-run growth. Moreover, as seen in Chapter 2, direct empirical tests reject the hypothesis of outcomes on a vertical contract curve (as well as outcomes on the labor demand curve).

Unions and technical efficiency

It has been argued that union restrictive/protective practices are potentially a much greater source of output loss than their relative wage effects. For example, Rees (1963) guesses that direct restrictions on output through control of manning requirements, the work pace, and other working practices probably exceed 0.3 percent of GNP. Indeed, he cites management's claim in railroads that obsolete work rules were costing the industry $500 million or a little over 0.1 percent of 1959 national output. There is a veritable litany of stories graphically describing the adverse effects of the 'rule book' and other restrictive working practices on productivity, but few if any reliable estimates. The British experience with productivity bargaining – for a case study, see Flanders (1964) – provides interesting insights into the possible cost savings resulting from the abandonment of restrictive practices (in return for higher pay); unfortunately, almost all workers covered by such agreements were already unionized prior to buy-out agreements of this type, thereby precluding a direct comparison of unionized and nonunionized workers. Yet such a comparison is necessary because it has long been recognized that nonunion workers are not averse to erecting barriers to efficient working (Mathewson, 1931), even though a union presence is likely to assist a more effective policing of any output-restricting cartel (Pencavel, 1977).

Economy-wide losses from union work rules are not known. Gollop (1976), in estimating a time-series translog production function for US manufacturing, finds that union coverage has little effect on substitution possibilities, as measured by the curvature of production isoquants. (However, unions are found to reduce productivity – see Section 7.4 below.) One study that rigorously quantifies the misallocation attendant upon union work rules is Allen's (1984c) study of factor allocation in two branches of US construction. Allen exploits the argument that union work rules will produce lower demand elasticities in the union sector, as reported in Freeman and Medoff (1982). Whereas Freeman and Medoff's highly aggregative data set did not enable them to test whether this result merely reflected the tendency of unions to organize in sectors possessing low demand elasticities to begin with, Allen sidesteps this problem to the extent that product and technology are more likely to be constant across the firms in his sample.

Allen derives union and nonunion factor demand elasticities from translog cost system parameters. This approach allows elasticities of substitution to differ between the various factors. Elasticities of substitution and own-price elasticities are then computed for union and nonunion contractors. In a three-factor model (total labor, material, and equipment costs) in which the amount of the contract is the output measure, it emerges that factor demand elasticities vary little between union and nonunion contractors. However, in a model that splits up the labor input into three categories (skilled, supervisory, and semiskilled/unskilled workers), it is found that own-price elasticities for labor are larger for nonunion contractors while labor–labor substitution elasticities tend to be smaller in the union sector. This evidence provides some support for the notion that union work rules inhibit managerial discretion to assign workers to jobs in the most efficient fashion.

The next step is to calculate the effect of these lower elasticities in the union sector on employment, costs, and productivity. Here, Allen undertakes a simulation exercise based on a typical subcontract for his office building sample. Specifically, he determines the change in factor allocation in the union sector when wages fall to nonunion levels, using first union and then nonunion elasticities. The first method, Allen contends, yields a measure of allocative inefficiency resulting simply from union wage effects. The second provides a composite measure of allocative *and* technical inefficiency, reflecting price effects and work rules respectively. Comparing the two sets of estimates reveals that the removal of work rules (as indirectly measured) would reduce staffing levels by 3.2 percent, increase productivity in the same proportion, reduce labor costs by 5 percent, and reduce total costs by 2 percent.

Now, while nontrivial gains in productivity might thus accrue from the elimination of occupational jurisdictions in the union sector, it is important to note that Allen's estimates fall far short of those commonly alleged to obtain in craft-oriented industries (but for a similar conclusion, see Mandelstamm, 1965). Moreover, Allen argues that the effect he identifies pertains to only one among a number of union job regulatory practices that have opposing effects on efficiency. In particular, he notes that offsetting efficiency gains are available in the form of superior training and reduced hiring costs (see Section 7.4 below).

The effect of work rules on productivity has also been examined by Ichniowski (1984b) using monthly data on ten unionized paper mills between 1976 and 1982. As a proxy for the number and complexity of union work rules, he measures the number of pages in collective bargaining agreements. He finds a strong inverse relationship between this measure and productivity, suggesting that productivity is inhibited by the proliferation of work rules. However, one cannot necessarily attribute this productivity decrease to unionism. Ichniowski finds that productivity in his one nonunion mill is about 9.5 percent lower than in union mills for the same level of inputs. Ichniowski is unable to compare explicitly the impact of formalized (union) with informal (nonunion) work rules or, for that matter, to identify those rules that most affect productivity. Rule proliferation may, alternatively, be associated with reduced strike activity (see Chapter 4).

Output and strikes

Finally, what of the effect of strikes on output and productivity? With the exception of the study by Neumann and Reder (1984), there is little in the way of systematic analysis of this question, although statistics on the direct cost of strikes (e.g. working days lost) are widely available. Unfortunately, here as elsewhere, the facts do not speak for themselves. As discussed in Chapter 4, the cost of strikes will depend on the extent to which substitution in production and consumption is possible. Note also that strikes, even if they can be attributed exclusively to unionism, are but one of several forms of exit behavior encountered in both union and nonunion regimes. Again, since it takes two parties to precipitate a strike, it is rather one-sided to label unions as the cause of strikes, although this has proved popular in the literature. As our analysis in Chapter 4 reveals, strikes might best be interpreted as accidents or bargaining failures, although the incidence of these accidents may be expected to differ systematically across industries.

Nevertheless, the possibility that production functions in economies with high levels of strike activity may differ from those in economies with lower levels of industrial conflict has been examined. For example, Maki (1983b) has attempted to explain differential growth rates in total factor productivity across a sample of 20 countries, 1967–75. Maki's simple regressions of productivity growth on mandays lost owing to labor disputes suggest that on average strikes retard productivity growth by 0.5 percentage points. Since average total factor productivity growth over the sample period amounted to only some 1.4 percent a year, this study points to sizeable strike effects. However, as Maki himself admits, there are a number of factors other than strikes that influence productivity or the growth rate of total factor productivity – some of which will be discussed below – and so these results are subject to omitted variable bias. For example, it is likely that both productivity growth and strikes are jointly determined by a third variable, namely inflation uncertainty/variability. That said, we note that Gollop (1976), while finding union coverage to have little effect on substitution possibilities in US manufacturing, does find (surprisingly) that strike activity affects substitution and factor demand elasticities.

Perhaps the best analysis of the relation between strike activity and output is that of Neumann and Reder (1984; summarized in Chapter 4) which allows for struck firms to substitute production over time and for strike-free employers to increase their output and hence offset welfare losses. Neumann and Reder's results reinforce our tentative conclusion that strikes are unlikely to represent a significant source of output loss. The issue of strike *threat* power is altogether another matter, but, as we have seen, this effect will be reflected primarily in the union wage premium and hence captured in the measure of allocative inefficiency.

From this discussion, it is apparent that systematic testing of the conventional union monopoly model is still needed. What has been forthcoming, however, is a large number of production function studies suggesting that the acknowledged allocative costs of unions may in practice be offset by a positive union productivity differential. Before proceeding with this empirical discussion, however, we first investigate briefly the wider theoretical background to this new view of unions.

7.3 Union-Induced Improvements in Productivity – A Theoretical Backdrop

The core of the new view of unionism, articulated primarily by Richard Freeman, James Medoff, and their students at Harvard, is grounded in a labor market application of Hirschman's (1970) exit-voice paradigm. On this view, unions provide workers with an effective 'collective voice' at the workplace that may generate productivity improvements given appropriate institutional responses from management. Yet elements of this unions-raise-productivity thesis are also encountered in rather more traditional models. Thus, for example, one popular explanation for positive union effects on productivity (over and above those stemming from predictable price-theoretic responses) is the so-called 'shock' effect, whereby management is induced to reduce organizational slack or technical inefficiency. Indeed, the Harvard analysts Brown and Medoff (1978, p. 359) and Clark (1980a, pp. 465–7) refer explicitly to 'union-shocked' management, while more recent discussion by Freeman and Medoff (1984, Chapter 11) increasingly stresses the importance of management response to union voice. Below, we explore several potential explanations for positive union productivity effects.

X-efficiency and shock effects

Leibenstein's (1966) characterization of X-inefficiency portrays situations in which least-cost combinations of labor and capital are not employed or are not utilized in a technically efficient manner. Motivational and information factors underpin the concept of X-efficiency. Leibenstein argues that neither individuals nor firms work as hard or search for information as effectively as they could. He suggests an approach to the theory of the firm that does not depend on the assumption of cost minimization by all firms; rather, the level of unit cost depends in part on the degree of X-efficiency, which in turn rests on the degree of competitive pressure and other motivational factors. Many of the sources of X-efficiency noted by Leibenstein − incentives to employers, organizational variables, managerial supervision, and working conditions − are likely to be influenced by unionism. Indeed, as we shall see, it is this very potential that the new view of unions has sought to exploit.

Unfortunately, X-efficiency is an ambiguous concept. Factors such as motivation or organizational structure, which Leibenstein views as determining X-efficiency, may alternatively be modeled as determined by maximizing behavior subject to the relevant constraints (see, for example, Stigler, 1976; De Alessi, 1983; Kuhn, 1985). Viewed from this perspective, the task is to model explicitly those factors (e.g. property rights and transaction costs) that explain differences in behavior. In other words, unionism can be viewed as either moving firms closer to or further from a given frontier (in nonmaximizing models) or moving firms along a given frontier that includes, say, productivity and on-the-job utility (in maximizing models).

If we accept that the correct amounts of the various inputs are being employed initially, then the introduction of a union that restricts, say, managers' ability to take on-the-job leisure, *inter alia*, is in fact economically inefficient. Only if, for some reason, optimization is lacking prior to unionization is it theoretically the case that such changes in managerial effort will be welfare improving. And, as we have seen, the basic ambiguity in X-efficiency theory – namely the absence of a distinct theory of worker (and manager) motivation – inhibits progress in this latter area.

The traditional shock effect model, then, simply presumes pre-union slack or X-inefficiency. Having to pay higher wages shocks management into looking for cost savings elsewhere, eliminating or reducing pre-existing slack within the organization in the process. Union-shocked management is supposed to be able to extract more output from a given quantity of inputs than is management free of the union challenge.

Collective voice/institutional response

With these preliminaries behind us, let us now turn to the collective voice model itself. The basic model is presented in Freeman (1976) and Freeman and Medoff (1979b, 1984). Freeman's starting point is in many ways similar to the internal labor market argument of Williamson, Wachter, and Harris (1975), on which we shall briefly comment below (see also Chapter 8). Because on-the-job skills specific to the firm increase the costs of mobility and turnover, there are gains to be had from regular employment. A continuing relation develops between firms and much of their workforce in which allocation and remuneration decisions are not controlled directly by the external price mechanism. This results in contracts of a multidimensional nature that encompass many issues other than the wage. Such contracts develop because workers care about nonpecuniary conditions and because different conditions, rules, and methods of organization have different costs. Also, since workers have some control over their own activities and can affect the productivity of others, especially in team settings where the monitoring of individuals is costly, their attitudes and morale become potentially important inputs into the production process (Freeman, 1976, pp. 361–2).

Freeman and Medoff argue cogently that the productivity-enhancing potential of unionism is grounded in the public goods nature of the workplace. First, nonrival consumption of shared working conditions (job safety, work pace, and so on) raises questions about possible mechanisms for choosing levels of the good and compensation of the workers (on this point, see Chapter 2). They speak of the necessity of a collective voice mechanism, which is at all times equated with autonomous unionism. Unions, so the argument runs, collect information about the preferences of all workers and enable firms to choose a more efficient mix of wage and personnel policies. More specifically,

Freeman (1976) contrasts the efficiency properties of collective voice with exits or quits. Collective voice may outperform the standard quit mechanism as a source of information about conditions and preferences because it substitutes an average (since the union is hypothesized to represent most closely the preferences of the median voter) for a marginal supply calculus in the presence of externalities. This distinction is important because those who are most likely to quit (e.g. young workers) typically differ markedly from the average worker. Thus, in work settings involving significant public goods, unionism may lead to a more efficient contract than would result from primary reliance on the preferences of marginal workers with its attendant selectivity bias problems.[3]

A second public goods dimension of the workplace concerns the nature of the input of effort. Without some collective form of organization, the incentive of the individual to take into account the effects of his actions on others may, just as with preference revelation, be too small. This problem arises where there are significant complementarities in worker effort inputs. In such circumstances output may depend on the lowest level of effort by any one worker (Duncan and Stafford, 1980). Accordingly, collective organization may potentially increase output through a joint determination of effort inputs. This does not necessarily imply that the union will be the employer's monitor of the employees.

Clearly, we must be wary of applying the public goods argument to all workplace situations. For the public goods argument to be relevant, two further conditions extending beyond complementaries in consumption and effort input also have to be satisfied. First, there must be costs attaching to the use of external markets. For example, if quitting was costless the individual worker could simply select the employer whose working conditions most closely mirrored his own preferences. Second, the workplace environment must be subject to unforeseen shocks, otherwise there would be no need for the union's demand-revealing function after the initial match of worker and firm. Both of these elements are recognized by Freeman (1976, p. 362), who stresses the ongoing nature of the employment relation and the role of exogenous (technological) shocks in altering the nature of the workplace in an informational context. (He also notes that changes in real income will lead workers to demand new conditions of employment and methods of compensation.)

By way of summary, the collective voice/institutional response model argues that the public goods dimension of the workplace requires collective organization, which is taken to be synonymous with unionism. In providing a means of expressing discontent other than through quits, collective voice is said to reduce exit behavior, lower hiring and training costs, and increase firm-specific investments.[4] The expression of collective voice through the agency of the union also creates an institutional mechanism for aggregating worker preferences in collective bargaining, allowing the firm to choose a more appropriate mix of compensation and personnel practices, while improving communication between the two sides. Collective voice also offers the prospect of raising productivity by encouraging cooperation among workers and improving workplace morale. Moreover, the presence of a union is said to be a vehicle for inducing management to alter methods of production and select more efficient practices. Note, finally, that the gains from collective bargaining depend importantly on both management's response to collective bargaining and also the union's response to reorganization of the work process – hence the institutional response component. In short, improvements are potential rather than guaranteed. Whether unions enhance or retard productivity is thus ultimately an empirical question.

Idiosyncratic exchange

Interestingly, the labor market situation described by Freeman in constructing the collective voice model is very similar to that analyzed in the idiosyncratic exchange or 'obligational contracting' model of Williamson, Wachter, and Harris (1975). The essence of this treatment is that the parties to nonstandardized or idiosyncratic exchange have an incentive to regularize trading relations in labor (and product) markets. Where workers possess nonstandard or imperfectly transferable skills, the firm and the worker have an interest in devising a governance structure to assure a continuing cooperative relation between them. The idiosyncratic exchange model is discussed in more detail in Chapter 8. Here we simply note that the efficiency benefits ascribed to unionism in the collective voice view are basically those described by the governance apparatus of the internal labor market in the idiosyncratic exchange model – both have a basis in the informational problem in certain sectors of the job market. What is interesting about the latter model is that there is little explicit discussion of unions (with the exception of Williamson, 1982). Also, the institutions of the labor market – in particular, the internal labor market – are treated as outcomes resulting from optimizing behavior. In contrast, the conventional neoclassical approach studies the optimal allocation of resources, while treating labor market institutions as a datum.

One immediate problem therefore is whether the beneficial governance structures described in both the idiosyncratic exchange and collective voice literatures attach to unionism *per se* or rather vary with the continuity needs of the parties. To the extent that Freeman (1976, p.

361n) himself argues that the public goods analysis motivating collective voice applies to 'regular work relations' (i.e. where workers do not change employers frequently), there is some real ambiguity attaching to the assumed exogeneity of unionism in the collective voice model. A second and related question, given the omission of a union argument in the idiosyncratic exchange model, is the degree to which productivity gains from internal labor market structuring and formalized governance procedures are obtainable with and without unionism.[5]

In conclusion, it would appear to be the case that if we are to ascribe to unions a positive impact on productivity, we have either to explain suboptimal decisionmaking in their absence or to view unions as a partial solution to public goods problems attaching to the workplace (the collective voice/institutional response model). An additional possibility is that unions may be a more efficient monitor of managers than is achievable via direct monitoring by the principal (i.e. owner). This agency problem is discussed in some detail by Kuhn (1985), in whose model the union's lower monitoring costs lead to higher managerial effort (and higher measured labor productivity) and a positive wage effect (see also Kuhn, 1982). The higher union wage represents the nonunion wage plus compensation for the union's monitoring services. However, bargaining power again enters the picture since unions may in reality expropriate all the efficiency gains and, although increasing the size of the pie (at least in the short run), make both managers and owners worse off. In the absence of direct empirical evidence, however, we are reluctant to attach much credence to such monitoring cost arguments.

7.4 Unions, Productivity, and Productivity Growth – Evidence

In this section we examine the effects of unionism on both the level and growth rate of productivity. Our discussion is in four parts. First, we briefly examine the production function technique and methods of measurement employed in the large majority of the productivity studies. Second, we document the evidence of union impact on levels of productivity. Third, we review a very different literature that focuses on productivity growth. Finally, since the extant literature focuses on unionism's net effects, we peek inside the black box wherein union status is supposedly transformed into productivity improvement.

Measurement

The production function studies in general employ some variant of the Cobb–Douglas production function (the principal exception is Gollop,

1976, who estimates a time-series translog production function for US manufacturing, 1947–71. After Brown and Medoff (1978), the starting point is the function:

$$Q = AK^{\alpha}(L_n + cL_u)^{1-\alpha}, \tag{7.1}$$

where Q is output, K is capital, L_u and L_n are union and nonunion labor, respectively, A is a constant of proportionality, and α and $(1-\alpha)$ are the output elasticities with respect to capital and labor. The parameter c reflects productivity differences between union and nonunion labor. If $c > 1$, then union labor is more productive, in line with the collective voice/institutional response and shock effect models. If $c < 1$, then union labor is less productive, in line with conventional arguments regarding union work rules and the like.

In estimating form, Brown and Medoff approximate equation *(7.1)* by:

$$\ln(Q/L) \simeq \ln A + \alpha \ln(K/L) + (1-\alpha)(c-1)P, \tag{7.2}$$

where L is $(L_u + L_n)$ and P is union density or L_u/L.

Equation *(7.2)* is derived from *(7.1)* as follows:

$$\begin{aligned}
Q &= AK^{\alpha}[L_n + L_u + (c-1)L_u]^{1-\alpha} \\
&= AK^{\alpha}[L + (c-1)L_u]^{1-\alpha} \\
&= AK^{\alpha}L^{1-\alpha}[1+(c-1)L_u/L]^{1-\alpha} \\
&= AK^{\alpha}L^{1-\alpha}[1 + (c-1)P]^{1-\alpha}.
\end{aligned}$$

Dividing both sides by L and taking logs yields:

$$\ln(Q/L) = \ln A + \alpha \ln K - \alpha \ln L + (1-\alpha)\ln[1+(c-1)P]$$

or,

$$\ln(Q/L) = \ln A + \alpha \ln(K/L) + (1-\alpha)\ln[1+(c-1)P].$$

Using the first-order Taylor series approximation that $\ln(1+x) \simeq x$ for small values of x, we thus obtain *(7.2)*.

Equation *(7.2)* requires some amplification. First, it assumes constant returns to scale (since the sum of the output elasticities equals unity). This assumption may be relaxed by including $\ln L$(establishment size), although this variable has in fact proved insignificant in the empirical literature. Second, the coefficient on P, namely $(1-\alpha)(c-1)$, measures the logarithmic productivity differential of unionized establishments, which in percentage terms is $[e^{(1-\alpha)(c-1)}-1]100$. If we assume that the union productivity effect reflects the greater efficiency only of labor and not of all inputs, then the union productivity effect is $(c-1)$ and is calculated by dividing the coefficient on P by $(1-\alpha)$. Third, that $c > 1$ implies that unions have higher total factor productivity, TFP, can be seen by subtracting $\alpha \ln(K/L)$ from both sides of equation (7.2):

$$\ln Q - \alpha \ln K - (1-\alpha)\ln L = TFP = \ln A + (1-\alpha)(c-1)P. \quad (7.3)$$

Fourth, the $\ln(K/L)$ term in equation (7.2) controls for factor substitution attendant upon a rise in the wage rate under unionism. If this effect is not controlled for, an upward bias is likely to be imparted to the union coefficient. Similarly, another standard price-theoretic response of employers must also be accounted for, namely the employment of higher-quality labor. This is achieved either by running an auxiliary earnings function and adjusting the labor input in the production function so that workers with greater schooling, experience, and other earnings-related characteristics are weighted to represent more efficiency units, or simply by including human capital variables as additional arguments.

Before proceeding with a review of the literature, some basic limitations of the production function test given in (7.2) might usefully be introduced. They are discussed in some detail by Brown and Medoff (1978) and in the subsequent literature and may be itemized as follows:

1 The use of value added as the dependent variable confounds price and quantity effects; that is, part of the measured union productivity differential may in fact result from higher product prices in the unionized sector.[6]

2 The assumption of identical production functions in the two sectors, apart from the productivity of labor parameter ($Q_n = AK_n^\alpha L_n^{1-\alpha}$; $Q_u = AK_u^\alpha h6 (cL_u)^{1-\alpha}$), masks the possibility that the two sectors may have different production function parameters (i.e. $\alpha_u \neq \alpha_n$).

3 Union and nonunion establishments may differ systematically in the quality of management or other unmeasured organizational factors. In short, 'firm effects' may not be independent of union status.

4 Nonunion labor inputs (e.g. managerial supervision) are not adequately represented in the model. If these are correlated with the unionism variable, as might be expected on price-theoretic grounds, then the union coefficient may be upwardly biased. Thus, one cannot disentangle the direct effect of unionism *per se* from its indirect effects via management response.

With these preliminaries behind us, we can now turn to the empirical evidence directly.

Effects on productivity

The array of production function studies is summarized in Table 7.1. We discuss in turn the manufacturing/economy-wide studies and the industry-level studies.

The pioneering study is that of Brown and Medoff (1978), who estimate an equation similar to *(7.2)*, using as their unit of observation 20 two-digit SIC manufacturing industries cross-classified by 29 Current Population Survey (CPS) state groupings (they had sufficient data for 341 out of a potential 580 observations). Data are obtained directly or derived from the 1972 Census of Manufactures, the Annual Survey of Manufactures for 1964 (which provides base capital stock figures by state) through 1971, and the May 1973–5 CPS micro files. As noted in the table, the dependent variable is measured as value added per worker. Right-hand variables in addition to proportion union, $\ln(K/L)$, and $\ln(L/\text{establishment})$, are regional and industry dummies, and a variable measuring the 'recentness' of the capital stock.

Brown and Medoff obtain estimates of a positive and statistically significant effect of unions on total factor productivity of more than 20 percent in their preferred specifications. If one attributes these gains exclusively to the labor input, then the union effect on productivity is about 30 percent (i.e. the union coefficient divided by 1 minus the capital–labor ratio coefficient). The estimates shown in the table are insensitive to adjustments for labor quality, the assumption regarding returns to scale (inclusion of the $\ln(L/\text{establishment})$ term), and several other experiments for which the authors do not report detailed results (Brown and Medoff, 1978, p. 369). The union coefficient is, however, insignificantly different from zero when the 19 industry dummy variables are omitted. This result suggests that unions are organized in the less productive industries nationally, but that, *within* a given SIC industry, establishments in a highly unionized state group are more productive.

The deficiencies of the production function test noted earlier apply with some force to Brown and Medoff's study. They themselves investigate the problems associated with the assumption of identical production function parameters in union and nonunion establishments, and for all manufacturing industries and areas. It emerges after relaxing this assumption in a number of specifications that the estimated union coefficient is sensitive to different assumptions and is sharply lower in most cases. Brown and Medoff admit that it is difficult to conclude just how much of the positive union productivity effect would survive if these differences could be taken into account correctly.

Finally, Brown and Medoff (1978, p. 368) emphasize that 'the estimated productivity and the estimated wage effect are of the same

Table 7.1 *Selected production function estimates of union–nonunion productivity differences*

Study/sample	Type of data	Output measure	Union effect (logarithmic productivity differential)	
Manufacturing/economy-wide				
Brown and Medoff (1978); manufacturing, 1972	State-by-industry aggregates	Value added	0.22 to	0.24
Brown, Medoff, and Leonard (as cited in Freeman and Medoff, 1984); manufacturing	State-by-industry aggregates	Value added		
1972				0.10
1977				0.27
Clark (1984); North American manufacturing, 1970–80	Product line businesses	Value added	−0.02 to	−0.03
Warren (1985); private domestic business economy, 1948–73	Time-series	Real gross private domestic product		−0.81
Industry-level (private sector)				
Frantz (1976); wooden household furniture, 1974	Establishments	Value added		0.15
Connerton, Freeman, and Medoff (1979) – updated estimates reported in Freeman and Medoff (1984); underground bituminous coal, 1965–80	Mines	Physical output in tons		

1965			0.29	to	0.32
1970			−0.04	to	0.08
1975			−0.18	to	0.16
1980			−0.17	to	0.13
Ichniowski (1984a) paper mills, 1976–82 (monthly data)	Establishments, 10 union and 1 nonunion	Physical output in tons	0.10	to	0.15
Clark (1980a); cement, 1953–76	Before-and-after comparison of (6) establishments that changed from nonunion to union status	Physical output in tons	0.06	to	0.08
Clark (1980b); cement, 1973–76	Establishments, 9 nonunion and 119 union generating 29 and 436 observations respectively	Physical output in tons	0.07	to	0.10
Allen (1984d); construction, 1972	State-by-industry aggregates	Value added deflated by price/cost index	0.14	to	0.18
Allen (forthcoming); commercial office buildings, 1974	Structures	Square footage of projects	0.26	to	0.32
Allen (forthcoming); elementary and secondary schools, 1972	Structures	Square footage of projects	insignificant		
Industry-level (public sector)					
Ehrenberg, Sherman, and Schwarz (1983); municipal libraries, 1977	Libraries	Eight separate measures of 'output' (e.g. interlibrary loans per capita, number of borrowers per capita, total circulation per capita)	insignificant		
Noam (1983); regulatory agencies in construction, 1970	Building departments	Building permits granted or construction volume supervised	insignificant		

Note: The percentage differential can be calculated by $(e^d - 1)100$, where d is the logarithmic differential.

order of magnitude.' This finding is, frankly, implausible. Given the statement that labor's share of value added in manufacturing is 0.53, per unit costs would increase by approximately 0.53 times 0.24 (their estimate of the union wage premium), or roughly 13 percent. Yet total factor productivity is estimated to have increased by over 20 percent. Although we are unable to say anything precise about profitability in the absence of further information on the parameters of production and demand (see Clark, 1984, and the discussion below), it seems safe to conclude that these figures, if correct, would imply a significant increase in profitability. Unfortunately, as we shall see, all the available evidence suggests that unionism reduces profitability. Further doubt on the finding that union wage and productivity effects are of similar magnitude is provided by Wessels (1985). He contends that the evidence of large union productivity effects is contradicted by other evidence showing that union effects on employment are small. He concludes that one of these estimated effects must be wrong: either unions do not substantially increase productivity or they substantially reduce employment.

Subsequently, Brown, Medoff, and Leonard (as reported in Freeman and Medoff, 1984) have detected an even larger union productivity effect for 1977, although not for 1972. (But note that this study employs a different measure of capital from that utilized by Brown and Medoff.) Similar reservations hold with respect to these estimates.

Clark (1984) reports small negative union productivity effects, using the 1970–80 Profit Impact of Market Strategy (PIMS) sample of some 902 product-line business units of large manufacturing companies. Clark's data set includes 4,681 observations since reporting by the companies is voluntary and many do not report yearly. (We shall again encounter Clark's study in subsequent subsections because he examines union impact along two additional dimensions of economic performance.) His productivity equation regresses the log of output (value added or sales) per worker on a union dummy, $\ln(K/L)$, and a plethora of firm- and industry-level control variables. As can be seen from the table, Clark finds that unionized firms have 2–3 percent *lower* productivity, a result that is insensitive to specification. Although the magnitude of this estimate is small and is at most marginally significant, it stands in marked contrast to the large positive productivity effects estimated by Brown and Medoff (and Brown, Medoff, and Leonard) for manufacturing. Clark's productivity finding is consistent with the theoretical model of a vertical contract curve in which unions have no effect on output or employment, but simply redistribute profits to labor (for an amplification of this model, see Chapter 2).

The suggestion of widespread beneficial union productivity effects is further undermined by Warren's (1985) findings. Warren estimates an economy-wide, time-series variant of the Brown–Medoff Cobb–Douglas production function for the US over the period 1948–73. He obtains a negative and statistically significant coefficient on union membership, suggesting that increases in unionization markedly decrease labor productivity. The finding that union labor is less productive than nonunion labor contradicts the results reported above obtained with cross-section manufacturing data, but is consistent with Gollop's (1976) estimates (not reported in the table) from a time-series translog production function for US manufacturing, 1947–71. Gollop includes four inputs – labor, capital, intermediate goods, and energy – and seeks to measure the impact of union coverage (and strikes) on productivity. He finds that union coverage significantly decreases factor productivity, as manifested in outward shifts of the production isoquants.[7]

Turning next to the industry-level studies, we distinguish between the private and public sectors. Of the private sector studies, only one, namely Frantz's (1976) investigation of establishments in wooden household furniture, uses a value-added measure of output or otherwise fails to correct for price and productivity effects. The studies by Clark (1980a, b) of the cement industry, on the other hand, represent a state of the art treatment in their attempt to control for the remaining biases noted in our remarks on measurement. Thus, Clark allows the production function parameters to vary between union and nonunion plants, controls for 'firm effects', and introduces a nonunion labor input (the ratio of supervisory to production worker hours) to disentangle the direct effect of unionism from its indirect effects via management response.

Clark (1980b) does not find strong evidence of statistically significant union productivity effects in the cement industry, which may in part be explained by the fact that nonunion establishments constitute only some 6 percent of his sample observations. The most significantly positive union effects appear to be in the southwest, where nonunion firms are most prevalent. One possible interpretation of this particular result is that positive productivity effects stimulated by union wage gains are largest when competitive pressures are most severe.

Somewhat stronger results are reported in Clark's (1980a) time-series study of six cement plants that over the sample period 1953–76 changed from nonunion to union status. The measured union productivity differential of approximately 6–8 percent is marginally significant and, moreover, does not appear to vary much over time. His results are thus consistent with the view that unionization of a plant and accompanying wage increases induce a response by management that yields a modest productivity advance that is maintained through time.[8] Unfortunately, Clark's sample of firms does not encompass plants changing union status in a reverse direction, although there is no presumption that such a change would result in a symmetrical decrease in productivity.

Clark's findings are also consistent with the view that unionism has little effect on unit costs. He estimates a union wage effect ranging from 12 to 18 percent and labor's share at around 0.43. Thus, a 6–8 percent productivity increase, in line with his actual estimate, would just offset the wage increase and leave unit costs approximately unchanged.

Of the other Harvard studies shown in Table 7.1, perhaps the most interesting is that of Connerton, Freeman, and Medoff (1979). They detect a large productivity advantage among union mines in 1965, but this was virtually eliminated by 1970, and by 1975 a substantial negative differential had opened up. The authors attribute this abrupt reversal of the union effect to the emergence of serious industrial relations problems in the industry associated with younger and less experienced supervisors, the emergence of internal problems within the United Mine Workers union, and the failure of the national bargaining framework to adapt to increasingly complex problems at the local level. While the negative union effect sharply differentiates this study from the other industry-level studies shown in the table, it graphically illustrates the point that union effects are not a datum.[9]

Further evidence of this diversity is reported by Allen (forthcoming), who finds very different union effects in two branches of construction: a productivity effect of at least 30 percent for office buildings but one that is effectively zero for schools. This latter case might better be considered a public sector study. Although the construction industry is private, there may be decreased competition, less monitoring, and more rents to capture on public sector projects (also see Allen, 1984a, d). Note also the findings of an earlier construction study by Mandelstamm (1965) that presaged the production function literature. Mandelstamm elicited contractor bid prices during 1957 for a standard small house in two Michigan cities, one of which was highly unionized. His findings, based on these hypothetical rather than actual cost figures, point to unionized labor being more productive than nonunion labor.

Turning finally to the public sector studies, in almost no case is there evidence of a positive union productivity differential. The pioneering public sector study is that of Ehrenberg, Sherman, and Schwarz (1983), who employ a reduced-form output equation based on a model of the equilibrium level of public services, in addition to the now conventional production function test. In this model, which is estimated across some 260 municipal libraries in 1977, it is assumed that demand is set equal to average costs to yield the optimal level of library output. Unions affect output through their wage and productivity effects on average costs. The inclusion of a wage variable in the reduced-form output equation implies that the coefficient on a union status variable will pick up the net effect of unions on productivity. If the wage variable is excluded, inferences may still be drawn about union impact on productivity, after suitable correction is made for worker quality differences. Thus, if it is found that unionism does not affect output but does raise wages, it may be inferred that unions also raise productivity, since the indirect negative effect of unions on output via increased average costs has been offset by factors directly increasing output. In any event, the authors find that unions in their municipal libraries sample have affected neither wages nor output, the one exception among some eight measures of library 'output' being interlibrary loans, where a small union productivity differential is observed. These results hold for both the reduced-form output and production function models.

Similar findings with respect to the union output effect are reported in a study by Sloan and Adamache (1984; not reported in the table), using wage and cost data for 367 hospitals in 1974 and 1977. The authors do not examine productivity directly, but instead seek to infer union net effects from a model of hospital costs that includes a predicted wage variable and a union status variable. The argument, analogous to that employed in Ehrenberg, Sherman, and Schwarz, is that unions affect costs directly via their wage effects and indirectly via their productivity effects. Unlike the municipal libraries study, however, Sloan and Adamache find that unions raise wages significantly in their hospitals sample: after correction for selectivity bias, it is found that the overall impact of unions on the pay of all hospital employees (other than doctors) is 8.8 percent. This wage effect adds significantly to hospital costs, whereas the coefficient on union status is insignificant. Sloan and Adamache thus conclude that unions influence hospital costs solely through their impact on wages. Costs are raised by 3.5–4.1 percent according to whether output is measured by adjusted patient days or adjusted admissions. The cost effects differ markedly by department, ranging from 0.6 percent for plant operations to 8.9 percent for housekeeping services. That said, the authors are at pains to point out that the cost-inflating role of unionism is minor when compared with the contribution of other factors – in particular, health insurance.

Finally, Noam's (1983) illuminating study of the effects of unionism on productivity within a sample of 1,100 building departments in 1970 is based on a more conventional production function test. Output is defined either by the number of building permits issued or by the total construction volume supervised by these regulatory agencies. Noam attempts to provide a simultaneous analysis of the wage and productivity effects of unionism, but his study is more notable for its public choice theoretic variables (see Chapter 9). He finds that unions raise salaries by approximately 18 percent, *ceteris paribus*, but their impact on productivity is insignificant – a result that is invariant to specification.

The evidence surveyed above points to a wide diversity of findings regarding unionism's impact on productivity. This is not altogether unexpected at the industry level. More worrying, however, is the disagreement among studies using manufacturing data and the evidence from economy-wide, time-series studies that appears flatly to contradict the notion that unions in general raise productivity. As we shall see subsequently, other time-series data cast further doubt on the robustness and generality of the unions-raise-productivity thesis.

The sources of productivity improvement

The data presented in Table 7.1 simply identify net effects. As Brown and Medoff (1978, p. 374) themselves state: 'The idea that unions make firms . . . more productive would be more persuasive if the mechanisms by which productivity is improved could be isolated.' It is of course a central tenet of the new view of unions that the substitution of collective voice for classical exit behavior will reduce quits and improve morale and cooperation among workers. Similarly, related theoretical arguments suggest that improved governance structures in jobs characterized by public goods and production complementarities can lead to productivity gains. What, then, can be said about the specific routes through which unionism affects productivity?

In general, the cross-section evidence reveals that quits are indeed significantly lower among union workers, after taking into account earnings, the alternative wage, and other arguments (Freeman, 1980a, 1980b; Blau and Kahn, 1981, 1983; Mincer, 1983). Furthermore, longitudinal analyses by Freeman (1980b) and Mincer (1983) seeking to control for person-specific effects reveal that for given workers the likelihood of quitting decreases for union joiners and increases for union leavers. There is some ambiguity, however, as to the wage effect in longitudinal analyses of quits. Freeman (1980b), for example, finds that the coefficient on wages in his quits equation changes from negative and significant in a cross-section to positive and insignificant in the fixed effects model, suggesting that it is more unionism *per se* than higher wages that reduces quits. Mincer (1983), on the other hand, reports that both unionization and the union wage premium lead to a reduction in quits.

The production function studies reported in the table do not in general seek to identify the sources of productivity improvement. However, Brown and Medoff do introduce a quits variable into their production function and attribute the reduction in the union coefficient to the effects of lower quits on productivity. This procedure reduces the union coefficient by one-fifth – the residual four-fifths presumably are associated with 'better management, morale, motivation, communication, etc.' (Brown and Medoff, 1978, p. 374). In sharp contrast with the economy-wide studies reviewed above, Clark (1980a) reports either no change or even higher quits following unionization in three of the six cement plants he followed over time.

One obvious route through which union voice might improve productivity is the establishment of procedures to handle grievances. Few would question the proposition that worker performance is positively affected by quality-of-work factors. For example, Katz, Kochan, and Gobeille (1983) and Ichniowski (1984a), using data on union plants at General Motors and from ten unionized paper mills, respectively, find the number of grievances to be inversely related to productivity. Left unanswered in such comparisons, however, is the effectiveness of union voice in reducing and/or arbitrating grievances relative to the *unobserved* grievances occurring in otherwise similar nonunion plants.

One interesting result in the literature is that unionism seems to be associated with *lower* job satisfaction (Borjas, 1979; Freeman, 1978; Kochan, 1980), which at first blush may appear inconsistent with the union voice hypothesis. This finding, however, is explained as a direct result of the increased reliance on voice in unionized settings, since formal grievance procedures may make workers more conscious of job problems and more willing to express discontent (Freeman, 1976, 1978). Relatedly, one could argue that there are basic differences in job satisfaction and preferences for unionization between union and nonunion workers, thus making direct comparisons in job satisfaction across the two sectors less meaningful.

A recent study by Leigh (1984a) shows support for this latter interpretation of the evidence. Using data drawn from the Young Men's National Longitudinal Survey (NLS) on the voting responses of union and nonunion workers to a hypothetical union representation election, Leigh compares the relationship between willingness to express job-related discontent and preferences for union representation among the two groups. He argues that the degree of job dissatisfaction, after controlling for job characteristics such as pay and working conditions, can be taken as a proxy for the willingness of workers to express discontent. Leigh reports significant differences between the two groups of workers. For nonunion workers, increased job dissatisfaction (discontent) is associated with a weaker preference for remaining nonunion or, equivalently, an increased demand for unionism. Among union workers, however, both dissatisfied and highly satisfied workers express a preference for remaining unionized. The differences between union and nonunion workers are most pronounced for dissatisfied workers and least pronounced for relatively satisfied workers. Leigh contends that this evidence provides indirect support for the collective voice view that unionism encourages the expression of discontent.

Although the job satisfaction evidence can be interpreted as broadly consistent with the voice interpretation of how unions function, we still might expect to observe more positive and direct indications of the operation of collective voice. Further unease results from Allen's (1984b) finding that absenteeism is at least 30 percent *higher* among union workers. Allen interprets this result to mean that unionism may not be successful in changing working conditions that produce job dissatisfaction and thus lead to higher absenteeism. We should also note, however, that Allen reports that the decrease in productivity resulting from increased absenteeism is probably quite small – a fraction of 1 percent.

What of the other routes through which a union productivity effect might manifest itself? On the basis of interviews from among his sample of cement plants before and after unionism, Clark (1980a) finds that management adjustments to unionism exhibit some fairly consistent patterns (although no systematic improvement in worker 'morale' is detected). In all six cases, new plant managers were hired, and in most cases there was increased emphasis on cutting costs, establishing production targets and goals, and improving monitoring and communication. These responses appear on the surface more to support the traditional 'shock' effect interpretation of unionism than the collective voice view.

By contrast, in the construction industry, Allen (1984d) discerns no evidence of higher managerial efficiency (as measured by salary) in more heavily unionized settings. In fact, Allen does not attribute the higher productivity of unionized construction workers to union voice, most notably of course because union workers are attached more to their trade than to any individual employer. Rather, he argues that the union hiring hall and uniform wage scales economize on search time for both parties, while union status provides a productivity quality signal or trademark. Having said this, Allen is unable to proxy this effect with either precision or success in his regression analysis.

In sum, a glimpse inside the black box of union-induced productivity improvement reveals few insights into the behavioral changes resulting from unionism. Apart from the evidence on quits and grievances, direct empirical support for the collective voice explanation of productivity change is far from overwhelming. Subsequently, we contend that management response to decreased profit expectations under unionism may provide the primary explanation for observed productivity improvements in the union sector.

Unions and productivity growth

Interestingly, there is little discussion in the unions-raise-productivity literature of a very different set of research findings on union impact revealed in research and development (R&D) studies of total factor productivity growth (but see Freeman and Medoff, 1984, Chapter 12). This literature is primarily concerned with modeling the impact of R&D on the growth in total factor productivity, but all studies that include unionism as a control variable report negative and often significant coefficients on the level of unionization (e.g. Mansfield, 1980; Terleckyj, 1980; Link, 1981; Sveikauskas and Sveikauskas, 1982).[10]

Following the approach developed by Terleckyj (1974), the R&D studies assume a three-factor Cobb–Douglas production function written in terms of output, Q, physical capital, K, and technical capital, T:

$$Q = Ae^{\lambda t}K^{\alpha}L^{(1-\alpha)}T^{\beta}, \qquad (7.4)$$

where A is a constant, λ is a disembodied rate of growth parameter, α and β are output elasticities, and t represents time.

Defining total factor productivity as a Solow-type residual, namely $TFP = \ln Q - \alpha \ln K - (1-\alpha)\ln L$, we see that:

$$TFP = \ln A + \lambda t + \beta \ln T. \qquad (7.5)$$

The time derivative of TFP, ϱ, which measures the growth rate in total factor productivity is therefore:

$$\varrho = \lambda + \beta(dT/dt)/T, \qquad (7.6)$$

where $\beta = (\partial Q/\partial T)(T/Q)$.

Thus

$$\varrho = \lambda + \Phi(dT/dt)/Q, \qquad (7.7)$$

where Φ is $\partial Q/\partial T$, the marginal product of technical capital, and dT/dt approximates net investments into the stock of R&D. The variable $(dT/dt)/Q$ is typically measured by R&D investment intensity – dollars of expenditure divided by sales.

As noted earlier, the R&D studies typically include the level of unionization as a control variable and find that total factor productivity growth is slower in industries and firms with higher levels of unionism. Are the results of these studies *necessarily* inconsistent with the results of the Harvard studies? The latter studies imply that the *level* of TFP is higher in unionized settings while the R&D studies find that TFP *growth* is lower the greater the extent of unionism. Hirsch and Link (1984) show that these results need not be inconsistent. If one specifies the standard Harvard model in difference form, then changes in total factor productivity should be a function of *changes* in union density, ΔP. They thus estimate the equation:

$$\varrho = \lambda + (1-\alpha)(c-1)\Delta P + \Phi(dT/dt)/Q, \qquad (7.8)$$

using data from 19 two-digit manufacturing industries over the period 1957–73. However, contrary to the prediction of the collective voice model, they report that total factor productivity growth is negatively related to the change in unionism. When the authors also include a level of unionism variable, both it and the change in unionism are negatively and significantly related to total factor productivity growth. Although their sample is highly aggregated and of very small size, Hirsch and Link's results imply that unionism not only reduces total factor productivity (as reflected in the sign of the union change variable), but also slows the rate of productivity increase. (See also the analysis by Kendrick and Grossman, 1980, which Hirsch and Link, 1984, p. 34n, believe to be unreliable.)

Related yet somewhat different results are reported in an empirical study by Maki (1983a) of the growth in TFP in Canadian manufacturing, 1926–78, although Maki also reaches the conclusion that unions on balance retard total factor productivity growth. Maki argues that unions have both impact or shock effects and longer-term effects. He anticipates that the impact effects will be positive whereas the longer-term effects (e.g. legacy or heritage effects of work rules) will be negative. The former effects are proxied by annual changes in unionization while the latter are measured by levels of unionization. Maki finds that these predictions are borne out in the data. It takes 5–8 years (the coefficient on the change in unionization divided by that on the level of unionization) for the positive impact effect of any given increase in unionization on disembodied growth to be offset by the longer-term effect of unionism in slowing growth.

We believe the results reported by Hirsch and Link (1984) and Maki (1983a), taken in conjunction with Warren's (1985) time-series evidence reported earlier, cast considerable doubt on the robustness and generality of the cross-section findings of the Harvard studies. The scale of this challenge might be somewhat attenuated were we able to go beyond the net effects and identify the specific routes of productivity improvement. As we have seen, however, little progress has been made in this area. That unions may even impact negatively on long-term performance and productivity growth appears to us a strong possibility and one closely related to union effects on firm profitability.

Interpretation

Despite the disparate findings of the productivity studies, two patterns are, we believe, discernible in the literature. First, estimated productivity effects appear to be largest in those industries where union–nonunion wage differentials are most pronounced. The largest union wage and productivity effects are found in construction (Allen, 1983a, 1984d), moderate effects on both are detected in the cement industry (Clark, 1980a,b), while no positive productivity or wage effects are discernible in public libraries (Ehrenberg, Sherman, and Schwarz, 1983) or British coalfields (Pencavel, 1977).

Second, and relatedly, measured union productivity effects appear to be restricted to the private sector and are largest where competitive pressures are most intense. This latter point was noted by Clark (1980b), who found the largest union productivity effect in the southwest region of his sample where nonunion competition was most pronounced, and by Mandelstamm (1965) who identified competition from outside contractors as the chief source of greater efficiency observed in his more highly unionized submarket. Indeed, one might view the large union–nonunion productivity differential in construction as a response to both large wage differentials and a large (and growing) nonunion sector (for an analysis of the recent decline in construction industry productivity, see Allen, 1984e). By contrast, in the hospital industry and among government bureaus, where competitive pressure is typically weak, no productivity effect is observable despite the presence of a significant union wage premium (Sloan and Adamache, 1984; Noam, 1983). In a more direct test of this thesis, Allen (1984a) concludes that union contractors are much more productive on privately owned than on publicly owned construction projects in the hospital and nursing home industry.

That said, there is little doubt that the large productivity gains attributed to unionism by Brown and Medoff (1978) and others across manufacturing industry as a whole are of an implausible magnitude. This interpretation is underscored by the economy-wide, time-series production function studies of Gollop (1976) and Warren (1985) in which union labor is shown to be *less* productive than nonunion labor; by productivity growth studies that include a change in unionism variable (e.g. Hirsch and Link, 1984); and by the unanimous finding of the profits literature, reviewed below, that unions reduce profitability. Indeed, our reading of the evidence leads us to conclude that the *average* union productivity effect is just as likely to be negative as positive.

Moreover, the argument that unions raise productivity (in a static if not a dynamic context) appears to us to owe more to traditional shock effects than to the expression of collective voice. Although unionism does appear to reduce quits, independent of the wage differential, there is little evidence to show that this or indeed any other voice mechanism is the primary source of the measured productivity gain. Furthermore, higher absenteeism if not lower job satisfaction among union workers makes us wary of accepting the union voice argument in an unqualified fashion. Union productivity gains appear to be generated by management responses to unionism not so much because of improved voice as in response to situations in the private sector where there are large wage increases, significant nonunion competition, and deteriorating profit expectations.

Although we have no difficulty with the conclusion that union wage gains lead to price-theoretic adjustments, and also shock management so that greater output is obtained from given quantities of inputs, we are not completely comfortable with the X-efficiency argument. Unionized firms may on average derive greater physical output from a given set of inputs but in so doing forgo other valued outputs. In these circumstances, it is doubtful that large efficiency gains are available to the parties, and this conclusion is reinforced for the case of society at large. Our conclusion is, then, that evidence of a union productivity effect is underwhelming, and that those productivity gains that do exist are most likely attributable to management's response to decreased profit expectations. It is to the evidence on unions and profitability that we turn next.

7.5 Unions and Profitability

Union rent seeking: what are the routes?

Union wage gains must come at the expense of either nonunion labor in the form of lower wages, consumers through higher product prices, or capital owners via lower rates of profit. Each route is circumscribed by the forces of competition. Large wage differentials between similarly skilled union and nonunion workers tend to be partially eroded by selective hiring, threat effects raising wages in the nonunion sector, and cost advantages enjoyed by nonunion firms. Cost increases cannot easily be passed through to consumers in the form of higher prices unless a union has organized an entire industry or local market where exclusion of foreign and nonunion competitors is possible. And, as discussed in Section 6.7, the conventional wisdom has it that the share of profits in national income is too small to be the primary source for union gains.

(Conversely, even modest union wage gains at the expense of profits will show up as large percentage decreases in profits.)

It is within this context that the unions-raise-productivity literature was initially received. Brown and Medoff (1978, p. 377), who estimate union productivity and union wage effects of roughly equal magnitude, conclude: 'Union and nonunion establishments (in U.S. manufacturing) can compete in the same product market despite the fact that the former pay their workers more because unionized workers (establishments) are more productive by roughly offsetting amounts.' As we saw earlier, their estimates, if correct, would most probably imply higher profitability under unionism. The more important point here is that a union-induced productivity gain does *not* in and of itself imply increased profits, a fact commonly missed even by antagonists of the new view of unions (e.g. Burton and Tullock, 1983).

The relationship between the rate of return on capital and union effects on wages and factor productivity is in fact rather complex (Clark, 1984). Only where the factor mix is not affected by union wage increases (e.g. where bargaining outcomes lie on a vertical contract curve and not on the demand curve) can one directly translate unit cost changes into profit rate changes. For example, assuming an unchanged factor mix and that labor's share is 0.70, a union wage increase of 10 percent coupled with an increase in factor productivity of 7 percent would leave both unit costs and the profit rate unchanged. In general, however, union effects on profitability depend not only on their wage and productivity effects, but also on the parameters of production and demand – in particular, product demand elasticity (and thus market structure), labor's share in total cost, and changes in the capital stock due to substitution and scale effects (see Clark, 1984). Hence the need for direct empirical evidence on unions and profitability.

If unions are to obtain rents from *potential* firm profits, the source of these rents is likely to be supra-competitive or above-normal profits resulting from market power or governmental regulation and quasi- or Ricardian rents deriving from fixed capital and firm-specific advantages (e.g. location, R&D, and the like).[11] We briefly discuss each of these potential sources.

Governmental regulation that simultaneously restricts entry and price competition (by means of rate setting) can create a potential pool of economic profits that may be captured in part by labor. This is precisely what happened in the US airline and trucking industries (Olson and Trapani, 1981; Moore, 1978), evidence of which is provided by widespread union wage concessions and membership losses following deregulation of these industries.

Unions may also be expected to capture some share of economic profits associated with market power. The relationship between profits and market power is disputed by economists at the levels of theory and evidence (for a summary, see Scherer, 1980). The most commonly used measures of market structure – industry concentration ratios and firm market share – need not (and many would argue typically do not) measure market power or potential profits. The ambiguity that attaches to the profits–market power relationship in industrial organization studies is also evident in the recent union and profits literature (reviewed below). However, the issue is of some importance. If unions decrease profitability primarily or exclusively in, say, highly concentrated industries with above-normal returns, their negative effects on long-run growth and performance may be less important. As we shall see, evidence on this point is far from conclusive.

While union capture of profits associated with market power may have relatively benign effects, no such presumption applies if quasi-rents from fixed physical and intangible capital investments provide the major source for union rent seeking. The case of physical capital is discussed in Baldwin's (1983) amplification of Simons' (1944) analysis of the market power of trade unions. When the capital replacement cycle is long relative to the union's time horizon, the 'surplus' that provides the return on durable and specialized capital, and that occurs only after costs are sunk, is vulnerable to capture by monopoly labor. Informed investors respond rationally by decreasing investment and maintaining inefficient plant in production so as to discourage higher wage demands. Specifically, Baldwin shows that a firm may have increased incentive to develop labor-intensive rather than labor-saving technologies and to maintain some inefficient plant, since technology with a high marginal cost of output provides an effective deterrent to inflated wage demands. (We note that Baldwin believes her model to be particularly applicable to the US steel industry.) Of course this low-investment strategy, although protecting investors' returns, is costly because it reduces productivity and the incentives to innovate and grow. As a result, both sides have an incentive to design alternative methods of contract enforcement that might effectively extend workers' horizons or otherwise more closely match their interests with those of the firm.

Using similar reasoning, Connolly, Hirsch, and Hirschey (CHH, 1985) develop a rent-seeking model in which unions capture returns from intangible capital investments; in particular, research and development (R&D) expenditures. In their model, unions capture some portion of the returns from intangible capital investments that are long-lived and nonmarketable. Thus, unions are able to capture a portion of rents accruing from nontransferable firm-specific product and process innovations resulting from R&D. By contrast, unions are less able to capture rents resulting from marketable patents or short-lived advertising capital. CHH predict (and find) that investors place a lower stock

210

market value on R&D investments by union firms than by otherwise similar nonunion enterprises. Consequently, union firms invest less intensively in R&D. They find no such union effect with respect to advertising and 'unanticipated' patents (those not predicted by R&D spending and other variables).

Both the Baldwin and CHH models of union rent seeking suggest that unions have a real effect on capital investment, leading to too little investment and reduced long-run growth. Note, however, that such an outcome is 'inefficient' for *both* parties (see Section 2.2). The firm and union members could be better off maximizing the size of the pie and then bargaining over division of the pie. CHH liken union rent seeking to a tax on profits that can be either lump-sum (in the special case of settlements on a vertical contract curve) or distortionary (if union gains vary directly with firm investment behavior). However, we doubt whether efficient contracts can evolve and be enforced in settings where the capital replacement cycle is long and the enforceability of property rights is costly (on this issue see Baldwin, 1983; CHH, 1985; Pakes and Nitzan, 1983).

For those who believe that economic profits cannot be sustained indefinitely, including those associated with market share or concentration, decreased profit expectations associated with union rent seeking are believed likely to decrease investment and long-run growth. Hence, empirical evidence as to overall union effects on profits, as well as the routes through which rents are obtained, must be examined alongside the productivity evidence considered previously.

What is the evidence?

Rather surprisingly, empirical studies examining union effects on profitability have become available only recently. They have been authored primarily by labor economists interested in union impact on economic performance and not by researchers in the industrial organization area where profitability studies have long been commonplace. Despite substantial differences in methodology, data sources, units of observation, and measures of profitability, all studies of which we are aware find unionism to be associated with lower profits.

The US studies include: Freeman (1983a), Karier (1985), and Voos and Mishel (1985), who use aggregate manufacturing data and the price–cost margin (similar to a rate of return on sales) as a profitability measure; Clark (1984), who uses accounting profit measures (rates of return on capital and sales) for his sample of product-line businesses; Salinger (1984), Hirsch and Connolly (1985), and Connolly, Hirsch and Hirschey (1985), who use manufacturing firm data and similar forward-looking stock market measures of profitability (Tobin's q in the first two studies and excess value divided by sales in the latter); and Ruback and Zimmerman (1984), who analyze stock price changes in response to National Labor Relations Board (NLRB) certification and representation election results.[12] We now turn to a more detailed examination of these studies.

A particularly important paper in this area is that of Clark (1984), primarily because of its attempt to investigate union impact along a number of dimensions of firm performance (productivity, profits, and growth). Focusing here on the profits analysis, Clark reports evidence of significantly negative union effects. After including an extensive array of firm, worker, industry, and market structure controls, unionism is found to decrease the pre-tax rate of return on capital by 4.1 percentage points, or by 19 percent relative to the sample mean. Rather more dramatic results are obtained when Clark partitions his sample into firms possessing 'low' or 'high' market shares (less than 10 percent and greater than 35 percent shares, respectively). For firms with *low* market shares, unions reduce profits by 4.7 percentage points or by 40 percent relative to the sample mean of 11.1 percent! No change is discernible in the case of high market share firms, which earn a mean rate of return of 34.7 percent. However, Clark's surprising result with respect to market share finds no support elsewhere, which raises the question of the representativeness and accuracy of the PIMS data.

Freeman (1983a), using data from the Survey of Manufactures for 1958–76 and from the Internal Revenue Service (IRS) for 1965–76, also finds that significant decreases in industry profitability result from increased union density. In apparent contrast to Clark, however, this reduction in profits is restricted almost entirely to highly concentrated industries. Freeman concludes that unions effectively capture rents associated with market power, as proxied by concentration, and that previous profitability studies in the industrial organization area are seriously flawed owing to their omission of a union variable. An identical conclusion is reached by Karier (1985), who uses 1972 state-by-manufacturing industry data provided by Brown and Medoff. Voos and Mishel (1985), who allow for the simultaneous determination of profitability and unionism, find an even stronger negative impact of unionism in their profits equation where the union variable is endogenous. Unlike Freeman and Karier, they (fn. 5) do not conclude that unions' major impact on profits is in highly concentrated industries. Finally, Salinger (1984) concludes that investor-determined market value (Tobin's q) is reduced by unions most sharply among firms in concentrated industries and contends that unions capture most of the monopoly rents in the American economy. (Because monopoly rents are small to begin with and because of a complex set of interactions in his nonlinear profits equation, we are not convinced that his interpretation of the results is correct.)

Like Salinger's, the papers by Hirsch and Connolly (1985) and Connolly, Hirsch and Hirschey (CHH, 1985) use firm data (367 firms drawn from the 1977 *Fortune* 500) and stock market value measures of profitability (the market value measure in the latter paper is highly correlated with Tobin's q; $r = .94$). However, the focus and results of these papers differ from those of the previous studies. Although they find unions to be associated with lower overall profitability, the effect is estimated to be smaller (and often insignificant) and sensitive to specification. Unlike the other studies, Hirsch and Connolly examine the union interaction with both industry concentration and firm market share. Using Leamer's (1978) SEARCH analysis, these relationships are found to be sensitive to specification and one's priors; they find only weak evidence that unions decrease profits more among firms with high market shares and no evidence that unions capture profits from concentration.

The primary focus of the CHH paper is on the ability of unions to capture rents associated with intangible capital investments in R&D. Consistent with their model, they find that R&D adds significantly less to the market value of union firms and that such firms invest less intensively in R&D. These results support the belief that unions act as a distortionary tax on firm rents rather than as a neutral lump-sum tax. They find no evidence that unions are able to capture rents associated with short-lived advertising expenditures or with marketable patents.

Finally, in an innovative study, Ruback and Zimmerman (1984) relate stock price movements to NLRB certification and representation election outcomes. Consistent with the more direct evidence reviewed above, they report substantial decreases in equity value associated with union representation. Particularly interesting is the finding that investors are reasonably good at predicting the outcome of representation elections and that both union wins and losses decrease market value, losses by a much smaller amount. Their interpretation of this latter finding is that an NLRB election loss still signifies some possibility of there being a future election or that the holding of an election signals to investors the existence of labor relations problems within the firm.

Implications

We believe several tentative conclusions may be offered in the light of the profit studies. First, management reticence to embrace unions is a rational response to decreased profit expectations. Second, while some positive union productivity effects are both possible and likely, they are not sufficient to offset the increase in costs from union wage increases and possible increases in capital stock (for an identical conclusion, see Freeman and Medoff, 1984). Third, such large and widespread productivity effects as reported by Brown and Medoff (1978) are implausible in the light of the consistently negative union effect on profits found in these studies.

Less settled, however, are the routes through which unions capture rents and the effect of decreased profits on long-run productivity and sales growth. Freeman, Karier, and Salinger provide arguments and evidence that unions primarily capture monopoly rents associated with industry concentration, but we remain unconvinced. Our unease stems in part from the fragility of these relationships, as evidenced by the Hirsch and Connolly study. More fundamental, however, is the general lack of corroborative evidence. As pointed out in Hirsch and Connolly, if unions capture rents associated with concentration, this should be manifested in larger union–nonunion compensation (wages plus fringes) differentials among workers in more concentrated industries. But, as seen in Chapter 5, the evidence is that the compensation differential is no greater (indeed, perhaps smaller) in highly concentrated industries. Of course, increased compensation could take the form of improved working conditions or enhanced job security among union workers in concentrated industries. Yet we know of no such evidence. In addition, economists do not even agree that concentration makes possible greater profits, although here Freeman and Karier are surely correct that the neglect of unions in this literature calls into question the status of previous empirical studies.

We find particularly intriguing CHH's suggestion that unions capture rents associated with long-lived non-transferable capital investments and that effective union rent seeking has real effects on firm investment behavior. Although we are reluctant to place too much emphasis on the results of any single study, their findings, if correct, imply that unions may impact negatively on long-run growth. As seen earlier, results reported in the productivity growth studies do not encourage us to take a sanguine view of the long-run implications of unionism. That said, evidence of union effects on sales or output growth is sparse. While Clark (1984), Freeman and Medoff (1984), and CHH (1985) find the growth in sales or value added to be negatively related to unionization, all conclude that this relationship is quite weak.

In the end, interpretation of the union–profits nexus may depend most crucially on one's priors regarding the importance of X-efficiency and the sustainability of above-normal profits. If one believes that many firms operate with substantial slack or inefficiency and that economic profits can be sustained over long periods of time, then union rent seeking may be largely benign and may even act to improve productivity, redistributing rents from owners to workers but registering little impact on long-run investment and growth. By contrast, if one views the economy as highly competitive in a dynamic context so that slack and economic profits are relatively short-lived, effective union rent seeking (where possible) is likely to impact negatively on investment behavior and long-run economic performance. We readily admit that our own leanings are toward this latter view. However, the need for further evidence in this area is obvious.

7.6 Final Reflections

In this chapter, we have examined the impact of unionism on economic performance. It now seems clear that the (static) allocative costs of unionism are of more modest magnitude than was earlier thought to be the case. It also seems that the scale of output losses stemming from the union 'rule book' and strikes have been somewhat overstated. (Note that this interpretation is applicable to the US situation. Pending empirical analysis of union effects in countries with a more strongly entrenched craft system and higher union density, we are reluctant to generalize this statement.)

On the benefits side, we have reviewed an important theoretical and empirical literature that exploits the public goods dimensions of the workplace to argue that unions raise productivity, other things being equal. Our conclusion is that both the orthodox literature and the new collective voice literature have alternately exaggerated the costs and benefits of unionism. The collective voice model has rightly emphasized that unionism need not necessarily detract from productivity, and this is an important finding in itself. What is in doubt is the generality and robustness of the unions-raise-productivity thesis. Equally important, it is not clear how the productivity gains reported in the least controversial studies have arisen. Our own interpretation is that the evidence is more consistent with a shock effect than with union voice.

Having said this, we have also investigated union impact on productivity growth and profitability. The results of the profitability studies are particularly disturbing. If unions do in fact reduce present and future rates of profit (even assuming such reductions are concentrated among firms with market power), then long-run investment in R&D and physical capital may well decline. The time-series evidence pointing to negative union effects on productivity and productivity growth lends support to this view.

We have sought to accentuate the positive in discussing the new view of unions, even though we have just argued that the longer-term effects of unionism are not encouraging. It may of course be objected that the positive union productivity results offered by supporters of the collective voice model are a chimera. But such objections have to be confronted with data. To their credit, the Harvard analysts have done this, even though their findings are not particularly compelling.

For the future, two general areas of research are warranted. The first concerns the specific channels or mechanisms through which unionism affects the workplace. Such research should seek to distinguish between the effects of unionism *per se* and the effects of governance structures achievable in the absence of unionism. To what extent is unionism necessary to achieve rules leading to efficient contracts? Does unionism provide a more effective voice than does the market or any alternative agent? Or does the legal environment artificially create a public goods case for unionism? Finally, and relatedly, since unionism is clearly much more likely and effective in some job settings than others, future research must at some point address more adequately the statistical problems arising from the simultaneous determination of unionism and union effects on the workplace (see Freeman and Medoff, 1983) and of unionism, working conditions, and productivity (see Duncan and Stafford, 1980).

A second major area of future research concerns the longer-term or dynamic effects of unionism. Much more information is required on profit and growth effects. Moreover, any such investigation should encompass union activities in nonpecuniary markets. The main issue here is whether or not the pursuit by unions of their sectional interests in political markets has adverse consequences for economic performance. A subsidiary question is whether or not unions' political activities dilute membership control. Discussion of these issues is remitted to our final chapter.

Notes

1 The pioneering study is that of Slichter, Healy, and Livernash (1960). Recent evidence is surveyed by Freeman and Medoff (1984) and Addison and Hirsch (1984). Our discussion relies heavily on the latter paper. Further commentary is provided in Addison (1985) and Hirsch (1985).

2 See, for example, Tullock (1967), Krueger (1974), Posner (1975), and Bellante and Long (1981).

3 Although the market may 'fail' in the presence of public goods, the collectively determined outcome from the median voter model is not generally the efficient outcome since the intensity of preferences is not fully reflected in the process (see Chapter 2).

4 There is, of course, no guarantee that firm-specific training will be provided in optimal quantities. Indeed, quits may be artificially reduced with adverse consequences for overall labor mobility.

5 Approximately 30 percent of nonunion firms provide formal grievance procedures. This statistic, reported in Freeman (1980b, p. 645), is from a 1968 survey of the Bureau of National Affairs Personnel Policies Forum.

6 Following a suggestion by Gregg Lewis, Addison and Hirsch (1984) have

argued further that the union coefficient in value-added studies may crudely track the union–nonunion wage differential.

7 For completeness, we should refer in passing to Maki's (1983c) study of value-added productivity in 17 Canadian two-digit industries employing pooled data for 1961–71. Using both Cobb–Douglas and translog production functions that allow for time trends and cyclical and energy price effects, Maki finds a positive union productivity differential of some 30 percent. However, Maki demonstrates the sensitivity of his results to the functional form used. Thus, in a specification that allows factor shares (proxied by $\ln(K/L)$) to be a function of unionization, the union productivity effect abruptly changes in sign though not in magnitude or significance!

8 Clark (1980a, p.461n) crudely tests his assumption that the union effect does not vary through time by specifying the coefficient on the union (dummy) variable as a linear function of time. An insignificant negative trend in the union effect is reported with the production parameters set at their cross-section values.

9 Interestingly, in a study of union impact in British coal mining, 1900–13, Pencavel (1977) also reports sizeable negative union productivity effects on the basis of a CES production function model. For an alternative explanation of the downturn of productivity in British coal mining, see Hirsch and Hausman (1983).

10 For a detailed survey of the literature on technological change, productivity growth, and R&D, see Link (forthcoming).

11 As summarized in Chapter 2, Lazear (1983a, b) models a competitive market (i.e. with free entry of firms) in which firms differ in the costs of preventing unionism (owing, say, to differences in worker tastes). In equilibrium, although marginal union and nonunion firms will have equal profit rates, the average union profit rate may be lower than the average nonunion profit rate.

12 Caves et al. (1980) find profitability among Canadian industries to be negatively related to union density. They do not examine the interaction between unionization and concentration in their profit equations.

CHAPTER 8

Unions and Inflation

8.1 Introduction

Considerable controversy attaches to the role of trade unions in the
inflationary process. One debate turns on the question of whether or
not unions are a cause of inflation. Another, rather less controversial,
issue is the effect of unions on the mechanisms through which inflation
is transmitted through the economy. On the former question, debate is
clouded because there are two levels of causation – direct and indirect –
such that it is possible to exonerate unions at one level but not at the
other. Here we shall have to distinguish carefully between the issues of
proximate (i.e. direct) and fundamental (i.e. indirect) causation. On the
latter question, debate is also clouded to the extent that unionism may
be as much determined (by optimizing processes) as determining. The
task here is to isolate the separate contributions of various institutional
mechanisms to wage (and price) inertia. Although the precise contribution of unionism is not transparent, considerable progress has been
made in analyzing the responsiveness of inflation to aggregate demand
pressures in a framework that explicitly allows for the frictions of real
world labor markets.

Our treatment proceeds as follows. First, the notion that unions may
be a direct cause of inflation is evaluated. Second, more recent
arguments focusing on the role of labor market institutions as
mediating influences through which more basic economic forces operate
are analyzed. Third, the possibility that unions may after all be a cause
of inflation in the fundamental sense is discussed. In all cases, empirical
evidence bearing on these issues is reviewed.

8.2 Unions as a Direct Cause of Inflation

The orthodox view of trade unions is that they do not constitute a
direct source of inflationary pressure. The direct cause of inflation is
said to be an excessive rate of growth in the money supply relative to
the growth rate of aggregate output.[1] In Milton Friedman's (1951, p.
222) words: 'Unions are simply the thermometers registering the heat

218

rather than the furnaces producing the heat [of the inflationary process].' On this view, unions are essentially a passive force, responding to but not themselves generating inflation. The reaction functions in wage change–excess demand space is believed to be broadly the same in both union and nonunion sectors. Excess monetary growth stimulates output (in the short run) and prices. The output component creates an excess demand for labor in both sectors, wages in each of which react in 'similar' fashion. Price changes feed into the inflationary expectations of workers in both sectors in an identical manner.[2]

Orthodoxy recognizes that differences of degree attach to the wage reaction functions in the two sectors. It is accepted that unions may influence the 'market' reaction function in two principal ways. First, they may dampen the responsiveness of wage change to excess demand because of the time-consuming nature of union negotiation procedures. (Alternatively, there may simply be a longer lag on the unemployment term.)[3] Second, unions may impart some degree of inflationary bias to the system such that for all levels of excess demand the rate of wage inflation in the union sector will exceed the 'market' rate by a constant amount. This latter possibility occupies something of a middle ground between orthodoxy proper and what we shall term 'counter-orthodoxy', but it still retains the orthodox proposition that wage change in the union sector is largely determined by market forces – the inflationary bias operating through the intercept term of the reaction function.

Counter-orthodoxy reverses the chain of causation in the orthodox model. Unions can and do affect the rate of change in wages independently of demand. Union wage gains (and higher product prices) are simply validated by the monetary authorities. The money supply is now an endogenously determined variable responding to the going rate of wage and price inflation dictated by the union sector.[4] Attention thus focuses on the rate of wage inflation, which is variously described as being determined by union power, union militancy, and union spillover forces.

Each variant will be examined in turn. But before turning to the three models, it is useful to introduce the following identity. The arithmetically weighted wage level, W, may be written:

$$W = (1 - T)W_n + TW_u, \qquad (8.1)$$

where W_n is the average nonunion wage, W_u is the union wage, and T is union density.

Expressing the union–nonunion wage differential as

$$\lambda = \frac{W_u - W_n}{W_n},$$

the union wage may be written:

$$W_u = W_n (1 + \lambda). \tag{8.2}$$

Substituting (8.2) into (8.1) yields:

$$W = W_n (1 + T\lambda). \tag{8.3}$$

Differentiating (8.3) with respect to time gives:

$$dW/dt = dW_n/dt + W_n T \; d\lambda/dt + W_n\lambda \; dT/dt + T\lambda \; dW_n/dt$$
$$= dW_n/dt \cdot (1 + T\lambda) + W_n T \cdot d\lambda/dt + W_n\lambda \cdot dT/dt. \tag{8.4}$$

And the proportional time derivative $dW/dt \cdot 1/(W_n(1+T\lambda))$ or $\dot{W}$ is:

$$\dot{W} = \dot{W}_n + [T/(1+T\lambda)]d\lambda/dt + [\lambda/(1+T\lambda)]dT/dt, \tag{8.5}$$

where the dot operator signifies a proportional time derivative.

Equation (8.5) provides a useful backdrop to our discussion, suggesting as it does that unions can influence wage inflation by raising the nonunion wage, by increasing the union–nonunion differential,[5] and by raising union density. But note that equation (8.5) is at root an identity and so it is difficult to discriminate between it and a causal economic mechanism (Pencavel, 1977).

Union 'power'

There are two basic concepts of union power. The first is that of union monopoly power, as indexed by the Marshallian rules for the elasticity of derived demand (see Chapter 2) and the costs of enforcing union monopoly. If union monopoly power is to provide an explanation for continuing wage inflation, the minimum requirement would seem to be a sustained rise in the degree of monopoly power through time; presumably there will also need to be some imperfection in nonunion wage determination, otherwise wages in that sector may fall *pari passu* with wage increases in the union sector. Unfortunately, there is no evidence of a sustained rise in union monopoly power through time, although there have been occasions of 'wage push' allied to factors reducing the cost of enforcing union monopoly – for example, Friedman and Schwartz (1963, p. 419) identify the New Deal episode as one such interval. However, one swallow does not make a spring. Moreover, as Ashenfelter (1978) has noted, an awkward corollary of the argument is that decreases in union monopoly power imply that trade unions may in certain periods be responsible for deflation.

To proceed further with the union monopoly power version one has presumably to drop the assumption that changes in monopoly power are immediately reflected in union (i.e. relative) wages. But to argue thus is to alter fundamentally the monopoly power model and to undermine the objectivity of the measure of power.

The second model has a basis in the bargaining power of the union to extract wage gains from the employer. This ability is determined by the relative power of the two parties in collective bargaining.[6] In perhaps the best-known theoretical model, Johnston (1972) argues that the employer will seek to minimize the expected costs of the union wage claim given the union's 'real claim' (not the actual claim but rather an estimate of what the union would settle for without a strike), an estimate of the relationship between strike probability and the wage offer, and a judgment of the length of strike needed to secure acceptance of that offer. Johnston predicts that the rate of change in wages will be a function of the rate of change in the real wage claim, the rate of profit per worker, union ability to endure a strike, and strike costs to the firm by length of strike. Yet, in an empirical test of the model (Johnston and Timbrell, 1973), many of the variables specified in the theoretical model are dispensed with, and the rate of change in wages is simply modeled as a function of the rate of change in the real claim.[7] The latter is itself a function of inflationary expectations (crudely drawn) and either a 'catch-up' variable measuring the degree to which real wages have fallen behind an assumed target growth rate or a variable measuring a three-year moving average of the rate of change in the ratio of post-tax to gross wages.

The basic problem confronting this empirical application of the bargaining power model is that of differentiating it from the expectations-augmented Phillips curve. Thus price expectations adorn both models while the catch-up variable may be viewed as reflecting an excess demand influence (Christofides, Swidinsky, and Wilton, 1980a). Note, too, that counter-orthodoxy, strictly interpreted, requires union behavior to be determined independently of economic variables.

The catch-up variable employed by Johnston and Timbrell in their empirical analysis has attracted considerable attention in Britain, if not the US, under the guise of the real wage hypothesis (RWH). A large number of British observers have argued that unions' targets for real wage growth provide perhaps the major explanation of contemporary wage inflation (e.g. Miller, 1976; Williamson and Wood, 1976; Henry and Ormerod, 1978; Henry, 1981). However, not only is the theoretical pedigree of the model obscure, but its explanatory (as opposed to predictive) power is weak. On the former point, it is not clear whether

221

the RWH is a bargaining equilibrium real wage model after Johnston (1972), a state of worker expectations model (which, though potentially of interest, has yet to be defined), or a simple frustration thesis.[8] On the latter point, it is admitted by even the most sophisticated protagonist of the RWH that it does not seem possible to frame a critical test of the model vis-à-vis orthodoxy (Henry, 1981). These and other problems[9] lead us to conclude that the RWH is descriptive of rather than analytical on the phenomenon for which an explanation is sought. However, the notion that workers have some target wage in mind is, as we shall subsequently argue, worthy of formal elaboration.

Union militancy

This variant of counter-orthodoxy contends that wage inflation is a function of the aggressiveness or militancy of trade unions in collective bargaining. Clearly, 'militancy' is a much more subjective variable than the construct of union 'power' considered earlier. Indeed, some analysts have denied that consistent proxies can be developed for the propensity of unions to engage in wage push. Unfortunately, their own socio-logically based arguments that describe the process or stage of militancy emerge on closer inspection to comprise inductive propositions about past events. As such, they have no predictive power and are irrefutable (for a review, see Addison and Burton, 1984a). However, other analysts have sought to develop proxies for union militancy, of which the most popular have been measures of union membership.

Thus, in a controversial series of articles, the British economist A. G. Hines (1964, 1968, 1969, 1971) postulates that the rate of change in union density ($\dot{T}$) can be employed as a proxy for militancy on the grounds that when unions are aggressive they will simultaneously increase their membership and enter wage claims.[10] Hines reports a positive and statistically significant relationship between wage inflation and $\dot{T}$ in each of his studies. Unemployment, on the other hand, emerges as an insignificant factor in wage determination.

Much of the controversy surrounding Hines' model can better be understood by referring to the identity given in equation (8.5). From that equation it is quite possible that the $\dot{T}$ variable is tracking not militancy but, rather, the fact that a weighted average changes when its weights change. On this interpretation, $\dot{T}$ has no behavioral content unless it is argued that union militancy is geared to increasing the number of workers covered by the union wage. Hines eschews this possibility, arguing that the relation between the rate of change in wages and $\dot{T}$ is a direct one. However, this hypothesis is simply *ad hoc*, and is not derived from any well-developed theory of union behavior.

Mulvey and Gregory (1977a) conjecture that union militancy

operates through the second term on the RHS of equation *(8.5)*, namely by increasing the union–nonunion differential. They argue that Hines is correct in emphasizing the role of militancy in union wage change but incorrect in identifying the channel of that influence. Using US data for the period 1920–58, Mulvey and Gregory replicate and test Hines' basic estimating equation, together with equation *(8.5)*. They report that including the change in the union–nonunion differential, in addition to the change in the proportion of the labor force unionized, improves the fit of Hines' equation but renders insignificant the sign of his militancy variable ($\dot{T}$). Unfortunately, in all of this it is difficult to distinguish between the different types of behavior postulated and the mere shuffling of identities. Clearly, the union–nonunion differential may fluctuate for a number of reasons other than militancy (e.g. it will vary with the cycle – see Chapter 5 and Section 8.4 below), while its size may affect unionization to as great an extent as the converse. Perhaps the safest conclusion is that the coefficient on $\dot{T}$ at best provides an extremely rough measure of the union wage differential, but tells us little, if anything, about the structural relation between unions and inflation (Pencavel, 1977).

As noted earlier, a central problem confronting the Hines' militancy hypothesis is that it is not derived from a well-developed theory of union behavior. Accordingly, the hypothesis may possess predictive power but not explanatory power (Burton, 1972). Also, of course, a variety of explanations unrelated to union militancy may be offered for the positive association between $\dot{T}$ and wage change. For example, the association may simply reflect an aggregation phenomenon noted earlier, or perhaps a passive security motive on the part of hitherto nonunion workers.[11] Moreover, empirically the Hines hypothesis has not traveled well, having yet to be replicated with any success outside Britain (Swidinsky, 1972; Ward and Zis, 1974). And even for that country, Hines' equation has been shown to perform badly in a number of industry- and macro-level studies (see, for example, Wilkinson and Burkitt, 1973; Henry, Sawyer, and Smith, 1976).

These and other problems have encouraged other analysts to employ a variety of alternative proxies for union militancy; in particular, various measures of strike activity. Again, the empirical results have been mixed (see Ashenfelter, Johnson, and Pencavel, 1972; Ward and Zis, 1974), the relationship between the chosen measure of strikes and wage inflation being fairly unstable. This instability is not surprising because strike activity is unlikely to be a reliable indicator of union militancy. This is underscored by the recent argument of Geroski, Hamlin, and Knight (1982) that strikes are a symptom of bargaining power *weakness* rather than strength, as implied by the union militancy hypothesis. In fact, at a theoretical level, the association between strikes

223

(over wage issues) and wage inflation is ambiguous, most notably because it takes two to precipitate a strike. It therefore seems likely that the positive association between strikes and wage inflation observed in a number of studies is not causal, but rather reflects the joint determination of both variables by underlying economic forces. Although the evidence is opaque, there are grounds for believing that wage change is positively related to inflation uncertainty (Riddell, 1979b) and that uncertainty, by complicating the inferential task facing the bargaining parties, precipitates more strikes (Siebert and Addison, 1981).

Wage spillover and wage imitation

Counter-orthodoxy denies that market forces play a major role in union wage determination. What is it that enables such analysts to ignore employer resistance to union wage claims? Here, we encounter the union spillover hypothesis, which points to a uniformity of wage increase across unionized sectors of the labor market. With all union employers affected equally, so the argument runs, employer resistance will be minimized. Thus the focus shifts to the factors producing uniform wage settlements. The story of wage spillover does not end here, however, because union settlements may either directly or indirectly (via third-party wage-fixing machinery) spill over into the nonunion sector – indeed, as we have already suggested, some transmission of wage rigidity would seem to be required by the model if union spillovers are to produce wage inflation. (For a discussion of union effects on union and nonunion wage *levels*, see Chapter 5.)

First consider the union spillover hypothesis. The central idea is that the level of money wages in any sector is determined by the reference comparisons that sector participants make with an institutionally given set of wages in other sectors. Thus, nominal wage changes are visualized as being transmitted across the labor market not by a market adjustment function but by a spillover process of the form:

$$\dot{W}^s_{it} = \sum_{r=1}^{n} \beta_{ir} \dot{W}_{rt} \quad \beta_{ir} > 0, \tag{8.6}$$

where $\dot{W}^s_i$ is the spillover induced rate of growth in money wages in sector i, $\dot{W}_r$ is the rate of growth in wages in reference sector r, $r = 1 \ldots n$ constituting the *reference wage set* for ith sector participants, and β_{ir} is a spillover coefficient defining the degree of pattern following dependency of ith sector wage increases on rth sector wage increases (Addison and Burton, 1979).

224

Ignoring a number of ambiguities in equation *(8.6)*,[12] what microbehavioral relationships underpin this sparse formal representation? One candidate is the notion of relative deprivation (Baxter, 1973). This construct is intimately related to the process of reference group selection, for the choice of reference groups by *i* will dictate the magnitude of relative deprivation experienced by *i*. If the relation between *i*'s wage level and its referents is disturbed, then *i* will feel relatively deprived and will attempt to restore the preexisting parity. In this manner, so the argument runs, wage increases obtained by specific groups of workers will become generalized throughout the labor market. Unfortunately, as Burton (1977) has shown, relative deprivation emerges as a weak reed on which to hang the transmission mechanism. Thus reference group theory does not contain any restrictions on the form or arguments of individual relative deprivation functions and accordingly cannot generate any predictions about the nature, size, or direction of wage spillover effects. Moreover, there is no means of measuring relative deprivation in a manner that allows aggregation across individuals and that permits a direct test of the assumed relation between changes in the stock of relative deprivation and wage inflation. In short, the relative deprivation hypothesis poses much the same sort of methodological problems as does introspective cardinal utility theory.

Confronted with this difficulty, empirical studies have sought to infer reference group comparisons from data on wage changes. Some measure of the problem is indicated in two British studies, which use much the same procedures to elicit the pattern of reference groups and also cover similar time periods. Each claims considerable support for spillover in wage determination. Unfortunately, the reference sectors identified in the studies exhibit practically no overlap (Hines, 1969; Sargan, 1971). This outcome is of course a reflection of *post hoc* rationalization of the data in terms of the hypothesis since the theory cannot predict the direction and pattern of spillover wage effects.

We note that we should expect to observe interconnections between wages in different sectors of the labor market owing to the operation of market forces, even in the absence of a spillover process. For example, a simple Marshallian model would include both the firm's own wage rate as well as competing wage rates as determinants of labor supply and hence wage change, while the *direct* influence of comparisons on wage offers and reservation wages is quite consistent with standard models of market behavior once the fiction of the Walrasian auctioneer and tâtonnement is dispensed with (see Phelps, 1968; Addison and Burton, 1978, 1979).

One alternative option in discussing equation *(8.6)* is the so-called union politics hypothesis, first articulated by Ross (1948), in which it is assumed that failure of a union leadership to match the wage increases secured in other jurisdictions will lead to rank-and-file disaffection and either challenges to the union leadership or membership loss. Seeking to deflect either such challenge, union leaderships will lodge comparable wage claims. This model exploits differences in the objective functions of union leadership and membership (see Chapter 9), while providing a transmission mechanism, albeit predicated on bargaining *goals*, missing from the relative deprivation hypothesis.

Evidence on inter-union spillovers is available in the 'wage round' and 'pattern bargaining' literatures. In the British case, the most comprehensive study finds that there is no such animal as the national wage round, whether that phenomenon is defined in terms of wage contract uniformity, periodicity, or entry pattern (Elliott, 1976). Although we do observe 'coalitions' or contract subsets evincing imitative wage behavior, there is emphatically no such thing as a single, homogeneous wage round (Burton and Addison, 1977).

The early US literature purported to show evidence of a pattern bargaining phenomenon, associated with a primary or first-order round of wage increase in the hard goods industries followed by a second-order round in the rest of manufacturing industry (Levinson, 1960a, b; Maher, 1961). Eckstein and Wilson (1962) provided what seemed at the time to be powerful econometric corroboration of the uniform wage patterning discerned in these earlier, descriptive studies. However, it gradually became clear that the close correspondence of wage movements was a chimera. This was underlined by the failure of Eckstein (1968) to replicate his earlier results with updated data (see below). More recent studies confirm the variation in wage settlements. One of the better studies is that of Mehra (1976). Using quarterly time-series data for manufacturing industries, Mehra fits a wage *level* equation in terms of consumer prices, unemployment rates, and profit rates at the two-digit industry level. After having removed any autocorrelation in the error term for each specific industry, Mehra performs a number of statistical tests designed to detect any remaining correlation patterns in the residuals across industries; cross-industry serial correlation is attributed to spillovers. Such correlation is detected for some (high-wage, noncompetitive) industries but not for others. Further evidence against the pattern bargaining hypothesis is supplied by Flanagan (1976) who, unlike Mehra, distinguishes explicitly between the union and nonunion sectors of US manufacturing. In neither sector does Flanagan detect any evidence that wage change is explained by a rigid uniformity of wage settlements. Similar results are also reported by Mitchell (1980).

Given the statistical elusiveness of wage imitation, other analysts have adopted what might be termed an 'agnostic' union spillover model. In an empirical analysis notable for its use of a very large body of (Canadian) data on individual agreements, Christofides, Swidinsky, and Wilton (1980b) advance a model of the form:

$$\dot{W}^A_i = \dot{W}^*_i + \lambda(\dot{W}^s_i - \dot{W}^*_i), \qquad (8.7)$$

where $\dot{W}^A_i$ is the actual wage settlement of the ith bargaining group, $\dot{W}^*_i$ is the hypothetical wage change that would have occurred in the absence of wage spillovers and interdependencies, and $\dot{W}^s_i$ is the spillover wage settlement(s) relevant for the ith bargaining group.

The nonspillover component of the actual wage settlement, $\dot{W}^*_i$, is assumed to be determined by excess demand, price expectations, and price catch-up (see Section 8.4 below). As for the specification of $\dot{W}^s_i$, the authors define four reference sets of wage settlements from which union spillover might emanate: regional spillovers, regional spillovers from large firms, broad industry–regional spillovers, and specific-industry–regional spillovers. The basic technique employed is to add the last j settlements (in chronologically reverse order) according to each measure until their explanatory power is exhausted. The authors report that the more narrowly defined the industry classification, the sharper the statistical results; that is, localized spillover unsurprisingly dominates the results.

Christofides, Swidinsky and Wilton candidly admit that they must of necessity remain agnostic about the theoretical rationale for wage spillovers. The basic problem with the mixed market–spillover model is that it suffers from simultaneous equations bias. Neoclassical theory indicates that the labor supply to any sector is a function of wages in the alternative wage set. Thus the excess demand for labor in any sector and its assumed proxy, the unemployment rate in that sector, is not theoretically independent of wages in all other sectors. The avoidance of simultaneous equations bias in estimating a mixed market–spillover model requires that $\dot{W}^*$ be given by a specific functional form derived from underlying supply and demand equations recognizing interdependence. The estimation of a simple spillover-augmented Phillips curve thereby introduces an identification problem (Addison and Burton, 1979).

Other analysts less cautious than Christofides, Swidinsky, and Wilton have attempted to sidestep the deficiencies of reference group theory and the union politics model (which, recall, argues that each individual union will seek to match the rate of increase achieved in other union jurisdictions but fails to explain the 'going rate' of union wage inflation) by postulating some form of wage leadership. Equation *(8.6)* is thus rewritten:

$$\dot{W}_{it}^s = \beta_{iL} \dot{W}_{Lt}, \qquad (8.8)$$

where $\dot{W}_L$ refers to the proportional rate of change in money wages in the leading sector. This introduction of wage leadership, while not solving the wage claim–wage settlement dichotomization, nevertheless appears to order causally the spillover system and to render the union wage sector outcome theoretically determinate.

Yet to proceed further one has to be able to predict the identity of the leading sector *and* supply a theory of wage determination for that sector. On the former point, our previous discussion of reference group theory indicates that there are no rigorous criteria for classifying the leading sector. Analysts have in consequence resorted to *ad hoc* judgment. For example, Eckstein and Wilson (1962) diagnose the leading sector to be a 'key group' of eight two-digit durable goods industries which they draw up on the basis of inspection of the data and the testimony of labor economists! In much the same manner, McGuire and Rapping (1968) identify the leading sector as some subset of the Eckstein–Wilson key group, namely the auto and steel industries. Interestingly, in a subsequent attempt to fit his model to 1960s data, Eckstein (1968) is forced to admit that the cohesion of wages in the key group had loosened considerably, while a new spillover channel – from construction to durable goods manufacturing – had opened up. In short, the leading sector had changed its identity.

On the second point, although measurement has tended to outpace theory, a number of models of key sector wage determination have been developed (for a review, see Burton and Addison, 1977). To take just one example, Eckstein and Wilson present an *ad hoc* bargaining model in which wage increases within the key group, identified earlier, are set by a bargaining process in which the relative opportunity costs of concession to unions and employers in that group are related to the unemployment and profit rates of the group as a whole. Wages in the rest of manufacturing (i.e. the non-key group) are determined by spillovers from the key group and industry-specific unemployment and profit rates.

This representation of the union wage determination process as dichotomized may have a very simple explanation. As Wachter and Wachter (1978) note, and as the evidence appears to suggest, the key industries may simply be those enjoying the most favorable excess demand positions, and spillover may simply represent similarly shared excess demand conditions and the input–output nexus. It now seems clear that there is no such thing as monosectoral or single-industry leadership, which lends credence to this interpretation; and also that there is little if any evidence of 'institutional' spillover somehow detached from product and labor market considerations (Mehra, 1976).

Unfortunately, as we shall subsequently argue, there are further ramifications of spillover, but for present purposes we can conclude that little is to be gained from further experimentation with retrospective key group analysis and the notion that comparison and wage imitation are 'institutionally' as opposed to 'economically' determined. This is not to say that the notion of key sector wage leadership has lost its appeal to empirical analysts. Thus, Vroman (1984) has recently pointed to the coercive influence of key national agreements reached in the auto and steel industries on contract wage determination in US manufacturing between 1957 and 1980. But he himself notes the (additional) problems of differentiating spillover effects from those resulting from catch-up and the distortions introduced by the arbitrary imposition of incomes policies in the bargaining cycle.

A not uncritical component of any model of unionism's role in wage inflation is the behavior of the nonunion wage in response to changes in the union wage. It is, as we have seen, typically assumed that the (average) nonunion wage is determined independently of the (average) union wage. Only one treatment – the threat effect model – explicitly models wage interdependence between the two sectors. As will be recalled from Chapter 5, nonunion wages are said to be positively related to union wages because a widening union wage differential implies a rising threat of organization to the nonunion sector, whose employers notch up wages to preempt this outcome. Similarly, wages in the union sector cannot be divorced from nonunion wage developments since a rising nonunion wage lowers the employment costs to unions of an increase in their own wages, and conversely.

The threat effect model as applied to wage inflation has been formalized by Ashenfelter, Johnson, and Pencavel (1972). The attraction of the model is that it provides a determinate theory of wage inflation and relative wage formation that encompasses *both* sectors of the labor market. The question at issue, however, is the degree of support it offers counter-orthodoxy. This is most obviously because once the union–nonunion differential has achieved its stable equilibrium value, the rate of wage inflation will be determined by excess demand and price expectations, namely by the standard augmented Phillips curve arguments. It follows that unions can add independently to inflation only if their preference for wage increases over members' job security becomes stronger (Burton, 1985). Ashenfelter, Johnson, and Pencavel argue that changes in this preference may be captured empirically by militancy indicators, namely strike frequency and changes in union membership, which variables returns us to the controversy opened up earlier.

Although there is some support for the threat effect model in cross-section work (see Rosen, 1969; Ehrenberg and Goldstein, 1975;

229

Freeman and Medoff, 1981), some doubt has been cast on the Ashenfelter–Johnson–Pencavel treatment by more recent time-series studies. These have suggested that the steady-state wage inflation produced by the model (when either sector is unhappy with the equilibrium union–nonunion differential) is zero. This result follows if either the union–nonunion or the nonunion–union spillover coefficient is insignificantly different from zero. Thus, in an analysis of wage developments in US manufacturing from 1961 to 1975, Flanagan (1976) reports an absence of spillover from the union to the nonunion sector. In a separate analysis using data constructed from industry unionization rates and average hourly earnings from 1954 to 1971, Johnson (1977) obtains a similar result and, like Flanagan, also reports that the union sector, seeking to maintain its desired wage differential, follows wage movements in the nonunion sector. These findings have occasioned no small controversy, and there are signs that both sets of results are sensitive to the choice of model specification and sample period (Vroman, 1980, 1982; Mitchell, 1980). Clearly, however, the model does not provide a general explanation for wage inflation. Also, the unemployment occasioned by dissatisfaction with the equilibrium union–nonunion differential should be modeled explicitly since this may be expected ultimately to help equalize desired differentials in the two sectors.

Taken in the round, then, the evidence does not offer much support for this particular spillover model. This conclusion is perhaps under-written by the small size of the union sector in the US. Interestingly, the British evidence points in much the same direction despite the consider-ably higher level of union density in that country. In Britain, almost one-quarter of the male manual labor force is covered by the terms of a collective agreement without actually belonging to a union. Yet Mulvey (1978) reports that, although the wage differential of union members over uncovered workers is around 15 percent, that of nonunion covered workers is in the range 0–5.3 percent. Mulvey argues that this is because the threat response of nonunion employers who pay the full union rate is primarily to match the nationally negotiated union wage rate rather than the rates fixed in supplementary or company agreements in the two-tier collective bargaining framework (see Section 5.9).

Unions may of course also influence the nonunion wage via the operation of legal wage minima and third-party wage fixing. Hard evidence on this 'indirect' effect is sparse. We comment on the controversy surrounding the impact of Davis–Bacon in US construction in Chapter 9. Suffice it to say here that the influence of union wages on wage minima, though evident, is rather less than heretofore alleged. Minimum wages not only influence the wages of those below the minimum but also impact on union wages via a traditional demand–

supply route following substitution by employers away from low-wage labor toward skilled (union) labor. For the US, Gramlich (1976) and Linneman (1982) report that higher wages do indeed respond to change in wage minima. Linneman, for example, estimates that the average (expected) earnings gain for a union member from the presence of a minimum wage law in 1974 amounted to $400 (−$8 for nonunion workers). But again there are few signs of *institutional* spillover. Using Canadian wage contract data, Christofides, Swidinsky, and Wilton (1978) are unable to identify any wage spillover from adjustments to wage minima on negotiated wages.

Turning finally to third-party arbitration, the basic problem is that the vast majority of arbitration cases involve the fixing of union wages. The only evidence available to us in this area concerns the determinants of wage increase by settlement stage. Auld, Christofides, Swidinsky, and Wilton's (1981) analysis of micro contract data for union contracts signed during the 1966–76 period in the Canadian public and private sectors suggests that these determinants are not invariant by settlement stage. Perhaps their most interesting finding is that mediation–conciliation diminishes the impact of labor market variables in the private sector. They also show that arbitrated wage settlements in the public sector are determined by considerations other than labor market forces and competitive wage pressures.

The arbitration issue is an important one from the perspective of spillover. The process might well yield greater uniformity of wage settlements than might otherwise result. More work is urgently needed here. Also, public sector wage increases generated by the mechanical application of comparability formulae confront the reality of a private sector wage structure that is not fixed and wage patterns that are not immutable. Such exercises underpin the urgency of ascertaining the rationale for such wage imitation as is observed in the private sector. The basic problem is that inability to pay may not always be as crucial a factor in the public sector as it is in the private sector. (For an amplification of this argument drawing on evolutionary theory, see Addison and Chilton, 1984.)

Summary

Our basic criticism of counter-orthodoxy has centered on its *ad hoc* specification and reliance one way or another on variables that are consistent with more orthodox market models. Empirically, the contribution of trade unions to wage inflation appears modest. This can be seen if we return to equation *(8.5)* and simply assume that nonunion wages are determined exogenously. Aggregate wage change is only minimally influenced by unions via changes in the wage differential and changes in density. Thus, for the US over the period 1967–73, Ashenfelter (1978) estimates that unionism increased wages by only 1.2 percent above what would have eventuated in their absence. Since the aggregate wage increased by 44 percent over this interval, the union contribution is evidently tiny. Similar results obtain for the UK: over the same time interval, unions contributed some 10 percentage points to an overall wage inflation of 170 percent (Mulvey and Gregory, 1977b). We earlier cautioned against treating *(8.5)* as a behavioral equation and also stressed that implicit in the 'model' was some notion of noncompetitive wage determination in nonunion labor markets. Nevertheless, in the light of our preceding empirical discussion, these may be not unreasonable ballpark estimates.

But is the orthodox view of trade unions and inflation vindicated by the failure of counter-orthodoxy? As formulated, orthodoxy provides only a rudimentary picture of the wage determination process and of the problems that arise in real world labor markets from phenomena associated with, though not necessarily determined by, trade unionism. Qualifications concerning the lags on wage setting introduced by unions and the possibility of dampened or even biased reaction functions do not really come to grips with the 'appearance' of cost-push inflationary pressures and the role of labor market institutions. Also, it would be difficult for the simple orthodox view to cope with the finding that unions apparently escalate the reaction of wages to price inflation while slowing wage responsiveness to labor market slack (see, for example, Mitchell, 1980). To delve deeper we shall have to introduce labor market institutions more concretely into the analysis than is admitted in the simple orthodox analysis, even though the manner of their incorporation is largely in the spirit of the neoclassical core.

In fact, the stimulus toward introducing real world institutions into wage change analysis was provided by the apparent demise of the Phillips curve in the middle to late 1960s. Empirical studies revealed a substantial weakening in the labor market tightness variable and a corresponding strengthening of the price term. Wages appeared to follow some combination of their own lagged values and the system thus reduced to a highly autoregressive process. In short, the Phillips relation appeared to be a horizontal line in wage change–unemployment space, although vertically displaced by changes in inflationary expectations. This apparent exogeneity of wages provided ammunition to counter-orthodoxy. However, much modern wage change analysis views the autoregressive model of wage determination as based on a very narrow interpretation of the data and has sought to model the processes producing observed changes in the Phillips relation and, in particular, the consequences of the lag structures built into the wage (and price) equation by contractual behavior.

In what follows, we first review recent theoretical and empirical refinements in the wage determination literature, before turning to consider the endogeneity of the money supply and the possibility that unions may after all constitute a fundamental or indirect cause of inflation.

8.3 Recent Theoretical Developments

Research resources have increasingly been devoted to explaining wage and price contracts, and hence sluggish price adjustments, from a neoclassical or at least close-to-optimizing microeconomic perspective. The bulk of this theoretical literature addresses the issue of why such contracts will dominate spot or auction markets in certain sectors of the labor (and product) market(s); comparatively little attention has been focused on the wage determination process in contractual markets. Moreover, there is little mention of unions in this literature, reflecting the fact the theory was initially developed to apply to unorganized labor markets. Not surprisingly, then, we shall observe a certain tension between theoretical and applied work in this area.

At least two strands in the developing contracts literature may be identified. One relies on costly information and heterogeneous workers, jobs, and products, and is associated with the notion of idiosyncratic exchange (Williamson, Wachter, and Harris, 1975; Wachter and Williamson, 1978).[13] The other, more formal approach is based on the purportedly differential risk aversion characteristics of otherwise homogeneous workers and employers, and is associated with the notion of implicit contracts that constrain behavior (Azariadis, 1975; Baily, 1974; D. F. Gordon, 1974). Of late, the two branches of the literature have perhaps drawn somewhat closer together, although clear differences in emphasis remain. Let us briefly examine each variant, beginning with the risk aversion model.

The basis of the neoclassical models, advanced by Azariadis and Baily in particular, is that labor services are traded for an insurance contract. If, as is assumed, workers are more risk averse than their employers, it will be mutually advantageous for the firm to offer workers a joint product comprising employment and insurance against income instability. An implicit contract results in which the worker's wage differs from his marginal revenue product – being greater than his contribution to output in bad times (adverse states of nature) and less than that contribution in good times (favorable states of nature). So the risk averse worker alternatively receives an insurance indemnity or pays an insurance premium. Efficiency requires that at all times the marginal product of labor and the worker's marginal rate of substitution between income and leisure be equated. The former is more variable than the latter and so the firm is permitted to determine employment. Firms and workers engage in long-term contracting relations that, although implicit, specify real wage rates in advance and the quantity of labor services to be supplied by the worker to the firm in each state of nature. The real wage is rigid over states of nature.

The implicit contracts model has not unnaturally attracted its fair share of criticism. The first problem for the theory is to explain why contracts do not simply produce worksharing (i.e. reductions in hours for all workers) rather than layoffs in adverse states of nature. No adequate explanation of layoffs is offered in the original contracts literature, other than the possibility of local nonconvexity in workers' preferences over leisure streams (Azariadis, 1977).[14] More recently, it has been recognized that layoffs may depend on the presence of some third-party insurance – namely, government-financed unemployment compensation, which typically does not compensate for reduced hours.

A second problem concerns the enforceability of such contracts. It is assumed that firms will adhere to contracts because a reputation as a 'good employer' will in the long run reduce the firm's wage bill – risk-reducing policies being the cheapest and most profitable way of attracting any given labor force. It is less clear why workers should adhere to an unwritten contract.[15] Recently, the question of enforceability has received greater attention from contract theorists. In particular, Holmstrom (1981, 1983) has argued that contracts will develop in which a worker accepts a wage in the first period of a multiperiod contract that falls below his alternative or opportunity wage, thereby assuring the employer against his terminating in favorable states of nature. In this way, Holmstrom argues, there are exploitable gains to both parties from the implicit contract, which will therefore come to dominate spot market trades. It is not clear, however, that both parties can indemnify each other simultaneously (Bull, 1983). Here a union presence may ensure against employer default.

A third and related problem concerns the information properties of the model. In the early treatments, it is assumed that there is a known distribution of states of nature and symmetric access to information by both parties about the state of nature that has eventuated. It now appears that contract theory hinges importantly on the presence of information asymmetries. If information is asymmetric – say the employer alone observes the demand for labor – the possibility emerges that the firm may 'cheat' and deliberately misrepresent the state of nature to its own advantage. For example, the literature distinguishes between two cases in which the employer may either understate (in good times) or generally overstate his labor demand so as alternatively to reduce his costs or increase his labor utilization. The focus thus shifts to contractual procedures geared to making truth revelation the value-maximizing strategy for employers. As Riordan and Wachter (1983) note, the solution is to establish a schedule relating the wage bill to the quantity of employment and then allow the firm to select a point on the curve based on its private information. This (second best) solution will stimulate the employer to reveal his private information and make him reluctant to misrepresent the demand for his product.

We have already traveled some distance from the assumptions of the basic risk aversion model to provide a rationale for layoffs and to establish that contracts may be more than a 'veil' (Barro, 1977a). Yet a basic problem remains: the implicit contracts model explains real wage rigidity, which though broadly in line with the stylized facts has nothing to say about the determination of money wages. At first blush, therefore, the theory does not seem to provide a convincing story of why we observe nominal wage and price rigidities in the face of nominal shocks. Why, then, are real variables not insulated completely from such disturbances? One argument is that transaction costs militate against full indexation. Gray (1976, 1978) provides one such theory of indexation. Her basic thesis is that the optimal degree of indexing depends on the ratio of the variances of nominal to real disturbances: the lower is this ratio, the greater the efficiency loss from indexing, and vice versa. Even if there are no indexing costs (i.e. those associated with monitoring the index and adjusting wage schedules), indexing will not take place unless nominal disturbances exceed some critical value. Gray's model also establishes optimal contract length. Contracting costs are assumed to decline with contract length but the forecast variances of real and monetary shocks will increase through time, thus increasing the possibility that output will deviate from its desired level. Accordingly, at some point the costs of contract renegotiation just equal the benefit of adjusting wages to their full information values.[16]

However, implicit contract theorists seem unwilling to rely on transaction costs to produce the rigidities observed in nominal wages in the face of changes in aggregate demand. Instead they prefer to focus on the risk-bearing properties of alternative contracting schemes to explain why the rigidity of the real wage does not necessarily imply complete time invariance (see Azariadis and Stiglitz, 1983).

In contrast, the idiosyncratic exchange variant of contract theory elevates in importance the role of transaction costs. In this model the key concepts are those of bounded rationality and opportunism. Bounded rationality refers to the cognitive limits (i.e. the limited computational and informational-processing abilities) of economic agents in relation to the complexity of the decisions that they face. Although economic agents are intendedly rational they are only limitedly so. The result is that it is either impossible or prohibitively costly to identity all future contingencies and to specify *ex ante* how transactions are to be determined under these different conditions, even abstracting from the problems of contract enforcement. For this reason, contracts are left incomplete and ignore many contingencies. The parties to the contract are said to adapt to new circumstances in a sequential fashion (Wachter and Williamson, 1978).

Unfortunately, although incomplete contracting economizes on bounded rationality – multiperiod contracts reduce the number of states that have to be considered in choosing an optimal strategy over a given planning period or, alternatively, permit a longer horizon for a fixed amount of computation – it poses special problems because of opportunism or 'self-interest seeking with guile' (Williamson, Wachter and Harris, 1975, pp. 258–9). We earlier discussed this problem from the perspective of the employer misrepresenting his private information. In the idiosyncratic exchange or obligational market contracting model the tendency of *workers* to behave opportunistically is emphasized. This arises directly from the idiosyncratic features of many ongoing exchange relationships. Consider the internal labor market of the firm. Because of firm-specific training, jobs are heterogeneous or idiosyncratic. Incumbent workers thus enjoy nontrivial advantages over outsiders, giving rise to a gap in the workers' current and opportunity wages and the firm's current and opportunity unit labor costs (Wachter and Wachter, 1978, p. 128), thereby insulating workers in the short run from changes in labor market conditions. However, precisely because the self-policing benefits of competition are lacking, incumbents can behave opportunistically. What emerges, then, is a bilateral monopoly problem. The solution to this hazard of unconstrained idiosyncratic trading takes the form of a governance apparatus, geared to the joint maximization of the firm's surplus. This apparatus is described in some detail by Williamson, Wachter, and Harris, but its key elements include the use of promotion ladders, formal grievance procedures, and the application of the seniority principle. In addition, Riordan and Wachter (1983) emphasize monitoring and auditing procedures. Here a specific role is reserved for unions. In this sense the industrial relations argument that unions are a counter to the ability of firms to take advantage of workers by manipulating the external environment as perceived by workers (the moral hazard problem) is formalized somewhat. Unions emerge as an efficient device for monitoring and processing information as well as constituting an instrument for collective bargaining. Yet in the basic model it is not the union *per se* but rather the bargaining power possessed by idiosyncratically trained job incumbents that produces the governance apparatus.[17] The specific contribution of unionism to the multiperiod contracts predicted for obligational contracting markets is unclear. Markets with continuity needs may, of course, provide an ideal environment for union organization and unions themselves may create continuity needs by stimulating investments in firm-specific human capital; but they are not the central element of this theory.

Wage fixity in the obligational market model is produced by the fact that it is prohibitively costly for both sides of the employment relation to monitor, verify, and adapt to all new information. The rules governing wage changes (and the wage–employment relation) are thus invariant over the contract period, although they are changed at recontracting. It is in this sense that Wachter (1976, p. 124) writes: 'This model is still rational but only after complete recontracting occurs.' We shall examine the consequences of this adjustment process below. But note the explicit recognition in the model that institutions are not a datum and will themselves change if the circumstances on which they were predicated change. Wachter and Williamson (1978) discuss this institutional adaptation, arguing that subjecting contracting relations to inflation will produce shorter-term contracting, escalator clauses, additional standardization (i.e. greater reliance on auction markets), and greater vertical integration. It is not higher inflation *per se* that produces these results but, rather, relative price uncertainty or an increased variance of the inflation rate. Thus, Wachter and Williamson (1978, pp. 564–5) speak of such changes being brought about by the increased dispersion of relative prices associated with a higher mean rate of inflation, while Wachter and Wachter (1978, pp. 130–1) discuss the changes in terms of a high variance inflation rate. In either case, the argument is that there is a permanent loss in potential output as the economy moves into a high-inflation regime because, although the new contractual arrangements are 'optimal' in the changed circumstances, the move to shorter-period contracts dissipates the advantages of obligational market contracting.

Up to this point, we have not explicitly considered the life cycle of earnings in continuity markets. Most recently, theorists have paid more attention to this phenomenon and analyzed somewhat more formally the role of firm-specific human capital and seniority rules (see Section 6.6). The general tenor of the theoretical arguments is that seniority rules can have the same effect as separation penalties designed to reduce the incentive of either side to cheat and hence lead to suboptimal training investments (see, for example, Carmichael, 1983). Perhaps a more interesting development, however, from the perspective of life-cycle earnings is the approach of Lazear (1979, 1981), whose analysis is not predicated on specific human capital consideration but, rather, on the role of the age–earnings profile as a device to reduce worker shirking behavior. Lazear argues that it pays both sides to agree on a long-term wage profile that pays workers less than their value marginal product when young and more than their value marginal product when old. This more steeply sloped age–earnings profile dominates contracts in which wages are set equal to current value marginal product because a worker's incentive to shirk (or cheat) is reduced. The productivity of each hour spent working is increased when the bulk of wage payment is delayed relatively late in life since workers are more anxious to act as a responsible agent of the firm principal (i.e. to avoid a job termination). The actual slope of the age–earnings profile reflects the incentives of both sides to cheat. If a steeper function serves to reduce the worker's incentive to shirk and a flatter profile to reduce the firm's incentive to default, there is some optimal profile that minimizes total offenses and maximizes lifetime earnings/productivity.

Lazear's model parallels the human capital model in certain important respects (including hours constraints) but not in others. In addition, there is an explicit role for unions in the Lazear model via their monitoring function. Where unions are viewed as the monitor of the employees, this will flatten the age–earnings profile for union workers, though that profile will lie above that of nonunion workers. Where unions are the monitor of the employer, this will serve to steepen the (higher) profile among union workers.

The contract literature, as a whole, provides important insights into why quantity adjustments rather than continuous price changes may be efficient for the (immediate) parties to the contract. Taken together, the various strands of the theory may be read as arguing that implicit contracts have the function of allocating risk and resources in a manner that economizes on transaction costs (Riordan and Wachter, 1983). Yet, a number of ambiguities attach to the theory. First, it is by no means clear how money wages are determined in the model. In part, this lack of clarity stems from the controversy over real wage versus nominal wage rigidity. We shall return to this point below, but for the moment let us focus on the process of wage adjustment in the contract models. Although there is general consensus that implicit contracts insulate wages from the current state of demand (and value marginal product) and that contracts are made over the economic climate rather than the economic weather, there is no substantive agreement as to the process of wage determination. In part, this reflects benign neglect attendant upon the view that the labor market may be likened to an asset market in which wages are simply treated as installments on long-term financial obligations. Some contract theorists, however, have gone so far as to argue that the ruling criterion in wage determination is that of fairness, leading to the emergence of a wage–wage spiral (e.g. Okun, 1981). Most analysts resist the interpretation that there is something economically arbitrary in the wage determination process and agree that wages cannot remain permanently out of line with their long-run market valuation, namely at a level in excess of that justified by underlying neoclassical forces. But this agreement is achieved at the price of imprecision.

Robert Hall's (1980) analysis is instructive in this regard. Noting the installment nature of wages in a contractual framework and the long-term horizon over which contracts are 'written', Hall (p. 112) cautions that

> ... the magnitudes of the obligations cannot be set unambiguously in advance, if only because of uncertainty about the future value of the dollar. Adjustments need to take place to accommodate surprises in monetary and fiscal policy, shifts in the relative prices of food and oil, and many other unforeseen developments. Annual rates of wage inflation will reflect whatever changes have been made in long-term obligations, changes that were planned in advance, changes that have occurred in contracts with compensation formulas linked to current employment, and full market-clearing movements among the minority of workers in the open labor markets with short-term employment arrangements. Plainly such a hodgepodge of sources of wage movements will not have a simple relation to a single measure of demand.

Hall is, however, wary of jettisoning the Phillips curve concept. He concedes that the longer-run terms offered to new workers may follow something like the Phillips relation.

Possibly a little more guidance into the process of wage change is offered by Wachter and Williamson. But this is achieved via the introduction of explicit (albeit incomplete) contracts. The length of the explicit contract is apparently less than that of the implicit contract, the former adapting slowly to changes in underlying conditions so that the process producing 'full rationality' in contracts extends beyond any explicit contract period. Bounded rationality and opportunism underpin this sequential process. One problem here is that there may be little more than a difference of degree between explicit contracts and implicit contracts as formulated by contract theory, although Jacoby and Mitchell (1982) do query whether implicit contracting explains explicit contracting. We return to this point below. Meantime, we note that the arguments producing wage change in the Wachter–Williamson model are conventional enough. The novelty of the analysis is the endogeneity of labor market institutions – an element that is only hinted at in the conventional implicit contracts model.

A second difficulty with contract theory is the ambiguous role of unions in the theoretical apparatus. We should recall that contract theory was originally devised to reflect relationships between worker and firm in unorganized markets. The relevance of the model appeared confirmed by Hall's (1980, 1982) empirical analysis of continuity markets, which reports that a very substantial proportion of all workers have close-to-lifetime tenure on the job. However, union workers also have very considerable lifetime tenure, which on average exceeds that of nonunion workers (Addison and Castro, 1984). Despite this reality, we have seen that one has to search hard to discover specific reference to unionism in the various strands of contract theory. Only now are unions being accorded a role with respect to contract enforcement and their monitoring function. Ironically, modern empirical analyses (see Section 8.4), while paying almost ritual obeisance to contract theory, have focused on union wage contract data. The issue of why nonunion wages, the focus of contract theory, are adjusted at more frequent intervals than union (typically three-year) contracts is seldom addressed at the level of theory.

A third problem is the issue of nominal versus real wage rigidity. Although some analysts appear to believe that demand-induced unemployment requires nominal wage rigidity, contract theorists clearly feel that the dichotomy has been overdrawn and that *both* real wages and nominal wages display considerable rigidity. As we have seen, there is some dispute about the factors producing incomplete indexing, but if the insurance function can never be complete then nominal wages will also be partly rigid. The presence of long-term, overlapping explicit contracts will of course add to this rigidity. That said, analysts have still satisfactorily to address the issue of contract length and the incidence and scale of indexing arrangements. We will report some progress in this area in Section 8.4.

Finally, we note that it is nowhere claimed in the theoretical literature that implicit contracts dominate in each and every labor market setting, even though Hall's remarks, noted above, indicate that he feels spot markets constitute the very considerable minority of cases. The general point would seem to be that there are either different types of continuity markets or varying requirements for them across the spectrum of labor markets. With the exception of the Wachter and Williamson (1978) analysis, there are few clues in the literature to the determinants of different contractual regimes. Even neglecting the issue of union impact in this regard, it is clear that the institutional detail in the theoretical models is meager.

8.4 Recent Empirical Analyses of Wage Change

Inevitably, given the state of flux in contract theory, the extant empirical literature, while claiming affinity with the theory, is primarily concerned with modeling the effects of actual or hypothetical contractual arrangements on wage change. Most recently, however, there has been a shift of resources toward testing the implications of contract theory within the framework of the risk aversion model. In what follows, we trace the developing themes in the empirical literature.

Aggregative studies

As noted earlier, the stimulus toward the incorporation of real world institutions into wage change analysis was provided by the apparent collapse of the Phillips relation in the middle to late 1960s. One of the first to criticize this alleged demise of the Phillips curve was Wachter (1976), who argued that the lagged response of obligational markets to excess demand merely gave the appearance of a weakening in the role of the latter. In reality the Phillips curve was not dead. To the contrary, Wachter's empirical analysis of aggregate wage change in the US over the period 1954–74 suggested that there was not only more inflation for any given volume of unemployment, but also evidence of a steepening in the US Phillips curve over the sample period. The former result was obtained by constructing an improved measure of labor market slack (adjusting the unemployment rate for the changing demographic and structural features of the labor market to obtain a time-consistent measure of excess demand) and imposing a distributed lag on this variable to reflect the fact that current wage increases generated by contracts negotiated in the past should be explained by demand conditions ruling at the time the particular contract was negotiated rather than by current demand conditions. The latter result was observed by allowing the parameters of the wage change function to shift through time. (It was assumed for estimating purposes that changes in parameters proceeded monotonically; i.e. following a trend.)

Wachter's estimating equation is of the form:

$$\dot{W}_t = \alpha_o(\gamma) + \sum_{i=0}^{m} \beta_i(\gamma) U_{t-i}^* + \sum_{i=1}^{n} \tau_i(\gamma) \dot{P}_{t-i} + \varepsilon_i, \quad (8.9)$$

where $\dot{W}$ is the percentage rate of change in wages, U^* is a measure of labor market tightness, $\dot{P}$ is the percentage rate of change in prices, m and n denote lag lengths, and γ is a parameter shift operator. The model was also estimated with changes in the money supply substituted for the price term, on which more below.

Wachter notes that the responsiveness of wages to unemployment is not merely through the direct effect of unemployment (the $\Sigma\beta_i$) but also through its indirect effect (the $\Sigma\tau_i$). The latter effect operates through a price change equation (not shown) in which wage change is one argument. In a reduced-form equation, therefore, unemployment has an indirect effect via the influence of wage change on price change. The price term in equation (8.9), which as can be seen enters with a one-period lag, may thus be viewed as reflecting excess demand conditions and as a distributed lag generator for the unemployment rate. Given the inertia of contractual wage determination, the $\Sigma\tau_i$ capture the slow feedback response of demand variables through the price mechanism. It is for this reason that Wachter criticizes the interpretation (though not the use) of an autoregressive wage term in modern wage determination equations. The association between wage change and lagged wages does not imply a wage–wage spiral but, rather, mirrors the lagged or long-term response of wages to their conventional determinants in a world of slowly adjusting contracts. This provides the rationale for his subsequently substituting an autoregressive money supply term for the price (or wage) term – assuming, of course, that the causation runs from changes in the money supply to wages and prices rather than the converse (see Section 8.5).

In summary, it is argued that the direct or short-run effect of excess demand on wage inflation is picked up by the unemployment term, while the indirect or long-term effect is captured by the price (or money supply) term. The latter may be viewed as capturing inertia or expectational effects (see below). Wachter reports that the short-run responsiveness of wages to excess demand (the $\Sigma\beta_i$) has not weakened, that the system displays considerable inertia (with the lag structure on prices extending up to some 24 quarters), and that the wage equation has some unstable parameters. The effect of unemployment (direct and indirect) is shown to have increased over the postwar period.

Why, then, have more conventional analyses concluded that the Phillips curve has become less responsive to demand forces? This is partly because such analyses have not adequately controlled for changes in the composition of unemployment. Also, there is the question of the indirect or expectational effects. Shifts in the Phillips curve are induced by changes in expectations. But, if these are slow to adjust, it is entirely possible that inertia causes the price term to continue rising even at a time of downward movement along a given Phillips curve. (According to Wachter, this 'perverse' behavior characterized the last two recessions in his sample period, whereas in earlier recessions downward movements along the curve coincided with downward shifts in the curve.)

Wachter's final (and more contentious) point is that the Phillips curve has become steeper as it has shifted out (i.e. become more responsive to unemployment). This is the changing coefficient point, achieved by running the equation for the whole sample period with a fixed weight on the lagged price term and a variable weight on the unemployment term. Wachter's rationale for this observation is simply that contracts have gradually been altered to cope with a higher expected rate of inflation or to make up for past rates of inflation and their very structure has been changed in response to greater uncertainty surrounding the permanence of new inflation rates.

In a subsequent analysis by Wachter and Wachter (1978), these points are clarified somewhat. The strengthening response of wage change to current conditions is measured by rising values on the autoregressive wage term for more recent time periods (i.e. low i) observed over successive sample intervals. This occurs simultaneously with quantitatively large values for long lag terms in the autoregressive variable.

Wachter and Wachter also experiment with a lagged money supply growth term, which, as in Wachter (1976), replaces the lagged wage (or price) change variable. Unlike the latter study, a distinction is made between the anticipated and unanticipated component of money growth (Barro, 1977b).[18] Systematic changes in the rate of growth of the money supply are shown to have no significant effect on unemployment, but the residuals from the money growth equation are positively and significantly associated with unemployment. Conversely, anticipated changes in the money supply impact significantly on wage change with a positive sign, although the lags in the system extend back up to 20 quarters. Wachter and Wachter conclude that, given a long enough time horizon, slower monetary growth can secure its objective without necessarily requiring the extended period of high unemployment that conventional autoregressive models appear to suggest. The requirement here is to pursue stable monetary rules over an extended period, although this is clearly much complicated by the occurrence of real shocks.

Unions, it appears, constitute an important subset of Wachter's obligational markets. This is made more transparent in Wachter's (1974) analysis of interindustry wage dispersion in US manufacturing over the period 1947–73. The argument here is that movements in the differential between high-wage and low-wage sectors (identified with union and nonunion settings respectively)[19] are rooted in the longer planning (or contract) periods of the former. Longer planning periods generate lags in adjustment and lags in expectational effects. During periods of unusually low unemployment and high inflation the higher-wage sectors with longer planning periods are said to underestimate the economy-wide rate of change in wages with the result that the interindustry dispersion of wages narrows. When labor markets are slack, on the other hand, the converse holds.

Wachter finds that the evidence on wage dispersion is consistent with this explanation. Using an Almon lag structure, Wachter regresses the coefficient of variation of interindustry manufacturing wages (CV) on the reciprocal of the unemployment rate (U^{-1}), the rate of price inflation ($\dot{P}$), together with a time trend (TR) and two dummies. His fitted equation is as follows ($|t|$ in parentheses):

$$CV = .2253 - .3319\dot{P} - .2662U^{-1} + .0300TR + \text{dummies} \quad R^2 = .96$$
$$ (5.39) \quad (.31) \quad (1.97) \phantom{+.0300TR + \text{dummies}} DW = 1.7$$
$$(8.10)$$

Note that the coefficients shown are the sum of the lag weights – the full lag structure being five years.

Thus, distortions of usual sectoral differentials are determined coincidentally with wage inflation by current and lagged values of unemployment and price inflation. Although it has been conventional to regard a rising union–nonunion differential as a source of (cost-push) inflation, Wachter's analysis suggests that (cyclical) changes in wage dispersion have no causal role in wage inflation; they merely serve as a proxy for the lagged response of wage change to its determinants. That said, Wachter and Wachter (1978) note that escalator clauses now enable the union sector to keep up with inflation. And during the 1970s it does indeed appear to have been the case that the wages of employees in heavily unionized industries who were covered by escalators grew significantly relative to the wages of other employees in the economy (see, for example, Kosters, 1977; Mitchell, 1980). We shall return to the role of escalators in the inflation process below.

The evidence from these aggregate-level studies is that obligational markets (of admittedly uncertain composition) do not cause inflation, although the nature of the adjustment process may on occasion give the appearance of cost-push inflationary pressures. Such markets do, however, introduce long and variable lags in the reaction of wages to their determinants, and such lags complicate the task of economic management, not least because of the potentially misleading signals offered policymakers. In a very real sense there is a very limited scope for policy activism since the institutions of the labor market are not a datum.

Micro contract data

Let us now explore in somewhat greater detail the process of wage change at the micro level, since this would appear to offer the most appropriate milieu for wage determination studies seeking to introduce institutional realities. (This point will be developed in somewhat more detail in the context of British wage change analysis.)

The pathbreaking micro studies in which each wage settlement is treated as an observation are Canadian in origin.[20] All such studies test the hypothesis that wages are determined by current labor market conditions, inflationary expectations, and a price catch-up variable. The latter requires some explanation. The argument turns on the issue of unexpected inflation. In the new-microeconomics literature (Friedman, 1968; Phelps, 1968) workers are assumed to bargain for 100 percent of price expectations *ex ante*, while the market process corrects for unexpected inflation *ex post*. The correction mechanism is via excess demand – if prices increase faster than had been anticipated in the wage bargain then the real wage paid labor will be too low. The falling real wage will create an excess demand for labor and bid up the now inappropriate real wage. The interesting question is whether expectational errors will in fact be reflected in measured excess demand in a world of long-term contracts and worker attachments. It is possible in these circumstances that unexpected inflation forces both parties into a disequilibrium situation that cannot be fully corrected until recontracting. At this point, the rate of change in wages will exceed that predicted on the basis of measured excess demand and by an amount that is directly related to the length of the previous contract. In short, price catch-up is a measure of latent firm-specific excess demand arising from unexpected inflation that is to be included along with price expectations and some measure of aggregate excess demand in modeling wage change.

It can be seen that, if this argument is correct, catch-up will produce additional inertia in wage determination. In fact, the unemployment, price expectations, and catch-up variables employed in the various Canadian studies (e.g. Riddell, 1979b; Christofides, Swidinsky, and Wilton, 1980a) appear to provide a good explanation of wage change and to resurrect the Phillips curve, although there is some disagreement about whether the long-run curve is vertical.

Having said this, Riddell (1983), drawing on the data of his more aggregative contracts study (Riddell and Smith, 1982), notes that not all the persistence in wage settlements is explained by 'real wage' variables. In other words, there appears to be more persistence in wage settlements than can be accounted for by the state of the labor market, expectations of future price or wage inflation, and price catch-up. The continued presence of autocorrelation (i.e. the persistence in the unexplained part of wage change through time) suggests to Riddell the possibility of wage spillover between settlements.[21] In a world of staggered or nonsynchronized wage bargaining, it is clear that relative wage considerations will add to inertia in wage inflation. This can be seen most readily following Riddell (1983). Assume that there are just two bargaining groups, A and B, with staggered or overlapping two-period contracts. Suppose A settles in even years and B in odd years, with the wage predetermined in each case until contract renewal. If only the real wage mattered, then, in the event of an inflationary disturbance in period 0, the economy would return to equilibrium by period 2. There is inertia in wage change to the extent that it takes two years for the inflationary shock to be reflected in all wages, B having adjusted fully at the beginning of period 1. Next consider relative wage setting and the introduction of a neutral disinflationary shock in period 0. When B comes to negotiate in period 1, it will lower its wage but by less than is required to yield equilibrium since A has a predetermined wage (until period 2) which has not yet incorporated the disinflationary shock. Hence, B will resist full downward adjustment of its wage on relative wage grounds. In turn, its predetermined wage will influence A's behavior at recontracting in a similar manner. Clearly, the time taken to achieve the new equilibrium will be more protracted than in the real wage example. (Note that if wage settlements were synchronized there would be no difference between the two adjustment paths.)

Since the two cases are not mutually inconsistent, the real virtue of this much simplified example lies in its demonstration that at the time a given wage contract is being determined there will be an overhang from contracts set in the past, but which will continue to be in effect during part of the current contract period. In short, wage determination has both a backward-looking component and a forward-looking component. Past decisions will impact on current wage decisions to produce inertia in the wage determination process.

Taylor (1980) has sought to extract the contractual or inertia component from the (forward-looking) expectations component. In his two-period, staggered, nominal wage contracts model, labor supply behavior is fundamentally concerned with *relative* rather than with own wages, with an adjustment added to take account of expected excess demand. Given an endogenous monetary policy, and a zero steady-rate of price inflation, Taylor shows that the effect of a price shock on the time taken to bring the price level back to equilibrium depends crucially on the manner in which expectations are generated (and the ability of policy to influence expectations). If expectations are generated by backward-looking (i.e. adaptive or extrapolative) behavior, the time taken to return to equilibrium is much longer (and the loss in output much greater) than if expectations are rational.

Thus far, actual wage data have not been employed to distinguish between contract inertia and expectations, although Taylor (1983) has recently advanced a quantitative model of overlapping contracts reflecting the features of real world bargains in the union sector – namely, the distribution of workers by contract length, deferred wage increases, and escalator clauses. (His previous analysis assumed contracts of uniform length with a constant fraction of workers settling over any given time period and an absence of deferred increments or, equivalently, zero back-end loading.) Taylor's detailed simulations show the constraints that different real world contracts impose on a general disinflation (from 10 to 3 percent) effected solely by the change in expectations consistent with the new monetary policy. Although it is thus possible for such a disinflation to take place without any change in unemployment (compare Mitchell and Kimbell, 1982), Taylor shows that the adjustment path is extremely slow in the first two years of the disinflation program – by the eighth quarter of the program, wages have decreased by only 0.9 percentage points. Wage growth of 3 percent is ultimately achieved after some 16 quarters. Interestingly, Taylor's model implies that policy has to accommodate the overhang of previously negotiated wage increases to convince the bargaining parties that rapid deceleration will follow. And if wages do not adjust downward, then deferred wage increases in the future will also have to be accommodated!

Abraham (1983) uses the overlapping wage contracts model of Taylor (1980), but with rather more institutional detail (specifically, the importance of one-, two-, and three-year agreements across the economy), to chart the adjustment path accompanying a deceleration in the rate of growth in the money supply from 10 to 3 percent. In Abraham's model, 'almost perfect' foresight is assumed, in the sense that the change in monetary policy is unanticipated but that once the policy change is announced agents are again endowed with perfect foresight. As before, contracts are both backward and forward looking. Policy changes do not influence the former and so their effect depends on altering the latter. Abraham's simulations confirm that, in completely forward-looking contracts, the time taken to achieve the new steady state (wage and price inflation of 3 percent) is determined simply by the length of time it takes for all contracts to be renegotiated, namely three years. The larger the backward-looking component of expectations, the longer is the time taken to achieve a reduction in the rate of change in money wages to 3 percent and the greater the serial correlation in wages, although this does not exceed twice the length of the longest contract. Also, given the importance of backward-looking behavior, the time taken to reach this new steady state is almost invariant with respect to the precise policy followed in reducing monetary growth. However, the income distributional consequences differ markedly by disinflation path, being much less pronounced the more gradual the deceleration in monetary growth. If workers resist abrupt policy changes, they may be expected to shape contracts in a way that decreases the role of current and future economic conditions in wage setting, with fairly obvious consequences. Abraham conjectures that there is real potential for inducing a high responsiveness in wage setting by a phased disinflationary monetary policy.

The use of relative wages in the forgoing raises a number of difficulties. In particular, we note that Taylor's model does not possess the natural rate property (McCallum, 1982). Moreover, relative wage effects are not the only possible source of autocorrelation in time-series models (Riddell, 1979a). We would conclude that, although the use of relative wages is helpful in suggesting an additional source of inertia in wage determination, the concept should not be taken too literally pending further work on the stochastic structure of the wage equation and additional experimentation with industry-specific variables. We shall comment separately on the crucial assumption of contract exogeneity below.

British evidence

British research into the role of labor market institutions in wage determination has followed a somewhat different route. Much of the empirical discussion has focused on the adequacy of the official wage rate series as a measure of wage change. The 'failure' of the Phillips curve in the latter half of the 1960s led analysts to question whether part of the story was the index itself. The index does not give an accurate measure of the size of settlements because the bargaining calendar is not uniformly spread over the year. Since the time pattern of settlements varies across the economy, it is not surprising that aggregate wage change equations based on the index fail to display stability with respect to the addition or deletion of observations (Pencavel, 1982).

The first attempt to tackle the problem of a nonuniform bargaining calendar was that of Ashenfelter and Pencavel (1975), who simply scaled the dependent variable by the number of workers affected by wage settlements. The dependent variable became the (quarterly) change in wage rates normalized by the proportion of workers setting a new wage contract (during that quarter). Unfortunately, it emerged that conventional economic variables performed poorly in explaining the variance of this refined wage change measure. This result in turn prompted others to consider the limitations of Ashenfelter and Pencavel's scaling technique. In particular, Elliott and Dean (1978) note that the proportion of workers settling over a given period is not the same as the frequency of wage settlements and that the former measure could under certain circumstances obscure systematic changes in frequency. This criticism is reinforced by Smith and Wilton (1978), who extend the Ashenfelter–Pencavel model to include multiyear, variable-length contracts, and deferred increments. They demonstrate that such institutional considerations involve a more complex set of weights than envisioned by Ashenfelter and Pencavel. Nevertheless, Smith and Wilton's estimated wage change equations (using aggregate wage data for Canada) perform poorly.

Recognition of the wider array of institutional details led Elliott and Shelton (1978) to construct an 'adjusted' wage rate index for Britain. This new index averages wage changes only across those groups of workers who settle in the relevant periods. The authors offer their index so as to provide a more meaningful dependent variable in studies of the wage determination process (Elliott and Shelton, 1978, p. 260). We know of no independent studies using this index for Britain. One obvious problem with the index is that adjustment of the dependent variable may require a corresponding adjustment to aggregate explanatory variables (Addison and Burton, 1981). And, as Smith and Wilton note, data regarding some of the relevant micro explanatory variables may exist in a form that cannot readily be aggregated (e.g. the catch-up variable introduced earlier). Certainly, there will be a loss of information in aggregate studies that average individual observations.

Another problem with the use of aggregate data relates to the distinction between the occurrence of an event and the extent of the occurrence. As Pencavel (1982) has argued, the wage change process can be decomposed into two elements: first, the probability that wages will be adjusted and, second, the scale of the wage change conditional on wages being adjusted. Sample selection bias is thus possible in aggregate wage change exercises when the determinants or the parameters of each element are different.

Pencavel's study focuses on the impact of incomes policy on the frequency and magnitude of wage change in British coalmining, 1948–75. The first stage in this inquiry was to employ a probit equation to determine the probability of wages changing. From this equation, an inverse Mills ratio was constructed and duly plugged into a least-squares regression of wage change on the percentage change in consumer prices, output per manshift, the percentage change in the price of coal, aggregate unemployment, plus incomes policy dummies. It emerges from the first operation that the greater the increase in retail prices, the higher is the probability that wages will change. (The role of unemployment is discounted, and no support is given to the hypothesis that statutory incomes policies are more effective in reducing the frequency of wage settlements than 'voluntary' policies.) Turning to the selectivity-adjusted wage change equation, there is little support for any of the conventional Phillips curve arguments, from which Pencavel speculates that the apparent statistical significance of such variables reported in aggregate wage change analyses reflects primarily their effects on frequency rather than the magnitude of settlements. Clearly, further research is required here because Pencavel's study relates only to coalmining (part of the public sector) and records large standard errors on all coefficients (including the inverse Mills ratio term). But the procedure of analyzing wage change conditional upon a new agreement being negotiated seems eminently sensible, and returns us to the issue of contract endogeneity.

Contract endogeneity: cost-of-living adjustments and contract length

Of the US studies examined earlier, the most explicit allowance for institutional change is contained in the aggregate analyses of Wachter (1976) and Wachter and Wachter (1978). Interestingly, some support for Wachter's analysis is contained in Froyen and Waud (1984), who test Friedman's (1977) analogous proposition that inflation weakens the allocative efficiency of the price system, and is thus associated with a permanent loss in real output. Froyen and Waud estimate that, for Britain, the decline in the equilibrium level of real output due to inflation variability amounted to about 2.5 percent between the subperiods 1957–68 and 1969–80 (the variance of the inflation rate in the latter period was approximately two and a half times greater than in the former period).

Of the studies using micro contract data, only Riddell (1979b) and Christofides and Wilton (1978) examine the effects of inflation uncertainty on wage change. Riddell's study of Canadian wage determination uses US Livingstone–Carlson data on directly observed expectations. Inflation uncertainty is measured by the standard deviation of individual survey respondents' forecasts of the consumer price index (CPI). (It is assumed that individual decisionmakers have subjective probability distributions regarding future inflation – rather than precise notions of future inflation – so that the expected rate can be viewed as the mean of this distribution, and the standard deviation can be used as a measure of the amount of uncertainty associated with the point prediction.) Riddell finds that his inflation uncertainty variable exerts a significantly positive effect on wage inflation. Moreover, inclusion of the inflation uncertainty variable brings the coefficient on the price expectations term closer to unity. In other words, the vertical Phillips curve obtains once the amount of inflation uncertainty is held constant.

Christofides and Wilton (1978) argue that, because of uncertainty regarding the future rate of inflation, bargainers may not fully incorporate the expected (mean) rate of inflation into the contract; the shortfall can be taken into account *ex post*, via catch-up, if expectations turn out to be correct. They argue that, where both parties are risk averse, a Pareto-optimal risk-sharing arrangement will generally involve a coefficient on the price expectations term that is less than unity, and that this coefficient will itself fall with the variability of inflation (greater uncertainty) and possibly rise with the expected mean rate of inflation (via a threshold effect). Correspondingly, the coefficient on catch-up should rise with the variability and expected mean rate of inflation. Their empirical findings corroborate this conjecture, although it remains a puzzling feature of their analysis that total compensation for inflation emerges as less than complete (Riddell, 1979a).

Thus far all the studies we have examined, with the notable exception of Pencavel (1982), take contract length as a datum even though this is known to vary through time. Moreover, the various studies typically ignore cost-of-living adjustments (COLAs), presumably on the grounds that all wage contracts either implicitly or explicitly involve a COLA clause. Yet this assumption masks changes in the prevalence of COLAs through time and marked interindustry differences in their coverage (Card, 1983). There is also the empirical result, cited earlier, that during the 1970s the wages of workers in heavily unionized industries who were covered by COLAs grew significantly relative to other wages in the economy. Recently, analysts have begun to examine each issue.

The issue of contract length is critical to modeling the wage determination process and, of course, to the adjustment path set in train by macro disturbances. A recent study by Christofides and Wilton (1983) examines the determinants of contract length in a setting in which the degree of wage indexation and contract length are determined recursively (following Gray, 1978). The authors examine 1,749 Canadian contracts over the sample period 1966–75. Of these contracts, 1,440 are unindexed. Of the remaining contracts, 158 have an elasticity of the base wage with respect to the consumer price index of less than 0.5 and 151 have an elasticity equal to or greater than 0.5. Each of the three types of contract is examined separately in recognition of the possibility that the responsiveness of contract length to its determinants may vary according to the degree of indexation (see below).

Christofides and Wilton argue that contract length will vary directly with contracting costs and inversely with uncertainty regarding future price inflation. Contracting costs are proxied by the SIC group to which each micro observation is assigned and a dummy variable that distinguishes between contracts covering either more or less than 1,000 employees. Uncertainty about the course of future price inflation is measured by the square of the standard error of the estimate from an inflation equation, which describes expected inflation as a distributed lag of past rates of inflation. Note here that the authors use a 'sliding' regression approach to ensure that agents are provided with no more information than was available to them at the time contract negotiations took place (unlike Wachter and Wachter, 1978).

It is found that increased uncertainty significantly reduces contract length across all types of contracts (unindexed, and more or less indexed), and is the dominant argument for unindexed contracts. For the latter, as the uncertainty measure rises from its minimum to its maximum value, contract length is reduced by 14.2 months. The coefficient on uncertainty no longer dominates the contract length equations for the two groups of indexed contracts, and is lower in absolute size for the less indexed contracts. The authors rationalize this result on the grounds that the effect of increased inflation uncertainty on the variance of the real wage rate in indexed contracts will depend negatively on the scale of wage indexation, so that those enjoying less protection will be more prone to shorten contract length. The authors also find that contract length varies across industries but not by size of negotiating group. Interpretation of the former finding is clouded since the industry variable may also pick up uncertainty not modeled by the authors.

This analysis takes the optimal degree of indexing as a given and relates contract duration to price inflation prediction errors, although it is recognized that the effect of uncertainty (as measured) on contract length may differ by degree of indexation. Other analyses typically take contract length as a datum and examine the likelihood and extent of indexing.

A formal statement of the optimal degree of indexing is provided by Ehrenberg, Danziger, and San (EDS, 1983) and Card (1984b). Both emphasize the key role of unanticipated inflation, and each derives the extent of indexation from a model of firm profit maximization subject to a union utility function. The EDS model, of which only the fixed employment variant is considered here, shows that the optimal degree of indexation will be higher, the greater the elasticity of the firm's demand curve with respect to unanticipated inflation, and the greater employee risk aversion (where the initial degree of indexation is less than unity). The optimal degree of indexing will be lower, the larger the elasticity of other input prices with respect to unanticipated inflation, and the greater the extent of random shocks to productivity, demand, and other input prices (when employee-relative risk aversion exceeds employer-relative risk aversion). The model also shows that increases in expected inflation and inflation uncertainty (measured by the coefficient of variation in the expected value of the CPI) have no effect on the degree of indexation. Both results stem from the assumption that all real variables are affected not by the distribution of the aggregate price level, merely by its realized value (but see below).

EDS also consider the factors that influence the decision to index. In general, the same variables that affect the extent of indexation, once it occurs, also influence the probability of indexing. The main difference is that the probability of indexing rises with inflation uncertainty, given risk averse workers. Also, the probability of indexing falls unambiguously with the cost of indexing, while increases in the residual uncertainty of value added (caused by random shocks to productivity, demand, and other input prices) increase the probability of indexing given equal risk aversion of employers and employees.

The interesting aspect of Card's (1984b) study is that it directly derives estimates of the risk aversion of workers and firms (together with other parameters of the model) from contract-specific estimates of the correlations between input and output prices and aggregate price shocks. Card's objective is to explain the wide dispersion in the response of contract wages to price increases observed across different contracts or, more accurately, different industries. Specifically, Card seeks to explain differences in the marginal elasticity of wage indexation, which is defined as the cents per point increase in the CPI that the relevant escalator yields (while active) divided by the real contractual wage at the beginning of the contract. His sample comprises some 189 indexed labor contracts written in the Canadian manufacturing sector between 1968 and 1975.

It is assumed that unions and firms bargain over a contingent wage schedule, linking the contract wage to the CPI, and that the employer sets employment subject to the wage rate and to the prices it faces for inputs and outputs. The firm maximizes profits subject to the union utility function, which reflects the contractual real wage, the level of employment during the contract period, and the alternative real wage available to employees during that period. An optimal wage escalator is one that maximizes the expected utility of profits subject to a minimum expected utility requirement for workers.

The central feature of Card's analysis is that, if movements in the CPI yield information on contemporaneous shifts in the demand and supply of labor to the contract, the escalator will alter the contractual real wage with realized aggregate prices. Thus, if increases in the CPI signal an outward shift in the demand curve for labor or an inward shift in the supply curve (as the result of an improvement in alternative real wages), the contractual real wage will rise with the CPI and vice versa. Accordingly, much hinges on the information that aggregate prices convey for the market-specific prices of interest to the bargaining parties. If the conditional distributions of alternative wages and firm input and output prices are independent of the aggregate price level, then the optimal elasticity of indexation will be zero or, equivalently, the elasticity of the *nominal* contractual wage rate with respect to the aggregate price level will be unity. However, it is argued that movements in aggregate prices *will* signal shifts in alternative wages and firm-specific prices so that real wages will vary. More specifically, it is argued that the informational content of the CPI with respect to alternative wages and firm-specific prices of inputs and outputs will be a direct function of the correlation between unexpected changes in these variables and unexpected changes in the CPI. The greater the correlation between unanticipated changes in, say, the industry selling price and unanticipated changes in the aggregate price level, therefore, the more precise the conditional inference that may be drawn and, *ceteris paribus*, the more responsive the real wage will be to changes in the CPI. Conversely, the lower the informational content of aggregate prices, the closer will be the elasticity of nominal contractual wages to unity. Of course, the actual behavior of the marginal elasticity of indexation, as defined, will be a function of all three regression coefficients, and not simply that between unexpected changes in the industry selling price and the CPI. However, holding inferences of the alternative wage constant, if increases in consumer prices signal an outward shift in the demand curve for labor (either because the correlation between the industry selling price and the CPI is positive or because the correlation between input prices and the CPI is negative), then the real wage will rise in the presence of a positively sloped supply curve, and vice versa.

Card's empirical analysis shows that the marginal elasticity of indexation depends on the parameters of the firm's production function, the parameters of workers' and owners' utility functions, and the relationship between firm-specific prices and the aggregate price index (the latter being used to identify the parameters of the basic model). The chief finding is, of course, that the more information that aggregate prices convey for the market-specific prices of interest to the parties the greater will be the indexation of the real wage to the CPI or, equivalently, the greater the deviation of the optimal elasticity of indexation from zero.

Card's model provides valuable insights into the rigidity of the real wage and is a welcome empirical addition to the contracts literature. That said, it represents only a small step in the direction of modeling the effects of COLAs on wage determination, not least because it restricts its attention to only those contracts possessing an indexation clause and hence raises a selection bias problem. Moreover, no formal account is taken of contract length, although it is stated that contract length dummies are insignificant in a regression equation for the marginal elasticity of indexation, holding industry fixed effects constant.

Not all the subtleties of the preceding analyses are reflected in empirical studies that speak more directly to the question of COLA impact on wage change. In an analysis of 5,570 contracts in US manufacturing covering the period 1969–81, Hendricks and Kahn (1983) investigate the determinants of the likelihood of observing COLAs, the scale of indexation among contracts with COLAs, and the wage effects of COLA coverage. They find that the probability of observing a COLA clause is positively related to union coverage (a proxy for bargaining power) and inflation uncertainty, as measured by the variance of inflation forecasts in directly observed inflationary expectations. However, this probability is reduced the greater the unanticipated volatility of industry prices, as measured by the standard error of a regression of the relevant industry price on the CPI and a time trend.

The scale of indexing is also shown to be positively related to inflation uncertainty and negatively affected by industry price uncertainty. Note that the former result differs from that predicted by Ehrenberg, Danziger, and San (1983). However, the latter point out that, where the aggregate price shock has some joint distribution with the firm's demand and input price shock, conditional inferences about own demand and input prices with respect to a given change in the aggregate price level will be less well defined – that is, possess lower informational content – the greater price uncertainty and thus the closer will be the elasticity of indexing of the nominal wage to unity, *ceteris paribus*.

Turning next to the effect of COLAs on wage change, Hendricks and Kahn regress the annual change in wages for their sample of contracts on a large number of variables that include two dummies for indexed contracts according to whether the COLA is capped (i.e. subject to some maximum allowable increase) or uncapped, the reference category in each case being contracts in which there is no COLA prevision. They find that the effect of COLAs on wage change depends on the restrictions placed on them (see also Vroman, 1984). Contracts with uncapped COLAs yield significantly higher total wage growth. Moreover, in a separate analysis, they find that uncapped COLAs yield higher compensation for expected inflation than unindexed contracts – there were no differences between capped and unindexed contracts in this regard – and very much higher compensation for unanticipated inflation. Unfortunately, the determinants of the restrictions placed on COLAs are nowhere analyzed in this study, and the endogeneity of such provisions makes it difficult to interpret these findings. It may be conjectured that the liberality of COLAs is allied with union bargaining power, but it would be unwise to argue that the evidence supplied by Hendricks and Kahn establishes that COLAs are inflationary. At most the evidence provides a measure of the problems that can arise under uncapped COLAs during periods of unanticipated inflation. Such problems will presumably result in the subsequent modification of overly generous indexation clauses (see, for example, Freedman and Fulmer, 1982), but in the interim they may increase the persistence of inflation.

Only one study of which we are aware links frequency of wage adjustment and indexation. Using US data on wages for a sample of 157 major union collective bargaining agreements from 1957 to 1978, Cecchetti (1984) attempts to measure and explain changes in the frequency and degree of indexation of wage adjustments. Frequency is defined as the average speed at which contracts maintain relative wages (i.e. keep pace with current conditions) and not as the period of time between actual wage changes. Cecchetti infers frequency, as defined, from the dispersion of wage inflation produced by staggered and overlapping wage contracts. Very crudely put, the measured dispersion of wage inflation for a given average inflation will provide an inverse measure of frequency or the time taken for contracts to keep pace with current conditions. Cecchetti detects pronounced changes in frequency over his sample period, but these are not systematically related to movements in the price index.

Turning to indexation, Cecchetti notes that his frequency measure implies less than complete indexing of the relative wage. In the absence of discounting, the degree of indexing as defined will depend on the ratio of frequency to contract length; the closer the ratio to unity, the lower is the degree of indexing. Using supplementary Federal Mediation and Conciliation Service data on contract length and an assumed discount rate of 0.04, he again detects major change in the indexation parameter. It emerges, for example, that the degree of indexing increased rapidly after 1971; although contract length shortened, this was more than offset by an increase in frequency. Interestingly, movements in the degree of indexation apparently bear no relation to the variance of real and nominal shocks (unlike Gray, 1978) or to the reliability of aggregate prices in conveying information about movements in real input and output prices (unlike Card, 1984b).

Given the failure of other variables to explain movements in either frequency or indexation, to what does Cecchetti ascribe the abrupt changes in the respective series? Causation is laid at the door of incomes policy, the discrete applications of which tie in quite closely with breaks in the frequency and indexation series. Cecchetti concludes that US incomes policy, in its attempt to moderate inflation, created a world more prone to it. In particular, the rules of Phase II of the Nixon controls episode stimulated the inclusion of escalator provisions in both the initial and subsequent years of multiple-year agreements. This had the effect of increasing the speed at which price changes could be propagated through union wages while decreasing the sensitivity of these wages to real shocks.

Cecchetti provides a new story consistent with the widening in the union–nonunion differential in the 1970s (see Chapter 5). The inertia of union wage setting coupled with the increasing indexation of union wages is again perceived to have distorted the differential in the face of real wage shocks. Indication that some belated correction is under way is suggested by subsequent 'give-backs' in union contracts (on which, see Mitchell, 1982).

We would conclude that our knowledge of contract endogeneity is in a fairly rudimentary state. Although progress has been made in analyzing the determinants of COLAs in a risk aversion framework, a number of puzzles attach to the form taken by COLAs in this regard. Why, for example, are many COLAs written in the form of x cents per percentage point increase in the CPI when this has the effect of narrowing skill differentials? Also, what factors determine the various limitations placed on compensation under COLAs? These facts and the relationship between COLAs and contract length have yet to be addressed adequately in theoretical work.

At the empirical level, it is clear that *ex post* measures of COLA compensation are wrongly specified in terms of the theoretical models and also that better *ex ante* measures seem to be required (EDS, 1983). That said, it is a peculiarity of the literature that models designed to explain how union wages are negotiated (as opposed to determined) have failed to predict expected wages for non-COLA contracts (Kaufman and Woglom, 1984). Turning to wage determination *per se*, the role of COLAs is opaque. Most wage determination models have generally excluded COLA contracts. In studies that do include (*ex post*) COLAs, it is found that compensation for unanticipated inflation – the coefficient on unanticipated inflation plus that on catch-up – is considerably higher under COLA contracts than under unindexed contracts. However, it is difficult to draw inferences from such studies in the absence of any firm theoretical underpinning for the *ex post* unexpected inflation variable or, equivalently, the absence of a model of COLA endogeneity.

Finally, there is the interesting point raised by Wachter and Wachter (1978) that the response of obligational markets to an unanticipated increase in the inflation rate is likely to be lumpy or discontinuous, so that the adoption of escalator clauses of varying degrees of complexity does not proceed continuously with the variance of the inflation rate. However, once established, such clauses may remain in place long after the conditions that gave rise to them change. One obvious consequence of a more or less fully indexed nominal wage is that the economy becomes more prone to real disturbances. This may well have happened in the 1970s. The real problem is to model the next step, namely the adjustment of contract length.

Summary

This then is the current state of play in modern treatments seeking to introduce institutional detail into wage change analysis. Progress has been made on a number of fronts in discussing the rationality and consequences of wage contracts, but much remains to be done. This expectations-augmented Phillips curve appears to have been rehabilitated in US and Canadian micro studies. However, much hinges on the aggregate demand policy rule; thus direct estimation of Phillips curves may convey little information about the sensitivity of wage change to excess demand. Having said this, there is the nagging question of serial correlation. There appears to be more persistence in wage settlements than can be accounted for by traditional variables such as the state of the labor market, expectations of future wage inflation, and catch-up for differences in actual and expected inflation.

This persistence in wage settlements has been exploited in relative wage models. Potentially, relative wages are, as we have seen, an additional source of wage inertia even in a rational expectations framework. The notion that labor demand and supply behavior is rooted in relative rather than own wages returns us to the controversy surrounding wage spillover models encountered in Section 8.2. Although we are not enamored of the relative wage argument because of its failure to consider structural relationships, it is possible that in a world of uncertainty economic agents will draw inferences about future trends of nominal variables as much from labor market monitoring as from price forecasting. This of course complicates matters by giving a further twist to the problem of breaking inflationary expectations. However, there is nothing in this view to suggest that wage comparisons are a datum: there will be errors, learning, and adaptation. These subtleties are not captured in the simulation exercises of Taylor (1980) and Abraham (1983). Again, relative wage arguments are not inconsistent with orthodox explanations of wage change. The key issue is the manner of their incorporation in wage change analysis. Here we return to the observation that the relative wage models do not possess the natural rate property. It is therefore a moot point whether we have become unduly concerned with residual persistence. A less controversial conclusion would be that unions influence the mechanics of the inflationary process and introduce long and variable lags in the response of wages to its determinants. Such is the message of both aggregate and micro level studies.

The lags introduced by staggered, long-term contracts complicate the task of economic management while offering little scope for policy activism (assuming the interpretation of contracts as close-to-optimizing arrangements is accepted). There is, moreover, no suggestion that contracting practices cause inflationary pressure, although inflationary disturbances are more spread out on this account and the inertia in wage settlements may give the appearance of cost-push pressures. In short, the existence of such contracts affects the mechanics of inflation.

We have implied in the forgoing that the union role in all of this, if not transparent at the level of theory, is clear-cut empirically. After all, the vast majority of the data sets considered earlier use union contract data directly, or otherwise integrate the realities of union contracting relations in simulation exercises. Also, we know that nonunion wages tend to be adjusted at more frequent intervals than do union wages. The corollary is that unionized workers should experience greater fluctuation in employment and hours than their nonunion counterparts because of the implied greater rigidity of union wages. There is indeed evidence of greater cyclical variation of employment and hours in the union sector (e.g. Medoff, 1979; Raisian, 1979; Pearce, 1983).[22] But the nagging question remains: is there more than a difference of degree between the nonunion and union sectors? Nonunion workers also enjoy considerable continuity of employment, raising the possibility that their wages, too, are set over the economic climate rather than the economic weather. Thus, there is the possibility that the greater rigidity of the union wage (or rate of increase in wages) has been overemphasized in the literature, and that similar wage adjustment processes may obtain in all continuity markets, whether unionized or not.

8.5 Unions as a Fundamental Determinant[23]

We now consider the possibility that unions are a fundamental or indirect determinant of inflation. Since there is no incongruity in arguing that unions are a fundamental cause of inflation but not a proximate or direct cause, it is not surprising that the positions taken by economists on this issue have varied widely. Hayek (1959), for example, while espousing a conventional monetarist position on the identity of the direct cause of inflation, specifically indicts unions as a fundamental determinant. He argues that their wage actions have increased the natural rate of unemployment. Government responds by (mistakenly) expanding the budget deficit and money supply to mop up the induced unemployment. But this action relaxes the constraints on union action, leading to a wage push and hence a rise in unemployment. The process then repeats itself. As Burton (1980) has shown, the Hayekian model resembles the standard accelerationist treatment with the innovation that unemployment now oscillates between *two* natural rates: the lower being the natural rate in the absence of a full employment commitment, and the higher being that determined by more aggressive union wage behavior in the presence of a full employment commitment. The Hayek model thus produces a cycle of inflation around a rising trend.

Unfortunately, it is not clear why governments should persist with full employment policies that have this unenviable property. Surely they, no less than other economic actors, might be expected to learn. Also, the incentive for unions to push is less than obvious; we return to this point below. Both issues constitute unsatisfactory elements in the Hayekian analysis.

Rather more interesting an argument is that advanced by Gordon (1975a), who postulates that unions are *both* a proximate and a fundamental determinant of inflation. Gordon separately identifies a demand for and supply of inflation, which seems an eminently sensible approach and indeed one further elaborated on in Chapter 9. He argues that wage inflation is determined by conventional market forces *and* union pushfulness, although, as Burton (1980) notes, the logic of his model implies that a union push that fails to be accommodated by the monetary authorities will raise the natural rate of unemployment rather than the inflation rate (in dynamic equilibrium). His principal focus, however, is on fundamental rather than proximate determinants of inflation and specifically on the interaction of the demand for and supply of inflation in the political marketplace. On the one hand, Gordon examines the gains for different groups flowing from inflationary policies, with the political pressures from such groups constituting an implicit demand for inflation. On the other, governments are perceived as vote-maximizing entities that seek to capture the political profit from manipulating monetary and fiscal policies. In short, inflation is provided by vote-maximizing government in response to the political pressure exerted by those who would benefit from inflation. Thus, political realities and maximizing behavior rule out the simple monetarist solution to inflation.

Gordon identifies unions as the principal beneficiaries of inflation and their redistributive gains are said to result from upward movements in the wage level. However, what is the incentive for unions to 'push' in the model if, as Gordon assumes, there is unit elasticity of price change to wage change, so that labor's share is a datum? To proceed further, Gordon assumes an open economy, distinguishing between traded goods, nontraded goods with flexible prices, and nontraded goods with contractually fixed prices. The incentive to engage in wage push is that labor can gain at the expense of the two fixed-price sectors (assuming that the exchange rate remains constant). Unfortunately, as Brunner (1975) has shown, once all the relevant long-run conditions are introduced into the model — for example, the connection between the exchange rate and domestic and world inflation and adjustments in the domestic output market – the incentive for a continuous push on wages by unions evaporates. In short, it does not appear that the prevalence of secular inflations can be explained by Gordon's cost-push variable. Gordon (1975b) counters that it may still be rational for unions to indulge in wage push even if the gains are only transitory, provided that workers have a sufficiently high rate of time preference. However, this justification does not seem to tackle Brunner's central objection because it provides only a short-run rationale that cannot contribute much to an understanding of long-run inflationary trends (Burton, 1980).

An alternative suggestion is that the process of wage determination at the micro level can be likened to a prisoners' dilemma situation: all unions have an incentive to push to protect their relative incomes from the actions of other unions in an environment in which it is not possible to hold others to forgo pushing for a similar commitment. The overall outcome may appear irrational but in fact each 'player' is acting rationally.

What does the empirical evidence show? The major study on which we can draw is Gordon's (1977) analysis of the determinants of monetary growth *inter alia* for an eight-country sample over the period(s) 1958–73(76). In this analysis, Gordon pays close attention to the direction of causation issue, using the Granger (1969) test for exogeneity in a two-way relationship. To examine the exogeneity of money, the test involves regressing money growth on its own lagged values together with lagged values of wage change. The money supply is exogenous with respect to wage change if the lagged wage change term fails to contribute significantly to the explanation of monetary growth over and above the serial correlation process captured by the lagged values of monetary growth. The procedure is symmetric in determining the exogeneity of wage change.

Gordon seeks to compare the performance of an international monetarist model with a wage-push model along the dimensions of monetary growth, wage change, and price change. We focus here on the money and wage equations, the results for Britain and the US being reproduced in Table 8.1.

Before discussing these results, we should note that broad biases attach to Gordon's test procedures, despite the welcome attention paid to endogeneity and feedback. For the monetarist hypothesis to be supported, wages should be highly predictable and money should explain much of the variance in wage growth. Yet Gordon's wage equation introduces none of the institutional complexities that we have earlier argued should be incorporated into wage change analysis. Reflecting this point, Hall (1977, p. 469) notes: 'there is an evident bias ... in favor of the wage push hypothesis – every user of econometrics knows how easy it is to run unsuccessful regressions.'

Table 8.1 *Quarterly money and wage equations, the United States and the United Kingdom, 1958(3)–1973(1)*

| | Money supply | | Wage rate | | | |
| | US | UK | US | | UK | |
			(a)	(b)	(a)	(b)
Lagged dependent variable	−.544** (1.57)	−1.856** (3.63)	.816* (2.72)	.400* (1.27)	−.051 (.09)	−.442 (.80)
Money			.085* (1.07)	.258* (3.04)	.781* (3.77)	.652* (2.89)
Wage rate	1.999+ (1.19)	0.413 (.29)				
Output ratio (change)	.371 (1.11)	1.936* (2.56)				
Output ratio (level)	−.009 (.02)		.035* (.36)	.026* (.28)	.072 (.19)	−.198 (.55)
Traded goods prices		.300 (.28)	.020 (.25)	.144 (1.78)	.015 (.03)	−.137 (.29)
Full employment fiscal deficit	−1.012** (.74)	−.047 (.03)				
International reserves	−.092** (.72)	.348* (2.59)				
Control and wage push dummies:						
US – guideposts (1963(1)–1966(2))				−.237 (2.45)		
– restraint (1973(1))				−.523 (1.35)		
UK – restraint (four periods)						−1.493 (1.82)
– wage-push (1970(1)–1971(1))						2.197 (2.41)

|*t*| in parentheses

Notes: The superscripts denote significance at the 5 percent level – on a one-tailed test – of one or more positive individual coefficients (*); one or more negative coefficients (**); and one or more coefficients of both signs (+).

Source: Gordon (1977), Tables 4 and 12.

Gordon tests the argument that unions are both a proximate and a fundamental determinant of inflation. At the former level of causation, support for the wage-push hypothesis is adduced from a wage equation with large unexplained residuals and low coefficients for money and other arguments (e.g. domestic output). At the latter level of causation, wages should enter the money equation with a significantly positive coefficient.

Looking first at the results for the quarterly money supply change model, it appears that for the US (and the total sample excluding the US, not shown in the table) there is no sign that money accommodates previous wage movements. That is to say, the coefficient on wages is not significant. It is true that the sum of the coefficients on the wage variable is large, but, as we shall shortly see, there is no sign of autonomous wage push in the US. The evidence thus suggests that money supply is exogenous with respect to wages. This conclusion complements our earlier analysis discounting the wage–wage spiral.

For Britain, on the other hand, extending the sample period through to the fourth quarter of 1976 produces a significant coefficient on wages in the money equation (not shown in the table). This result suggests accommodation by the monetary authorities of the 1974–6 wage explosion in Britain. Gordon argues that British workers were simply trying to maintain their real wages in the aftermath of the 1973–4 oil price shock. He does not interpret this phenomenon as wage push *per se* since he views wage push as indicative of union aggressiveness. Perhaps we should view this particular episode as providing support for the more eclectic Friedman (1970) position that, on occasion, union pressure may lead to an expansion of the money supply. In general, then, there is little evidence to suggest that the money supply is endogenous with respect to money wages.

Turning to wage behavior, Gordon finds that the growth of the money supply enters positively and significantly in the equations for the US and for the total sample excluding the US (and for three of the seven countries in the latter). An interesting finding is that the strongest coefficient on lagged money growth obtains in the case of Britain, which, as Gordon notes (1977, p. 445), is somewhat remarkable in the light of the antimonetarist orientation of British economists.

The distinguishing feature of the wage equations themselves is the use of dummy variables to identify periods of autonomous wage push. We should not be surprised to learn that the dummies identified in part by 'peeking at the data' yield some evidence of wage push (Parkin, 1977, p. 473). Specifically, five (out of eight) significantly positive coefficients are obtained – though not for the US despite what Gordon terms the 'appearance' of some accommodation to wage change in that country's money equation. We also note that the estimated wage equations have large residuals, again with the exception of the US.

In summary, there is at most only weak evidence of accommodation and no direct evidence that *unions* cause the accommodation that exists. However, these results are suggestive rather than definitive and call for further analysis of the endogeneity of money issue. While little support can be adduced for the argument that unions cause inflation by their wage behavior, the possibility exists that unions seek to redistribute income in their favor through mechanisms other than the wage. This possibility is explored in Chapter 9. Suffice it to say here that Gordon's theoretical apparatus remains viable and his focus on the demand for and supply of inflation central to any investigation of the inflation process.

8.6   Conclusions

Our concluding comments may be kept brief. The weight of the evidence demonstrates fairly conclusively that unions are not a primary proximate determinant of inflation. Yet, while not originating inflationary pressures directly, they appear significantly to influence the mechanics of the process. We say 'appear' because although union contracts do have this effect it has yet to be established that unionism *per se* produces this outcome. Much more analysis of the nonunion sector in general, and continuity markets in particular, is required before we conclude that explicit contracts are more than a veil. In short, despite the lack of clarity of the theory in this regard, unionism may in part be determined by micro-optimizing arrangements.

Also, our knowledge of the precise manner in which the mechanics of inflation are influenced by unions is still rudimentary. The major difficulty here attaches to the assumption in much of the empirical literature that contracts are exogenous. Recent progress at the theoretical level in analyzing contract endogeneity (e.g. the determinants of COLAs and contract length) has yet to be satisfactorily integrated within the body of wage change analysis. Pending this integration, our ability to predict wage change will be severely hampered even if an interesting retrospective story of wage determination may be offered. For these reasons, and our presumption that existing contracts are close-to-optimal arrangements for the private parties to the contract, we have not explored how changes in the institutional structure might assist macro management. That would be premature.

Although our restructuring of the orthodoxy versus counter-orthodoxy debate with which we began our analysis has enabled us to provide answers to a number of puzzles in that earlier controversy, our discussion has raised rather more questions than it has answered. One important issue and source of controversy here is the role of relative rather than own wages in wages determination and the implications of relative wage models for the natural rate property. Another issue concerns instances of two-way feedback between wage change and monetary growth. Even though these do not constitute evidence that unions are a fundamental cause of inflation, the actions of policymakers require further analysis, not least because wage determination is highly contingent on policy and the consistency of policy. Failure to recognize this dependence means that little information on the responsiveness of wages or prices to excess demand can be gleaned from statistical Phillips curves that ignore the policy rule.

Notes

1 That is, $\dot{P} = \dot{M} + \dot{V} - \dot{Q}$, where $\dot{P}$ is the inflation rate, $\dot{M}$ is the rate of growth in the money supply, $\dot{V}$ is the rate of growth of velocity, and $\dot{Q}$ is the rate of growth of real output. Assuming that the growth in velocity is exogenous, the rate of inflation is thus proximately determined by the growth of money supply.
2 The equation given in note 1 does not indicate how much of the change in nominal income brought about by monetary growth takes the form of price increases versus output increases. Friedman's argument is summarized in the following equation:

$$\dot{P}_t = \alpha \dot{P}_t^e + f(U_t - U_t^N), \quad \alpha = 1$$

where $\dot{P}^e$ is the expected rate of inflation, U is actual unemployment, and U^N is the natural rate of unemployment that obtains when $\dot{P}_t = \dot{P}_t^e$. This 'natural rate hypothesis' states that, in equilibrium, there is no association between inflation and unemployment, that is, $\dot{P}_t - \dot{P}_t^e = 0 = f(U_t - U_t^N)$. If the authorities seek to reduce unemployment below its natural rate, which is determined independently of the equilibrium rate of inflation, they can do so only by operating on $\dot{P}_t$ without simultaneously affecting $\dot{P}_t^e$. If inflationary expectations are formed adaptively, there is scope for sudden increases in the rate of growth in the money supply to reduce unemployment. However, the price increases generated will ineluctably feed back into inflationary expectations. Ultimately, mistakes will be corrected and unemployment will return to its natural level and output will fall.

If inflationary expectations are formed rationally – in the sense that the expectations-generating mechanism is an unbiased predictor of $\dot{P}_t$ – then $\dot{P}_t$ and $\dot{P}_t^e$ will differ only by a white noise disturbance term; that is, the error term will be uncorrelated with past values of other variables. In this case, it would appear that monetary policy cannot cause even temporary changes in unemployment, unless the authorities behave in a totally unpredictable manner. However, it has been argued that, if wages and prices are set one or more periods ahead, the authorities will possess an informational edge. Some observers have seen some scope for policy activism against the backdrop of wage and price contracts that we observe in real world labor and product markets (Fischer, 1977). To anticipate the material covered in the latter half of this chapter, the source of this inertia is unlikely to offer the authorities a menu for policy choice. Institutions will adapt if the assumptions on which they are predicated change.

3   The wage reaction function simply equates wage change with excess demand. Given a nonlinear relationship between unemployment and excess demand, the simple Phillips curve obtains. The possibilities referred to in the text distinguish between a union reaction function and a market or nonunion reaction function. The dampening argument is that the slope of the nonunion function exceeds that of the union. This produces a flatter Phillips curve for the union sector, which cuts from below the nonunion curve at some unemployment rate. The possibility that unions may bias the reaction function translates into the statement that the wage change intercept of the union Phillips curve lies above that of the nonunion curve. The notion that there is a longer lag in the response of union wage change to its unemployment determinant is less obvious in that it may also imply dampening (see Burton, 1985; Mulvey and Trevithick, 1973).

4   Unfortunately, the validation hypothesis has been something of an article of faith to those who see unions as a direct cause of inflation. Attention has focused on wage inflation at the expense of the causal chains in the full model. One can find a parallel in the neglect by monetarists of the determinants of money growth.

5   Assuming that relative union–nonunion employment is inelastic with respect to the relative wage (Mulvey and Gregory, 1977a).

6   On the concept of relative power, see Chamberlain and Kuhn (1965); and for a discussion of the relationship between the various dimensions of power, see de Menil (1971).

7   Johnston and Timbrell also experiment with a variable capturing the bargaining cycle, namely the fraction of the labor force setting a wage increase in the relevant period. This empirical argument is elaborated upon in Section 8.4.

8   For a decisive rejection of the frustration thesis, see Nordhaus (1972).

9   For a detailed discussion of the model, see Addison and Burton (1984a).

10 The greater the wage increase sought, the greater is the required increase in union membership. This argument is consistent with the notion that the union wage differential is a positive function of union density (see Chapter 5). Of course, viewed from another causal perspective, the higher the union wage differential, the *lower* will be the equilibrium level of unionization, *ceteris paribus* (Lazear, 1983a, b).

11 That is, nonunion workers may seek to join unions prior to negotiating bouts because of the greater probability of strikes at such times. If a strike occurs, their immediate income loss will be reduced by the amount of the strike benefits they receive. However, this argument has little force for the US.

12 For example, are labor market participants concerned with the nominal or the real magnitudes of wage increases in reference sectors? For a discussion, see Addison and Burton (1979).

13 We do not separately discuss Okun's (1975, 1981) analysis of 'customer' product markets. Okun's model emphasizes the difficulties confronting buyers and sellers in ascertaining their current environment. The obligational market model, on the other hand, emphasizes limited knowledge of the future.

14 Azariadis (1977, p. 254) also notes that differences in firm-specific human capital provide an 'attractive alternative' to risk aversion as a source of layoffs.

15 Baily (1974) assumes that the worker faces mobility costs: in his model constant wage contracts are feasible only when short-run fluctuations in the wages available elsewhere are small relative to mobility costs. D. F. Gordon (1974) simply argues that the prospect of a future recession will effectively constrain workers from quitting in good times. Azariadis (1975) deals with a one-period model in which it is assumed that the worker cannot find alternative employment.

16 For a criticism of the underlying model, see Parkin (1980).

17 Williamson (1982) draws a sharp distinction between obligational markets and union markets.

18 For a criticism of this approach, see Baily (1978) and Kaufman and Woglom (1984).

19 Wachter, though using the term 'high-wage sector' and 'unionized sector' interchangeably, here recognizes that the theory relates more directly to high-wage industries. This provides a further example, if one were needed, of the somewhat ambiguous status of unions in contract models.

20 For an excellent review of the Canadian literature, see Riddell (1979a).

21 This is, of course, the substance of Mehra's (1976) approach.

22 But, for a very different set of results, see Raisian (1983a).

23 This section draws heavily on Burton's (1980) analysis of the spectrum of economists' views on the question of proximate versus fundamental causation. For an extended discussion of the causation issue, see Addison, Burton, and Torrance (1980).

CHAPTER 9

Unions and Politics

9.1 Introduction

In this final chapter we turn to the controversial question of the political influence of unionism, which we may refer to as its expression of 'external' voice. Although the subject is pregnant with implications for union democracy, economic growth, and inflation, the fact of the matter is that our knowledge of union impact in nonpecuniary markets is still rudimentary. We shall not be able to provide firm answers to many of the questions we raise, but the use of public choice theory (i.e. the economics of politics) allows us to make some progress in understanding unionism's political face.

It has been conventional to treat union political power as a benign if not positive force for change. More specifically it has been argued that much union political activity has been geared to promoting legislation of no obvious benefit to organized labor. Thus Rees (1977, p. 171) writes: 'Although the positions taken by unions on particular issues may not always be in the interests of the community as a whole, at least as it is construed by other groups, it does seem to be in the public interest to have some strong group that will act as champion of the underdog.' It is often noted, for example, that the AFL–CIO was instrumental in securing passage of the 1964 Civil Rights Act. As if to reinforce this interpretation, it is also noted that unions have failed to block particular pieces of legislation perceived to be contrary to their interests (e.g. the Landrum–Griffin and Taft–Hartley Acts of 1959 and 1947, respectively) or to secure specifically pro-union legislation (e.g. the ill-fated Labor Law Reform Bill of 1977). It is, however, usual to enter the caveat that when unions have acted in concert with analogous others (i.e. other producer group interests sharing momentarily a common identity of interests), greater success has been achieved (see, for example, Freeman and Medoff, 1984, p. 205).[1]

An alternative view is that union action in the political marketplace is best portrayed not in terms of ideology – voting behavior independent of any direct self-interest motivation – but, rather, in terms of the pursuit of narrow sectional interests. Supporters of this view are at times guilty of overstating the significance of union political power, but the public choice theoretic core on which such analysts draw provides a useful analytical perspective on union operation in the political marketplace and one that is not predicated on an assumed asymmetry between activities in the pecuniary market on the one hand and in the nonpecuniary market on the other.

To set the scene for our analysis of union political influence we begin with a discussion of public sector unions. Such unions perforce operate in the political market since their paymasters are politicians (and, ultimately, voters). Next, the rationale for the involvement of private sector unions in the political marketplace is discussed. Specific pieces of legislation at the state and federal levels are then analyzed in terms of union support/opposition. At this point, the analysis is broadened considerably to consider the possible ramifications of rent seeking in the political marketplace along the dimensions of economic growth, public expenditure, and inflation. Finally, the threads of the preceding arguments are drawn together.

9.2 Public Sector Unions

Public sector unions or employee associations, as well as bureaucrats, necessarily operate in the political market. However, the conventional analysis of labor demand in the public sector has typically applied the standard theory of household demand for inputs with little attention being given to those political factors that bear on government behavior (Reder, 1975). This is remarkable in view of the fact that voter-expressed demands for government services replace the marginal revenue product curve in such settings (although both reflect marginal valuations of the end products). Public sector employees are voters too, and we shall argue that they seek to increase, or prevent the erosion of, the demand for their own services.

Our starting point is the observation that there are important differences in motivation between the political entrepreneur and his counterpart in the private sector. The latter has an incentive to discover profit-enhancing strategies and methods of operation. Profit maximization necessarily implies cost minimization. By contrast, the incentive for the political entrepreneur to lower costs is ambiguous even assuming that he can identify cost savings when the necessary information is generated by the bureaucracy itself. Although there may indeed be situations in which vote-maximizing politicians perceive gains from reducing the costs of government, they must run the gauntlet of public sector employees who have been adversely affected by such decisions. It may therefore be to the politician's advantage to introduce measures that concentrate benefits on an important voting group, the costs of which are defrayed over taxpayers as a whole and, as in the case of underfunded pensions, possibly through time (Burton, 1982).

Now public sector employees are an important constituency for a number of reasons. For example, it has been shown that they vote more frequently than private sector voters (e.g. Bush and Denzau, 1977; Bennett and Orzechowski, 1983). They therefore exert greater influence than an equal-sized group of private sector voters. If bureaucrats view publicly provided goods as yielding higher wage income as well as utility from consumption and perceive this added dimension as a reduction in the price of the goods, these public employees will opt for a yet larger public sector (Borcherding, Bush, and Spann, 1977).

What of the politician's wider constituency and, in particular, the tax-paying public? This constituency is interested in ameliorating its tax burden, but its resistance may be weak and inchoate for the reasons described by Downs (1957). The taxpayer funds a veritable plethora of government activities and it would not be optimal for him to invest sufficient time and effort to discern just how much of his taxes are expended on public employee wages and employment relative to other expenditure items. The individual taxpayer has, moreover, an incentive to free ride in the provision of political opposition to the special pleading of public sector employees (Burton, 1982).

In short, the benefits of political support from public sector employees may exceed the costs in lost votes from higher taxation. This outcome might be expected to be more pronounced at the federal level than at state and local government levels both because the latter may be more constrained in their fiscal activities and also because local taxpayers face smaller information costs in isolating the 'price' of public sector services. That said, the existence of federal grants to state and local governments may attenuate these constraints. And although local or state taxpayers can vote with their feet (i.e. effect a locational shift), the costs of this 'market escape process,' as Burton (1984b, p. 141) terms it, are considerably higher than those faced by consumers in regular markets. The proliferation of Proposition 13 legislation in the US since 1978 (on which more below) might appear to suggest that the costs of forming a taxpayer coalition are less prohibitive than we have suggested. However, as Burton (1982) reminds us, a judiciously targeted reduction of public sector output can split the coalition, while outputs may be reduced more than inputs.

A more general analysis would suggest that voters, including taxpayers, will limit their 'awareness' to areas where intervention pays off most and costs least. Taxpayers will thus have producer group interests which may well dominate their interests as taxpayers. With a benefit for every interest group, the politician maximizes his vote prospects even though the costs of a package of programs may in the aggregate exceed the benefits.

Let us now turn directly to public sector unions. As noted in Chapter 3, there was a sharp increase in the membership of public sector unions in the 1960s and 1970s. Kurth (1983) observes that there is no shortage of 'explanations' for this development, although the proximate cause is often taken to have been permissive regulation, dating from 1962 and Executive Order 10988 in the case of federal employees, and from 1959 in the case of state and local government employees.[2] Kurth starts from the premise that unionism was imposed on the private sector whereas it evolved naturally in the public sector. Why did politicians as employers open the door to unionism? The answer lies in Kurth's representation of the public employee organization as a political 'firm' that reduces the cost of political transactions by monitoring compliance and metering performance. This device allows Kurth to chart a steady evolution of public employee organizations from a patronage system through a merit system to unionization. In all phases of this evolutionary development, the political firms in question are said to be efficient in the sense that politicians hire public employees to produce most efficiently those governmental services wanted by the public. There is, other things being equal, no scope for overpayment or rents in the public sector: if public employees are paid more than their counterparts in the private sector this is because of the services they provide and their political activity. This absence of rents is predicated on perfect political competition. A politician who accedes to union demands will, it is assumed, be defeated by an opponent who stands firm and resists these demands, thereby providing the service or good at lower cost.

How then does Kurth explain the existence of rents in the public sector and the success of militant public employee unions? He argues that other things have not remained equal; in particular, the role of union militancy in the public sector is equated with the post-1960 expansion of revenue sharing for mandated expenditures. Kurth reasons that such expenditures are directed toward ends not highly valued by local politicians, so that disruption by unions of these ends is of little cost to local politicians. However, if militancy succeeds in redirecting shared funds toward that which *is* valued by the politician (e.g. substituted for local taxes), then the politician obtains a positive gain from labor militancy among his employees.

This analysis runs counter to our earlier discussion. The interesting feature of Kurth's analysis is that it suggests that part of the public employee's wage is a payment for political services, so that we cannot necessarily equate wage differentials between the public and private sectors with rent. That said, his analysis neglects the power of bureaucrats to distort the voters' choice of the relative size of the public

271

sector. Admittedly, this power may be more circumscribed at the local than the national level because of the greater ease in ascertaining the costs of local services and the ability of voters to vote with their feet and escape to another jurisdiction. However, the notion that public expenditures faithfully reflect the demands and maximize the utility of voters is we feel no more tenable at the state than at the national level.

The alternative approach is, of course, that of the standard bureaucracy model (see Niskanen, 1971, 1975). This postulates that bureaucrats will attempt to obtain as large a budget as possible for the bureau in which they are employed. Even though there will be competition from other bureaus, this model points to a greater than optimal level of public expenditure 'because the nature of the budget process allows bureaus to act as price discriminating revenue maximizers' (Courant, Gramlich, and Rubinfeld, 1979, p. 806). If we graft on to this model the notion that, as the public sector grows, the voting power of public employees will generate further increases in the number of bureaucrats and their salaries (after Buchanan and Tullock, 1977), then the public sector comes to resemble a monster (or Leviathan) whose relative importance grows through time.

Courant, Gramlich, and Rubinfeld (1979) have sought to model the limits of this process at the local or state level. Assuming a balanced budget constraint, they argue that the power of a strong public sector will ultimately be constrained by private sector outmigration, and with it the erosion of the tax base. It is shown that the optimum public wage depends inversely on the size of public sector employment. Given the assumptions of the model, this implies that, even though wage bargaining power is endogenous, the ability to raise wages with employment is ultimately constrained. More specifically, it is shown that, in general, the optimum level of public sector employment from the perspective of political leverage is less than the level at which the public wage is maximized. In short, although public employee political power rises with public sector employment, the ability to translate this power into higher wages is still limited by the economic realities of the market escape process.[3]

Balanced budget requirements and expenditure- and tax-limitation legislation would appear to have a distinct chilling effect on the demand for public sector services. Not surprisingly, it appears that state and local government employees are strongly opposed to expenditure- and taxation-limitation legislation (Courant, Gramlich, and Rubinfeld, 1980). Unfortunately, we know of no studies that exploit the diversity of state and municipal fiscal constitutions and analogous legislation to test for their impact on either the demand for public sector employees or the union–nonunion differential. However, note that expenditure- and tax-limitation legislation, such as Proposition 13 in California or

Proposition 2½ in Massachusetts, will affect the demand for public services and demand for labor only in the specific context of the bureaucracy model. In theory, such legislation should not have any independent effect in a median voter model – such legislation merely reflecting changes in other variables influencing the demand for public services (Ehrenberg and Schwarz, 1983). Indeed, this distinction allows a discriminating test of the two models. Shapiro and Sonstelie (1982) examine changes in the parameters of demand for public services (expenditures on government, police, fire, and parks, although not labor demand *per se*) attendant upon the implementation of Proposition 13 in California in 1978. They find evidence of parameter shifts and hence support for this bureaucracy model. Ironically, it is revealed that, by removing one source of discretionary income, Proposition 13 actually attenuated the influence of voters on the allocation of revenue among expenditure categories.[4] In other words, voter influence on the bureaucracy was in some important sense weakened by Proposition 13.

At the federal level, the balanced budget assumption is, of course, breached. In addition, the market escape route that figures so prominently in the Courant, Gramlich, and Rubinfeld (1979) analysis is further eroded. Finally, the conflict between interest groups is considerably wider than the two-person game (public sector employee versus private sector taxpayer) envisioned in that model.

Clearly, more research is needed in which the role of the public sector union figures more centrally, but the public choice considerations introduced above cast some light on public sector wage differentials and the existence (and nature) of rents. Although the position of the union *per se* is opaque, it might reasonably be argued that the effectiveness of bureaucracies in promoting their own interests is in direct proportion to their organizational cohesiveness (Borjas, 1980), and hence a potentially important role can be reserved for unions in the public choice framework. Moreover, while unions need not always have large wage effects independent of public sector rents, they may have significant effects on expenditures and the nature of outputs.

9.3 Private Sector Unions

The economic analysis of private sector unions has traditionally focused on their impact in pecuniary markets. This is somewhat more understandable in the case of the US because it has long been an article of faith that American unions conform to the so-called 'business union' principle (see, for example, Estey, 1981, Chapter 3). British unions, on the other hand, soon found it expedient to establish a political party (the Labour Party) in order to secure a better representation of labor's interests in parliament.[5] Yet despite the significant differences in the links between unions and political parties in the two countries, the fact remains that unions (and other producer group interests) have a clear incentive to operate in both pecuniary and nonpecuniary markets, the relative mix of the two activities being determined by their relative costs and benefits (Faith and Reid, 1983; Burton, 1984a).

We have argued that unions are rent-seeking agencies that attempt to redistribute income in their favor at the expense of other groups in society. In the pecuniary market, unions can gain at the expense of profits, consumers, and other workers (generally nonunion labor, but conceivably other union workers too). The scope for redistribution via profits is believed to be quite limited – the share of profits in national income being too low to provide substantial gains for the average member (Phelps Brown, 1973; but see Sections 6.7 and 7.5 above). Because of this, it has long been considered that redistribution at the expense of nonunion workers is the more potent source of gain (e.g. Johnson and Mieszkowski, 1970).[6] That said, the monopoly rents achieved by unions are subject to erosion both via the rising price of unionism and through the incentives provided firms and consumers to make substitution in production and consumption. Of course, the strength of this market escape route to labor cartels may be attenuated or even blocked if unions can gain the assistance of the state. This is presumably the sense of Ross' (1948, p. 7) comment: 'No group can maintain significant power in present-day society without political influence,' even though he failed to develop this important insight.

If rent seeking can take place in both pecuniary and nonpecuniary markets, unions and other sectional interest groups will, as noted above, presumably devote resources to these activities according to their relative costs and returns. Rent seeking in the political marketplace operates through the coercive powers of government to regulate a market or industry. The gains accrue via direct money subsidies, control of entry, control of production of complements and substitutes, and control of market price. Union gains are thus typically achieved at the expense of taxpayers and consumers, although multiple-interest groups compete for regulation.[7]

It may be argued that rent seeking in the economic marketplace will be relatively more attractive to small, homogeneous unions (e.g. craft unions) because unions with a large and heterogeneous membership face substantial costs in first constructing and then policing the cartel. This difficulty in the economic marketplace is, however, offset by a compensating advantage of large membership in the political market-place, because the union may be able to offer a critical mass of voting support to 'accommodating' governments and politicians. Not only is such a union likely to evince a higher demand for state assistance because of the costs of private cartelization, then, but the government is likely to supply greater amounts of regulation where the voting rewards are greatest. This is none other than a straightforward application of Stigler's (1971) economic theory of regulation and recalls the analysis of Section 9.2.[8]

Although rent seeking via the political marketplace may be especially attractive to large unions, all unions have an incentive to operate in political markets to gain the protection of the state from the forces of competition. That assistance will often involve measures that buttress bargaining power in the economic marketplace through decreasing the cost of organizing or stimulating the demand for union labor (see Section 9.4 below). An important question, therefore, is the extent and impact of union political power. It is not enough simply to state the potential, the outcome has also to be assessed. In short, is union political power a problem? The answer to this question depends in part on ideology, and in practice upon the extent to which the market economy in general diverges from the competitive paradigm. The issue is a highly controversial one but, as we shall show in the next section, some progress can be made in isolating union influence and in identifying the nature of the problem.

In the interim, however, we have to consider the possibility that union political action may reflect the interests of the leadership rather than the membership. The precise identity of the union beneficiaries has been little discussed in the literature, but recently Burton (1984c) has exploited Ross' (1948) insight that union leadership like any other bureaucracy may be expected to pursue their own interests rather than those of the membership, subject to some minimally acceptable standard of performance. Burton argues that union bureaucrats will seek to maximize the size of union membership since their power, status, and income are likely to be a direct function of union size. (It is assumed that the member-dominated union 'club' will strive for the maximization of per capita rents.)[9]

He notes that, in a large union, the potential for 'executive discretion' may be enhanced for two reasons. First, the incentive for each individual member to participate in union affairs is less in large than in small unions because the influence of his vote on the outcome is correspondingly reduced. Since there are positive costs to voting, there is thus some scope for union leaderships to pursue their own goals. Burton predicts that the larger the union, the more expansion-minded will be its membership policy. Second, the ability of the union member to vote with his feet – the exit option – may in practice be severely circumscribed. In a world of loose or non-existent jurisdictional agreements, the Tiebout (1956) mechanism should eliminate any scope for executive discretion, but with more or less tight jurisdictional agreements there are distinct costs attaching to the exit option, since switching union affiliation may well imply an interindustry or interoccupational move. Burton argues that the average size of trade unions will be larger and their number fewer in the presence of restrictions on competition.

The costs of exiting from union to nonunion status will depend on the extent of closed shop and other union security agreements. The more widespread closed and union shops, the greater is the potential for executive discretion. Burton predicts that unions will tend to be larger in the presence of exclusive union membership agreements with employers.[10]

Burton's argument is, then, that union growth provides the key to executive discretion. Of course, union growth may also be in the interests of the membership. By increasing union density, union growth may be expected to reduce both the elasticity of product demand and also the substitution elasticity between union labor and other factors (see Freeman and Medoff, 1981). The empirical evidence reviewed in Chapter 5 suggests that there is a positive association between percentage organized and the union wage. This evidence is summarized by Voos (1983), who also computes the marginal benefit to union members from organizing, using estimates of the union coverage coefficient in the union wage equation provided by Freeman and Medoff. These marginal benefits range from $126 per year in textiles to $789 per year in transport equipment (1967 dollars) per person organized. When these gains are projected over, say, a five-year time horizon and discounted at, say, 15 percent, the relevant present values are $423 and $2,646 respectively. Against these benefits must be set the marginal costs of organizing. Voos measures organizing costs in terms of direct expenditures on salaries and expenses for a sample of 25 unions between 1964 and 1977. These data are matched with observations on new union members from National Labor Relations Board (NLRB) representation election records. Her regression analysis reveals that the marginal costs of winning bargaining rights for one more person range from $152 to $500 (1967 dollars), according to specification. Thus it seems that the expenditures of international unions on organizing programs can be justified by the benefits received by their members. Indeed, Voos argues that unions do not grow sufficiently.

This analysis takes no account of union dues, and so the gain to the membership from union growth cannot simply be equated with these marginal benefits. However, evidence supplied by Raisian (1983b) suggests that there is a positive relation between the union wage premium net of dues and the size of dues. It thus appears that much of the premium is a rent.

The US studies analyze an environment of low to moderate rather than high levels of unionization. There is therefore an obvious problem in extrapolating their findings beyond the range of observations and to other countries. The possibility that unions will use such methods as exclusive jurisdiction agreements and union security agreements to monopolize the provision of union services and appropriate some of the 'profits' of union strength cannot therefore be ruled out. Burton's analysis presumably needs to be recast in these terms. Alternatively, the switching point in union density at which leadership interests are better served than those of the membership by further growth has formally to be identified.

Union size may reasonably be expected to contribute to the erosion of the union member's position as principal. Some evidence of this is provided by the apparent dissonance between the political goals of the AFL–CIO and union members' preferences (see, in particular, Heldman and Knight, 1980). The monopolization of union services resulting from exclusive jurisdiction and compulsory union membership constitutes an important theoretical challenge to the median (union member) voter or pure union agent model assumed in the literature. In the absence of empirical evidence, however, we shall not further discuss the identity of the union beneficiaries although this may be of major importance in understanding the political activities and legislative goals of large unions.

9.4 Unions and Legislation

Despite the extension of collective bargaining rights to federal, state, and municipal workers in the 1960s and 1970s, it is tempting to conclude that US unionism has not been conspicuously successful in promoting its sectional interests through politics.[11] For example, in the early 1970s, when the AFL–CIO with the support of the Nixon administration sought backing for an expansion of the picketing rights of construction workers, it encountered stiff resistance in Congress. And even after Congress eventually passed the legislation, it was vetoed by President Ford. Again, in 1977 and 1978 organized labor strongly supported a bill that would have increased penalties on businesses committing unfair labor practices and reduced the time required to hold union representation elections. On both occasions Congress failed to pass this proposed Labor Law Reform Act, despite the increased number of labor-supported candidates in Congress.

In earlier times, too, labor suffered reversals with the passage of the Taft–Hartley Act in 1947 and the Landrum–Griffin Act in 1959. That said, from 1931 to 1938 Congress supplied six major pieces of labor legislation actively supported by the union movement. The Davis–Bacon Act (1931), the Walsh–Healey Public Contracts Act (1936), and the Fair Labor Standards Act (1938) authorized direct federal regulation of wages, hours, and working conditions in various sectors of the economy. The National Industrial Recovery Act (1933) was the first federal minimum wage statute, although its main purpose was to set up a system of industry codes or cartel arrangements.[12] More substantive gains accrued to labor via the Norris–LaGuardia Act (1932) and the National Labor Relations (Wagner) Act (1935). Norris–LaGuardia had the effect of greatly restricting employers' use of injunctions against union organization, and made the so-called yellow-dog contracts unenforceable. The Wagner Act ushered in the current era of labor legislation.[13] Under the Act, the rights of workers to organize, bargain, and strike were given clear legal sanction. Employers were required to bargain in good faith with unions that represented a majority of their employees, and representation and certification procedures were established. The National Labor Relations Board, the policing agency, supervised the representation election process and certified unions as exclusive bargaining representatives. It also acted as a tribunal for hearing 'unfair labor practice' charges against employers (five employer activities were made unlawful under Wagner).[14]

It is customary to view all six pieces of legislation as 'environmentally' determined by the mass of public sympathy toward unions at this time and a not uncommon perception that the Great Depression was unlikely to be cured by market forces. It is also often argued that the decade of the 1930s provides an example of enlightened labor legislation. A rather different view would be that the events of the Great Depression dramatically weakened the opposition faced by the beneficiaries of the legislation who were thus able to engineer changes in the legislative environment. An interesting discussion by Reynolds (1980a) of the Norris–LaGuardia and Wagner Acts reaches this very conclusion; one that is consonant with received theory (Stigler, 1971; Posner, 1971; Peltzman, 1976; Rubin 1975).

However, our task is to identify formally the influence of unions (*inter alia*) on the legislative process. In what follows, we first examine the effect of union membership and campaign contributions on the voting behavior of legislators before turning to consider the 'success' of union-favored legislation.

Identifying union influence with any degree of precision is no easy task. An immediate problem is to distinguish between the influences of ideology and self-interest in motivating the voting behavior of the legislator, after Kau and Rubin (1979). But how might ideology be measured? One possibility would be to use the annual ratings given congressmen by any one of a number of ideological groups on the basis of their voting behavior. Two liberal groups engaging in this rating exercise are Americans for Democratic Action (ADA) and the AFL–CIO Committee on Political Education (COPE). In their analysis of 26 congressional votes in 1974, Kau and Rubin use the ADA ratings of congressmen as their measure of ideology. The union economic interest – one among several sectional interests identified by the authors – is simply proxied by the percentage of residents in a congressman's state who belong to unions. Kau and Rubin report that unions have a significant influence on congressional voting on almost all issues. That said, something remains that is systematically associated with voting that correlates with the ideological variable, even after controlling for logrolling (achieved by eliminating those bills that appeal to the same economic interests).

However, the ideological variable may reflect economic interests in some unmeasured way. Relatedly, there are difficulties in using an ideological variable that is based on votes to predict votes (see, for example, Carson and Oppenheimer, 1984). For our purposes, however, it seems clear enough that the union variable is highly significant in explaining congressional votes.

This finding receives further support from a general equilibrium analysis of congressional voting on eight bills in 1979 that served to increase government regulation of the economy. Kau, Keenan, and Rubin (1982) again report that union strength – measured by membership and contributions – is significant in the majority of votes. Although ideology, this time based on a constituent rather than a legislator measure, is again found to be an important (indeed the dominant) argument, the union role in favoring regulation and increased intervention is clear-cut. Business interests, on the other hand, are shown to oppose such laws, but their influence appears to be less productive of votes than that of unions, at least for the sample of bills considered.

Most analysts have in fact eschewed an ideological variable and have narrowed their focus to voting issues in which the economic interest of unions is said to be more transparent. Minimum wage legislation has attracted the most scrutiny. All the early studies show that union voting strength or union contributions to political campaigns positively influence the probability that a legislator will vote in favor of such legislation (Silberman and Durden, 1976; Kau and Rubin, 1978; Bloch, 1980). In a paper that investigates the impact of union membership *and* political contributions on voting behaviour, while simultaneously investigating the determinants of union contributions, Kau and Rubin (1981) examine some eight pieces of labor-related legislation. They conclude that unions do possess significant power in influencing congressional votes in a manner that appears to reflect their economic

279

self-interest (e.g. opposing a two-tier minimum wage amendment and supporting extension of the minimum).[15] Both union financial contributions and union voting strength emerge as significant determinants of voting behavior, other things being equal – the former in all eight pieces of legislation, the latter in two. Contributions and membership appear, moreover, to be deployed in a systematic fashion: contributions are given to favored representatives who need assistance (proxied by low seniority) and to representatives from districts that have only an average number of union members.

An important criticism of the minimum wage literature has been offered by Uri and Mixon (1980), who have argued cogently that vote-maximizing legislators can appeal simultaneously to opposing constituencies in circumstances where the outcome of the final vote is not in doubt.[16] Voting with the majority on the final vote allows the legislator to appeal to the union constituency in the case of minimum wage legislation, while voting for an amendment that lessens the impact of that legislation on other constituencies (e.g. small businesses) also gains the support of the latter. The basic idea here is that amendments tend to concentrate benefits more closely on political groups than does the composite bill. Uri and Mixon's empirical analysis of four amendments to, as well as the final vote on, the 1977 Amendment to the Fair Labor Standards Act, which increased the level of the minimum wage, supports their contention that voting is not a simple binary choice. Focusing here on the union result, they find that union strength, although significant in influencing the final vote, was insufficient to overturn three of the four amendments lessening the impact of the legislation on other important constituencies, and in particular the small business community.

Of the minimum wage studies, perhaps the best attempt to integrate theory with measurement is that of Cox and Oaxaca (1982), who examine the influence of two interest groups, namely capitalists and organized labor, on state-legislated minimum wage rates in 1970 and 1975. They first present a general equilibrium analysis in which the economic interests of the two sides are made explicit. The model assumes two production sectors (and a household sector to reflect the assumption that their products are gross substitutes): one is nonunion and employs unskilled and skilled labor together with capital; the other is union and is relatively more skilled labor intensive relative to capital. Assuming constant real output, perfect capital markets, and full capital mobility, Cox and Oaxaca investigate the effects of imposing a binding wage floor on nonunion firms that increases the wage rate of unskilled labor. It is shown that employment in the union sector increases, that the real rental rate of capital decreases, and that the union wage rate increases relative to the capital rental rate.

Having demonstrated that the economic interests of high-wage union labor and owners of capital are involved in minimum wage legislation, the next step is to discover whether owners of capital do in fact oppose minimum wage legislation and unions support it. This is achieved via a political model of state-legislated wage minima. The state legislator is depicted as an optimizing individual seeking to maintain his tenure in office. His vote on minimum wages may thus be expected to reflect the relative importance of the two groups in the political marketplace; a vote that adversely affects the majority interest group will threaten the legislator's continued tenure in office. The views that prevail in the legislature are assumed to be those of the median voter.

Cox and Oaxaca estimate a Tobit model in which the dependent variable is the state minimum wage (i.e. including a zero minimum wage). There were 14 states in 1970 and 10 in 1975 without state minima. The independent variables are the proportion unionized, the proportion of income comprised of rents, dividends, and interest, and the proportion of earnings that is proprietor income. The last two variables are intended as proxies for capitalists' interest while the first is a proxy for labor's interests. Apart from these choice variables, a prevailing wage argument is also employed in the estimating equation.

Their results provide strong support for the economic model, despite the obvious limitations attaching to their proxies for union and capital influence.[17] It emerges, for example, that a 10 percentage point rise in the extent of organized labor raises the expected minimum by $0.22 per hour in 1975, whereas an equal percentage point fall in capital's income share increases it by $0.33 per hour. For the hypothetical state with average labor and capital representation, the expected minimum wage in 1975 is estimated to be 62 percent higher than it would otherwise be in the absence of any organized labor interest and 26 percent lower than in the absence of a capital income share. Given an actual state minimum wage averaging $1.80 at this time, these values imply minimum wages of about $1.10 and $2.45, respectively.

Discernible in the literature, therefore, is an increasing tendency to focus on the outcomes of union-favored legislation rather than simply on the voting records of individual congressmen. This is made most explicit in a still unpublished analysis by Freeman, summarized in Freeman and Medoff (1984, pp. 195–8). The basis of the study is a time-series analysis of the influence of union density in a state on the votes of senators for union-favored legislation (as defined by COPE ratings). The controls include median income in the state, percentage of state residents black, and region of the country. Consonant with the studies reviewed earlier, Freeman finds that union density is an important determinant of a legislator's vote. More specifically, he reports that an across-the-board 5 percentage point increase in union density would have improved the 'success' of union-favored bills by approximately 7 percentage points, while a corresponding decrease in union strength would have reduced 'success' by about 13 points. However, Freeman cautions that the success rate should not be interpreted too literally in so far as the content of a bill figures centrally in its acceptance or rejection. Freeman interprets his results as meaning that improved union density or penetration would typically be reflected in the strength of a bill's pro-union provisions, and vice versa. This interpretation, taken in conjunction with the findings of Uri and Mixon (1980), underscores the degree of refinement required in exercises seeking to assess union influence on legislation.

In a separate analysis of 280 union-favored bills, 1947–80, Freeman and Medoff (1984) conclude that unions have in fact, if not in intent, been more successful as the instrument of voice for all workers and lower segments of society than as a special interest group seeking to enhance its own position. They structure the legislation in question according to the following taxonomy: 'legislation pertaining to unionism' (77 bills), 'legislation pertaining to general labor issues' (72 bills), and 'all non-labor-related legislation' (131 bills). The first group is subdivided into four categories: national labor legislation, restrictions on union political power, alterations in Davis–Bacon, and bills regulating workers in industries covered by the Railway Labor Act. Freeman and Medoff report that only 20 percent of national labor legislation was in the 'right direction' as perceived by organized labor, considerably lower than the success rate for general labor- and non-labor-related legislation of around 55 percent. On the other hand, bills to restrict unions' political expenditures or to weaken Davis–Bacon were almost always successfully deflected by labor's political influence.

These are interesting statistics, which the authors explain in terms of the degree of opposition faced by unions in promoting legislation with concentrated costs and not simply concentrated benefits. The argument that legislation that deepens labor monopoly at the national level evokes an active response from business lobbies is an eminently sensible one. However before we conclude that organized labor has been conspicuously unsuccessful in promoting national labor legislation, we must recall that, in the interval preceding Freeman and Medoff's sample period, Congress had supplied six major pieces of legislation favored by the union movement (see Section 9.1 above). This is to make the obvious point that, in assessing the success or otherwise of union political activism, one has to consider the degree of base period success. Moreover, just as Freeman and Medoff (1984, p. 202) refer to the ill-fated Labor Law Bill of 1977 as 'relatively mild' legislation, so too could one speak of 'modest reversals' under Landrum–Griffin and Taft–Hartley (see, for example, Reynolds, 1980a). The point is that such labels are not particularly helpful. The relatively uncontroversial conclusion would be that unions have to some extent been on the defensive in the postwar period, at least in the US.[18]

A second difficulty is encountered with respect to the taxonomy itself. The argument that 'minimum wages . . . benefit virtually no union member directly and few indirectly' (Freeman and Medoff, 1984, p. 199), although it explains the positioning of minimum wage legislation in the category of 'general labor legislation', is one that few observers would accept without qualification. The basic difficulty confronting any analysis of this nature is that unions have an incentive to dress special-interest legislation in general-interest clothing. Consider, for example, Occupational Safety and Health Administration (OSHA) legislation. Is such legislation in the interest of labor as a whole, or might not unions have a narrow sectional interest in supporting such legislation? On the first question, the answer is ambiguous. If workers are well informed about the dangers inherent in the job and are sufficiently mobile to avoid risks they do not wish to embrace, then some workers (i.e. those less sensitive to risk) will of course suffer as a result of an effective safety/health standard. On the second question there is at least the possibility that organized labor may support OSHA because it imposes standards on nonunion firms already attained in unionized establishments. As such, application of the union standard will increase the demand for union labor. Unfortunately, there is insufficient information to test this hypothesis. Another possibility, explored by J. Miller (1984), is that OSHA standards raise the cost of capital relative to the cost of labor and, while decreasing industry output and productivity, actually increase the demand for labor. In short, a simple categorization of bills does not really come to grips with the problem of explaining the rationality of organized labor in supporting legislation.

It is ironic that similar studies have not been conducted for countries in which the level of unionization considerably exceeds that obtaining in the US. As Freeman and Medoff note, the counter-response of other sectional interests to monopoly-deepening union legislation is less likely to be successful where organized labor constitutes a majority of the labor force.

Given the current state of play in the empirical literature, no general quantitative statement concerning the extent of union power can be given. This is perhaps less than surprising given that union power is not a datum but may be expected to fluctuate through time as a result of shifting coalitions and the complexion of governments. Unions are but one of the sectional interest groups that operate and compete in the political marketplace. However, there are signs that unions are a singularly important case of the general phenomenon because of the large number of voter members involved, even in the US. Unions do, it would appear, exert significant influence on the legislative process, and their power to oppose may be equally if not more important than their power to initiate, which is one reason why one should not dwell unduly on the recent failure of union-sponsored bills. Having said this, we would not conclude that the political power of American unions is in the ascendancy at this time. Indeed, given the interactive and mutually reinforcing character of economic and political power, the opposite may be true.

The material we have analyzed demonstrates that it is unprofitable to assume benevolent preferences on the part of union workers for nonunion members, as the industrial relations literature sometimes appears to suggest (e.g. Bok and Dunlop, 1970). That is not to argue that ideology is unimportant but simply to make the point that interpreting union political action as motivated by self-interest is as viable a notion in the context of the political market as it is in regular markets. This ground has now been conceded. Interestingly, Freeman and Medoff (1984, p. 202), while arguing that unions have achieved greater success in the areas of general and non-labor-related legislation, recognize that unions have attained this status 'through no virtue of their own.' In short, the debate over union influence, though as divisive as ever, has been restructured and is now conducted within a framework of public choice theory. We should expect to see considerable progress in identifying unionism's political influence in this new milieu.

9.5   Unions, Growth, and Inflation Revisited

Less progress has been made in charting the wider consequences of the exertion of political power for economic ends. Yet there are pointers to suggest that consideration of the political activities of unions and other powerful producer group interests assists our understanding of the inflation problem and the process of economic growth. That said, we are currently very far from being able to quantify union impact along the dimensions of growth, public expenditure, and inflation. In all that follows we again emphasize that unions are but one of the players in the processes we describe.

Unions and growth

As noted earlier, all unions, and not merely large unions or public sector unions, have an incentive to lobby for government measures that redistribute resources in their favor. This lobbying pressure may be pronounced in the case of industries or firms that have historically grown large but that are currently in decline. Union lobbying will presumably take the form of a demand for subsidies, bail-out operations, trade protection, and other forms of assistance. Unions may find common cause with the relevant representatives of capital in this endeavor. Such lobbying activities, if successful, threaten to hinder economic growth through propping up obsolete industries, and slowing the movement of resources from less to more highly valued uses.

The issue is wider than this, however. According to Alchian's (1950) analysis, a private enterprise economy in which government subsidies do not exist has a Darwinian survival-of-the-fittest aspect. Enterprises that make at least a normal rate of return survive and perhaps grow, while those making economic losses sooner or later are evolved out of the economic system.[19] Concurrently, 'new' enterprises are being created, some of which succeed and others fail. Note that in this evolutionary process not only the generation of profits but also the making of losses is viewed as central to the efficiency of the economic system. In a system that insulates firms from losses, however, the process of economic natural selection would be much attenuated and inefficient enterprises would continue in existence. Note, too, the implication that producer groups have an incentive to lobby in the political market to gain the assistance of the state to impair this process in their own interest. In Alchian's terms, such measures would dampen the possibilities of economic evolution.

Elements of this view are contained in Mancur Olson's (1982) analysis of comparative growth rates. Olson's thesis is that the comparatively slow growth rate of the British and US economies is intimately related to the greater prevalence and significance of collectively organized sectional interests, not only trade unions but also professional associations, trade associations, and various other lobbies and cartels. Olson argues that the phenomenon of 'market closure' has both static efficiency effects (Chapter 7) and dynamic or evolutionary effects. The latter dampen the prospects for economic growth. The mechanism is relatively straightforward: the peaceful evolution of political democracy fosters the growth of special interest groups, and interest group politics leads to legislation that protects sectional interests and inhibits resource allocation and growth. The measure of retardation is said to be in direct proportion to the length of time interest groups have had to evolve without upheaval and dislocation. Thus, for example, West Germany and Japan should have higher growth rates than Britain and the US. Moreover, parts of the US (e.g. the northeast) should have slower growth rates than others (e.g. the south).

Although Olson provides crude econometric results consonant with his explanation, the explanation of economic growth is unlikely to have a basis in simple theories. One problem with Olson's analysis is that it does not allow for fluctuations in the political power of interest groups. Thus, as Nelson (1981, pp. 1058–9) notes: 'his hypothesis cannot easily explain a number of recent political developments which have torn down, or significantly reduced, the levels of protection carefully raised over the years by various interest groups to shield themselves.' Again, Olson's theory neglects international effects that impinge on the rise and decline of nations. That said, his analysis usefully might be viewed as an informal component of a wider growth model that includes a public choice element, the thrust of which is that the sheltering of special interests renders economic change more costly and difficult.

The crucial issue would seem to be the interplay between market forces on the one hand and attempts to impair or block their operation on the other. Interestingly, it is precisely the workings of the democratic political market that provide the threat to the market economy. No one would seriously entertain the notion that the complex tangles of special-interest legislation obtained by unions and others from the democratic process have succeeded in totally blunting the operation of market forces. The market escape process can undermine even the erection of government measures to protect monopolies. But it seems reasonable to assume that measured economic growth is retarded as a result of attempts to intervene in the market at the behest of producer interest groups, including unionism. To repeat, the precise allocation of responsibility for the retarded growth outcome is an interesting but unknown matter. However, unions would seem to be participants in the process.

Unions, public expenditure, and inflation

The message of Chapter 8 was that unions are not a proximate (or direct) determinant of inflation. The proximate cause is, rather, an excessive rate of growth in the money supply relative to the growth rate of real output (though unions may play a subsidiary role by reducing the growth rate of output). The inflation debate has now shifted firmly to the level of fundamental causation, namely to a consideration of what causes the money supply to increase in the first place. Discussion of the fundamental determinants of inflation raises important questions for policy: if monetary growth is viewed as the result of deeper-set forces, then presumably these must be treated if inflation is to be contained.

Our preceding discussion of the union as a rent-seeking agency is of direct relevance to the inflation problem. Political actions by trade unions, among others, may be viewed as geared to redistributing resources from taxpayers towards the union. Despite the power of producer group interests vis-à-vis taxpayers, however, much hinges on whether or not governments are subject to a balanced budget rule. If they are subject to a constitutional limitation of this nature, then higher expenditure must be balanced by higher taxation. In the absence of any such restraints, expenditures can exceed income and the excess covered by debt creation or inflationary finance. The former route has the disadvantage of harming politically powerful constituencies (e.g. the householder lobby). The latter route is more attractive to the extent that it is a partially hidden tax on net money holders that does not require legislative sanction. On this reasoning, unions may be expected to have an implicit 'demand' for inflation and governments a motive to 'supply' it. The inflation tax is, then, subsequently redistributed to powerful political groups.

All of this constitutes a very informal statement of a demand-for-and-supply-of-inflation model, but it would appear to offer a more fruitful line of inquiry than the political business cycle model or models that employ union political power merely to ratify inflationary developments in pecuniary markets (see Chapter 8). As Brunner (1975) has argued cogently, formalization of such a model requires establishing the links between the political process and the budget, the behavior and ruling precepts (as well as the independence) of central banks, and the resulting interaction between budget and central banks. These elements provide the basic building blocks for a systematic analysis of the inflation problem. Brunner himself provides a not dissimilar general framework from that supplied in this chapter, exploiting asymmetries of information costs and potential rewards between the various voter groups and viewing politicians as competitive entrepreneurs.

Yet the modeling of this process is extremely difficult and little real progress has been made to date. To identify the role of unions *per se* at this point in the development of the political economy model is an impossibility. Nevertheless, we can assemble some empirical material that in general supports the model. In what follows, we first consider the effects of unions on public spending before briefly returning to the notion that governments respond more to powerful interest groups than to the median voter.

There has been much discussion of the union demand for government spending but very little in the way of systematic inquiry. Organized labor has of course lobbied vigorously for all manner of spending programs that provide jobs for union members (e.g. railroad jobs, federal housing projects, dam construction, shipbuilding projects, and loan guarantees to ailing corporations and cities). The union movement has also consistently applied pressure for easy money policies and for a restructuring of the Federal Reserve System to make its members 'more responsive to the needs of the American people.'[20] Then there is the plethora of public assistance and job creation programs that to a greater or lesser extent bear the imprimature of the labor movement. Indeed, it is difficult in practice to point to public spending programs that have not been supported by organized labor. Accordingly, any evaluation of union impact quickly promises to involve ideological issues and discussion of the proper role of government. Less controversy is occasioned if we take two specific examples of union impact on the public purse. The first concerns union opposition to the contracting-out of publicly provided goods, and the second involves a consideration of Davis–Bacon.

Unions actively oppose contracting-out for obvious reasons of self-interest. One method of protecting union (and other) employees from displacement is to require relatively high wages on all service contracts, thereby diminishing the attraction of contracting-out in the first place. Here it is interesting to note that amendments to the Service Contract Act (SCA) in 1972 and 1976 stipulated that prevailing wage determinations for service contracts should take 'due consideration' of the federal wage levels for comparable jobs. As Goldfarb and Heywood (1982) point out, the *purpose* of the due consideration clause was to eliminate the existing gap between the wages and fringes of federal (blue-collar) employees and service contract employees (see below). Be this as it may, our interest here is not in prevailing wage legislation *per se* but, rather, in the cost reductions, potential and actual, from contracting-out. This is because we know even less about the application of SCA than about Davis–Bacon.

What, then, are the potential cost savings to the taxpayer? There are grounds for believing these are nontrivial on the basis of property rights theory and the empirical observation that public enterprise tends to be overly labor *and* capital intensive relative to the private sector (Crain and Zardkoohi, 1978).

Summarizing the results of seven General Accounting Office (GAO) studies, Bennett and DiLorenzo (1983) find public provision of services to be invariably more costly than private provision. Unfortunately, few of their data relate to contracting-out *per se*, the bulk of the material concerning the comparative costs of 'similar' services in the two sectors (e.g. a comparison of the repair costs of naval and commercial vessels). There is a real problem of comparing like with like here and accordingly the GAO estimates must be treated with considerable caution. However, more direct comparisons are possible in the case of weather forecasting and military base support services where contracting-out is practiced. Cost savings of 36–64 percent and 15 percent respectively are reported.

Bennett and DiLorenzo further argue that the sizeable cost disparities they report actually understate the cost advantage of the private sector, largely because the SCA forces private firms to pay higher wages when entering into government contracts. They argue that this spillover effect artificially adds 15 percent to the costs of private sector contractors (assuming a public sector wage differential of 20 percent and a labor share of 75 percent). However, in a separate case study of the application of SCA to research and development contracts, Goldfarb and Heywood (1982) estimate a wage impact of only 4.55 percent.

Controversy also attaches to the public expenditure implications of the Davis–Bacon Act. This established the principle of 'prevailing wages', specifying that workers on federally financed construction projects were to be paid wages (and fringes) at local prevailing rates for comparable construction work. Much of the criticism of Davis–Bacon has focused on the manner in which the concept of prevailing wages was applied until very recently by the administering agency, the Department of Labor (DOL). It defined prevailing wages as:

(a) the rate of wage paid in the relevant area to the majority of those employed in the relevant classification;
(b) in the event that a majority is not paid at the same rate, then the rate paid to the greatest number, provided that these constitute 30 percent of those employed; or,
(c) the average paid when less than 30 percent of those employed received the same rate.[21]

Referring to the immense task of making over 2,000 area determinations and 15,000 project wage determinations (but see below) with only a handful of wage specialists, Goldfarb and Morrall (1981) argue that it is not surprising that such determinations tend to produce 'prevailing wages' that favor employer and employee groups possessing the strongest incentives to supply wage information to DOL. Indeed, it does appear to be the case that prevailing wages often came to mean union wage scales or wage levels that exceeded the average. Conventional cost estimates based on these findings vary quite widely, however. Goldfarb and Morrall (1981), using a different Davis–Bacon rule (namely, setting the prevailing wage at the arithmetic mean wage), produce cost estimates/savings from switching to the average from the union wage in 1972 of $222–571 million for commercial and residential construction. If it is assumed that Davis–Bacon determinations *below* the actual average have no effect, the above cost savings are increased to $423–962 million. The GAO (1979) obtain cost increases in the range $228–513 million for 1976 in an analysis that seeks to compare actual Davis–Bacon determinations with 'correct' Davis–Bacon rates computed on the basis of its own wage survey data. Finally, Thieblot (1975), in an interesting study of project rebids occurring at the time of the one-month suspension of Davis–Bacon by the Nixon administration in 1971, produces an estimate of the cost of the Act to government of $240 million. Additional estimates of the indirect or administrative costs of Davis–Bacon lie in the $100–200 million range.

Yet, in the most sophisticated attempt to date to compute the costs of Davis–Bacon, Allen (1983) notes that since 1964 the DOL has relied predominantly on *area* determinations. If these prove to be more accurate than project determinations, the bias toward union rates noted in the literature may have lessened. Allen first seeks to ascertain the accuracy of Davis–Bacon area determinations in effect during 1980. His sample comprises the area determinations for 77 Standard Metropolitan Statistical Areas (SMSAs) applied in three categories of construction. The technique employed compares the actual behavior of the DOL with its supposed behavior. A statistical model describing the actual behavior of the DOL is developed to determine the exact point at which it switches from average to union wages in determining prevailing wages. Next, using data for construction from the May 1973–8 Current Population Surveys (CPS), the actual percentage unionized is calculated for the 77 SMSAs. If the point at which the DOL switches from average to union wages falls below (above) the *appropriate* union density figure derived from CPS data, then the DOL method is biased in favor of (against) union rates. (The appropriate level of union density is that compatible with a majority of workers in the relevant sector being union members.) Allen finds that the switching point for two of the three sectors (residential construction, and heavy and highway construction) occurs at a higher level of unionization than is required to make union wages the prevailing wage. Here, then, there is no bias in favor of union wage scales. Only in the third sector, building construction, is this bias evident (i.e. the switching point is well below what is consistent with the union rate covering a majority of workers). So, for Allen, the real problem with DOL administration of Davis–Bacon is one of inconsistent application of existing regulations rather than one of bias in adopting union rates irrespective of union density.

His next step is to compute the costs of Davis–Bacon. Unlike other studies, Allen allows for substitution in production resulting from payment of wages on public projects that exceed market levels. The method involves estimation of a system of factor demand equations for the construction industry, together with the percentage of inaccurate determinations. Allen's simulations reveal that, as of 1977, public construction costs were inflated in the range $41–224 million. These estimates fall well below those reported by other observers. Although Allen's sample over-represents areas in which union density is high, so that inappropriate adoption of union pay scales is less likely, these results provide arguably the best indication of the *current* costs of

Davis–Bacon. Moreover, the sharp decrease in the share of union construction should reduce the cost of Davis–Bacon in future years.

It is difficult to resist the conclusion that Davis–Bacon is supported by the construction unions (and, of course, unionized firms) for reasons of economic self-interest, not least because we have seen that organized labor has succeeded in deflecting *legislative* attempts to weaken the Act and, indeed, even increased its effect in earlier years (Goldfarb and Morrall, 1981, p. 205). Yet this is but one piece of legislation. Moreover, it has to be explained why union influence has, at least until recently, been so much more successful with respect to Davis–Bacon than in the case of an analogous piece of legislation – the Walsh–Healey Act. (This established governmental administration of employment conditions for all government contracts exceeding $10,000 by directing the Secretary of Labor to set minimum wage scales among most government contractors.) Walsh–Healey appears to have been palpably unsuccessful as a protective device for unions. Reynolds (1982) suggests that the favorable wage-fixing circumstances of Davis–Bacon were conspicuous in their absence in the case of Walsh–Healey.[22] In particular, union political pressure was diffuse because of jurisidictional conflicts between industrial unions, while administration was vastly complicated by the diversity of product and technology in firms providing services to the government. The part of Reynolds' analysis dealing with the relationship between the bureaucracy and its clientele is particularly suggestive, but presumably requires some modification in the light of the changed operation of the bureaucracy under the Reagan administration.

The resistance of unions to contracting-out and their continuing support for Davis–Bacon, though rational, clearly has adverse consequences for the public purse even if the precise magnitudes are uncertain. Further analyses of the costs of regulation are justified on nonideological grounds so as to provide taxpayers, consumers, and even government with estimates of the true costs of regulation. Arguably, the partial deregulation of trucking and the airlines owes much to economic analyses of these costs. The fact remains that any discussion of unionism's inflationary consequences cannot at present draw directly on its public expenditure implications.

Conventional economic analysis has largely failed to establish a clear link between inflation and either the tax/public expenditure share of GNP or public sector growth. Equally, attempts to endogenize policy have been less than successful. In the latter context, consider the political business cycle model favored by individual monetarists and nonmonetarists alike (see, for example, Parkin, 1975; Nordhaus, 1975). Governments, so the argument runs, induce political business cycles and an inflationary bias in pursuit of electoral popularity. Although there is *some* measure of empirical support for the existence of such cycles (see Tufte, 1978; Frey and Schneider, 1978; Maloney and Smirlock, 1981), the models in question presuppose voter ignorance of the basic structure of the economy or voter myopia. This voter naiveté is what provides the incentive for politicians to behave in the hypothesized manner.

Recently, however, it has been argued that voters do not in fact misperceive their own long-run interests or, equivalently, that voters are indeed sophisticated agents. MacRae (1977, 1981), assuming that political administrations choose policies that maximize a vote function, seeks to determine whether actual policy choices more closely resemble the solution to a vote-maximization problem in which voters are assumed to be naive or one in which they are assumed to be sophisticated. He finds that the sophisticated voter hypothesis performs as well or better than the naive voter hypothesis across a variety of time periods. However, as Chappell (1983) has pointed out, if political administrations do not actually choose policies that maximize a vote function, then MacRae's results are ambiguous: the failure to bring about political business cycles could mean that voters are not naive but, equally, it could undermine the notion that politicians implement policies that maximize votes. Chappell's own research, focusing on presidential popularity rather than actual voting behavior, indicates that the sophisticated voter model performs marginally better than the myopic voter model. Chappell's results thus suggest that the potential for politically motivated business cycles is limited.

Yet all such studies assume that political outcomes/popularity reflect the pattern of interests of the median voter, whereas our analysis has pointed to the dominance of sectional interest groups in the political marketplace. The median voter assumption is, then, likely to be overly restrictive, and there is evidence from the public choice and political science literatures to corroborate this contention (see also the discussion in Chapter 2). Thus, Dudley and Montmarquette (1982), in an analysis of government spending across a sample of 52 countries, test whether public spending is determined by the vote of the individual with median income or by a special interest group (which is the public sector bureaucracy rather than unionism *per se*). Dudley and Montmarquette separately test the median voter and Leviathan models (see Section 8.2), and a nested variant that includes each as a special case. They report that, while tests of the single models do not permit rejection of either approach, a key hypothesis of the median voter hypothesis is rejected in the nested version. On their test, then, the Leviathan model has the stronger empirical credentials. And from a political science perspective, Hibbs' (1982a, 1982b) sophisticated analyses seem to confirm that the rational or sophisticated voter model is best understood in the context of partisan models; that is, there is systematic covariation between macroeconomic outcomes and the political orientation of governments.

The fragmented nature of the empirical literature indicates that little progress has been made in analyzing the determinants of public expenditure and inflation. Although the evidence seems to be consistent with the arguments deployed in this chapter as to unionism's contributory role, that evidence is opaque on their *specific* contribution. This is almost inevitable because the 'game' being played in the political marketplace involves multiple interest groups and coalitions and hence a complex mix of political demands. Added to which there is ceaseless change in political markets no less than in pecuniary markets. These factors complicate but do not preclude empirical inquiry into unionism's role.

One implication of the informal demand-for-and-supply-of-inflation model, operating through public expenditure and the inflation tax, is that the redistributive game is akin to a prisoners' dilemma. This provides its micro rationality since the overall outcome ultimately looks nonoptimal. This is perhaps the unkindest cut of all: it is possible that the players in the political market game will be unable to devise a binding rule to defuse the expenditure and/or inflation problems. Indeed, the large number of groups involved may militate against a solution because of the costs and difficulties of organizing collective action (Burton, 1984b).

9.6 Conclusions

Inevitably, given the embryonic nature of the subject area of this chapter, we have raised rather more questions than we have answered. We have sought to challenge the assumption that the environment of union operation is exclusively or necessarily predominantly one of private sector pecuniary markets. This assumption is, of course, breached by the reality of public sector unions, which perforce operate in political markets. More important perhaps, we have shown that rent seeking by private sector unions may sometimes rest more on regulatory capture by the state than on the direct enforcement of an above-competitive price for labor services by the union itself.

Union influence on the legislative process was considered in the context of specific pieces of legislation. It was found that union strength, measured by membership and/or contributions, is generally a significant determinant of the votes of legislators. The success of union-favored legislation is another question, however, and the subject of no small controversy. It does nevertheless seem that US unions have in recent years been more successful in defending their existing monopoly power than in extending it. It is difficult at this stage to conclude, as have some observers, that unions have been more 'successful' in pursuing general-interest legislation rather than their own sectional interest either because non-labor-related legislation is potentially as important, if not more important, a target for rent seeking as other categories of legislation, or because such legislation may be deployed to disguise the harmful effects of unionism in the economic marketplace (e.g. job creation measures that mop up union-induced unemployment).

A number of contemporary economic problems – slow growth, rising levels of public expenditure, and inflation – were informally attributed to unionism *and* other pressure groups via their impact on vote-maximizing politicians. The specific contribution of unionism is as yet opaque, reflecting the rudimentary state of the political economy model. Nevertheless, a number of empirical regularities consistent with the hypothesized role of unionism were offered.

It follows from our discussion that coercive action against any single interest group is unlikely to remedy the problems alluded to in this chapter, even if this action were practicable. This is perhaps the sense of Rees' (1977, p. 12) comment: 'if some producer groups are to have strong political influence it is good for the consumer for all of them to have influence.' Here Rees is envisaging a situation in which unions and business do not act in concert. But this is of course no solution to the problem of organized sectional interests.

It remains an important research agenda to assess the contribution of union influence in political markets; one hitherto unexploited area is their influence at state and municipal levels. Such evidence as we have uncovered here may indeed be fairly trivial compared with nonunion distortions. But it is a question of fact. Unfortunately, discussion of unionism's role has in the past relied more on rhetoric than hard analysis – on both sides of the divide. The open-ended nature of this chapter underlines the need for further research on this extremely sensitive issue.

Notes

1 See also Navarro (1980) and Ackerman and Hassler (1981).
2 The first state legislation permitting collective bargaining was passed in Wisconsin. By the 1970s, most industrial states had laws permitting state and local government employees to bargain over the terms and conditions of employment, although not all public employees were covered by this legislation (US Department of Labor, 1981).
3 Note, however, that the model assumes identical voting participation rates for public and private sector employees.
4 A further twist is that state expenditures continued to rise in California in the wake of Proposition 13 because revenues from other sources offset the property tax shortfall.

5   The British TUC, the counterpart of the AFL–CIO, decided in 1900 to set up a distinct Labour Group in Parliament, its task being 'to cooperate with any other party which for the time being may be engaged in promoting legislation in the direct interest of labour, and be equally ready to associate itself with any party in opposing measures having an opposite tendency' (Simpson, 1973, p. 39). This led to the formation of the Labour Representation Committee, which changed its name to the Labour Party in 1906.

6   See also Section 6.7.

7   On the gains to unions from regulation, see Moore (1980) and Olson and Trapani (1981).

8   For a generalization of Stigler's regulatory model, see Peltzman (1976).

9   For another test of the bureaucratic union vs. member-dominated club, see Block and Saks (1979).

10 For an empirical analysis of the role of exclusive representation and other union security agreements in promoting union growth, see Reid and Kurth (1984).

11 The British evidence is analyzed in Addison and Burton (1984b) and is not discussed here.

12 The wage regulatory aspect of this Act was declared unconstitutional in 1937.

13 The Wagner Act generalized the organization rights obtained by the politically powerful railroad unions some nine years earlier under the Railway Labor Act.

14 Taft–Hartley added a like number of unfair union activities.

15 It should be noted that the economic interest of the union is not formally identified in this study and is at times ambiguous.

16 We note in passing that there is some debate in the literature about whether or not politicians seek to maximize votes. An alternative is that they seek a winning majority. For a discussion, see Riker (1962).

17 Two further limitations attach to this study: one is the deliberate exclusion of other variables affecting state minimum wages; the other concerns the appropriateness of analyzing state laws in isolation from the federal minimum wage.

18 The same cannot be said of British unions; see Addison and Burton (1984b).

19 For an amplification of this argument in the context of industrial policy, see Burton (1983).

20 See *Labor Looks at the 94th Congress*, AFL–CIO Department of Legislation, January 1977, p. 27.

21 The DOL has recently changed the prevailing wage definition by eliminating category (b) and revising category (c) so that it applies when less than 50 percent receive the same rate. In principle, this should deflect much of the criticism of the Act.

22 Reynolds (1982, p. 306) identifies these favorable elements as follows: '(1) its application to a single industry, (2) the concentrated political clout of the old-line building trade unions, (3) the historically diffuse opposition, and (4) the relative ease of administration.'

References

Aaron, Benjamin, Joseph R. Grodin, and James L. Stern (eds) (1979), *Public-Sector Bargaining* (Washington, DC: Bureau of National Affairs).

Abbott, Michael G. (1982), 'An Econometric Model of Trade Union Membership Growth in Canada, 1925–1966,' Working Paper No. 154, Industrial Relations Section, Princeton University, September.

Abbott, Michael G. (1984), 'Specification Tests of Quarterly Econometric Models of Aggregate Strike Frequency in Canada,' *Research in Labor Economics* 6, 177–250.

Abowd, John M. and Henry S. Farber (1982), 'Job Queues and the Union Status of Workers,' *Industrial and Labor Relations Review* 35(3), April, 354–67.

Abraham, Jesse M. (1983), 'Income Redistribution During a Disinflation and Its Effect on the Disinflation Path,' Working Paper No. 165, Industrial Relations Section, Princeton University, June.

Ackerman, Bruce A. and William T. Hassler (1981), *Clean Coal/Dirty Air: or How the Clean Air Act Became a Multibillion-Dollar Bail-Out for High-Sulfur Coal Producers and What Should be Done about It* (New Haven, CT, and London: Yale University Press).

Addison, John T. (1984), 'Trade Unions, Corporatism, and Inflation,' *Journal of Labor Research* 5(1), Winter 39–62.

Addison, John T. (1985), 'What Do Unions Really Do? A Review Article,' *Journal of Labor Research* 6(2), Spring, 127–46.

Addison, John T. and John Burton (1978), 'Wage Adjustment Processes: A Synthetic Treatment,' *British Journal of Industrial Relations* 16(2), July, 208–23.

Addison, John T. and John Burton (1979), 'The Identification of Market and Spillover Forces in Wage Inflation: A Cautionary Note,' *Applied Economics* 11(1), March, 95–103.

Addison, John T. and John Burton (1981), 'On Institutions and Wage Determination,' *Journal of Labor Research* 2(1), Spring, 99–109.

Addison, John T. and John Burton (1984a), 'The Sociopolitical Analysis of Inflation,' *Weltwirtschaftliches Archiv* 120(1), March, 90–120.

Addison, John T. and John Burton (1984b), *Trade Unions and Society: Some Lessons of the British Experience* (Vancouver, BC: The Fraser Institute).

Addison, John T., John Burton, and Thomas S. Torrance (1980), 'On the Causation of Inflation,' *Manchester School* 48(2), June, 140–56.

Addison, John T. and Alberto C. Castro (1984), 'The Importance of Lifetime Jobs in the U.S. Economy: Some Additional Evidence,' mimeographed, University of South Carolina, November.

Addison, John T. and John B. Chilton (1984), 'Wage Patterns: Fragments of an Evolutionary Theory,' mimeographed, University of South Carolina, October.

Addison, John T. and Barry T. Hirsch (1984), 'Union Effects on Efficiency,

Productivity, and Profits: Alternative Views and Evidence,' mimeographed, University of North Carolina at Greensboro, February.

Alchian, Armen A. (1950), 'Uncertainty, Evolution, and Economic Theory,' *Journal of Political Economy* 58(3), June, 211–21.

Allen, Steven G. (1983), 'Much Ado about Davis–Bacon: A Critical Review and New Evidence,' *Journal of Law and Economics* 26(3), October, 707–36.

Allen, Steven G. (1984a), 'The Effect of Unionism on Productivity in Privately and Publicly Owned Hospitals and Nursing Homes,' mimeographed, North Carolina State University, October.

Allen, Steven G. (1984b), 'Trade Unions, Absenteeism, and Exit-Voice,' *Industrial and Labor Relations Review* 37(3), April, 331–45.

Allen, Steven G. (1984c), 'Union Work Rules and Efficiency in the Building Trades,' mimeographed, North Carolina State University, July.

Allen, Steven G. (1984d), 'Unionized Construction Workers Are More Productive,' *Quarterly Journal of Economics* 99(2), May, 251–74.

Allen, Steven G. (1984e), 'Why Construction Industry Productivity is Declining,' mimeographed, North Carolina State University, August.

Allen, Steven G., 'Unionization and Productivity in Office Building and School Construction,' *Industrial and Labor Relations Review*, forthcoming.

Anderson, John C., Charles A. O'Reilly, III, and Gloria B. Busman (1980), 'Union Decertification in the U.S.: 1974–77,' *Industrial Relations* 19(1), Winter, 100–7.

Antos, Joseph R. (1983), 'Union Effects on White-Collar Compensation,' *Industrial and Labor Relations Review* 36(3), April, 461–79.

Antos, Joseph R., Mark Chandler, and Wesley Mellow (1980), 'Sex Differences in Union Membership,' *Industrial and Labor Relations Review* 33(2), January, 162–9.

Ashenfelter, Orley (1972), 'Racial Discrimination and Trade Unionism,' *Journal of Political Economy* 80(3), May/June, 435–64.

Ashenfelter, Orley (1978), 'Union Relative Wage Effects: New Evidence and a Survey of their Implications for Wage Inflation,' in Richard Stone and William Peterson (eds), *Econometric Contributions to Public Policy* (New York: St Martin's Press), 31–60.

Ashenfelter, Orley and David E. Bloom (1984), 'Models of Arbitrator Behavior: Theory and Evidence,' *American Economic Review* 74(1), March, 111–24.

Ashenfelter, Orley and James N. Brown, 'Testing the Efficiency of Employment Contracts,' *Journal of Political Economy*, forthcoming.

Ashenfelter, Orley and George E. Johnson (1969), 'Bargaining Theory, Trade Unions, and Industrial Strike Activity,' *American Economic Review* 59(1), March, 35–49.

Ashenfelter, Orley and George E. Johnson (1972), 'Unionism, Relative Wages, and Labor Quality in U.S. Manufacturing Industries,' *International Economic Review* 13(3), October, 488–508.

Ashenfelter, Orley, George E. Johnson, and John H. Pencavel (1972), 'Trade Unions and the Rate of Change of Money Wages in United States Manufacturing Industry,' *Review of Economic Studies* 39(1), January, 27–54.

Ashenfelter, Orley and John H. Pencavel (1969), 'American Trade Union Growth: 1900–1960,' *Quarterly Journal of Economics* 83(3), August, 434–48.

Ashenfelter, Orley and John H. Pencavel (1975), 'Wage Changes and the Frequency of Wage Settlements,' *Economica* 42(166), May, 162–70.

Atherton, Wallace N. (1973), *Theory of Union Bargaining Goals* (Princeton, NJ: Princeton University Press).

Auld, Douglas A. L., Louis N. Christofides, Robert Swidinsky, and David A. Wilton (1981), 'The Effect of Settlement Stage on Negotiated Wage Settlements in Canada,' *Industrial and Labor Relations Review* 34(2), January, 234–44.

Axelrod, Robert (1984), *The Evolution of Cooperation* (New York: Basic Books).

Azariadis, Costas (1975), 'Implicit Contracts and Underemployment Equilibria,' *Journal of Political Economy* 83(6), December, 1183–202.

Azariadis, Costas (1977), 'R. J. Gordon on Unemployment Theory,' *Journal of Monetary Economics* 3(2), April, 253–5.

Azariadis, Costas and Joseph E. Stiglitz (1983), 'Implicit Contracts and Fixed Price Equilibria,' *Quarterly Journal of Economics* 98(392), Supplement, May, 1–22.

Baily, Martin N. (1974), 'Wages and Employment under Uncertain Demand,' *Review of Economic Studies* 41(1), January, 37–50.

Baily, Martin N. (1978), 'Discussion', in *After the Phillips Curve: Persistence of High Inflation and High Unemployment* (Edgartown, MA: Federal Reserve Bank of Boston, June), 156–63.

Bain, George Sayers and Farouk Elsheikh (1976), *Union Growth and the Business Cycle: An Econometric Analysis* (Oxford: Blackwell).

Bain, George Sayers and Farouk Elsheikh (1979), 'An Inter-Industry Analysis of Unionisation in Britain,' *British Journal of Industrial Relations* 17(2), July and 137–57.

Baldwin, Carliss Y. (1983), 'Productivity and Labor Unions: An Application of the Theory of Self-enforcing Contracts,' *Journal of Business* 56(2), April, 155–85.

Ballentine, J. Gregory and Wayne R. Thirsk (1977), 'Labor Unions and Income Distribution Reconsidered,' *Canadian Journal of Economics* 10(1), February, 141–8.

Barro, Robert J. (1977a), 'Long-Term Contracting, Sticky Prices, and Monetary Policy,' *Journal of Monetary Economics* 3(3), July, 305–16.

Barro, Robert J.(1977b), 'Unanticipated Money Growth and Unemployment in the United States,' *American Economic Review* 67(2), March, 101–15.

Bartel, Ann and David Lewin (1981), 'Wage and Unionism in the Public Sector: The Case of Police,' *Review of Economics and Statistics* 63(1), February, 53–9.

Baxter, J. L. (1973), 'Inflation in the Context of Relative Deprivation and Social Justice,' *Scottish Journal of Political Economy* 20(3), November, 262–82.

Bazerman, Max H. and Henry S. Farber, 'Arbitrator Decision Making: When are Final Offers Important?' *Industrial and Labor Relations Review*, forthcoming.

Becker, Brian E. and Richard U. Miller (1981), 'Patterns and Determinants of Union Growth in the Hospital Industry,' *Journal of Labor Research* 2(2), Fall, 309–28.

Becker, Gary S. (1959), 'Union Restrictions on Entry,' in Philip D. Bradley (ed.), *The Public Stake in Union Power* (Charlottesville, VA: University of Virginia Press).

Bellante, Don and James Long (1981), 'The Political Economy of the Rent-Seeking Society: The Case of Public Employees and Their Unions,' *Journal of*

Labor Research 2(1), Spring, 1–14.

Bennett, James T. and Thomas J. DiLorenzo (1983), 'Public Employee Unions and the Privatization of "Public" Services,' *Journal of Labor Research* 4(1), Winter, 33–45.

Bennett, James T. and Manuel H. Johnson (1979), 'Free Riders in U.S. Labour Unions: Artifice or Affliction,' *British Journal of Industrial Relations* 17(2), July, 158–72.

Bennett, James T. and William Orzechowski (1983), 'The Voting Behavior of Bureaucrats: Some Empirical Evidence,' *Public Choice* 41(2), 271–83.

Berkowitz, Monroe (1954), 'The Economics of Trade Union Organization and Administration,' *Industrial and Labor Relations Review* 7(4), July, 575–92.

Bishop, Robert L. (1964), 'A Zeuthen–Hicks Theory of Bargaining,' *Econometrica* 32(3), July, 410–17.

Black, Dan A. and Darrell F. Parker (1984), 'Public Choice, Seniority and the Decline of Union Membership,' mimeographed, University of Kentucky, September.

Black, Dan A. and Darrell F. Parker (1985), 'The Division of Union Rents,' *Journal of Labor Research* 6(3), Summer, 281–8.

Blair, Douglas H. and David L. Crawford (1984), 'Labor Union Objectives and Collective Bargaining,' *Quarterly Journal of Economics* 99(3), August, 547–66.

Blau, Francine D. and Lawrence M. Kahn (1981), 'Race and Sex Differences in Quits by Young Workers,' *Industrial and Labor Relations Review* 34(4), July, 563–77.

Blau, Francine D. and Lawrence M. Kahn (1983), 'Unionism, Seniority, and Turnover,' *Industrial Relations* 22(3), Fall, 362–73.

Blejer, Mario I. (1981), 'Strike Activity and Wage Determination Under Rapid Inflation: The Chilean Case,' *Industrial and Labor Relations Review* 34(3), April, 356–64.

Bloch, Farrell E. (1980), 'Political Support for Minimum Wage Legislation,' *Journal of Labor Research* 1(2), Fall, 245–53.

Bloch, Farrell E. (1982a), 'The Endogeneity of Union Membership in a Pay Model,' *International Economic Review* 23(3), October, 695–8.

Bloch, Farrell E. (1982b), 'Formalization, Collectivization, and the Demand for Union Services,' *Journal of Labor Research* 3(1), Winter, 31–7.

Bloch, Farrell E. and Mark S. Kuskin (1978), 'Wage Determination in the Union and Nonunion Sectors,' *Industrial and Labor Relations Review* 31(2), January, 183–92.

Block, Richard N. and Daniel H. Saks (1979), 'Union Decision-Making and the Supply of Union Representation: A Preliminary Analysis,' *Proceedings of the Thirty-Second Annual Meetings* (Madison, WI: Industrial Relations Research Association, December), 218–25.

Bloom, David E. (1981), 'Is Arbitration *Really* Compatible with Bargaining?' *Industrial Relations* 20(3), Fall, 233–44.

Bok, Derek C. and John T. Dunlop (1970), *Labor and the American Community* (New York: Simon & Schuster).

Borcherding, Thomas E., Winston C. Bush, and Robert M. Spann (1977), 'The Effects of Public Spending on the Divisibility of Public Outputs in Consumption, Bureaucratic Power, and the Size of the Tax-Sharing Group,' in Thomas E. Borcherding (ed.), *Budgets and Bureaucrats: The Sources of Government Growth* (Durham, NC: Duke University Press), 211–28.

Borjas, George J. (1979), 'Job Satisfaction, Wages, and Unions,' *Journal of*

Human Resources 14(1), Winter, 21–40.

Borjas, George J. (1980), 'Wage Determination in the Federal Government: The Role of Constituents and Bureaucrats,' *Journal of Political Economy* 88(6), December, 1110–43.

Bowlby, Roger L. and William R. Schriver (1978), 'Bluffing and the "Split-the-Difference" Theory of Wage Bargaining,' *Industrial and Labor Relations Review* 31(2), January, 161–71.

Brown, Charles and James Medoff (1978), 'Trade Unions in the Production Process,' *Journal of Political Economy* 86(3), June, 355–78.

Brown, James N. (1982), 'How Close to an Auction is the Labor Market?' *Research in Labor Economics* 5, 189–235.

Brunner, Karl (1975), 'Comment [on Gordon],' *Journal of Law and Economics* 18(3), December, 837–57.

Buchanan, James M. and Gordon Tullock (1977), 'The Expanding Public Sector: Wagner Squared,' *Public Choice* 31, Fall, 147–50.

Bull, Clive (1983), 'Implicit Contracts in the Absence of Enforcement and Risk Aversion,' *American Economic Review* 73(4), September, 658–71.

Burton, John (1972), *Wage Inflation* (London: Macmillan).

Burton, John (1977), 'A Critique of the Relative Deprivation Hypothesis of Wage Inflation,' *Scottish Journal of Political Economy* 24(1), February, 67–76.

Burton, John (1980), 'Unionism, Inflation and Unemployment,' *Vie et Sciences Economiques* 86, July, 37–48.

Burton, John (1982), *The Political Future of American Trade Unions*, Heritage Lecture 12 (Washington, DC: Heritage Foundation).

Burton, John (1983), *Picking Losers . . . ? The Political Economy of Industrial Policy*, Hobart Paper 99 (London: Institute of Economic Affairs).

Burton, John (1984a), 'The British Disease and Trade Unionism: Conventional Wisdom and Political Economy,' in Addison and Burton, *op. cit.*, 1–24.

Burton, John (1984b), 'Capitalism, Democracy, and the Problem of Organized Sectional Interests,' in Addison and Burton, *op. cit.*, 129–53.

Burton, John (1984c), 'The Economic Analysis of the Trade Union as a Political Institution,' in Jean-Jacques Rosa (ed.), *The Economics of Trade Unions: New Directions* (Boston, MA: Kluwer-Nijhoff), 123–54.

Burton, John (1985), *Trade Unions, Stagflation, and Economic Policy* (London: Macmillan).

Burton, John and John T. Addison (1977), 'The Institutionalist Analysis of Wage Inflation: A Critical Appraisal,' *Research in Labor Economics* 1, 333–76.

Burton, John and Gordon Tullock (1983), 'Concluding Comments,' in Joseph D. Reid, Jr (ed.), *New Approaches to Labor Unions* (Greenwich, CT: JAI Press), 347–53.

Burton, John F., Jr and Charles Krider (1970), 'The Role and Consequences of Strikes by Public Employees,' *The Yale Law Journal* 79(3), January, 418–40.

Bush, Winston C. and Arthur T. Denzau (1977), 'The Voting Behavior of Bureaucrats and Public Sector Growth,' in Thomas Borcherding (ed.), *Budgets and Bureaucrats: The Sources of Government Growth* (Durham, NC: Duke University Press), 90–9.

Butler, Richard J. and Ronald G. Ehrenberg (1981), 'Estimating the Narcotic Effect of Public Sector Impasse Procedures,' *Industrial and Labor Relations Review* 35(1), October, 3–20.

Cain, Glen G., Brian E. Becker, Catherine G. McLaughlin, and Albert E. Schwenk (1981), 'The Effect of Unions on Wages in Hospitals,' *Research in Labor Economics* 4, 191–320.

Card, David (1983), 'Cost-of-Living Escalators in Major Union Contracts,' *Industrial and Labor Relations Review* 37(1), October, 34–48.

Card, David (1984a), 'Efficient Contracts and Costs of Adjustment: Short-Run Employment Determination for Airline Mechanics,' Working Paper No. 180, Industrial Relations Section, Princeton University, November.

Card, David (1984b), 'An Empirical Model on Wage Indexation Provisions in Union Contracts,' National Bureau of Economic Research Working Paper No. 1388, June.

Carlson, John A. (1977), 'A Study of Price Forecasts,' *Annals of Economics and Social Measurement* 6(1), Winter, 27–56.

Carmichael, Lorne (1983), 'Firm-Specific Human Capital and Promotion Ladders,' *Bell Journal of Economics* 14(1), Spring, 251–8.

Carson, Richard A. and Joe Oppenheimer (1984), 'A Method of Estimating the Personal Ideology of Political Representatives,' *American Political Science Review* 78(1), March, 163–78.

Cartter, Allan M. (1959), *Theory of Wages and Employment* (Homewood, IL: Irwin).

Caves, Richard E., Michael E. Porter, A. Michael Spence, and John T. Scott (1980), *Competition in the Open Economy* (Cambridge, MA: Harvard University Press).

Cecchetti, Stephen G. (1984), 'Indexation and Incomes Policy: A Study of Wage Adjustment in Unionized Manufacturing,' mimeographed, New York University, February.

Chamberlain, Gary (1982), 'Multivariate Regression Models for Panel Data,' *Journal of Econometrics* 18(1), January, 5–46.

Chamberlain, Neil W. and James W. Kuhn (1965), *Collective Bargaining* (New York: McGraw Hill).

Chappell, Henry W., Jr (1983), 'Presidential Popularity and Macroeconomic Performance: Are Voters Really So Naive?' *Review of Economics and Statistics* 65(3), August, 385–92.

Christensen, Sandra and Dennis Maki (1983), 'The Wage Effect of Compulsory Union Membership,' *Industrial and Labor Relations Review* 36(2), January, 230–8.

Christofides, Louis N. and David A. Wilton (1978), 'Long Term Contracts, Uncertain Inflation and Short Run Wage Adjustment: Evidence from Canadian Contract Data,' mimeographed, University of Guelph.

Christofides, Louis N. and David A. Wilton (1983), 'The Determinants of Contract Length – An Empirical Analysis Based on Canadian Micro Data,' *Journal of Monetary Economics* 12(2), August, 309–19.

Christofides, Louis N., Robert Swidinsky, and David A. Wilton (1978), 'Minimum Wages, Inflation, and the Relative Wage Structure,' mimeographed, University of Guelph.

Christofides, Louis N., Robert Swidinsky, and David A. Wilton (1980a), 'A Micro Econometric Analysis of the Canadian Wage Determination Process,' *Economica* 47(186), May, 165–78.

Christofides, Louis N., Robert Swidinsky, and David A. Wilton (1980b), 'A Microeconometric Analysis of Spillovers within the Canadian Wage Determination Process,' *Review of Economics and Statistics* 62(2), May, 213–21.

Clark, Kim B. (1980a), 'The Impact of Unionization on Productivity: A Case

Study,' *Industrial and Labor Relations Review* 33(4), July, 451–69.

Clark, Kim B. (1980b), 'Unionization and Productivity: Micro-Econometric Evidence,' *Quarterly Journal of Economics* 95(4), December, 613–39.

Clark, Kim B. (1984), 'Unionization and Firm Performance: The Impact on Profits, Growth, and Productivity,' *American Economic Review* 74(5), December, 893–919.

Close, Frank A. and David E. Shulenburger (1971), 'Labor's Share by Sector and Industry, 1948–1965,' *Industrial and Labor Relations Review* 24(4), July, 588–602.

Comay, Yochanan and Abraham Subotnik (1977), 'A Reinterpretation of Hicks' Bargaining Model,' in Orley C. Ashenfelter and Wallace E. Oates (eds), *Essays in Labor Market Analysis* (New York: John Wiley), 45–52.

Connerton, Marguarita, Richard B. Freeman, and James L. Medoff (1979), 'Productivity and Industrial Relations: The Case of U.S. Bituminous Coal,' mimeographed, Harvard University.

Connolly, Robert A., Barry T. Hirsch, and Mark Hirschey (1985), 'Union Rent Seeking, Intangible Capital, and Market Value of the Firm,' mimeographed, University of North Carolina at Greensboro, January.

Courant, Paul N., Edward M. Gramlich, and Daniel L. Rubinfeld (1979), 'Public Employee Market Power and the Level of Government Spending,' *American Economic Review* 69(5), December, 806–17.

Courant, Paul N., Edward M. Gramlich, and Daniel L. Rubinfeld (1980), 'Why Voters Support Tax Limitation Amendments: The Michigan Case,' *National Tax Journal* 33(1), March, 1–20.

Cousineau, Jean-Michel and Robert Lacroix (1983), 'Why Does Strike Activity Vary Over Time and Between Industries?' mimeographed, University of Montreal, February.

Cox, James C. and Ronald L. Oaxaca (1982), 'The Political Economy of Minimum Wage Legislation,' *Economic Inquiry* 20(4), October, 533–55.

Crain, W. Mark and Asghar Zardkoohi (1978), 'A Test of the Property Rights Theory of the Firm: Water Utilities in the U.S.,' *Journal of Law and Economics* 21(2), October, 395–408.

Crawford, Vincent P. (1979), 'On Compulsory Arbitration Schemes,' *Journal of Political Economy* 87(1), February, 131–59.

Crawford, Vincent P. (1981), 'Arbitration and Conflict Resolution in Labor–Management Bargaining,' *American Economic Review Papers and Proceedings* 71(2), May, 205–10.

Crawford, Vincent P. (1982a), 'Compulsory Arbitration, Arbitral Risk and Negotiated Settlements: A Case Study in Bargaining under Imperfect Information,' *Review of Economic Studies* 49(1), January, 69–82.

Crawford, Vincent P. (1982b), 'A Theory of Disagreement in Bargaining,' *Econometrica* 50(3), May, 607–37.

Cross, J. G. (1965), 'A Theory of the Bargaining Process,' *American Economic Review* 55(1), March, 67–94.

Crouch, Colin J. (1980), 'The Conditions for Trade Union Wage Restraint,' mimeographed, London School of Economics, April.

Dahrendorf, Ralf (1959), *Class and Conflict in Industrial Society* (Stanford, CA: Stanford University Press).

Dalton, James A. and E. J. Ford, Jr (1977), 'Concentration and Labor Earnings in Manufacturing and Utilities,' *Industrial and Labor Relations Review* 31(1), October, 45–60.

Davies, Robert J. (1981), 'The Political Economy of Strikes: An Empirical Analysis of the Group of Ten,' paper prepared for the International Conference on the Economics of Trade Unions, Fondation pour la Nouvelle Economie Politique, Paris, March.

De Alessi, Louis (1983), 'Property Rights, Transaction Costs, and X-Efficiency: An Essay in Economic Theory,' *American Economic Review* 73(1), March, 64–81.

DeFina, Robert H. (1983), 'Unions, Relative Wages, and Economic Efficiency,' *Journal of Labor Economics* 1(4), October, 408–29.

DeFina, Robert H. (1985), 'Union–Nonunion Wage Differentials and the Functional Distribution of Income: Some Simulation Results from a General Equilibrium Model,' *Journal of Labor Research* 6(3), Summer, 263–79.

Delaney, John Thomas (1981), 'Union Success in Hospital Representation Elections,' *Industrial Relations* 20(2), Spring, 149–61.

Delaney, John Thomas (1983), 'Strikes, Arbitration, and Teacher Salaries: A Behavioral Analysis,' *Industrial and Labor Relations Review* 36(3), April, 431–46.

de Menil, George (1971), *Bargaining: Monopoly Power versus Union Power* (Cambridge, MA: MIT Press).

Denison, Edward F. (1954), 'Income Types and the Size Distribution,' *American Economic Review Papers and Proceedings* 44(2), May, 254–69.

Dertouzos, James N. and John H. Pencavel (1981), 'Wage and Employment Determination under Trade Unionism: The International Typographical Union,' *Journal of Political Economy* 89(6), December, 1162–81.

Dickens, William T. (1983), 'The Effect of Company Campaigns on Certification Elections: *Law and Reality* Once Again,' *Industrial and Labor Relations Review* 36(4), July, 560–75.

Dickens, William T. and Jonathan S. Leonard (1985), 'Accounting for the Decline in Union Membership, 1950–1980,' *Industrial and Labor Relations Review* 38(3), April, 323–34.

Diewert, W. E. (1974), 'The Effects of Unionization on Wages and Employment: A General Equilibrium Analysis,' *Economic Inquiry* 12(3), September, 319–39.

Donn, Clifford B. (1977), 'Games Final-Offer Arbitrators Might Play,' *Industrial Relations* 16(3), October, 306–14.

Donn, Clifford B. and Barry T. Hirsch (1983), 'Making Interest Arbitration Costly: A Policy Proposal,' *Journal of Collective Negotiations* 12(1), Spring, 21–32.

Downs, Anthony (1957), *An Economic Theory of Democracy* (New York: Harper & Row).

Dudley, Leonard and Claude Montmarquette (1982), 'The Representative Voter Versus Leviathan,' Cahier 8141, Department of Economic Science, University of Montreal.

Duncan, Greg J. and Frank P. Stafford (1980), 'Do Union Members Receive Compensating Wage Differentials?' *American Economic Review* 70(3), June, 355–71.

Duncan, Greg J. and Frank P. Stafford (1982), 'Do Union Members Receive Compensating Wage Differentials? Reply,' *American Economic Review* 72(4), September, 868–72.

Duncan, Gregory M. (1983), 'Sample Selectivity as a Proxy Variable Problem: On the Use and Misuse of Gaussian Selectivity Corrections,' in Joseph D. Reid, Jr (ed.), *New Approaches to Labor Unions* (Greenwich, CT: JAI Press), 333–45.

Duncan, Gregory M. and Duane E. Leigh (1980), 'Wage Determinaton in the Union and Nonunion Sectors: A Sample Selectivity Approach,' *Industrial and Labor Relations Review* 34(1), October, 24–34.

Duncan, Gregory M. and Duane E. Leigh (1985), 'The Endogeneity of Union Status: An Empirical Test,' *Journal of Labor Economics* 3(3), July, 385–402.

Dunlop, John T. (1944), *Wage Determination under Trade Unions* (New York: Macmillan).

Dworkin, James B. and Marian Extejt (1979), 'Recent Trends in Union Decertification/Deauthorization Elections,' *Proceedings of the Thirty-Second Annual Meetings* (Madison, WI: Industrial Relations Research Association), December), 226–34.

Eaton, B. Curtis (1972), 'The Worker and the Profitability of the Strike,' *Industrial and Labor Relations Review* 26(1), October, 670–9.

Eberts, Randall W. (1984), 'Union Effects on Teacher Productivity,' *Industrial and Labor Relations Review* 37(3), April, 346–58.

Eberts, Randall W. and Joe A. Stone (1983), 'On the Contract Curve: A Test of Alternative Models of Collective Bargaining,' mimeographed, University of Oregon, January.

Eckstein, Otto (1968), 'Money Wage Determination Revisited,' *Review of Economic Studies* 35(102), April, 133–43.

Eckstein, Otto and Thomas A. Wilson (1962), 'The Determination of Money Wages in American Industry,' *Quarterly Journal of Economics* 76(3), August, 379–414.

Edwards, Linda N. and Franklin R. Edwards (1982), 'Wellington–Winter Revisited: The Case of Municipal Sanitation Collection,' *Industrial and Labor Relations Review* 35(3), April, 307–18.

Edwards, P. K. (1977), 'Strikes in the United States, 1881–1972: A Critical Examination of the Theory of the Institutionalization of Conflict,' D.Phil. Thesis, Oxford University.

Edwards, P. K. (1978), 'Time Series Regression Models of Strike Activity: A Reconsideration with American Data,' *British Journal of Industrial Relations* 16(3), November, 320–34.

Ehrenberg, Ronald G., Leif Danziger, and Gee San (1983), 'Cost-of-Living Adjustment Clauses in Union Contracts: A Summary of Results,' *Journal of Labor Economics* 1(3), July, 215–45.

Ehrenberg, Ronald G. and Gerald S. Goldstein (1975), 'A Model of Public Sector Wage Determination,' *Journal of Urban Economics* 2(3), July, 223–45.

Ehrenberg, Ronald G. and Joshua L. Schwarz (1983), 'Public Sector Labor Markets,' National Bureau of Economic Research Working Paper No. 1179, August.

Ehrenberg, Ronald G., Daniel R. Sherman, and Joshua L. Schwarz (1983), 'Unions and Productivity in the Public Sector: A Study of Municipal Libraries,' *Industrial and Labor Relations Review* 36(2), January, 199–213.

Ehrenberg, Ronald G. and Robert S. Smith (1985), *Modern Labor Economics: Theory and Public Policy*, 2nd edn (Glenview, IL: Scott, Foresman and Co.).

Elliott, Ralph D. and Benjamin M. Hawkins (1982), 'Do Union Organizing Activities Affect Decertification?' *Journal of Labor Research* 3(2), Spring, 153–61.

Elliott, Robert F. (1976), 'The National Wage Round in the United Kingdom: A

Sceptical View,' *Oxford Bulletin of Economics and Statistics* 38(3), August, 179–201.

Elliott, Robert F. and Andrew J. H. Dean (1978), 'The Official Wage Rates Index and the Size of Wage Settlements,' *Oxford Bulletin of Economics and Statistics* 40(3), August, 249–61.

Elliott, Robert F. and Hilary C. Shelton (1978), 'A Wage Settlements Index for the United Kingdom, 1950–75,' *Oxford Bulletin of Economics and Statistics* 40(4), November, 303–19.

Ellwood, David T. and Glen Fine, 'Effects of Right-to-Work Laws on Union Organizing,' *Journal of Political Economy*, forthcoming.

Epple, Dennis, Allan Zelenitz, and Michael Visscher (1978), 'A Search for Testable Implications of the Tiebout Hypothesis,' *Journal of Political Economy* 86(3), June, 405–25.

Estey, Marten (1981), *The Unions: Structure, Development, and Management*, 3rd edn (New York: Harcourt Brace).

Faith, Roger and Joseph D. Reid, Jr (1983), 'The Labor Union as Its Members' Agent,' in Joseph D. Reid, Jr (ed.), *New Approaches to Labor Unions* (Greenwich, CT: JAI Press), 3–25.

Farber, Henry S. (1978a), 'Bargaining Theory, Wage Outcomes, and the Occurrence of Strikes: An Econometric Analysis,' *American Economic Review* 68(3), June, 262–71.

Farber, Henry S. (1978b), 'Individual Preferences and Union Wage Determination: The Case of the United Mine Workers,' *Journal of Political Economy* 86(5), October, 923–42.

Farber, Henry S. (1978c), 'The United Mine Workers and the Demand for Coal: An Econometric Analysis of Union Behavior,' *Research in Labor Economics* 2, 1–74.

Farber, Henry S. (1980a), 'An Analysis of Final-Offer Arbitration,' *Journal of Conflict Resolution* 24(4), December, 683–705.

Farber, Henry S. (1980b), 'Does Final-Offer Arbitration Encourage Bargaining?' *Proceedings of the Thirty-Third Annual Meetings* (Madison, WI: Industrial Relations Research Association, December), 219–26.

Farber, Henry S. (1981), 'Splitting-the-Difference in Interest Arbitration,' *Industrial and Labor Relations Review* 35(1), October, 70–7.

Farber, Henry S. (1983a), 'The Determination of the Union Status of Workers,' *Econometrica* 51(5), September, 1417–38.

Farber, Henry S. (1983b), 'Worker Preferences for Union Representation,' in Joseph D. Reid, Jr (ed.), *New Approaches to Labor Unions* (Greenwich, CT: JAI Press), 171–206.

Farber, Henry S. (1984a), 'Right-to-Work Laws and the Extent of Unionization,' *Journal of Labor Economics* 2(3), July, 319–52.

Farber, Henry S. (1984b), 'The Analysis of Union Behavior,' National Bureau of Economic Research Working Paper No. 1502, November.

Farber, Henry S. (1984c), 'Threat Effects and the Extent of Unionization in the United States,' mimeographed, Massachusetts Institute of Technology.

Farber, Henry S., and Harry C. Katz (1979), 'Interest Arbitration, Outcomes, and the Incentive to Bargain,' *Industrial and Labor Relations Review* 33(1), October, 55–63.

Farber, Henry S. and Daniel H. Saks (1980), 'Why Workers Want Unions: The Role of Relative Wages and Job Characteristics,' *Journal of Political Economy* 88(2), April, 349–69.

Fellner, William J. (1947), 'Prices and Wages under Bilateral Monopoly,' *Quarterly Journal of Economics* 61(3), August, 503–32.

Fiorito, Jack (1982), 'American Trade Union Growth: An Alternative Model,' *Industrial Relations* 21(1), Winter, 123–7.

Fiorito, Jack and Charles R. Greer (1982), 'Determinants of U.S. Unionism: Past Research and Future Needs,' *Industrial Relations* 21(1), Winter, 1–32.

Fischer, Stanley (1977), 'Long-Term Contracts, Rational Expectations, and the Optimal Money Supply Rule,' *Journal of Political Economy* 85(1), February, 191–205.

Flanagan, Robert J. (1976), 'Wage Interdependence in Unionized Labor Markets,' *Brookings Papers on Economic Activity* 3: 635–73.

Flanders, Allan (1964), *The Fawley Productivity Agreements* (London: Faber & Faber).

Foulkes, Fred K. (1980), *Personnel Policies in Large Nonunion Companies* (Englewood Cliffs, NJ: Prentice-Hall).

Frantz, J. R. (1976), 'The Impact of Trade Unions on Production in the Wooden Household Furniture Industry,' Senior Honors Thesis, Harvard University, March.

Freedman, Audrey and William E. Fulmer (1982), 'Last Rites for Pattern Bargaining,' *Harvard Business Review* 60(2), March/April, 30–48.

Freeman, Richard B. (1976), 'Individual Mobility and Union Voice in the Labor Market,' *American Economic Review Papers and Proceedings* 66(2), May, 361–8.

Freeman, Richard B. (1978), 'Job Satisfaction as an Economic Variable,' *American Economic Review Papers and Proceedings* 68(2), May, 135–41.

Freeman, Richard B. (1980a), 'The Effect of Unionism on Worker Attachment to Firms,' *Journal of Labor Research* 1(1), Spring, 29–62.

Freeman, Richard B. (1980b), 'The Exit-Voice Tradeoff in the Labor Market: Unionism, Job Tenure, Quits and Separations,' *Quarterly Journal of Economics* 94(4), June, 643–74.

Freeman, Richard B. (1980c), 'Unionism and the Dispersion of Wages,' *Industrial and Labor Relations Review* 34(1), October, 3–23.

Freeman, Richard B. (1981), 'The Effect of Unionism on Fringe Benefits,' *Industrial and Labor Relations Review* 34(4), July, 489–509.

Freeman, Richard B. (1982), 'Union Wage Practices and Wage Dispersion Within Establishments,' *Industrial and Labor Relations Review* 36(1), October, 3–21.

Freeman, Richard B. (1983a), 'Unionism, Price–Cost Margins, and the Return to Capital,' National Bureau of Economic Research Working Paper No. 1164, July.

Freeman, Richard B. (1983b), 'Unions, Pensions, and Union Pension Funds,' National Bureau of Economic Research Working Paper No. 1226, November.

Freeman, Richard B. (1983c), 'Why are Unions Faring Poorly in NLRB Representation Elections?' mimeographed, Harvard University.

Freeman, Richard B. (1984a), 'Longitudinal Analyses of the Effects of Trade Unions,' *Journal of Labor Economics* 2(1), January, 1–26.

Freeman, Richard B. (1984b), 'Unionism Comes to the Public Sector,' National Bureau of Economic Research Working Paper No. 1452, September.

Freeman, Richard B. and James L. Medoff (1979a), 'New Estimates of Private Sector Unionism in the United States,' *Industrial and Labor Relations Review* 32(2), January, 143–74.

Freeman, Richard B. and James L. Medoff (1979b), 'The Two Faces of Unionism,' *Public Interest* No. 57, Fall, 69–93.

Freeman, Richard B. and James L. Medoff (1981), 'The Impact of the Percent Organized on Union and Nonunion Wages,' *Review of Economics and Statistics* 63(4), November, 561–72.

Freeman, Richard B. and James L. Medoff (1982), 'Substitution between Production Labor and Other Inputs in Unionized and Nonunionized Manufacturing,' *Review of Economics and Statistics* 64(2), May, 220–33.

Freeman, Richard B. and James L. Medoff (1983), 'The Impact of Collective Bargaining: Can the New Facts be Explained by Monopoly Unionism?' in Joseph D. Reid, Jr (ed.), *New Approaches to Labor Unions* (Greenwich, CT: JAI Press), 293–332.

Freeman, Richard B. and James L. Medoff (1984), *What Do Unions Do?* (New York: Basic Books).

Frey, Bruno and Friedrich Schneider (1978), 'An Empirical Study of Politico-Economic Interaction in the U.S.,' *Review of Economics and Statistics*, 60(2), May, 174–83.

Friedman, Milton (1951), 'Some Comments on the Significance of Labor Unions for Economic Policy,' in David M. Wright (ed.), *The Impact of the Union* (New York: Harcourt Brace), 204–34.

Friedman, Milton (1968), 'The Role of Monetary Policy,' *American Economic Review* 58(1), March, 1–17.

Friedman, Milton (1970), *The Counter-Revolution in Monetary Theory*, Occasional Paper 33 (London: Institute of Economic Affairs).

Friedman, Milton (1977), 'Nobel Lecture: Inflation and Unemployment,' *Journal of Political Economy* 85(3), June, 451–72.

Friedman, Milton and Rose Friedman (1980), *Free to Choose: A Personal Statement* (New York: Harcourt Brace Jovanovich).

Friedman, Milton and Anna J. Schwartz (1963), *A Monetary History of the United States, 1867–1960* (Princeton, NJ: Princeton University Press).

Froyen, Richard T. and Roger N. Waud (1984), 'The Changing Relationship between Aggregate Price and Output: The British Experience,' *Economica* 51(201), February, 53–67.

Fudenberg, Drew, David Levine, and Paul Ruud (1983), 'Strike Activity and Wage Settlements,' UCLA Department of Economics Working Paper No. 249, March.

Garen, John E. (1985), 'Worker Heterogeneity, Job Screening, and Firm Size,' *Journal of Political Economy* 93(4), August, 715–39.

General Accounting Office (1979), *The Davis–Bacon Act Should Be Repealed*, Report HRD–79–18 (Washington, DC: US Government Printing Office, April).

Geroski, Paul A., A. P. Hamlin, and K. G. Knight (1982), 'Wages, Strikes and Market Structure,' *Oxford Economic Papers* 34(2), July, 276–91.

Geroski, Paul A. and Mark B. Stewart (1982), 'Trade Union Wage Differentials in the U.K.: A Strange and Sad Story,' Working Paper No. 157, Industrial Relations Section, Princeton University, October.

Goldfarb, Robert S. and John S. Heywood (1982), 'An Economic Evaluation of the Service Contract Act,' *Industrial and Labor Relations Review* 36(1), October, 56–72.

Goldfarb, Robert S. and John F. Morrall (1981), 'The Davis–Bacon Act: An

Appraisal of Recent Studies,' *Industrial and Labor Relations Review* 34(2), January, 191–206.

Gollop, Frank M. (1976), 'The Effect of Unionization on Productivity in U.S. Manufacturing,' Working Paper 7614, Social Systems Research Institute, University of Wisconsin, September.

Gollop, Frank M. and Dale W. Jorgenson (1980), 'U.S. Productivity Growth by Industry, 1947–73,' in John W. Kendrick and Beatrice N. Vaccara (eds), *New Developments in Productivity Measurement and Analysis* (Chicago, IL: University of Chicago Press), 17–124.

Gordon, Donald F. (1974), 'A Neo-Classical Theory of Keynesian Unemployment,' *Economic Inquiry* 12(4), December, 431–59.

Gordon, Robert J. (1975a), 'The Demand for and Supply of Inflation,' *Journal of Law and Economics* 18(3), December, 807–36.

Gordon, Robert J. (1975b), 'Reply to Brunner's Comments,' *Journal of Law and Economics*, 18(3), December, 871–4.

Gordon, Robert J. (1976), 'Recent Developments in the Theory of Inflation and Unemployment,' *Journal of Monetary Economics* 2(2), April, 185–219.

Gordon, Robert J. (1977), 'World Inflation and Monetary Accommodation in Eight Countries,' *Brookings Papers on Economic Activity* 2: 409–68.

Gordon, Robert J. (1982), 'Why U.S. Wage and Employment Behaviour Differs from That in Britain and Japan,' *Economic Journal* 92(365), March, 13–44.

Gould, John P. (1973), 'The Economics of Legal Conflicts,' *Journal of Legal Studies* 2(2), June, 279–300.

Gramlich, Edward M. (1976), 'Impact of Minimum Wages on Other Wages, Employment, and Family Incomes,' *Brookings Papers on Economic Activity* 2: 409–51.

Granger, C. W. J. (1969), 'Investigating Causal Relations by Econometric Models and Cross-Spectral Methods,' *Econometrica* 37(3), July, 424–38.

Gray, Jo Anna (1976), 'Wage Indexation: A Macroeconomic Approach,' *Journal of Monetary Economics* 2(2), April, 221–35.

Gray, Jo Anna (1978), 'On Indexation and Contract Length,' *Journal of Political Economy 86(1)*, February, 1–18.

Grossman, Gene M. (1983), 'Union Wages, Temporary Layoffs, and Seniority,' *American Economic Review* 73(3), June, 277–90.

Gujarati, Damodar (1969), 'Labor's Share in Manufacturing Industries, 1949–1964,' *Industrial and Labor Relations Review* 23(1), October, 65–77.

Hall, Robert E. (1970), 'Why is the Unemployment Rate So High at Full Employment?' *Brookings Papers on Economic Activity* 3: 369–402.

Hall, Robert E. (1977), 'Comments and Discussion [on Gordon]', *Brookings Papers on Economic Activity* 2: 469–71.

Hall, Robert E. (1980), 'Employment Fluctuations and Wage Rigidity,' *Brookings Papers on Economic Activity* 1: 91–123.

Hall, Robert E. (1982), 'The Importance of Lifetime Jobs in the U.S. Economy,' *American Economic Review*, 72(4), September, 716–24.

Hall, Robert E. and David M. Lilien (1979), 'Efficient Wage Bargains under Uncertain Supply and Demand,' *American Economic Review* 69(5), December, 868–79.

Halvorsen, Robert and Raymond Palmquist (1980), 'The Interpretation of Dummy Variables in Semilogarithmic Equations,' *American Economic Review* 70(3), June, 474–5.

Hamermesh, Daniel S. (1971), 'White-Collar Unions, Blue-Collar Unions, and

Wages in Manufacturing,' *Industrial and Labor Relations Review* 24(2), January, 159–70.

Hamermesh, Daniel S. (1973), 'Who "Wins" in Wage Bargaining?' *Industrial and Labor Relations Review* 26(4), July, 1146–9.

Hamermesh, Daniel S. (ed.) (1975), *Labor in the Public and Nonprofit Sectors* (Princeton, NJ: Princeton University Press).

Harberger, Arnold C. (1954), 'Monopoly and Resource Allocation,' *American Economic Review Papers and Proceedings* 44(2), May, 77–87.

Harsanyi, John C. (1956), 'Approaches to the Bargaining Problem before and after the Theory of Games,' *Econometrica* 24(2), April, 144–57.

Hartman, Robert W. (1983), *Pay and Pensions for Federal Workers* (Washington, DC: Brookings Institution).

Hayek, F. A. (1959), 'Unions, Inflation, and Profits,' in Philip D. Bradley (ed.), *The Public Stake in Union Power* (Charlottesville, VA: University of Virginia Press), 46–62.

Hayes, Beth (1984), 'Unions and Strikes with Asymmetric Information,' *Journal of Labor Economic* 2(1), January, 57–83.

Heckman, James J. (1976), 'The Common Structure of Statistical Models of Truncation, Sample Selection and Limited Dependent Variables and a Simple Estimator for Such Models,' *Annals of Economic and Social Measurement* 5(4), Fall, 475–92.

Heckman, James J. and Solomon W. Polachek (1974), 'Empirical Evidence on the Functional Form of the Earnings–Schooling Relationship,' *Journal of the American Statistical Association* 69(346), June, 350–4.

Heldman, Dan C. and Deborah L. Knight (1980), *Unions and Lobbying – The Representative Function* (Arlington, VA: Foundation for the Advancement of the Public Trust).

Hendricks, Wallace E. (1977), 'Regulation and Labor Earnings,' *Bell Journal of Economics* 8(2), Autumn, 483–96.

Hendricks, Wallace E. (1981), 'Unionism, Oligopoly and Rigid Wages,' *Review of Economics and Statistics* 63(2), May, 198–205.

Hendricks, Wallace E. and Lawrence M. Kahn (1982), 'The Determinants of Bargaining Structure in U.S. Manufacturing Industries,' *Industrial and Labor Relations Review* 35(2), January, 181–95.

Hendricks, Wallace E. and Lawrence M. Kahn (1983), 'Cost of Living Clauses in Union Contracts: Determinants and Effects,' *Industrial and Labor Relations Review* 36(3), April, 447–60.

Heneman, Herbert G., III and Marcus H. Sandver (1983), 'Predicting the Outcome of Union Certification Elections: A Review of the Literature,' *Industrial and Labor Relations Review* 36(4), July, 537–59.

Henry, S. G. B. (1981), 'Incomes Policy and Aggregate Pay,' in J. L. Fallick and R. F. Elliott (eds), *Incomes Policies, Inflation and Relative Pay* (London: Allen & Unwin), 23–44.

Henry, S. G. B. and P. Ormerod (1978), 'Incomes Policy and Wage Inflation: Empirical Evidence for the U.K. 1961–1977,' *National Institute Economic Review* 85, August, 31–9.

Henry, S. G. B., M. C. Sawyer and P. Smith (1976), 'Models of Inflation in the United Kingdom: An Evaluation,' *National Institute Economic Review* 77, August, 60–71.

Hibbs, Douglas A., Jr (1976), 'Industrial Conflict in Advanced Industrial Societies,' *American Political Science Review* 70(4), December, 1033–58.

Hibbs, Douglas A., Jr (1982a), 'On the Demand for Economic Outcomes:

Macroeconomic Performance and Mass Political Support in the United States, Great Britain, and Germany,' *Journal of Politics* 44(2), May, 426–62.

Hibbs, Douglas A., Jr (1982b), 'The Dynamics of Political Support for American Presidents among Occupational and Partisan Groups,' *American Journal of Political Science* 26(2), May, 312–32.

Hicks, John R. (1963), *The Theory of Wages*, 2nd edn (New York: Macmillan).

Hines, A. G. (1964), 'Trade Unions and Wage Inflation in the United Kingdom, 1893–1961,' *Review of Economic Studies* 31(3), October, 221–52.

Hines, A. G. (1968), 'Unemployment and the Rate of Change of Money Wage Rates in the United Kingdom, 1862–1963: A Reappraisal,' *Review of Economics and Statistics* 50(1), February, 60–7.

Hines, A. G. (1969), 'Wage Inflation in the United Kingdom, 1948–62: A Disaggregated Study,' *Economic Journal* 79(313), March, 66–89.

Hines, A. G. (1971), 'The Determinants of the Rate of Change of Money Wage Rates and the Effectiveness of Incomes Policy,' in H. G. Johnson and A. R. Nobay (eds), *The Current Inflation* (London: Macmillan), 143–75.

Hirsch, Barry T. (1980), 'The Determinants of Unionization: An Analysis of Interarea Differences,' *Industrial and Labor Relations Review* 33(2), January, 147–61.

Hirsch, Barry T. (1981), 'The Interindustry Structure of Earnings and Unionization,' mimeographed, University of North Carolina at Greensboro, July.

Hirsch, Barry T. (1982), 'The Interindustry Structure of Unionism, Earnings, and Earnings Dispersion,' *Industrial and Labor Relations Review* 36(1), October, 22–39.

Hirsch, Barry T. (1985), 'What Do Unions Do? Comment,' *Industrial and Labor Relations Review* 38(2), January, 247–50.

Hirsch, Barry T. and Mark C. Berger (1984), 'Union Membership Determination and Industry Characteristics,' *Southern Economic Journal* 50(3), January, 665–79.

Hirsch, Barry T. and Robert A. Connolly (1985), 'Do Unions Capture Monopoly Profits?' mimeographed, University of North Carolina at Greensboro, June.

Hirsch, Barry T. and Clifford B. Donn (1982), 'Arbitration and the Incentive to Bargain: The Role of Expectations and Costs,' *Journal of Labor Research* 3(1), Winter, 55–68.

Hirsch, Barry T. and William J. Hausman (1983), 'Labour Productivity in the British and South Wales Coal Industry: 1874–1914,' *Economica* 50(198), May, 145–58.

Hirsch, Barry T. and Albert N. Link (1984), 'Unions, Productivity, and Productivity Growth,' *Journal of Labor Research* 5(1), Winter, 29–37.

Hirschman, Albert O. (1970), *Exit, Voice, and Loyalty* (Cambridge, MA: Harvard University Press).

Holcombe, Randall G. (1980), 'An Empirical Test of the Median Voter Model,' *Economic Inquiry* 18(2), April, 260–74.

Holmstrom, Bengt (1981). 'Contractual Models of the Labor Market,' *American Economic Review Papers and Proceedings* 71(2), May, 308–13.

Holmstrom, Bengt (1983), 'Equilibrium Long-Term Labor Contracts,' *Quarterly Journal of Economics* 98(392), Supplement, May, 23–54.

Holzer, Harry J. (1982), 'Unions and the Labor Market Status of White and Minority Youth,' *Industrial and Labor Relations Review* 35(3), April, 392–405.

Hutchins, Michael T. and Solomon W. Polachek (1981), 'Do Unions Really Flatten the Age–Earnings Profile? New Estimates Using Panel Data,' mimeographed, University of North Carolina, June.

Hyclak, Thomas (1979), 'The Effect of Unions on Earnings Inequality in Local Labor Markets,' *Industrial and Labor Relations Review* 33(1), October, 77–84.

Hyclak, Thomas (1980), 'Unions and Income Inequality: Some Cross-State Evidence,' *Industrial Relations* 19(2), Spring, 212–5.

Ichniowski, Casey (1984a), 'Industrial Relations and Economic Performance: Grievances and Productivity,' National Bureau of Economic Research Working Paper No. 1367, June.

Ichniowski, Casey (1984b), 'Ruling Out Productivity? Labor Contract Pages and Plant Performance,' National Bureau of Economic Research Working Paper No. 1368, June.

Jacoby, Sanford M. and Daniel J. B. Mitchell (1982), 'Does Implicit Contracting Explain Explicit Contracting?' *Proceedings of the Thirty-Fifth Annual Meetings* (Madison, WI: Industrial Relations Research Association, December), 319–28.

Johnson, George E. (1975), 'Economic Analysis of Trade Unionism,' *American Economic Review Papers and Proceedings* 65(2), May, 23–8.

Johnson, George E. (1977), 'The Determination of Wages in the Union and Non-Union Sectors,' *British Journal of Industrial Relations* 15(2), July, 211–25.

Johnson, George E. (1984), 'Changes over Time in the Union–Nonunion Wage Differential in the United States,' in Jean-Jacques Rosa (ed.), *The Economics of Trade Unions: New Directions* (Boston, MA: Kluwer-Nijhoff), 3–19.

Johnson, Harry G. and Peter Mieszkowski (1970), 'The Effects of Unionization on the Distribution of Income: A General Equilibrium Approach,' *Quarterly Journal of Economics* 84(4), November, 539–61.

Johnston, J. (1972), 'A Model of Wage Determination under Bilateral Monopoly,' *Economic Journal* 82(327), September, 837–52.

Johnston, J. and M. Timbrell (1973), 'Empirical Tests of a Bargaining Theory of Wage Rate Determination,' *Manchester School* 41(2), June, 141–67.

Jones, Ethel B. (1982), 'Union/Nonunion Wage Differentials: Membership or Coverage?' *Journal of Human Resources* 17(2), Spring, 276–85.

Kahn, Lawrence M. (1978a), 'The Effects of Unions on the Earnings of Nonunion Workers,' *Industrial and Labor Relations Review* 31(2), January, 205–16.

Kahn, Lawrence M. (1978b), 'Unions and the Employment Status of Nonunion Workers,' *Industrial Relations* 17(2), May, 238–44.

Kahn, Lawrence M. (1979), 'Unionism and Relative Wages: Direct and Indirect Effects,' *Industrial and Labor Relations Review* 32(4), July, 520–32.

Kahn, Lawrence M. (1980), 'Union Spillover Effects on Unorganized Labor Markets,' *Journal of Human Resources* 15(1), Winter, 87–98.

Kalachek, Edward and Frederic Raines (1980), 'Trade Unions and Hiring Standards,' *Journal of Labor Research* 1(1), Spring, 63–75.

Kalleberg, Arne L., Michael Wallace, and Lawrence E. Raffalovich (1984), 'Accounting for Labor's Share: Class and Income Distribution in the Printing Industry,' *Industrial and Labor Relations Review* 37(3), April, 386–402.

Karier, Thomas (1985), 'Unions and Monopoly Profits,' *Review of Economics and Statistics* 67(1), February, 34–42.

Katz, Harry C., Thomas A. Kochan, and Kenneth R. Gobeille (1983), 'Industrial Relations Performance, Economic Performance, and QWL Programs: An Interplant Analysis,' *Industrial and Labor Relations Review* 37(1), October, 3–17.

Kau, James B., Donald Keenan, and Paul H. Rubin (1982), 'A General Equilibrium Model of Congressional Voting,' *Quarterly Journal of Economics* 97(2), May, 271–93.

Kau, James B. and Paul H. Rubin (1978), 'Voting on Minimum Wages: A Time-Series Analysis,' *Journal of Political Economy* 86(2), April, 337–42.

Kau, James B. and Paul H. Rubin (1979), 'Self-Interest, Ideology, and Logrolling in Congressional Voting,' *Journal of Law and Economics* 22(2), October, 365–84.

Kau, James B. and Paul H. Rubin (1981), 'The Impact of Labor Unions on the Passage of Economic Legislation,' *Journal of Labor Research* 2(1), Spring, 133–45.

Kaufman, Bruce E. (1981), 'Bargaining Theory, Inflation, and Cyclical Strike Activity, in Manufacturing,' *Industrial and Labor Relations Review* 34(3), April, 333–55.

Kaufman, Bruce E. (1982), 'The Determinants of Strikes in the United States, 1900–1977,' *Industrial and Labor Relations Review* 35(4), July, 473–90.

Kaufman, Bruce E. (1983), 'The Determinants of Strikes Over Time and Across Industries,' *Journal of Labor Research* 4(2), Spring, 159–75.

Kaufman, Bruce E. and Jorge Martinez-Vazquez (1984), 'Union Wage Concessions and the Ross–Dunlop Debate: A Median Voter Analysis,' Department of Economics Working Paper No. 84-4, Georgia State University, May.

Kaufman, Roger T. and Geoffrey Woglom (1984), 'The Effect of Expectations on Union Wages,' *American Economic Review* 74(3), June, 418–32.

Kendrick, John W. and Elliot S. Grossman (1980), *Productivity in the United States: Trends and Cycles* (Baltimore, MD: The Johns Hopkins University Press).

Kennan, John (1980), 'Pareto Optimality and the Economics of Strike Duration,' *Journal of Labor Research* 1(1), Spring, 77–94.

Kennedy, Peter E. (1981), 'Estimation with Correctly Interpreted Dummy Variables in Semilogarithmic Equations,' *American Economic Review* 71(4), September, 801.

Kerr, Clark and Abraham Siegel (1954), 'The Interindustry Propensity to Strike – An International Comparison,' in Arthur Kornhauser, Robert Dubin, and Arthur M. Ross (eds), *Industrial Conflict* (New York: McGraw-Hill), 189–212.

Kiefer, Nicholas M. and Sharon P. Smith (1977), 'Union Impact and Wage Discrimination by Region,' *Journal of Human Resources* 12(4), Fall, 521–34.

Killingsworth, Mark R. (1983), 'Union–Nonunion Wage Gaps and Wage Gains: New Estimates from an Industry Cross-Section,' *Review of Economics and Statistics* 65(2), May, 332–6.

Kochan, Thomas A. (1979), 'How American Workers View Labor Unions,' *Monthly Labor Review* 102(4), April, 23–31.

Kochan, Thomas A. (1980), *Collective Bargaining and Industrial Relations: From Theory to Policy and Practice* (Homewood, IL: Irwin).

Kochan, Thomas A. and Jean Baderschneider (1978), 'Dependence on Impasse

Procedures: Police and Firefighters in New York State,' *Industrial and Labor Relations Review* 31(4), July, 431–49.

Kochan, Thomas A. *et al.* (1979), *Dispute Resolution under Fact Finding and Arbitration: An Empirical Analysis* (New York: American Arbitration Association).

Kokkelenberg, Edward C. and Donna R. Sockell (1985), 'Union Membership in the United States, 1973–1981,' *Industrial and Labor Relations Review* 38(4), July, 497–543.

Korpi, Walter and Michael Shalev (1979), 'Strikes, Industrial Relations and Class Conflict in Capitalist Societies,' *British Journal of Sociology* 30(2), June, 164–87.

Kosters, Marvin (1977), 'Wage and Price Behavior: Prospects and Policies,' in William Fellner (ed.), *Contemporary Economic Problems* (Washington, DC: American Enterprise Institute), 159–201.

Kotowitz, Y. and F. Mathewson (1982), 'The Economics of the Union-controlled Firm,' *Economica* 49(196), November, 421–34.

Krueger, Anne O. (1974), 'The Political Economy of the Rent-Seeking Society,' *American Economic Review* 64(3), June, 291–303.

Kuhn, Peter (1982), 'Malfeasance in Long Term Employment Contracts: A New General Model with an Application to Unionism,' National Bureau of Economic Research Working Paper No. 1045, December.

Kuhn, Peter (1985), 'Union Productivity Effects and Economic Efficiency,' *Journal of Labor Research* 6(3), Summer, 229–48.

Kurth, Michael M. (1983), 'Public Employee Organizations as Political Firms,' in Joseph D. Reid, Jr (ed.), *New Approaches to Labor Unions* (Greenwich, CT: JAI Press), 101–25.

Kwoka, John E., Jr (1983), 'Monopoly, Plant, and Union Effects on Worker Wages,' *Industrial and Labor Relations Review* 36(2), January, 251–7.

Lacroix, Robert (1983), 'The Effects of Strikes on Wages,' Cahier 8405, University of Montreal, December.

Lazear, Edward P. (1979), 'Why is There Mandatory Retirement?' *Journal of Political Economy* 87(6), December, 1261–84.

Lazear, Edward P. (1981), 'Agency, Earnings Profiles, Productivity, and Hours Restrictions,' *American Economic Review* 71(4), September, 606–20.

Lazear, Edward P. (1983a), 'A Competitive Theory of Monopoly Unionism', *American Economic Review* 73(4), September, 631–43.

Lazear, Edward P. (1983b), 'A Microeconomic Theory of Labor Unions,' in Joseph D. Reid, Jr (ed.), *New Approaches to Labor Unions* (Greenwich, CT: JAI Press), 53–96.

Leamer, Edward E. (1978), *Specification Searches: Ad Hoc Inferences with Non-experimental Data* (New York: Wiley).

Lee, Lung-Fei (1978), 'Unionism and Wage Rates: A Simultaneous Equations Model with Qualitative and Limited Dependent Variables,' *International Economic Review* 19(2), June, 415–34.

Leibenstein, Harvey (1966), 'Allocative Efficiency vs. "X-Efficiency",' *American Economic Review* 56(3), June, 392–415.

Leigh, Duane E. (1980), 'Racial Differentials in Union Relative Wage Effects – A Simultaneous Equations Approach,' *Journal of Labor Research* 1(1), Spring, 95–114.

Leigh, Duane E. (1981), 'Do Union Members Receive Compensating Wage Differentials? Note,' *American Economic Review* 71(5), December, 1049–55.

Leigh, Duane E. (1984a), 'Union Preferences, Job Satisfaction and the Union Voice Hypothesis,' mimeographed, Washington State University, June.

Leigh, Duane E. (1984b), 'Why Is There Mandatory Retirement? An Empirical Reexamination,' *Journal of Human Resources* 19(4), Fall, 512–31.

Leigh, J. Paul (1982), 'Are Unionized Blue Collar Jobs More Hazardous than Nonunionized Blue Collar Jobs?' *Journal of Labor Research* 3(3), Summer, 349–57.

Leontief, Wassily W. (1946), 'The Pure Theory of the Guaranteed Annual Wage Contract,' *Journal of Political Economy* 54(1), February, 76–9.

Levinson, Harold M. (1954), 'Collective Bargaining and Income Distribution,' *American Economic Review Papers and Proceedings* 44(2), May, 308-16.

Levinson, Harold M. (1960a), 'Postwar Movements of Prices and Wages in Manufacturing Industries,' Study Paper No. 21, *Study of Employment, Growth, and the Price Level*, Joint Economic Committee (Washington, DC: United States Congress).

Levinson, Harold M. (1960b), 'Pattern Bargaining: A Case Study of the Automobile Workers,' *Quarterly Journal of Economics* 74(2), May, 296–317.

Lewis, H. Gregg (1959), 'Competitive and Monopoly Unionism,' in Philip D. Bradley (ed.), *The Public Stake in Union Power* (Charlottesville, VA: University of Virginia Press), 181–208.

Lewis, H. Gregg (1963), *Unionism and Relative Wages in the United States: An Empirical Inquiry* (Chicago, IL: University of Chicago Press).

Lewis, H. Gregg (1983), 'Union Relative Wage Effects: A Survey of Macro Estimates,' *Journal of Labor Economics* 1(1), January, 1–27.

Lewis, H. Gregg, *Union Relative Wage Effects: A Survey*, forthcoming.

Link, Albert N. (1981), 'Basic Research and Productivity Increase in Manufacturing: Additional Evidence,' *American Economic Review* 71(5), December, 1111–2.

Link, Albert N., 'Technological Change and Productivity Growth,' in F. M. Scherer (ed.), *The Economics of Technological Change*, a volume of *The Encyclopaedia of Economics* (Harwood Academic Publishers, forthcoming).

Linneman, Peter (1982), 'The Economic Impacts of Minimum Wage Laws: A New Look at an Old Question,' *Journal of Political Economy* 90(3), June, 443–69.

Linneman, Peter and Pablo T. Spiller (1983), 'On Estimating Unions' Motives,' mimeographed, University of Pennsylvania, March.

Long, James E. (1982), 'Are Government Workers Overpaid? Alternative Evidence,' *Journal of Human Resources* 17(1), Winter, 123–31.

Long, James E. and Albert N. Link (1983), 'The Impact of Market Structure on Wages, Fringe Benefits, and Turnover,' *Industrial and Labor Relations Review* 36(2), January, 239–50.

Lumsden, Keith and Craig Petersen (1975), 'The Effect of Right-to-Work Laws on Unionization in the United States,' *Journal of Political Economy* 83(6), December, 1237–48.

McCallum, Bennett T. (1982), 'Macroeconomics after a Decade of Rational Expectations: Some Critical Issues,' *Federal Reserve Bank of Richmond* 68(6), November/December, 3–12.

MacDonald, Glenn M. (1983), 'The Size and Structure of Union–Non-union Wage Differentials in Canadian Industry: Corroboration, Refinement, and Extension,' *Canadian Journal of Economics* 16(3), August, 480–5.

McDonald, Ian M. and Robert M. Solow (1981), 'Wage Bargaining and Employment,' *American Economic Review* 71(5), December, 896–908.

McGuire, Timothy W. and Leonard A. Rapping (1968), 'The Role of Market Variables and Key Bargains in the Manufacturing Wage Determination Process,' *Journal of Political Economy* 76(5), September/October, 1015–36.

MacRae, C. Duncan (1977), 'A Political Model of the Business Cycle,' *Journal of Political Economy* 85(2), April, 239–64.

MacRae, C. Duncan (1981), 'On the Political Business Cycle,' in Douglas A. Hibbs and Heino Fassbender (eds), *Contemporary Political Economy* (Amsterdam: North Holland), 169–84.

MaCurdy, Thomas E. and John Pencavel, 'Testing between Competing Models of Wage and Employment Determination in Unionized Markets,' *Journal of Political Economy*, forthcoming.

Magenau, John M. (1983), 'The Impact of Alternative Impasse Procedures on Bargaining: A Laboratory Experiment,' *Industrial and Labor Relations Review* 36(3), April, 361–77.

Maher, John E. (1961), 'The Wage Pattern in the United States, 1946–1957,' *Industrial and Labor Relations Review* 15(1), October, 3–20.

Maki, Dennis R. (1983a), 'The Effects of Unions and Strikes on the Rate of Growth of Total Factor Productivity in Canada,' *Applied Economics* 15(1), February, 29–41.

Maki, Dennis R. (1983b), 'Strike Activity and Productivity Growth: Evidence from Twenty Countries,' *Columbia Journal of World Business* 18(2), Summer, 95–100.

Maki, Dennis R. (1983c), 'Trade Unions and Productivity: Conventional Estimates,' *Relations Industrielles* 38(2), 211–28.

Maloney, Kevin and Michael L. Smirlock (1981), 'Business Cycles and the Political Process,' *Southern Economic Journal* 48(2), October, 377–92.

Maloney, Michael T., Robert E. McCormick, and Robert D. Tollison (1979), 'Achieving Cartel Profits through Unionization,' *Southern Economic Journal* 46(2), October, 628–34.

Mancke, Richard B. (1971), 'American Trade Union Growth, 1900–1960: A Comment,' *Quarterly Journal of Economics* 85(1), February, 187–93.

Mandelstamm, Allan B. (1965), 'The Effects of Unions on Efficiency in the Residential Construction Industry: A Case Study,' *Industrial and Labor Relations Review* 18(4), July, 503–21.

Mansfield, Edwin (1980), 'Basic Research and Productivity Increase in Manufacturing,' *American Economic Review* 70(5), December, 863–73.

Martin, Donald L. (1980), *An Ownership Theory of the Trade Union* (Berkeley, CA: University of California Press).

Mathewson, Stanley B. (1931), *Restriction of Output among Unorganized Workers* (New York: Viking Press).

Mauro, Martin J. (1982), 'Strikes as a Result of Imperfect Information,' *Industrial and Labor Relations Review* 35(4), July, 522–38.

Medoff, James L. (1979), 'Layoffs and Alternatives under Trade Unions in U.S. Manufacturing,' *American Economic Review* 69(3), June, 380–95.

Medoff, James L. and Katharine G. Abraham (1980), 'Experience, Performance, and Earnings,' *Quarterly Journal of Economics* 95(4), December, 703–36.

Medoff, James L. and Katharine G. Abraham (1981), 'Are Those Paid More Really More Productive?: The Case of Experience,' *Journal of Human Resources* 16(2), Spring, 186–216.

Mehra, Yash P. (1976), 'Spillovers in Wage Determination in U.S. Manufacturing Industries,' *Review of Economics and Statistics* 58(3), August, 300–12.

Mellow, Wesley (1981), 'Unionism and Wages: A Longitudinal Analysis,' *Review of Economics and Statistics* 63(1), February, 43–52.

Mellow, Wesley (1983), 'Employer Size, Unionism, and Wages,' in Joseph D. Reid, Jr (ed.), *New Approaches to Labor Unions* (Greenwich, CT: JAI Press), 253–82.

Mellow, Wesley and Hal Sider (1983), 'Accuracy of Response in Labor Market Surveys: Evidence and Implications,' *Journal of Labor Economics* 1(4), October, 331–44.

Miller, Berkeley (1984), 'Industrial Structure and Unionization: Evidence from U.S. Manufacturing Sectors,' paper presented at the American Sociological Association Meetings, San Antonio, Texas, August.

Miller, James C., III (1984), 'Is Organized Labor Rational in Supporting OSHA?' *Southern Economic Journal* 50(3), January, 881–5.

Miller, Marcus H. (1976), 'Can a Rise in Import Prices be Inflationary and Deflationary? Economists and U.K. Inflation, 1973–74,' *American Economic Review* 66(4), September, 501–19.

Mincer, Jacob (1974), *Schooling, Experience, and Earnings* (New York: National Bureau of Economic Research).

Mincer, Jacob (1976), 'Unemployment Effects of Minimum Wages,' *Journal of Political Economy* 84(4, part 2), August, S87–S104.

Mincer, Jacob (1983), 'Union Effects: Wages, Turnover, and Job Training,' in Joseph D. Reid, Jr (ed.), *New Approaches to Labor Unions* (Greenwich, CT: JAI Press), 217–52.

Mitchell, Daniel J. B. (1980), *Unions, Wages, and Inflation* (Washington, DC: Brookings Institution).

Mitchell, Daniel J. B. (1982), 'Recent Union Contract Concessions,' *Brookings Papers on Economic Activity* 1: 165–201.

Mitchell, Daniel J. B., and Larry Kimbell (1982), 'Labor Market Contracts and Inflation,' in Martin N. Baily (ed.), *Workers, Jobs, and Inflation* (Washington, DC: Brookings Institution), 199–238.

Mitchell, Olivia S. and Emily S. Andrews (1981), 'Scale Economies in Private Multi-Employer Pension Systems,' *Industrial and Labor Relations Review* 34(4), July, 522–30.

Moore, Thomas Gale (1970), 'The Beneficiaries of Trucking Regulation,' *Journal of Law and Economics* 21(2), October, 327–43.

Moore, William J. (1980), 'Membership and Wage Impact of Right-to-Work Laws,' *Journal of Labor Research* 1(2), Fall, 349–68.

Moore, William J. and Robert J. Newman (1975), 'On the Prospects for American Trade Union Growth: A Cross-Section Analysis,' *Review of Economics and Statistics* 57(4), November, 435–45.

Moore, William J., Robert J. Newman, and R. William Thomas (1974), 'Determinants of the Passage of Right-to-Work Laws: An Alternative Interpretation,' *Journal of Law and Economics* 17(1), April, 197–211.

Moore, William J. and Douglas K. Pearce (1976), 'Union Growth: A Test of the Ashenfelter–Pencavel Model,' *Industrial Relations* 15(2), May, 244–7.

Moore, William J. and Douglas K. Pearce (1982), 'A Comparative Analysis of Strike Models during Periods of Rapid Inflation: 1967–1977,' *Journal of Labor Research* 3(1), Winter, 39–53.

Moore, William J. and John Raisian (1980), 'Cyclical Sensitivity of Union/ Nonunion Relative Wage Effects,' *Journal of Labor Research* 1(1), Spring, 115–32.

Moore, William J. and John Raisian (1983), 'The Level and Growth of Union/Nonunion Relative Wage Effects, 1967–1977,' *Journal of Labor Research* 4(1), Winter, 65–79.

Mulvey, Charles (1976), 'Collective Agreements and Relative Earnings in UK Manufacturing in 1973,' *Economica* 43(172), November, 419–27.

Mulvey, Charles (1978), 'Unions, Spillovers and Relative Wages,' Working Paper No. 3, Industrial Relations Section, Princeton University, March.

Mulvey, Charles and Mary Gregory (1977a), 'The Hines Wage Inflation Model,' *Manchester School* 45(1), March, 29–40.

Mulvey, Charles and Mary Gregory (1977b), 'Trade Unions and Inflation in the U.K. – An Exercise,' Discussion Paper in Economics No. 22, University of Glasgow.

Mulvey, Charles and James A. Trevithick (1973), 'Trade Unions and Inflation,' *Economic and Social Review* 4(2), January, 209–29.

Nash, John F., Jr (1950), 'The Bargaining Problem,' *Econometrica* 18(2), April, 155–62.

National Labor Relations Board (annual), *Annual Reports* (Washington, DC: US Government Printing Office).

Navarro, Peter (1980), 'The Politics of Air Pollution,' *Public Interest* No. 59, Spring, 36–44.

Nelson, Richard R. (1981), 'Research on Productivity Growth and Productivity Differences: Dead Ends and New Departures,' *Journal of Economic Literature* 19(3), September, 1029–64.

Nelson, William B., Gerald W. Stone, Jr, and J. Michael Swint (1981), 'An Economic Analysis of Public Sector Collective Bargaining and Strike Activity,' *Journal of Labor Research* 2(1), Spring, 77–98.

Neumann, George R. (1980), 'The Predictability of Strikes: Evidence from the Stock Market,' *Industrial and Labor Relations Review* 33(4), July, 525–35.

Neumann, George R. and Melvin W. Reder (1984), 'Output and Strike Activity in U.S. Manufacturing: How Large Are the Losses?' *Industrial and Labor Relations Review* 37(2), January, 197–211.

Neumann, George R. and Ellen R. Rissman (1984), 'Where Have All the Union Members Gone?' *Journal of Labor Economics* 2(2), April, 175–92.

Niskanen, William A. (1971), *Bureaucracy and Representative Government* (Chicago, IL: Aldine).

Niskanen, William A. (1975), 'Bureaucrats and Politicians,' *Journal of Law and Economics* 18(3), December, 617–43.

Noam, Eli M. (1983), 'The Effect of Unionization and Civil Service on the Salaries and Productivity of Regulators,' in Joseph D. Reid, Jr (ed.), *New Approaches to Labor Unions* (Greenwich, CT: JAI Press), 157–70.

Nordhaus, William D. (1972), 'The Worldwide Wages Explosion,' *Brookings Papers on Economic Activity* 2: 431–64.

Nordhaus, William D. (1975), 'The Political Business Cycle,' *Review of Economic Studies* 42(130), April, 169–90.

Oaxaca, Ronald L. (1975), 'Estimation of Union/Nonunion Wage Differentials within Occupational-Regional Subgroups,' *Journal of Human Resources* 10(4), Fall, 529–36.

Okun, Arthur M. (1975), 'Inflation: Its Mechanics and Welfare Costs,' *Brookings Papers on Economic Activity* 2: 351–90.

Okun, Arthur M. (1981), *Prices and Quantities: A Macroeconomic Analysis*

(Washington, DC: Brookings Institution).

Olsen, Randall J. (1978), 'Comment on "The Effect of Unions on Earnings and Earnings on Unions: A Mixed Logit Approach",' *International Economic Review* 19(1), February, 259–61.

Olson, C. Vincent and John M. Trapani, III (1981), 'Who Has Benefited from Regulation of the Airline Industry?' *Journal of Law and Economics* 24(1), April, 75–93.

Olson, Craig A. (1980), 'The Impact of Arbitration on the Wages of Firefighters,' *Industrial Relations* 19(3), Fall, 325–39.

Olson, Craig A. (1981), 'An Analysis of Wage Differentials Received by Workers on Dangerous Jobs,' *Journal of Human Resources* 16(2), Spring, 167–85.

Olson, Craig A. and Chris J. Berger (1983), 'The Relationship between Seniority, Ability, and the Promotion of Union and Nonunion Workers,' in David B. Lipsky and Joe M. Douglas (eds), *Advances in Industrial and Labor Relations* (Greenwich, CT: JAI Press), 91–129.

Olson, Mancur (1980), 'Comment on Reynolds' "The Public Goods Argument for Compulsory Dues",' *Journal of Labor Research* 1(2), Fall, 319–22.

Olson, Mancur (1982), *The Rise and Decline of Nations: Economic Growth, Stagflation, and Social Rigidities* (New Haven, CT: Yale University Press).

Oswald, Andrew J. (1982), 'The Microeconomic Theory of the Trade Union,' *Economic Journal* 92(367), September, 576–95.

Oswald, Andrew J. (1984), 'Efficient Contracts are on the Labor Demand Curve: Theory and Facts,' Working Paper No. 178, Industrial Relations Section, Princeton University, July.

Oswald, Andrew J. and Alan A. Carruth (1984), 'Miners' Wages in Post-War Britain: An Application of a Model of Trade Union Behaviour,' Working Paper No. 175, Industrial Relations Section, Princeton University, July.

Pakes, Ariél and Shmuel Nitzan (1983), 'Optimum Contracts for Research Personnel, Research Employment, and the Establishment of "Rival" Enterprises,' *Journal of Labor Economics* 1(4), October, 345–65.

Paldam, Martin and Peder J. Pedersen (1982), 'The Macroeconomic Strike Model: A Study of Seventeen Countries, 1948–1975,' *Industrial and Labor Relations Review* 35(4), July, 504–21.

Parkin, Michael J. (1975), 'The Politics of Inflation,' *Government and Opposition* 10(2), Spring, 189–202.

Parkin, Michael J. (1977), 'Comments and Discussion [on Gordon],' *Brookings Papers on Economic Activity* 2: 471–75.

Parkin, Michael J. (1980), 'Unemployment and Inflation: Facts, Theories, Puzzles and Policies,' in Edmond Malinvaud and Jean-Paul Fitoussi (eds), *Unemployment in Western Countries* (New York: St Martin's Press), 278–308.

Parsley, C. J. (1980), 'Labor Union Effects on Wage Gains: A Survey of Recent Literature,' *Journal of Economic Literature* 18(1), March, 1–31.

Pearce, James E. (1983), 'Unionism and the Cyclical Behavior of the Labor Market in U.S. Manufacturing,' *Review of Economics and Statistics* 65(3), August, 450–8.

Peltzman, Sam (1975), 'The Effects of Automobile Safety Regulation,' *Journal of Political Economy* 83(4), August, 677–725.

Peltzman, Sam (1976), 'Toward a More General Theory of Regulation,' *Journal of Law and Economics* 19(2), August, 211–40.

Pencavel, John H. (1971), 'The Demand for Union Services: An Exercise,' *Industrial and Labor Relations Review* 24(2), January, 180–90.

Pencavel, John H. (1974), 'Relative Wages and Trade Unons in the United Kingdom,' *Economica* 41(162), May, 194–210.

Pencavel, John H. (1977), 'The Distributional and Efficiency Effects of Trade Unions in Britain,' *British Journal of Industrial Relations* 15(2), July, 137–56.

Pencavel, John H. (1982), 'The Effects of Incomes Policies on the Frequency and Size of Wage Changes,' *Economica* 49(194), May, 147–59.

Pencavel, John H. (1984), 'The Tradeoff between Wages and Employment in Trade Union Objectives,' *Quarterly Journal of Economics* 99(2), May, 215–32.

Pencavel, John H. and Catherine E. Hartsog (1984), 'A Reconsideration of the Effects of Unionism on Relative Wages and Employment in the United States, 1920–1980,' *Journal of Labor Economics* 2(2), April, 193–232.

Perloff, Jeffrey and Robin C. Sickles (1983), 'FIML Estimation of Union Wages, Hours, and Earnings Differentials in the Construction Industry: A Nonlinear Limited Dependent Variable Approach,' mimeographed, University of California, March.

Pettengill, John S. (1980), *Labor Unions and the Inequality of Earned Income* (Amsterdam: North-Holland).

Phelps, Edmund S. (1968), 'Money Wage Dynamics and Labor Market Equilibrium,' *Journal of Political Economy* 76(4, pt 2), July/August, 678–71.

Phelps Brown, E. H. (1973), 'New Wine in Old Bottles: Reflections on the Changed Working of Collective Bargaining in Great Britain,' *British Journal of Industrial Relations* 11(3), November, 329–37.   668–71.
.678–81.

Phillips, A. W. (1958), 'The Relation between Unemployment and the Rate of Change in Money Wage Rates in the United Kingdom, 1861–1957,' *Economica* 25(100), November, 283–99.

Podgursky, Michael (1983), 'Unions and Family Income Inequality,' *Journal of Human Resources* 18(4), Fall, 574–91.

Posner, Richard A. (1971), 'Taxation by Regulation,' *Bell Journal of Economics* 2(1), Spring, 22–50.

Posner, Richard A. (1975), 'The Social Cost of Monopoly and Regulation,' *Journal of Political Economy* 83(4), August, 807–27.

Quan, Nguyen T. (1984), 'Unionism and the Size Distribution of Earnings,' *Industrial Relations* 23(2), Spring, 270–7.

Quinn, Joseph F. (1979), 'Wage Differentials among Older Workers in the Public and Private Sectors,' *Journal of Human Resources* 14(1), Winter, 41–62.

Rabinovitch, Ramon and Itzhak Swary (1976), 'On the Theory of Bargaining, Strikes, and Wage Determination under Uncertainty,' *Canadian Journal of Economics* 9(4), November, 668–84.

Raisian, John (1979), 'Cyclic Patterns in Weeks and Wages,' *Economic Inquiry* 17(4), October, 475–95.

Raisian, John (1983a), 'Contracts, Job Experience, and Cyclical Labor Market Adjustments,' *Journal of Labor Economics* 1(2), April, 152–70.

Raisian, John (1983b), 'Union Dues and Wage Premiums,' *Journal of Labor Research* 4(1), Winter, 1–18.

Reder, Melvin W. (1975), 'The Theory of Employment and Wages in the Public

Sector,' in Daniel S. Hamermesh (ed.), *Labor in the Public and Nonprofit Sectors* (Princeton, NJ: Princeton University Press), 1–48.

Reder, Melvin W. (1984), 'Strike Cost and Wage Rates: Cross-Industry Differences,' in Jean-Jacques Rosa (ed.), *The Economics of Trade Unions: New Directions* (Boston, MA: Kluwer-Nijhoff), 27–37.

Reder, Melvin W. and George R. Neumann (1980), 'Conflict and Contract: The Case of Strikes,' *Journal of Political Economy* 88(5), October, 867–86.

Rees, Albert (1963), 'The Effects of Unions on Resource Allocation,' *Journal of Law and Economics* 6(2), October, 69–78.

Rees, Albert (1977), *The Economics of Trade Unions*, 2nd edn (Chicago, IL: University of Chicago Press).

Reid, Joseph D., Jr. and Michael M. Kurth (1983), 'The Importance of Union Security to the Growth of Unionism,' mimeographed, George Mason University, December.

Reid, Joseph D., Jr and Michael Kurth (1984), 'The Contribution of Exclusive Representation to Union Strength,' *Journal of Labor Research* 5(4), Fall, 391–412.

Reynolds, Morgan O. (1980a), 'The Norris–LaGuardia Act, Wagner Act, and the Labor Representation Industry,' mimeographed, University of California–Davis, December.

Reynolds, Morgan O. (1980b), 'The Public Goods Argument for Compulsory Dues,' *Journal of Labor Research* 1(2), Fall, 295–313.

Reynolds, Morgan O. (1982), 'Understanding Political Pricing of Labor Services: The Davis–Bacon Act,' *Journal of Labor Research* 3(3), Summer, 295–309.

Riddell, W. Craig (1979a), 'Recent Research on Wage Inflation in Canada,' presented to the annual meetings of the Eastern Economics Association, Boston, MA, 10–12 May.

Riddell, W. Craig (1979b), 'The Empirical Foundations of the Phillips Curve: Evidence from Canadian Wage Contract Data,' *Econometrica* 47(1), January, 1–24.

Riddell, W. Craig (1983), 'The Responsiveness of Wage Settlements in Canada and Economic Policy,' *Canadian Public Policy* 9(1), March, 9–23.

Riddell, W. Craig and Philip M. Smith (1982), 'Expected Inflation and Wage Changes in Canada, 1967–81,' *Canadian Journal of Economics* 15(3), August, 377–94.

Riker, William H. (1962), *The Theory of Political Coalitions* (New Haven, CT: Yale University Press).

Riordan, Michael H. and Michael L. Wachter (1983), 'What Do Implicit Contracts Do?' mimeographed, University of Pennsylvania.

Robinson, Chris and Nigel Tomes (1984), 'Union Wage Differentials in the Public and Private Sectors: A Simultaneous Equations Specification,' *Journal of Labor Economics* 2(1), January, 106–27.

Romer, Thomas and Howard Rosenthal (1978), 'Political Resource Allocation, Controlled Agendas, and the Status Quo,' *Public Choice* 33(4), 27–43.

Romer, Thomas and Howard Rosenthal (1979), 'The Elusive Median Voter,' *Journal of Public Economics* 12(2), October, 143–70.

Roomkin, Myron and Harvey A. Juris (1978), 'Unions in the Traditional Sectors: The Mid-Life Passage of the Labor Movement,' *Proceedings of the Thirty-First Annual Meetings* (Madison, WI: Industrial Relations Research Association), 212–22.

Rose, Joseph B. (1972), 'What Factors Influence Union Representation

Elections?' *Monthly Labor Review* 95(10), October, 49–51.

Rosen, Sherwin (1969), 'Trade Union Power, Threat Effects and the Extent of Organization,' *Review of Economic Studies* 36(106), April, 185–96.

Rosen, Sherwin (1970), 'Unionism and the Occupational Wage Structure in the United States,' *International Economic Review* 11(2), June, 269–86.

Ross, Arthur M. (1948), *Trade Union Wage Policy* (Berkeley and Los Angeles, CA: University of California Press).

Ross, Arthur M. and Paul T. Hartman (1960), *Changing Patterns of Industrial Conflict* (New York: John Wiley).

Ruback, Richard and Martin B. Zimmerman (1984), 'Unionization and Profitability: Evidence from the Capital Market,' *Journal of Political Economy* 92(6), December, 1134–57.

Rubin, Paul H. (1975), 'On the Form of Special Interest Legislation,' *Public Choice* 21, Spring, 79–90.

Salinger, Michael A. (1984), 'Tobin's q, Unionization, and the Concentration–Profits Relationship,' *Rand Journal of Economics* 15(2), Summer, 159–70.

Samuelson, Paul A. (1955), 'Diagrammatic Exposition of a Theory of Public Expenditure,' *Review of Economics and Statistics* 37(4), November, 350–6.

Sandver, Marcus Hart (1982), 'South–Nonsouth Differentials in National Labor Relations Board Certification Election Outcomes,' *Journal of Labor Research* 3(1), Winter, 13–30.

Sargan, J. D. (1971), 'A Study of Wages and Prices in the U.K., 1944–1968,' in H. G. Johnson and A. R. Nobay (eds), *The Current Inflation* (London: Macmillan), 52–71.

Schelling, Thomas C. (1963), *The Strategy of Conflict* (London: Oxford University Press).

Scherer, F. M. (1980), *Industrial Market Structure and Economic Performance*, 2nd edn (Boston, MA: Houghton Mifflin).

Schmidt, Peter (1978), 'Estimation of a Simultaneous Equations Model with Jointly Dependent Continuous and Qualitative Variables: The Union–Earnings Question Revisited,' *International Economic Review* 19(2), June, 453–65.

Schmidt, Peter and Robert P. Strauss (1976), 'The Effect of Unions on Earnings and Earnings on Unions: A Mixed Logit Approach,' *International Economic Review* 17(1), February, 204–12.

Shah, Anup (1984), 'Job Attributes and the Size of the Union/Non-union Wage Differential,' *Economica* 51(204), November, 437–46.

Shalev, Michael (1980), 'Trade Unionism and Economic Analysis – The Case of Industrial Conflict,' *Journal of Labor Research* 1(1), Spring, 133–73.

Shapiro, Perry and Jon Sonstelie (1982), 'Did Proposition 13 Slay Leviathan?' *American Economic Review Papers and Proceedings* 72(2), May, 184–90.

Sheflin, Neil, Leo Troy, and C. Timothy Koeller (1981), 'Structural Stability in Models of American Trade Union Growth,' *Quarterly Journal of Economics* 96(1), February, 77–88.

Siebert, W. Stanley and John T. Addison (1981), 'Are Strikes Accidental?' *Economic Journal* 91(362), June, 389–404.

Siebert, W. Stanley, Philip V. Bertrand, and John T. Addison (1985), 'The Political Model of Strikes: A New Twist,' *Southern Economic Journal* 52(1) July, 23–33.

Silberman, Jonathan I. and Garey C. Durden (1976), 'Determining Legislative Preferences on the Minimum Wage: An Economic Approach,' *Journal of*

Political Economy 84(2), April, 317–29.

Simler, N. J. (1961), 'Unionism and Labor's Share in Manufacturing Industries,' *Review of Economics and Statistics* 43(4), November, 369–78.

Simons, Henry C. (1944), 'Some Reflections on Syndicalism,' *Journal of Political Economy* 52(1), March, 1–25.

Simpson, Bill (1973), *Labour: The Unions and the Party* (London: Allen & Unwin).

Skeels, Jack W. (1982), 'The Economic and Organizational Basis of Early United States Strikes, 1900–1948,' *Industrial and Labor Relations Review* 35(4), July, 491–503.

Slichter, Sumner H., James J. Healy, and E. Robert Livernash (1960), *The Impact of Collective Bargaining on Management* (Washington, DC: Brookings Institution).

Sloan, Frank A. and Killard W. Adamache (1984), 'The Role of Unions in Hospital Cost Inflation,' *Industrial and Labor Relations Review* 37(2), January, 252–62.

Smith, Philip M. and David A. Wilton (1978), 'Wage Changes: The Frequency of Wage Settlements, The Variability of Contract Length and "Locked-in" Wage Adjustments,' *Economica* 45(179), August, 305–10.

Smith, Sharon P. (1977), 'Government Wage Differentials,' *Journal of Urban Economical* 4(3), July, 248–71.

Snyder, David (1975), 'Institutional Setting and Industrial Conflict: Comparative Analyses of France, Italy, and the United States,' *American Sociological Review* 40(3), June, 259–78.

Snyder, David (1977), 'Early North American Strikes: A Reinterpretation,' *Industrial and Labor Relations Review* 30(3), April, 325–41.

Solow, Robert M. (1958), 'A Skeptical Note on the Constancy of Relative Shares,' *American Economic Review* 48(4), September, 618–31.

Stern, Robert N. (1978), 'Methodological Issues in Quantitative Strike Analysis,' *Industrial Relations* 17(1), February, 32–42.

Stevens, Carl (1966), 'Is Compulsory Arbitration Compatible with Bargaining?' *Industrial Relations* 5(2), February, 38–52.

Stewart, Mark B. (1983), 'Relative Earnings and Individual Union Membership in the United Kingdom,' *Economica* 50(198), May, 111–25.

Stigler, George J. (1970), 'Director's Law of Public Income Redistribution,' *Journal of Law and Economics* 13(1), April, 1–11.

Stigler, George J. (1971), 'The Theory of Economic Regulation,' *Bell Journal of Economics* 2(1), Spring, 3–21.

Stigler, George J. (1976), 'The Xistence of X-Efficiency,' *American Economic Review* 66(1), March, 213–6.

Stiglitz, Joseph E. (1982), 'The Theory of Local Public Goods Twenty-Five Years after Tiebout: A Perspective,' *National Bureau of Economic Research Working Paper No. 954*, August.

Subbarao, A. V. (1978), 'The Impact of Binding Interest Arbitration on Negotiation and Process Outcome: An Experimental Study,' *Journal of Conflict Resolution* 22(1), March, 79–103.

Sveikauskas, Catherine Defina and Leo Sveikauskas (1982), 'Industry Characteristics and Productivity Growth,' *Southern Economic Journal* 48(3), January, 769–74.

Svejnar, Jan (1980), 'On the Empirical Testing of the Nash–Zeuthen Bargaining Solution,' *Industrial and Labor Relations Review* 33(4), July, 536–42.

Svejnar, Jan, 'Bargaining Power, Fear of Disagreement and Wage Settlements:

Theory and Empirical Evidence from U.S. Industry,' *American Economic Review*, forthcoming.

Swidinsky, Robert (1972), 'Trade Unions and the Rate of Change of Money Wages in Canada, 1953–1970,' *Industrial and Labor Relations Review* 25(3), April, 363–75.

Swint, J. Michael and William B. Nelson (1978), 'The Influence of Negotiators' Self-Interest on the Duration of Strikes,' *Industrial and Labor Relations Review* 32(1), October, 56–66.

Swint, J. Michael and William B. Nelson (1980), 'Self-Motivated Bargaining and Rational Strikes: A Multiparty Model and Its Implications for Industrial Strike Activity,' *Southern Economic Journal* 47(2), October, 317–31.

Taylor, John B. (1980), 'Aggregate Dynamics and Staggered Contracts,' *Journal of Political Economy* 88(1), February, 1–23.

Taylor, John B. (1983), 'Union Wage Settlements During a Disinflation,' *American Economic Review* 73(5), December, 981–93.

Terleckyj, Nestor E. (1974), *Effects of R&D on the Productivity Growth of Industries: An Exploratory Study* (Washington, DC: National Planning Association).

Terleckyj, Nestor E. (1980), 'What Do R&D Numbers Tell Us About Technological Change?' *American Economic Review Papers and Proceedings* 70(2), May, 55–61.

Thieblot, Armand (1975), *The Davis–Bacon Act*, Report No. 10, Industrial Research Unit, University of Pennsylvania.

Thompson, Earl A. (1980), 'On Labor's Right to Strike,' *Economic Inquiry* 18(4), October, 640–53.

Tiebout, Charles M. (1956), 'A Pure Theory of Local Expenditures,' *Journal of Political Economy* 64(5), October, 416–24.

Troy, Leo. (1965), *Trade Union Membership* (New York: National Bureau of Economic Research).

Troy, Leo and Neil Sheflin (1985), *Union Sourcebook: Membership, Structure, Finance, Directory* (West Orange, NJ: Industrial Relations Data and Information Services).

Tufte, Edward R. (1978), *Political Control of the Economy* (Princeton, NJ: Princeton University Press).

Tullock, Gordon (1967), 'The Welfare Cost of Tariffs, Monopolies, and Theft,' *Western Economic Journal* 5(3), June, 224–32.

Tullock, Gordon (1971), 'The Charity of the Uncharitable,' *Western Economic Journal* 9(4), December, 379–92.

Uri, Noel D. and J. Wilson Mixon, Jr (1980), 'An Economic Analysis of the Determinants of Minimum Wage Voting Behavior,' *Journal of Law and Economics* 23(1), April, 167–77.

US Department of Labor (1981), *Summary of Public Sector Labor Relations Policies*, Labor-Management Services Administration (Washington, DC: US Government Printing Office).

US Department of Labor (1983), *Handbook of Labor Statistics*, Bureau of Labor Statistics Bulletin 2175 (Washington, DC: US Government Printing Office, December).

Viscusi, W. Kip (1980), 'Unions, Labor Market Structure, and the Welfare

Implications of the Quality of Work,' *Journal of Labor Research* 1(1), Spring, 175–92.

Voos, Paula B. (1983), 'Union Organizing: Costs and Benefits,' *Industrial and Labor Relations Review* 36(4), July, 576–91.

Voos, Paula B. (1984), 'Trends in Union Organizing Expenditures, 1953–1977,' *Industrial and Labor Relations Review* 38(1), October, 52–63.

Voos, Paula B. and Lawrence R. Mishel (1985), 'The Union Impact on Profits: Evidence from Industry Price–Cost Margin Data,' mimeographed, University of Wisconsin, May.

Vroman, Susan (1980), 'A Note on Union–Non-Union Spillovers,' *British Journal of Industrial Relations* 18(3), November, 369–71.

Vroman, Susan (1982), 'The Direction of Wage Spillovers in Manufacturing,' *Industrial and Labor Relations Review* 36(1), October, 102–12.

Vroman, Wayne (1984), 'Wage Contract Settlements in U.S. Manufacturing,' *Review of Economics and Statistics* 66(4), November, 661–5.

Wachter, Michael L. (1974), 'The Wage Process: An Analysis of the Early 1970s,' *Brookings Papers on Economic Activity* 2: 507–24.

Wachter, Michael L. (1976), 'The Changing Cyclical Responsiveness of Wage Inflation,' *Brookings Papers on Economic Activity* 1: 115–59.

Wachter, Michael L. and Susan M. Wachter (1978), 'Institutional Factors in Domestic Inflation,' in *After the Phillips Curve: Persistence of High Inflation and High Unemployment* (Edgartown, MA: Federal Reserve Bank of Boston), June, 124–55.

Wachter, Michael and Oliver E. Williamson (1978), 'Obligational Markets and the Mechanics of Inflation,' *Bell Journal of Economics* 9(2), Autumn, 549–71.

Walton, Richard and Robert B. McKersie (1965), *A Behavioral Theory of Labor Negotiations* (New York: McGraw-Hill).

Ward, R. and Zis, G. (1974), 'Trade Union Militancy as an Explanation of Inflation: An International Comparison,' *Manchester School* 42(1), March, 46–65.

Warren, Ronald S., Jr (1985), 'The Effect of Unionization on Labor Productivity: Some Time Series Evidence,' *Journal of Labor Research* 6(2), Spring, 199–207.

Warren, Ronald S., Jr and Robert Strauss (1979), 'A Mixed Logit Model of the Relationship between Unionization and Right-to-Work Legislation,' *Journal of Political Economy* 87(3), June, 648–55.

Warren-Boulton, Frederick R. (1977), 'Vertical Control by Labor Unions,' *American Economic Review* 67(3), June, 309–22.

Weiler, Paul (1983), 'Promises to Keep: Securing Workers' Rights to Self-Organization under the NLRA,' *Harvard Law Review* 96(8), June, 1769–827.

Weiss, Leonard W. (1966), 'Concentration and Labor Earnings,' *American Economic Review* 56(1), March, 96–117.

Wellington, Harry H. and Ralph K. Winter, Jr (1969), 'The Limits of Collective Bargaining in Public Employment,' *Yale Law Journal* 78(7), June, 1107–27.

Wessels, Walter J. (1981), 'Economic Effects of Right to Work Laws,' *Journal of Labor Research* 2(1), Spring, 55–75.

Wessels, Walter J. (1984), 'A Model of Unions as Wage Taxing Institutions: Simulations and Results,' mimeographed, North Carolina State University.

Wessels, Walter J. (1985), 'The Effects of Unions on Employment and

Productivity: An Unresolved Contradiction,' *Journal of Labor Economics* 3(1), January, 101–8.

White, Michael D. (1982), 'The Intra-Unit Wage Structure and Unions: A Median Voter Model,' *Industrial and Labor Relations Review* 35(4), July, 565–77.

Wilkinson, R. K. and B. Burkitt (1973), 'Wage Determination and Trade Unions,' *Scottish Journal of Political Economy* 20(2), June, 107–22.

Williamson, John and Geoffrey E. Wood (1976), 'British Inflation: Indigenous or Imported?' *American Economic Review* 66(4), September, 520–31.

Williamson, Oliver E. (1979), 'Transaction Cost Economics: The Governance of Contractual Relations,' *Journal of Law and Economics* 22(2), October, 233–61.

Williamson, Oliver E. (1982), 'Efficient Labor Organization,' mimeographed, Center for the Study of Organizational Innovation, University of Pennsylvania, April.

Williamson, Oliver E., Michael L. Wachter, and Jeffrey E. Harris (1975), 'Understanding the Employment Relation: The Analysis of Idiosnycratic Exchange,' *Bell Journal of Economics* 6(1), Spring, 250–78.

Wolman, Leo (1936), *Ebb and Flow in Trade Unionism* (New York: National Bureau of Economic Research).

Zeuthen, Frederick (1930), *Problems of Monopoly and Economic Warfare* (London: Routledge).

Author Index

Subject Index